Walt Disney World For Dummies® 2001

D0288658

Downtown Disney

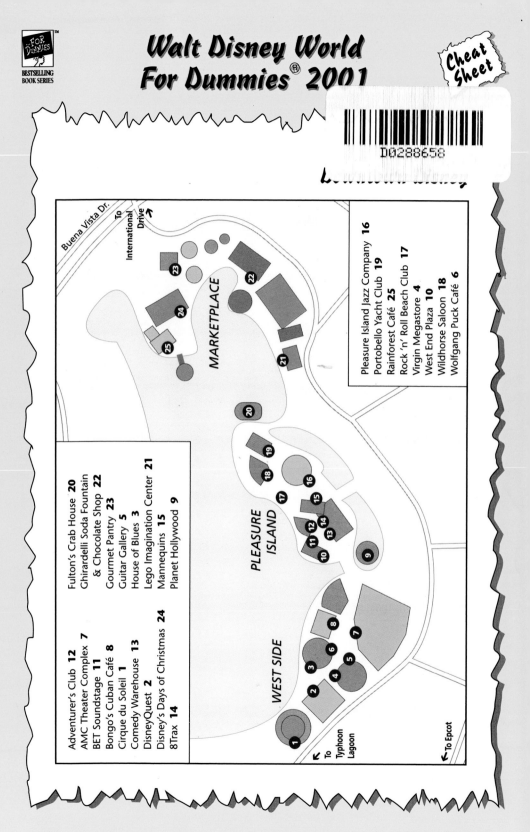

Marketplace / Pleasure Island / West Side map

Buena Vista Dr.

To International Drive

MARKETPLACE

PLEASURE ISLAND

WEST SIDE

To Typhoon Lagoon

To Epcot

Adventurer's Club **12**
AMC Theater Complex **7**
BET Soundstage **11**
Bongo's Cuban Café **8**
Cirque du Soleil **1**
Comedy Warehouse **13**
DisneyQuest **2**
Disney's Days of Christmas **24**
8Trax **14**

Fulton's Crab House **20**
Ghirardelli Soda Fountain
& Chocolate Shop **22**
Gourmet Pantry **23**
Guitar Gallery **5**
House of Blues **3**
Lego Imagination Center **21**
Mannequins **15**
Planet Hollywood **9**

Pleasure Island Jazz Company **16**
Portobello Yacht Club **19**
Rainforest Café **25**
Rock 'n' Roll Beach Club **17**
Virgin Megastore **4**
West End Plaza **10**
Wildhorse Saloon **18**
Wolfgang Puck Café **6**

For Dummies™: Bestselling Book Series for Beginners

Walt Disney World For Dummies® 2001

Cheat Sheet

Orlando & Walt Disney World

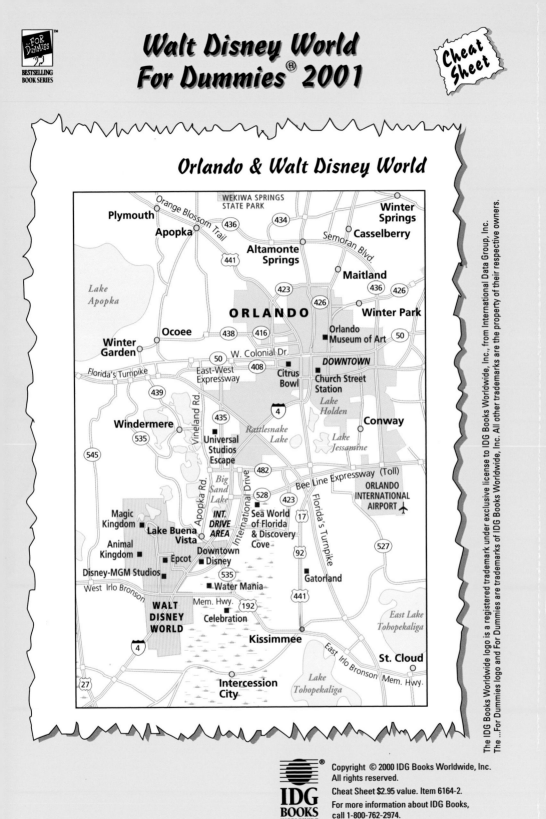

For Dummies™: Bestselling Book Series for Beginners

™

References for the Rest of Us!™

Walt Disney World® & Orlando
FOR
DUMMIES® 2001

by Jim and Cynthia Tunstall

IDG BOOKS WORLDWIDE

IDG Books Worldwide, Inc.
An International Data Group Company

Foster City, CA ✦ Chicago, IL ✦ Indianapolis, IN ✦ New York, NY

Walt Disney World® & Orlando For Dummies®, 2001

Published by
IDG Books Worldwide, Inc.
An International Data Group Company
919 E. Hillsdale Blvd.
Suite 400
Foster City, CA 94404
www.idgbooks.com (IDG Books Worldwide Web Site)
www.dummies.com (Dummies Press Web Site)

Library of Congress Control Number: 00-103386

ISBN: 0-7645-6164-2

ISSN: 1528-2112

Printed in the United States of America

10 9 8 7 6 5 4 3 2 1

1B/QR/QZ/QQ/IN

Distributed in the United States by IDG Books Worldwide, Inc.

Distributed by CDG Books Canada Inc. for Canada; by Transworld Publishers Limited in the United Kingdom; by IDG Norge Books for Norway; by IDG Sweden Books for Sweden; by IDG Books Australia Publishing Corporation Pty. Ltd. for Australia and New Zealand; by TransQuest Publishers Pte Ltd. for Singapore, Malaysia, Thailand, Indonesia, and Hong Kong; by Gotop Information Inc. for Taiwan; by ICG Muse, Inc. for Japan; by Intersoft for South Africa; by Eyrolles for France; by International Thomson Publishing for Germany, Austria and Switzerland; by Distribuidora Cuspide for Argentina; by LR International for Brazil; by Galileo Libros for Chile; by Ediciones ZETA S.C.R. Ltda. for Peru; by WS Computer Publishing Corporation, Inc., for the Philippines; by Contemporanea de Ediciones for Venezuela; by Express Computer Distributors for the Caribbean and West Indies; by Micronesia Media Distributor, Inc. for Micronesia; by Chips Computadoras S.A. de C.V. for Mexico; by Editorial Norma de Panama S.A. for Panama; by American Bookshops for Finland.

For general information on IDG Books Worldwide's books in the U.S., please call our Consumer Customer Service department at 800-762-2974. For reseller information, including discounts and premium sales, please call our Reseller Customer Service department at 800-434-3422.

For information on where to purchase IDG Books Worldwide's books outside the U.S., please contact our International Sales department at 317-572-3993 or fax 317-572-4002.

For consumer information on foreign language translations, please contact our Customer Service department at 800-434-3422, fax 317-572-4002, or e-mail rights@idgbooks.com.

For information on licensing foreign or domestic rights, please phone 650-653-7098.

For sales inquiries and special prices for bulk quantities, please contact our Order Services department at 800-434-4322 or write to the address above.

For information on using IDG Books Worldwide's books in the classroom or for ordering examination copies, please contact our Educational Sales department at 800-434-2086 or fax 317-572-4005.

For press review copies, author interviews, or other publicity information, please contact our Public Relations department at 650-653-7000 or fax 650-653-7500.

For authorization to photocopy items for corporate, personal, or educational use, please contact Copyright Clearance Center, 222 Rosewood Drive, Danvers, MA 01923, or fax 978-750-4470.

About the Authors

Jim and Cynthia Tunstall are the dummies behind this guide.

Jim has been an editor and writer for The *Tampa Tribune* since 1978. Cynthia is a freelance writer and photographer whose work has appeared in *Better Homes & Gardens, Elegant Bride,* and the *Atlanta Journal-Constitution,* among others. Together, they've authored six travel guides, including *Frommer's Walt Disney World & Orlando 2001* and *Florida for Dummies,* which you can find in bookstores in late 2000.

The Tunstalls are native Floridians who live in Lecanto, Florida — a radar blip that's 70 miles west of the Magic Mickey. They currently share space with two horses, two dogs, two cats, a parrot, and a lot of cranky wildlife, including a gopher tortoise named Ike.

ABOUT IDG BOOKS WORLDWIDE

Welcome to the world of IDG Books Worldwide.

IDG Books Worldwide, Inc., is a subsidiary of International Data Group, the world's largest publisher of computer-related information and the leading global provider of information services on information technology. IDG was founded more than 30 years ago by Patrick J. McGovern and now employs more than 9,000 people worldwide. IDG publishes more than 290 computer publications in over 75 countries. More than 90 million people read one or more IDG publications each month.

Launched in 1990, IDG Books Worldwide is today the #1 publisher of best-selling computer books in the United States. We are proud to have received eight awards from the Computer Press Association in recognition of editorial excellence and three from Computer Currents' First Annual Readers' Choice Awards. Our best-selling ...For Dummies® series has more than 50 million copies in print with translations in 31 languages. IDG Books Worldwide, through a joint venture with IDG's Hi-Tech Beijing, became the first U.S. publisher to publish a computer book in the People's Republic of China. In record time, IDG Books Worldwide has become the first choice for millions of readers around the world who want to learn how to better manage their businesses.

Our mission is simple: Every one of our books is designed to bring extra value and skill-building instructions to the reader. Our books are written by experts who understand and care about our readers. The knowledge base of our editorial staff comes from years of experience in publishing, education, and journalism — experience we use to produce books to carry us into the new millennium. In short, we care about books, so we attract the best people. We devote special attention to details such as audience, interior design, use of icons, and illustrations. And because we use an efficient process of authoring, editing, and desktop publishing our books electronically, we can spend more time ensuring superior content and less time on the technicalities of making books.

You can count on our commitment to deliver high-quality books at competitive prices on topics you want to read about. At IDG Books Worldwide, we continue in the IDG tradition of delivering quality for more than 30 years. You'll find no better book on a subject than one from IDG Books Worldwide.

John Kilcullen
Chairman and CEO
IDG Books Worldwide, Inc.

Eighth Annual Computer Press Awards ≥1992

Ninth Annual Computer Press Awards ≥1993

Tenth Annual Computer Press Awards ≥1994

Eleventh Annual Computer Press Awards ≥1995

IDG is the world's leading IT media, research and exposition company. Founded in 1964, IDG had 1997 revenues of $2.05 billion and has more than 9,000 employees worldwide. IDG offers the widest range of media options that reach IT buyers in 75 countries representing 95% of worldwide IT spending. IDG's diverse product and services portfolio spans six key areas including print publishing, online publishing, expositions and conferences, market research, education and training, and global marketing services. More than 90 million people read one or more of IDG's 290 magazines and newspapers, including IDG's leading global brands — Computerworld, PC World, Network World, Macworld and the Channel World family of publications. IDG Books Worldwide is one of the fastest-growing computer book publishers in the world, with more than 700 titles in 36 languages. The "...For Dummies®" series alone has more than 50 million copies in print. IDG offers online users the largest network of technology-specific Web sites around the world through IDG.net (http://www.idg.net), which comprises more than 225 targeted Web sites in 55 countries worldwide. International Data Corporation (IDC) is the world's largest provider of information technology data, analysis and consulting, with research centers in over 41 countries and more than 400 research analysts worldwide. IDG World Expo is a leading producer of more than 168 globally branded conferences and expositions in 35 countries including E3 (Electronic Entertainment Expo), Macworld Expo, ComNet, Windows World Expo, ICE (Internet Commerce Expo), Agenda, DEMO, and Spotlight. IDG's training subsidiary, ExecuTrain, is the world's largest computer training company, with more than 230 locations worldwide and 785 training courses. IDG Marketing Services helps industry-leading IT companies build international brand recognition by developing global integrated marketing programs via IDG's print, online and exposition products worldwide. Further information about the company can be found at www.idg.com. 1/26/00

Authors' Acknowledgments

Now we know why those folks babble on so much at the Academy Awards.

Angie Ranck at the Orlando/Orange County Convention & Visitors Bureau and Sandra Robert at Walt Disney World make sure that we survive our time in the trenches.

Our grandson Joshua Jacob Tourigny, whom you meet in the book as "J.J.," gives us a youthful perspective, as well as the energy to attack the theme parks time after time.

And Naomi Kraus, lord high czarina and our editor at IDG Books Worldwide, has soft hands. She keeps our style intact, while saving us, in a literary sense, from wearing the emperor's clothes.

Publisher's Acknowledgments

We're proud of this book; please register your comments through our IDG Books Worldwide Online Registration Form located at http://my2cents.dummies.com.

Some of the people who helped bring this book to market include the following:

Editorial and Media Development

Editors: Alissa Cayton, Naomi P. Kraus

Copy Editor: Billie Williams

Cartographer: Elizabeth Puhl

Editorial Manager: Jennifer Ehrlich

Editorial Assistant: Carol Strickland

Production

Project Coordinator: Nancee Reeves

Layout and Graphics: Sean Decker, Gabriele McCann, Shelley Norris, Tracy K. Oliver, Kristin Pickett, Renee Schmith, Rashell Smith, Julie Trippetti, Jeremey Unger

Proofreaders: Vickie Broyles, Henry Lazarek, Linda Quigley, Sossity Smith

Indexer: Becky Hornyak

Special Help Christine Meloy Beck, Jennifer Ehrlich, Allyson Grove

General and Administrative

IDG Books Worldwide, Inc.: John Kilcullen, CEO; Bill Barry, President and COO

IDG Books Consumer Reference Group

Business: Kathleen A. Welton, Vice President and Publisher; Kevin Thornton, Acquisitions Manager

Cooking/Gardening: Jennifer Feldman, Associate Vice President and Publisher

Education/Reference: Diane Graves Steele, Vice President and Publisher; Greg Tubach, Publishing Director

Lifestyles: Kathleen Nebenhaus, Vice President and Publisher; Tracy Boggier, Managing Editor

Pets: Dominique De Vito, Associate Vice President and Publisher; Tracy Boggier, Managing Editor

Travel: Michael Spring, Vice President and Publisher; Suzanne Jannetta, Editorial Director; Brice Gosnell, Managing Editor

IDG Books Consumer Editorial Services: Kathleen Nebenhaus, Vice President and Publisher; Kristin A. Cocks, Editorial Director; Cindy Kitchel, Editorial Director

IDG Books Consumer Production: Debbie Stailey, Production Director

IDG Books Packaging: Marc J. Mikulich, Vice President, Brand Strategy and Research

♦

The publisher would like to give special thanks to Patrick J. McGovern, without whom this book would not have been possible.

♦

Contents at a Glance

Cartoons at a Glance

By Rich Tennant

The 5th Wave — By Rich Tennant

"Of all the theme hotels in Orlando, you had to pick one whose theme was The Great Depression!"

page 7

The 5th Wave — By Rich Tennant

"Oh quit complaining. The tickets were a lot less expensive than some of the other attractions, and admit it— when was the last time you saw a really good figure-sliding exhibition on an indoor linoleum rink with kitchen dinette obstacles?"

page 41

The 5th Wave — By Rich Tennant

"The hotel said they were giving us the 'Indiana Jones' suite."

page 105

The 5th Wave — By Rich Tennant

YOUR CHILDS FANTASY RESTAURANT

"I'LL START WITH THE BOLOGNA AND COCOA PUFFS, FRUIT ROLL UPS, AND A BOWL OF FRENCH JELLY SOUP FOR AN ENTREE I'LL HAVE SPAGHETTIOS WITH PEANUT BUTTER, AND A SIDE OF CHOCOLATE...HOT DOGS."

VERY GOOD SIR.

page 123

The 5th Wave — By Rich Tennant

"I know these are your character's names, but when you're around guests at the theme park, you're neither sleepy, dopey, or grumpy."

page 171

The 5th Wave — By Rich Tennant

SWIM WITH THE GIANT SQUID

"SINCE WE LOST THE DOLPHINS, BUSINESS HASN'T BEEN QUITE THE SAME."

page 259

The 5th Wave — By Rich Tennant

Dueling Pianos

"Actually, they started out as just bickering pianos."

page 317

The 5th Wave — By Rich Tennant

"Tell them we work at one of the theme parks, and maybe they won't ask too many questions."

page 335

Fax: 978-546-7747
E-mail: richtennant@the5thwave.com
World Wide Web: www.the5thwave.com

Maps at a Glance

Table of Contents

Introduction

● ●

*W*elcome to **Walt Disney World,** a land dominated by a king-sized rodent and a modern utopia to many of the young and young-at-heart. For those of us who have been around a while, **Walt Disney World** is a mystery: Some day, it will run out of gas. (Won't it?) But to the millions who make the pilgrimage here — a group that includes Super Bowl champs, a prince or two, and regular folks — it's a national shrine. That we admit. A crowded shrine at that.

But charting a successful course through the home of Mickey Mouse shouldn't be a chore; you are, after all, on vacation. All you need to ensure an enjoyable trip to Orlando is some patience, some advance planning, and a little childlike wonder — now how hard is that?

About This Book

Pay full price? Read the fine print? Do it their way?

Excuse us. There's no need for any of that.

You picked this book because you know the . . . *For Dummies* label and you want to go to **Walt Disney World.** You also probably know how much you want to spend, the pace you want to keep, and the amount of planning you can stomach. You may not want to tend to every little detail, yet you don't trust just anyone to make your plans for you.

In this book, we boil down what has become a world unto itself — **Walt Disney World** — and the surrounding Orlando area. Walt Disney's Florida legacy is still growing 35 years after his death. At current count, **Walt Disney World** includes four theme parks and a dozen lesser attractions, two entertainment districts, tens of thousands of hotel rooms, scores of restaurants, and twin cruise ships.

Universal Studios Escape and **SeaWorld** add three, soon to be four theme parks. There are also 80 or so smaller attractions nearby, an avalanche of restaurants, and some 110,000 lodging rooms in Orlando.

How can anyone sort through that kind of mess, you ask?

It takes experience.

After three decades of stomping through the House of the Mouse, we know where to find the best deals (deals that are not rip-offs). In this book, we guide you through **Walt Disney World** and Orlando in a clear, easy-to-understand way, allowing you to find the best hotels, restaurants, and attractions without having to read this book like a novel —

cover to cover. Although you can read this book from cover to cover if you choose, you can also flip to only those sections that interest you. We also promise not to overwhelm you with choices. We simply deliver the best, most essential ingredients for a great vacation.

Please be advised that travel information is subject to change at any time — and this is especially true of prices. We therefore suggest that you write or call ahead for confirmation when making your travel plans. The authors, editors, and publisher cannot be held responsible for the experiences of readers while traveling. Your safety is important to us, however, so we encourage you to stay alert and be aware of your surroundings. Keep a close eye on cameras, purses, and wallets, all favorite targets of thieves and pickpockets.

Conventions Used in This Book

In order to make this book an easier reference guide for you, we use some handy abbreviations when we review hotels, dining, and attractions.

You'll probably notice first that we often substitute **WDW** for **Walt Disney World** in order to spare you from having to read those three words over and over again. Also, because almost everything in Orlando revolves around its theme parks, you often find that we refer to the section of the city that encompasses the theme parks as simply "the parks."

Also, because Orlando does its best to make you max them out, we use the following abbreviations for commonly accepted credit cards:

   AE: American Express

   CB: Carte Blanche

   DC: Diners Club

   DISC: Discover

   JCB: Japan Credit Bank

   MC: MasterCard

   V: Visa

We also include some general pricing information to help you as you decide where to unpack your bags or dine on the local cuisine. We have used a system of dollar signs to show a range of costs for one night in a double-occupancy hotel room or a meal at a restaurant. (Included in the cost of each meal is the main course; allow for the 6 to 7 percent sales tax as well as any appetizers, drinks, or other extras you desire.) Check out the following table to decipher the dollar signs:

Cost	Hotel	Restaurant
$	$50–$100	$15 and under
$$	$100–$200	$15–$25
$$$	$200–$250	$25–$40
$$$$	$250 and up	$40 and up

Foolish Assumptions

As we wrote this book, we made some assumptions about you and what your needs might be as a traveler. Here's what we assumed about you:

- ✔ You may be an inexperienced traveler looking for guidance when determining whether to take a trip to **Walt Disney World** and Orlando and how to plan for it.

- ✔ You may be an experienced traveler who hasn't had much time to explore Orlando and wants expert advice when you finally do get a chance to enjoy that particular locale.

- ✔ You're not looking for a book that provides all the information available about Orlando or that lists every hotel, restaurant, or attraction available to you. Instead, you're looking for a book that focuses on the places that will give you the best or most unique experience in Orlando.

If you fit any of these criteria, then *Walt Disney World & Orlando For Dummies* gives you the information you're looking for!

How This Book Is Organized

Walt Disney World & Orlando For Dummies is divided into eight parts. The chapters in each part lay out the specifics within each part's topic. Likewise, each chapter is written so that you don't have to read what came before or after, though we sometimes refer you to other areas for more information.

Here's a brief look at the parts:

Part I: Getting Started

Think of this part as the hors d'oeuvres. In this part, we tempt you with the best experiences, hotels, eateries, and attractions at Disney and the rest of Orlando. We throw in a weather forecast and a look at special events, and then help you plan a budget. We also provide special tips for families, seniors, travelers with disabilities, and gay and lesbian travelers.

Part II: Ironing Out the Details

Should you use a travel agent? How about buying a package tour? Where can you find the best airfare? We answer those questions, and then talk about booking tips and online sources in this part. We also give you a menu of area hotels and motels, and we talk about travel insurance, renting a car, and packing tips.

Part III: Settling into Orlando

After we get you to Orlando, we introduce you to the neighborhoods and explore some of the *modus transporto* (local buses, trolleys, taxis, shuttles, and other vehicles to get from hither to yonder). We also discuss money matters, such as ATMs and taxes.

Part IV: Dining in Orlando

Yummmmmy. In Part IV, we detail the pros and cons of dining in the parks and related properties, discuss the dress code (clothes are a must, but leave the formal stuff behind), and show you how to save a few bucks. We also rate the restaurants and tell you where you can eat with Disney and other characters.

Part V: Exploring Walt Disney World

Yippeeee-I-O! In Part V, we push through the turnstiles and drive up the dividends of Disney stockholders. After introducing you to this 47-square-mile fantasyland, we give you a thorough look at the four main theme parks — **Magic Kingdom, Epcot, Disney–MGM Studios,** and **Animal Kingdom** — as well as the **WDW** water parks, Disney Cruise Line, and the rest of the World.

Part VI: Exploring the Rest of Orlando

Part VI explores life outside Mickeyville. **Universal Studios Florida, Islands of Adventure, SeaWorld,** and a few of the smaller attractions are worth some of your time and money. There are also some inviting day trips, including **Busch Gardens** and the **Kennedy Space Center.** And don't forget to give yourself time to shop for souvenirs.

Part VII: Living It Up after the Sun Goes Down: Orlando Nightlife

Long considered to be kids' destinations, Disney and the rest of Orlando have discovered that many of you want to party into the night. In Part VII, we explore **Pleasure Island, CityWalk,** and other thriving Orlando hot spots, as well as dinner shows and the performing arts.

Part VIII: The Part of Tens

Every Dummies book offers The Part of Tens. Finding this part in a . . . *For Dummies* book is as certain as annual rate increases at Disney and Universal. In Part VIII, we give you parting knowledge about cheap attractions as well as places where you can kill an hour of your time.

You'll also find two other elements near the back of this book. We have included an *appendix* — your Quick Concierge — containing lots of handy information you may need when traveling in Orlando, like phone numbers and addresses of emergency personnel or area hospitals and pharmacies, contact information for babysitters, lists of local newspapers and magazines, protocol for sending mail or finding taxis, and more. Check out this appendix when searching for answers to lots of little questions that may come up as you travel.

We have also included *worksheets* to make your travel planning easier — among other things, you can determine your travel budget, create specific itineraries, and keep a log of your favorite restaurants so that you can hit them again next time you're in town. You can find these worksheets easily because they're printed on yellow paper.

Icons Used in This Book

You'll find seven icons throughout this guide:

The Tip icon tells you how to save time (including ways to beat the lines) as well as provides other handy facts.

Watch for the Heads Up icon to identify annoying or potentially dangerous situations such as tourist traps, unsafe neighborhoods, budgetary rip-offs, and other things to beware.

The Remember icon highlights information that bears repeating. Bears repeating.

We use this icon to identify particularly kid-friendly hotels, restaurants, and other places, although most of Orlando is quite receptive to small fries.

Keep an eye out for the Bargain Alert icon as you seek out money-saving tips and/or great deals.

You encounter these icons when we start barnstorming through the big parks. Joshua Jacob, also known as J.J., our grandson, has graciously agreed to give you an 8-year-old's perspective on some of the rides, shows, and more.

Where to Go from Here

We've briefed you on what to expect from this book and told you how to use it to plan a magical vacation to **Walt Disney World** — no pixie dust necessary. So start reading; there's lots to do before you arrive, from arranging a place to hang your Mouse ears each night to exploring the best Orlando's theme parks have to offer. Like the Boy Scouts' creed, the successful Orlando traveler needs to "be prepared"; follow the advice in this book and you will be. And, last but not least, smile — you're going to **Disney World!**

Part I

Getting Started

The 5th Wave   By Rich Tennant

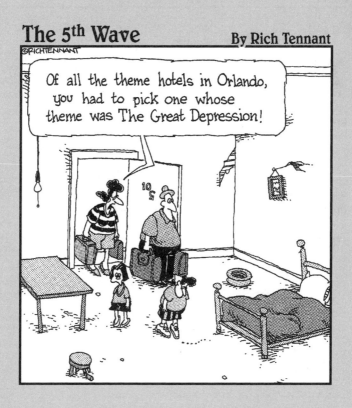

In this part . . .

To get the most enjoyment out of a vacation — with the least amount of hassle — it helps to know what awaits you in your chosen paradise before the landing gear lowers. Given its popularity, planning a trip to Walt Disney World as far in advance as possible is essential. In this part, we highlight the joys of a trip to Orlando and help you sort out the logistics of planning your trip, from choosing the best times of the year to go to planning your vacation budget. We also look at some of the best things to do while you're exploring Disney World and its environs.

Chapter 1

Discovering the Best of Walt Disney World and Orlando

In This Chapter

▶ Checking out must-do experiences and activities

▶ Finding great places to stay

▶ Locating the premier spots for dining

▶ Seeking the top thrill rides

▶ Finding hot things to do at night

*N*o matter what your interests — be it fine dining or finding out how fast you can go before losing your lunch — Orlando has something to offer you. There is a reason, after all, that this city is the number one domestic tourist destination in the United States. Thanks to its many offerings — theme parks, museums, and world-class resorts, just to name a few — the city manages to be all things to everybody, and consequently attracts visitors of all ages, from all backgrounds, and all countries. Yes, it can get crowded, and, in the summer, it's hot and sticky, but one thing you definitely won't be is bored.

All-Star Experiences

The major players in Orlando's vacation business (no surprise) are its numerous theme parks. You can spend your entire vacation inside these mega-amusement centers without running out of things to do. From *Cinderella's Castle* to *Big Thunder Mountain Railroad,* everyone loves the **Magic Kingdom,** Disney's original park, but there are also other great things to try inside Walt's World and around Orlando. Here's a list of exciting places to visit:

✔ At **Epcot,** you can travel around the globe in the *World Showcase,* pump up your adrenaline on such thrill rides as *Body Wars* and *Test Track in Future World*, and have a hands-on experience with the interactive games at *Innoventions*.

✔ **Disney–MGM Studios** is a ton of fun for all ages. Take a plunge down the *Tower of Terror,* ride the *Rock 'n' Roller Coaster,* and enjoy the spectacle of *Fantasmic!,* an after-dark mix of live-action, waterworks, and fireworks.

✔ **Universal Studios Florida** and its sister park, **Islands of Adventure,** combine cutting-edge, high-tech effects with great creativity. Their not-to-be-missed attractions include *Back to the Future, Terminator 2: 3-D Battle Across Time,* the *Incredible Hulk Coaster,* the *Amazing Adventures of Spider-Man,* and *Dueling Dragons.*

✔ With the opening of *Journey to Atlantis* and *Kraken,* **SeaWorld** has made headway in its battle to compete with Disney and Universal. But it's best to come here for the hands-on encounters with critters and the up-close views of polar bears, killer whales, and other creatures.

SeaWorld's new sister, **Discovery Cove,** offers a chance to swim with dolphins (for a premium) as part of a daylong package.

✔ If you're a night owl, you'll find it hard to call your trip complete without spending an evening at **Church Street Station.** Dance halls, old-fashioned saloons, dining rooms, and shopping make this downtown Orlando's prime place to party the night away.

Put Your Head on These Pillows

In the United States, Orlando is second only to Las Vegas in total number of hotel rooms, and with so many to choose from, no matter what kind of hotel you prefer, you'll find it here.

Walt Disney World has a vast selection of hotels from which to choose. Families find it hard to beat the woodsy **Fort Wilderness** or the **Wilderness Lodge,** whose features range from bunk beds to a geyser in the lobby. What more can a kid ask for?

Disney's **Dixie Landings** and **Port Orleans Resort** are the best choices among the moderately priced WDW properties. Both have plenty of amenities, including boat shuttles to nearby properties; swimming pools outfitted, respectively, with a waterfall and water slide; and multiple dining areas.

If you're on a leaner budget or not planning to spend much time in a room, you may prefer Disney's **All-Star Movie, All-Star Music,** and **All-Star Sports resorts.** With rates as low as $74 per night, they're the best bargain on WDW soil.

Don't need to stay in the World? Good. Booking a room in nearby Kissimmee, located only 10 to 15 minutes from **WDW,** can save you a lot of money. Although it doesn't have a lot of frills, the **Ramada Inn** on West Irlo Bronson Memorial Highway has rates as low as $40 per night. (See Chapter 3 for more suggestions on saving money on hotel rooms.)

Orlando & Walt Disney World

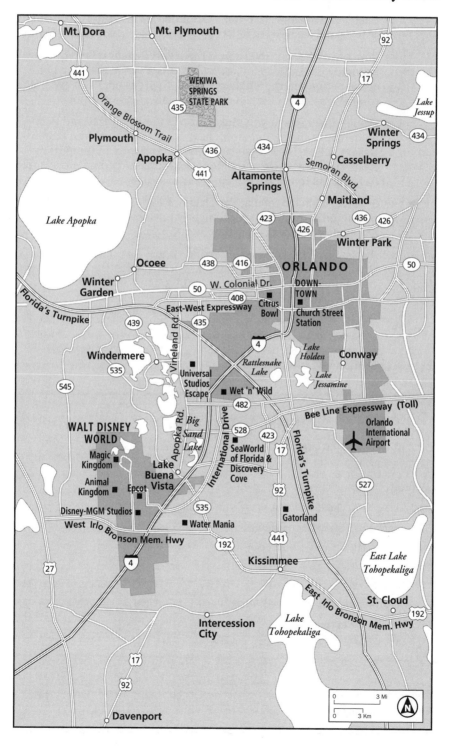

Here are other great hotels if you have special needs:

- ✔ **Business travelers: Marriott's Orlando World Center** has concierge service and an array of free-time ventures such as golf and tennis.

- ✔ **Romantics:** Set on 1,500 acres, the **Hyatt Regency Grand Cypress Resort,** with its swan-inhabited lakes, is a scenic place to get away. Better yet, the **Villas of Grand Cypress** offers an even more romantic setting, complete with fireplaces and whirlpools.

- ✔ **Disney Disciples:** If you must be on Disney property and in the epicenter of the action, don't miss the **Grand Floridian Beach Resort & Spa,** the **Polynesian Resort,** and the **Contemporary Resort.** All are on Disney's monorail route, providing quick and easy access to the parks.

- ✔ **Service:** It's hard to beat the elegant **Peabody Orlando's** 24-hour concierge and room service, nightly turndowns, and other attentive pampering perks.

- ✔ **Pools:** Disney resorts have terrific swimming pools, usually Olympic-size and based on themes. The pool at the **Caribbean Beach Resort,** for instance, resembles a fort with stone walls, cannons, and a water slide.

- ✔ **Health Club:** How can you beat a full Body by Jake club? The **Walt Disney World Dolphin** has one, complete with a weight room, aerobics classes, personal training, massages, body wraps, saunas, and more.

Who's going where?

The number of Florida theme-park visitors has dropped in recent years, according to *Amusement Business,* a trade magazine that estimates attendance.

Here are its 1999 figures and each park's national ranking:

1. Magic Kingdom, 15.2 million, down 3 percent.

3. Epcot, 10.1 million, down 5 percent.

4. Disney–MGM Studios, 8.7 million, down 8 percent.

5. Animal Kingdom, 8.6 million (first full year).

6. Universal Studios Florida, 8.1 million, down 9 percent (*Note:* Universal's Islands of Adventure didn't open until late summer 1999 but had 3.4 million visitors).

8. SeaWorld Florida, 4.7 million, down 4 percent.

9. Busch Gardens Tampa, 3.9 million, down 7 percent.

Sagging attendance is probably the reason that Disney, Universal, and SeaWorld raised one-day ticket prices $2 a head in January 2000. (The second time rates were hiked in less than a year.) Unless attendance suddenly explodes, don't expect rate hikes to stop any time soon.

Whet Your Appetite

Whether your prefer French cuisine or Italian, an elegant atmosphere or a rowdy one, there's probably a restaurant in Orlando that will cater to your every dining whim.

Think kids and it's hard to ignore the character meals at Walt Disney World parks and resorts. The best breakfast venue for character meals is the Garden Grill, a revolving restaurant in the *Land* pavilion at Epcot.

Do you prefer romance? The hands-down winner for romance-themed restaurants is Victoria & Albert's at Disney's Grand Floridian Resort. Dinner is an intimate, seven-course meal that retails for $85 a head (not including tax, tip, or wine — romance doesn't come cheap).

If you're dying for a view, Arthur's 27, which is on the 27th floor of the Wyndham Palace Resort in Lake Buena Vista, is hard to beat. You won't get a better angle for sunsets or Disney fireworks.

Here are some of the area's other bests:

- ✔ **Wine list:** Maison & Jardin in Altamonte Springs
- ✔ **California cuisine:** Pebbles in Lake Buena Vista
- ✔ **Italian chow:** Capriccio in the Peabody Hotel and Pacino's Italian Ristorante in Kissimmee
- ✔ **Seafood buffet:** the Cape May Café at Disney's Beach Club
- ✔ **Vegetarian fare:** the California Grill at Disney's Contemporary Resort

Chills and Thrills for Speed Freaks

If you're a speed freak who lives for the ups and downs of a good ride, Disney and the other parks will more than keep you busy.

The *Summit Plummet* water slide at Disney's **Blizzard Beach** starts pretty slow but finishes fast with a 120-foot, bathing suit-ripping free-fall. *The Amazing Adventures of Spider-Man* at **Islands of Adventure** is an amazing 3-D simulator that dips and twists through comic-book action. *The Incredible Hulk Coaster* at **Islands of Adventure** launches you from 0 to 40 mph in 2 seconds — and spins you through seven rollovers. *Dueling Dragons,* a set of twin coasters at **Islands of Adventure,** catapults your body through five inversions at 55 to 60 mph while coming within 12 inches of each other three times.

A twin-pack of rides at **Disney–MGM Studios** rounds out the adrenaline-inducing action. First up, *Rock 'n' Roller Coaster* rips from 0 to 60 mph in 2.8 seconds and goes directly into an inversion as 120 speakers blast Aerosmith at (yeeeow!) 32,000 watts in your stretch limo. If that doesn't send you into a tailspin, try the *Tower of Terror,* a free-fall experience that leaves your stomach hanging at several levels.

After the Sun Goes Down

Although Orlando is regarded primarily as a family destination, a red-eye culture has evolved thanks to those people who don't want to go to bed at the same time as the theme parks.

Pleasure Island in Downtown Disney is a six-acre complex of clubs and restaurants headlined by the high-energy Mannequins Dance Palace, the country flavor of the Wildhorse Saloon, and the rhythm and blues of the BET Soundstage. The adjoining **Disney West Side** offers the throaty sounds of the House of Blues, the renowned no-animals Cirque du Soleil, and the ultimate arcade, DisneyQuest.

The stars at Universal's **Citywalk** include the whimsical Jimmy Buffett's Margaritaville, Bob Marley — A Tribute to Freedom, Hard Rock Live, and the Motown Café Orlando.

In Downtown Orlando, **Church Street Station** is essentially one huge block party thanks to clubs such as Rosie O'Grady's Good Time Emporium and the Cheyenne Saloon and Opera House.

You can even ride a bucking bull (you don't need us to tell you that it's safer to watch) at another downtown nightspot, 8 Seconds, or rock the night away at The Globe Lounge.

Chapter 2

Planning Your Trip Schedule

. . . .

In This Chapter

▶ Considering the pros and cons of traveling in each season

▶ Checking out Orlando's weather patterns

▶ Consulting a calendar of special occasions

. . . .

*A*lthough, by most standards, Orlando remains a busy town throughout the year, some seasons are definitely busier than others. Deciding when to take your trip may affect what you see, how much you pay, and how long you stand in attraction lines. In this chapter, we analyze the advantages and disadvantages of visiting during various times of the year so that you can decide on the time of year that works best for your dream vacation plans.

The Secrets of the Seasons

In a nutshell, Orlando is Las Vegas for kids, so when they're out of school, the theme parks are a tangle of pushy, sweaty bodies. The busiest times to go are during spring break, summer (late May to Labor Day), and the winter holidays (mid-December to early January).

Obviously, your vacation experience is best when crowds are thinnest and the weather is mild. However, keep in mind that some attractions close down for refurbishing during these periods, so you may miss out on some stuff. In some cases, rooms are cheaper in the off-seasons, but unlike traditional vacation destinations, you won't get a major break on prices in Orlando when tourists aren't flocking to the parks. The city's convention, trade, and international visitors keep things busy year-round, so many hotels don't offer a high-low season rate scale. This year-round popularity also means that you need to book as early as possible.

Florida residents often scoot to the parks as a day trip or for a long weekend. Most out-of-state guests don't have that luxury. But if you have kids, take a hint from two families that we know and consider pulling them out of school for a few days during the off-season to avoid lines. Ask their teachers for schoolwork to take with you. You can also suggest that your kids write a report on some educational element of the vacation (yes, they will actually learn things while they're traipsing around the parks!), such as the *World Showcase* at **Epcot**.

Even if you come in the off-season, the parks run full tilt (though operating hours may be shorter). Orlando never turns out the lights, and each season has its perks and pitfalls.

Spring: Excitement blooms in Orlando

Spring is sensational in Orlando because

- The weather is mild.
- Accommodations that give discounts give them during spring.
- The lines at parks are relatively short.

But keep in mind that

- Without a winter, having a spring is hard. The temperature can get warm and sticky in April.
- The high pollen count can drive allergy sufferers crazy.
- Spring break cometh. Avoid this time period unless you're taking a break from the books.

Summer: Have fun in the Orlando sun

Summer is superb in Orlando because

- Sunrises and sunsets capped by fireworks. Need we say more?
- August means back-to-school sales at all Orlando's malls and outlets.
- All hotels, major restaurants, and indoor tourist attractions in Central Florida have air-conditioning.

However, keep in mind that

- The heat and humidity are oppressive.
- Crowds and sweat create a sometimes unpleasant perfume in the air.
- Discounts? Ha! Why cut prices with these crowds?

Fall: Harvest good times in Orlando

Fall is fabulous in Orlando because

- Ah, fall foliage. Orlando gets a 17-minute burst of fall colors. It's short but sweet.

> ✔ Accommodations that give discounts offer them in the fall.
>
> ✔ Lines in the parks begin to shrink to reasonable wait times.

But keep in mind that

> ✔ The weather is cooler, but the temperature doesn't get as mild as spring until Thanksgiving or later.
>
> ✔ Once mid-December arrives, so do the high prices.

Winter: You'll be warm and welcome in Orlando

Winter is wonderful in Orlando because

> ✔ Orlando doesn't have a true winter — just a few days at or near freezing, followed by mild, sunny weather.
>
> ✔ Lines at parks don't get much better than they are during winter.

However, remember that

> ✔ The many conventions held in Orlando throughout the year keep room rates reasonably high.
>
> ✔ During the mid-December to early January holidays, the parks are nearly as crowded as in the dead of summer.

Weather Warnings

You don't need to be paranoid, but knowing a little about Florida's weather-related temper tantrums is a good idea. Here's a list of weather events that you may experience during your stay:

> ✔ **Hurricanes:** The Gulf-and-Atlantic hurricane season runs from June 1 to November 30. In an average year, the Atlantic churns out ten of these storms, and one or two touch Florida. The good news is that Orlando's inland location means that the worst a storm will do is ruin a couple days of your vacation.
>
> ✔ **Lightning:** This scary but beautiful show courtesy of mother nature makes regular appearances during Orlando's frequent summer storms.
>
> However, don't let the presence of lightning ruin your trip. Unless you're standing in the wrong place (under an oak tree, wading in water, trying to hit a golf ball while wearing metal cleats and holding a metal club, or at the top of a roller coaster) at the wrong time, lightning's wrath is short-lived. (Summer thunderstorms are the largest providers of lightning in Florida.)

✔ **Sun:** Florida isn't called the Sunshine State for no reason. Make sure that you bring plenty of sunscreen on your trip. Florida tourism thrives on the sun, but you won't enjoy your vacation much if you're laid up with a painful sunburn or, even worse, sun poisoning.

Preventing your skin from turning a magnificent, and painful, shade of red is simple: Slather yourself with a 25-rated (or higher) sun block. And don't forget to keep re-applying it, especially after you hit the swimming pool. Likewise, remember to bring a wide-brimmed hat and don't forget a Florida native's favorite fashion statement — sunglasses.

Table 2-1 lists, by month, average high and low temperatures recorded in Central Florida.

Table 2-1		Central Florida Average Temperatures									
Jan	**Feb**	**Mar**	**Apr**	**May**	**June**	**July**	**Aug**	**Sept**	**Oct**	**Nov**	**Dec**
High °F											
71.7	72.9	78.3	83.6	88.3	90.6	91.7	91.6	89.7	84.4	78.2	73.1
High°C											
22.0	22.7	25.7	28.7	31.3	32.5	33.2	33.1	32.0	29.1	25.7	22.8
Low °F											
49.3	50.0	55.3	60.3	66.2	71.2	73.0	73.4	72.5	65.4	56.8	50.9
Low°C											
9.6	10.0	12.5	15.7	19.0	21.8	22.7	23.0	22.5	18.6	13.8	10.5

Orlando's Calendar: Attractions in Review

In this section, we list (by month) just a few of Orlando's many exciting festivals and special events. Please double-check with festivals and their organizations before planning your vacation around any of these events. Event dates are subject to change.

You can access Orlando's major daily newspaper, the *Orlando Sentinel,* at www.orlandosentinel.com for information about upcoming events.

✔ **January.** Enjoy the Zora Neale Hurston Festival celebrated in Eatonville, the first incorporated African-American town in America. The four-day festival highlights the life and works of author Zora Neale Hurston and is usually held the last weekend in January. Eatonville is 25 miles north of the parks. Admission is $3. Lectures or seminars require additional fees. Call ☎ **800-352-3865** or 407-647-3307 for details.

✔ **February.** Come and experience **Mardi Gras at Universal Studios.** Authentic parade floats from New Orleans, stilt walkers, and traditional doubloons and beads add to the fun of this event, which is included in the price of admission to the park. This event also includes special entertainment. It's in mid-February. For information call ☎ **800-837-2273** or 407-363-8000; www.uescape.com.

Also in mid-February, welcome the **Atlanta Braves** as they arrive for spring training at **Disney's Wide World of Sports Complex.** They play an 18-game spring season that begins in early March. Tickets are $8.50 and $15.50. For general information, call ☎ **407-828-3267.** To purchase tickets, call TicketMaster at ☎ **407-839-3900.** You can also get information online at www.majorleaguebaseball.com/springtraining/.

✔ **April.** More than 100 acts from around the world participate in **Orlando International Fringe Festival,** an eclectic event held for 10 days in April and May at various locations in downtown Orlando. Entertainers perform drama, comedy, political satire, experimental theater, and a seven-minute version of Hamlet, all on an outdoor stage. Ticket prices vary, but most performances are under $12. Call ☎ **407-648-0077** for more information.

✔ **June.** The first weekend in June draws tens of thousands of gay and lesbian travelers to Central Florida for **Gay Weekend.** This event grew out of "Gay Day," an unofficial event at **Disney World** dating to the early 1990s when it drew 50,000 people. **Universal Studios Escape** and **SeaWorld** also host this gay and lesbian weekend. You can find online information at www.gayday.com.

✔ **July.** Orlando is a hot spot in July. **Independence Day** is celebrated with bands, singers, dancers, and unbelievable fireworks displays at **Disney's Star-Spangled Spectacular.** The parks stay open late for the occasion (☎ **407-824-4321**). **SeaWorld** exhibits a dazzling laser/fireworks spectacular (☎ **407-351-3600**), and Orlando's Lake Eola Park shows a free display, too (☎ **407-246-2827**).

✔ **September.** One weekend each September, the **Magic Kingdom** hosts a contemporary Christian music festival featuring top artists. **Night of Joy** is a very popular event, so if it's on your dance card, get tickets ($25–$30) early. Ticket price also includes access to all **Magic Kingdom** attractions. Call ☎ **407-824-4321** for more information.

✔ **October.** Orlando is frightfully fun in October as **Universal Studios** hosts **Halloween Horror Nights** (☎ **800-837-2273** or 407-363-8000; www.uescape.com). The park transforms its grounds for 19 nights into a mass of haunted attractions, complete with live bands, special shows, a psychopath's maze, and hundreds of ghouls and goblins roaming the streets. The studio closes at dusk and then reopens in a new, chilling form at 7 p.m. The park charges special admission for this event and also serves alcohol. Guests aren't allowed to wear costumes to ensure that Universal employees can spot their peers.

Also in October, enjoy the **Epcot International Food & Wine Festival.** Here's your chance to sip and savor the food and beverages of 30 cultures. For information, call ☎ **407-824-4321.**

✔ **November.** The second weekend in November brings **The Walt Disney World Festival of the Masters.** For three days, **Downtown Disney Marketplace** is home to one of the largest art shows in the South. The exhibition features top artists, photographers, and craftspeople — all winners of juried shows throughout the United States. Admission is free. Call ☎ **407-824-4321** for details, or visit http://disney.go.com/DisneyWorld/intro.html.

✔ **December.** During the Disney Christmas festivities, Main Street in the **Magic Kingdom** is lavishly decked out with lights and holly, and carolers welcome visitors to **Christmas at Walt Disney World.** Thousands of colored lights illuminate an 80-foot tree. **Epcot, Disney–MGM Studios,** and **Animal Kingdom** also offer special embellishments and entertainment throughout the holiday season, as do all Disney resorts. Some holiday highlights include *Mickey's Very Merry Christmas Party,* an after-dark ticketed event, which takes place on weekends at the **Magic Kingdom** and offers a traditional Christmas parade and fireworks display. Admission, usually under $40, includes cookies, cocoa, and a souvenir photo. The best part? Shorter lines for rides. The *Candlelight Procession* at **Epcot** features hundreds of candle-holding carolers, a celebrity narrator telling the Christmas story, and a 450-voice choir that's very moving. Call ☎ **407-0824-4321** for details concerning all these events.

Also in December, **The Osborne Family Christmas Lights** spectacular is on display. This magnificent display came to **Disney–MGM Studios** in 1995 when the Arkansas family ran into trouble with hometown authorities over their multimillion-light display. In a twinkle, Disney moved the whole shebang to Florida. For online information on Christmas activities, go to http://disney.go.com/DisneyWorld/intro.html.

Chapter 3

Preparing Your Budget

● ●

In This Chapter

▶ Managing your dollars and cents

▶ Avoiding surprise expenses

▶ Debating traveler's checks, credit cards, ATMs, and cash

▶ Cost-cutting tidbits

● ●

Developing a realistic budget is an important key to enjoying your vacation — the last thing you want to experience when you get to Orlando is sticker shock, and the city is famous for its ability to exact a pound of flesh from even the most cost-conscious traveler. From the hotel rooms to dining to admission fees, you can ring up a high tally if you don't do your homework in advance. The good news is that we can help you make sure that you don't bust your bankroll.

Adding Up Your Costs

Budgeting your Walt Disney World vacation is easy, and using the worksheets that we include in the Appendix of this book gives you a pretty accurate estimate of its cost. The hard part is sticking to the budget that you create. Mickey and his pals are masters when it comes to separating you from your dollars. Vacationing at **Walt Disney World** makes you feel good, even giddy, and before you know it, you'll be out of dough.

If you avoid impulse bingeing — er, buying — and draft an honest budget, you'll avoid running out of money (or facing shock therapy when your credit-card bills arrive).

Make sure to include everything in your vacation budget. Add the cost of getting to the airport, airport parking (if you're driving yourself), airline tickets (you can find tips for getting the best airfare in Chapter 5), transportation from the Orlando airport to your room, your room rates, meals, shuttle or rental car charges, park admission (multiplied by the number of days you'll visit), the cost of any other attractions that you want to explore, and entertainment expenses. Tack on another 15 to 20 percent as a safety net. (How can you turn down your kids when they beg for Pluto slippers?)

Here are some things to expect in the way of prices when you get to Orlando:

- ✔ **Lodging.** The average room in Orlando costs $90 to $95 a night; in most cases, that rate includes any children staying in the room. The full range is $40 to $300 or more if you prefer suites or condos. If you choose to stay on Disney property, the average room sets you back $120 to $125 per night; the lowest-priced room costs $74, and prices for the most expensive rooms are in the stratosphere.

- ✔ **Transportation.** Some hotels offer free shuttles to the parks; others take you for a fee (see Chapter 8 for more information). If you stay at **Disney,** you can access its free transportation system (though it's plodding). Rental-car rates start at about $35 a day (don't forget to add the $6 daily charge to park your car at the theme parks if you don't stay on Disney property).

- ✔ **Dining.** Chowing down in Orlando will cost you an average of $80 per person, per day; $100 if you dine mostly in the theme parks or at Disney's and Universal's resorts (see Chapters 13 and 14 for more information on dining). Keep in mind that food in the parks and resorts is overpriced and occasionally mirrors the same quality as cardboard. Outside the parks, you can find delis for takeout and assorted budget eateries. Also, don't overlook the option of a room with a small kitchen or microwave.

- ✔ **Attractions.** Your expenses for attractions depend on what kind of parks you favor and how often you go. Disney, Universal, and SeaWorld theme parks charge $46 for adults and $37 for kids per day (see Chapters 17 though 25 for information on the individual parks). If you're going to visit regularly, buy one of the multiday, multipark passes that we outline in Chapters 17 though 25. Parts V and VI of this book also include some free and inexpensive attractions that you can visit if you want to lower your costs.

- ✔ **Shopping and Entertainment.** Orlando is no shopper's paradise, but there are two large malls and some outlets (see Chapter 27) where you can find a bargain. We don't recommend allowing yourself to gouge in the amusement-park gift shops unless you find a must-have souvenir.

Table 3-1 outlines various vacationing costs in Orlando.

Table 3-1 What Things Cost in Orlando

Transportation	U.S.$	U.K.£ (As of this writing, $1.65 = 1£)
Taxi from airport to WDW	42.00	25.43
Shuttle from airport to WDW (adult fare)	14.00	8.48
Accommodations	**U.S.$**	**U.K.£ (As of this writing, $1.65 = 1£)**
Double room at Days Inn, Kissimmee	39.00–59.00	23.61–35.72
Double room at Disney's All-Star Music Resort	74.00–104.00	45.28–63.63
Double room at Disney's Port Orleans Resort	124.00–189.00	75.87–115.65
Double room at Marriott's Orlando World Center	224.00–2,400.00	137.06–1,468.50
Double room at Disney's Grand Floridian Beach Resort & Spa	304.00–1,995.00	186–1,220.69
Food and Beverages	**U.S.$**	**U.K.£ (As of this writing, $1.65 = 1£)**
Coca-Cola (restaurant)	1.25	.76
Bottle of beer (restaurant)	2.50	1.51
All-you-can-eat buffet dinner at Akershus in Epcot, not including tip or wine	18.50	11.20
Seven-course fixed-price dinner for one at Victoria & Albert's, not including tip or wine	85.00–160.00	48.43–96.87
Attractions	**U.S.$**	**U.K.£ (As of this writing, $1.65 = 1£)**
Child 1-day, 1-park admission to Walt Disney World, Universal, or SeaWorld parks	37.00	22.46
Adult 1-day, 1-park admission to Walt Disney World, Universal, or SeaWorld parks	46.00	27.93
Child 3-day Universal Studios Escape Pass (unlimited access)	95.00	57.52
Adult 3-day Universal Studios Escape Pass (unlimited access)	114.95	69.60
Child 4-Day Park Hopper admission to Walt Disney World	142.00	86.21
Adult 4-Day Park Hopper admission (unlimited access) to Walt Disney World	176.00	106.85

Keeping a Rein on Runaway Expenses

Even the biggest of penny pinchers can forget to include certain items in their travel budget, resulting in a much larger tab than expected. A big reason these costs are hidden is that they are almost never quoted to you when you inquire about hotel or car-rental rates, unless you specifically ask about added charges. And visitors often underestimate the greed of the theme parks and their own inability to pass up those high-priced Mickey ears.

Look out for these surprises that can wreak havoc on your budget:

- ✔ **Sales Tax:** Florida has a 6 percent sales tax that's added to most things except groceries and medical services. In addition, expect another 5 percent, for a total of 11 percent, added to your hotel room in **Walt Disney World** and Orlando; 12 percent in nearby Kissimmee.

- ✔ **Car-Rental Charges:** Sales tax, surcharges, and various other required add-ons can add 20 to 25 percent to the quoted rates.

- ✔ **Tipping:** A 15 percent tip is the general rule for restaurant service and cab rides. The hotel housekeeper deserves $1 to $2 a day for cleaning your mess, making your beds, and keeping you stocked with towels. Baggage handlers usually receive $1 per bag.

- ✔ **A Prisoner of the Parks:** Whether you're visiting theme parks for the day or you're trapped for the length of your stay in a Disney or Universal resort without a car, expect to be charged more than your fair share for meals and more.

Paper, Plastic, or Pocket Change?

There are a number of options you can choose from to pay for your vacation, including meals, souvenirs, and so on. In this section, we explore the available options to help you determine the one that's right for you.

Traveling with traveler's checks

Traveler's checks are a throwback to the days before ATM machines gave you easy access to your money. Because you can replace them if they're lost or stolen, traveler's checks are a sound alternative to stuffing your wallet with cash. However, you may have trouble cashing them in some places. Common issuers include American Express, ☎ **800-221-7282,** and MasterCard, ☎ **800-223-9920.** (See Chapter 9 for more information on acquiring traveler's checks.)

Relying on ATMs

Many folks prefer to use ATMs when on vacation. At **Walt Disney World,** you can find ATMs on Main Street and in *Tomorrowland* in the **Magic Kingdom;** at the entrances to **Epcot, Disney–MGM Studios,** and **Animal Kingdom;** at **Pleasure Island;** and in **Downtown Disney Marketplace.** You can also find ATMs near Guest Services at **SeaWorld, Universal Studios Florida,** and **Islands of Adventure** (also at *The Lost Continent* near the bridge leading to *Jurassic Park*).

Outside of the amusement parks, you can find ATMs at most malls, convenience stores, and some grocery and drug stores. But remember that you frequently must pay an extra charge for using non-bank ATMs. In Florida, you're assessed an average charge of $2.60 if you use an ATM that isn't affiliated with your bank.

Cirrus (☎ **800-424-7787**) and Plus (☎ **800-843-7587**) are the two most popular networks; check the back of your ATM card to find out what network your bank affiliates with. (The 800-numbers also provide ATM locations where you can withdraw money.) Withdraw only as much cash as you need for incidentals — we recommend carrying no more than $50 or $60.

Be extremely careful when using ATMs, especially at night and in areas that are heavily traveled and aren't well lit. Don't let the land of Mickey lull you into a false sense of security. Goofy and Pluto won't mug you — but thieves working the theme parks may.

Charge! Carrying the cards

Traveling with credit cards is a safe alternative to carrying cash. Credit cards also provide you with a record of your vacation expenses once you return home. Most major credit cards are accepted throughout Central Florida, though WDW parks and resorts take only American Express, MasterCard, Visa, and the Disney Card, which you can use at any Disney store, restaurant, or vacation property. You can get cash advances from your major credit accounts, but make sure that you have your personal identification number (PIN) before leaving home. To get your PIN, call your credit card's issuer and ask them to send it to you.

Tips for Cutting Costs

You can conserve your cash in more than just a couple of ways when you vacation in Orlando. Use these tips to keep your vacation costs manageable:

> ✔ **Consider a package.** This doesn't mean an escorted tour, just a package that includes accommodations, airfare, and in some cases, additional perks. See Chapter 5 for more information on the ins and outs of package tours.

✔ **Visit during the off-season.** Hotel prices in the off-season cost almost half as much as during peak months. If possible, travel at non-peak times (September to November or April to June, for example).

✔ **Travel during off-days of the week.** Airfares vary depending on the day of the week that you fly. You can often cut your airfare in half if you stay over on a Saturday night. Likewise, you may find cheaper flights if you travel on a Tuesday, Wednesday, or Thursday. See Chapter 5 for more tips on getting the best airfare.

✔ **Find out if your kids can stay in your room with you free.** A room with two double beds usually doesn't cost more than a room with a queen-size bed. Many hotels don't charge you extra if the third and fourth persons are children. Reserving one room and paying an extra $10 to $15 for a rollaway can save you hundreds over the course of your vacation.

✔ **Reserve a room with a kitchen and do your own cooking.** Although the family chef may disagree with this suggestion, you can limit the amount of times per day that you eat out.

✔ **If you have a multiday pass to a theme park, utilize your in-and-out privileges.** Go back to your hotel for a picnic lunch and a swim or nap. You can eat economically, miss the midday sun, and refuel for an evening at the park.

✔ **Avoid splurging — pace yourself.** Your money goes fastest when you overexert yourself exploring the parks, and you end up too hungry, thirsty, or tired to care about how much you spend. Begin each day with a big breakfast at a fast-food restaurant or an all-you-can-eat buffet (you can find several outside the parks that cost around $3 to $5). Also, remember to stop often at drinking fountains, because cold sodas at attractions are extremely overpriced.

✔ **Brown-bag it.** Bringing your own food is extremely cost-effective. Remember, however, that parks are wise to this scheme, so make your operation covert — hide it.

✔ **Make lunch the most expensive meal of the day.** Trying out expensive restaurants makes more sense at lunchtime, rather than dinner. Most restaurants often have the same menu as at dinner, but at lower prices. Make sure that you also check out the early-bird specials.

✔ **Don't spend every day at a theme park.** Discover your hotel's pool, playground, workout room, and other freebies. Also, get out of town and head for one of the lower-priced attractions away from theme-park-central.

✔ **Skip souvenirs.** Make your photographs and memories the best mementos of your trip. If you're worried about money, do without the T-shirts, key chains, salt-and-pepper shakers, mouse ears, and other trinkets. Set a spending limit and stick to it!

✔ **Use your Magic Kingdom Club Gold Card.** The Magic Kingdom Club Gold Card provides a 10 to 20 percent discount at WDW resorts and on related packages and meals in the parks, and up to 30 percent off some rental cars. A two-year membership is $65 ($50 if you're 55 or older.) If you're a working stiff, ask if your company is a member, because many companies offer the card as a free benefit to employees. For more information, call ☎ **714-490-3200.** If you're a Disney stockholder, you can also ask Shareholder Relations (☎ **818-553-7200**) about discounts or incentives.

✔ **Receive instant discounts with an Orlando Magicard.** Another discount card, the Orlando Magicard is good for up to $500 in discounts on accommodations, car rentals, attractions, and more. You can retrieve a Magicard from the Orlando/Orange County Convention & Visitors Bureau, 8723 International Dr., Suite 101, Orlando, FL 32819 (☎ **800-551-0181** or 407-363-5871). You may also be eligible for other discounts if you're a member of AARP, AAA, the military, or some service clubs, so don't be bashful — just ask.

Chapter 4

Planning Ahead for Special Travel Needs

● ●

In This Chapter

▶ Travel tips for the whole family

▶ Travel advice for the senior set

▶ Travel tips for the disabled

▶ Travel advice for gays and lesbians

● ●

*W*orried that your kids are too young or that you're too old to enjoy Disney and beyond? Afraid you may experience barriers blocking your access or lifestyle? In this chapter, we dispense a little advice for travelers with specific needs.

Making Family Travel Fun

Orlando loves kids and welcomes them like no other city in the world. In addition to its theme parks, Orlando has plenty of smaller kid-friendly attractions. All but a few restaurants offer low-priced children's menus (see Chapter 14 for more info on kids and dining), and most hotels go crazy over their younger guests, providing pint-size pools and, in some cases, special gifts and programs (see Chapter 8 for kid-friendly hotels).

 However, despite Orlando's reputation as Kidsville, U.S.A., you may find that some attractions are a bit too sophisticated or intense for kids, including most of **Epcot's** exhibits (see Chapter 18) and many of the primo thrill rides at **Islands of Adventure** (Chapter 24). Likewise, you may find other attractions, such as **Discovery Cove** (Chapter 25), cost prohibitive.

Traveling with tots

Traveling with young children can often bring you more stress than relaxation on your vacation. Consider that younger children have special needs. They often eat on a routine basis, require frequent bathroom breaks, and have very short attention spans. (Does the phrase,

"Dad, are we there yet?" ring a bell?) Here are a few general suggestions for making travel plans for you and your youngsters:

✔ **Consider age — are your kids old enough?** Do you really want to bring an infant or a toddler to an overcrowded, usually overheated world that he or she may not appreciate because of his or her age? The large number of stroller-pushing, toddler-toting parents in the parks suggests that many people think the experience isn't too terrible, but we're warning you anyway. Our younger grandson, Andy, is 3 and just able to appreciate a few of the parks' offerings, especially those at **Disney's Magic Kingdom** (see Chapter 17). However, some of the costume-wearing characters frighten him, he wants a nap when we want to see the parade, and he's deadweight when we have to carry him when he gets too tired. No matter how organized you are, a little one is going to slow you down. Put your family in our position and ask yourself whether your family will enjoy a trip under such conditions that also costs the equivalent of a developing nation's GNP (gross national product)? Think of it this way — would you bring a toddler to the opera?

✔ **Accommodations for the little ones.** Kids under 12 (and older, in many cases) can stay for free in their parents' room in most hotels. Look for places that have pools and other recreational facilities so that your family can spend a no-extra-expense day or two away from the parks. If you want to skip a rental car and aren't staying at Disney, **International Drive** is the next-best place for centralized rooms, restaurants, and attractions. Public buses run there frequently, hotels often offer family discounts (see Chapter 8), and some provide free or moderate cost shuttles to **Walt Disney World, SeaWorld,** and **Universal Studios.**

✔ **Select a sitter service.** Most Orlando hotels offer baby-sitting services and several Disney properties have marvelous child-care facilities with counselor-supervised activity programs on the premises. **Walt Disney World** properties have used KinderCare sitters since 1981 (☎ **407-827-5444**). All their sitters are very carefully checked out, including a criminal background search, and if you're not staying at a Disney accommodation, you can call KinderCare on your own. In fact, they can even take your kids to the park or to any of the services at your resort, except swimming. Rates for in-room service are $12 per hour for one child, $13 per hour for two children, and $14 per hour for three kids, with a four-hour minimum — the first half-hour of which is travel time for the sitter. Call 24 hours in advance to make a reservation or to check rates for more than four kids.

✔ **Plan ahead for character dining.** If you would like to eat a meal with a cast of Disney characters while at **Walt Disney World,** then make character dining reservations when you reserve your hotel room. (See Chapter 15 for more details about character dining.)

Also, once you're in **WDW,** check the daily schedule for character appearances (all the major parks post them on maps or boards near the entrance) and make sure the kids know when they're going to meet their heroes, because doing so is often the highlight of their day. A little pre-planning can help you avoid running after every character you see, which only tires out your little ones and gives you sore feet. And remember — the "in" thing is getting character autographs, so take our advice: Buy an autograph book at home instead of paying premium park prices.

✔ **Establish ground rules.** Being firm when the object is fun is tough, but consider setting firm rules before leaving home on things like bedtime and souvenirs. Your kids will be on something akin to a sugar high while they're on vacation (you may be, too), so don't allow giddiness to take control of your senses.

✔ **Keep tabs on the little ones in the land of Mickey.** Getting lost inside a theme park is as easy as remembering your middle name. Getting found takes a bit more work. For adults and older kids, make sure that you arrange a lost-and-found meeting place as soon as you arrive in the park. Attach a name tag to younger kids, and find a park employee as soon as you're separated from your party. We list lost-and-found locations in our description of each of the major theme parks in Chapters 17 through 25.

✔ **Pack to toddler-proof your hotel room.** Although your home may be toddler-proof, hotel rooms aren't. Bring blank plugs to cover outlets and whatever else is necessary to prevent an accident from occurring in your room.

✔ **Staying safe in the sun.** Don't forget to bring sunscreen for the entire family. If you forget to bring it, buy sunscreen with a 25 or higher rating at a convenience store or a drugstore (some theme-park shops also carry it). Slather your young children — even if they're in a stroller — and make sure that you pack a hat for infants and toddlers. Likewise, make sure that everyone traveling with you drinks plenty of water to avoid dehydration.

✔ **Remember ride restrictions.** Most parks explain their height restrictions for certain attractions or identify those that may unsettle young children. (We also list these restrictions in our dis-cussions of the major theme parks in Chapters 17–25.) Save your-self and your kids some grief before you get in line and experience disappointment. Make your restriction rules firm — a bad trip down a darkened tunnel or a scary loop-de-loop can make your youngster cranky all day (and the fear of such rides can last a long while thereafter).

✔ **Take time out for a show.** Take time for an inside, air-conditioned show two or three times a day, especially during afternoons in the summer. They're a good way to beat the heat, and you may even get your littlest tikes to nap in the darkened theater. For all shows, arrive at least 20 minutes early to avoid the bad seats, but not so early that the kids go nuts waiting (most of the waiting areas are outside).

✓ **Pack a snack.** When dreaming of your vacation, you probably don't envision hours spent standing in lines, waiting and waiting. Unfortunately, doing so is an inevitability you can't avoid. Store some lightweight snacks in an easy-to-carry backpack, especially when traveling with small kids to save you headaches and save you money over park prices, which are sometimes double those in the free world.

✓ **Rent a stroller.** Unless you're particularly attached to your stroller, or it's specially designed for triplets, you won't have a problem using the ones provided by the parks, most of which charge about $6 a day for rentals. Renting a stroller from the parks allows you to avoid hauling yours to and from the car or on and off the trams, trains, or monorails. However, there are exceptions — the most notable being **Universal Studios Florida** and **Islands of Adventure,** where you face a long walk from the parking lot to the ticket booths. For infants and toddlers, you may want to bring a sling or backpack-type carrier to use when traveling to and from the parking lots as well as while you're standing in line for the shows and attractions.

✓ **Take a break.** The **Disney, Universal,** and **SeaWorld** parks maintain play areas that offer parents a rest while their kids continue to have fun. Schedule two or three visits to these spots a day, depending on your stamina. Many of these kid zones include water toys, and some parks have major water-related rides, so packing a change of clothes for the whole family is a good idea. Rent a locker ($5 or less) and store your spare duds until you need them. During summer months, the Florida humidity can keep you feeling soggy all day, so you'll appreciate the fresh clothing. (So will other visitors who enter your air space.)

✓ **Plan playtime for parents. Walt Disney World** and **Universal Studios** both offer a parent-swap program for parents traveling with small children. On many of the "big kid" rides, one parent can ride the attraction while the other stays with the kids, and then the adults can switch places without having to stand in line again. Notify a staff member that you want to take advantage of this program when you get in line.

Finding kid-friendly tours

Many theme parks specially design tours that appeal to the younger set, which include great sources of age-appropriate entertainment.

SeaWorld has justifiably earned its reputation as a park that makes education fun and offers a variety of tours. One of the most interesting is the *Polar Expedition Guided Tour.* This hour-long journey gives kids a chance to come face to face with a penguin and get a behind-the-scenes look at "Wild Arctic" support areas. Call ☎ **407-370-1380** to schedule a tour. *To the Rescue,* another hour-long tour, allows you to see some of the park's rescue and rehabilitation work with several species, including manatees and rare sea turtles. Both tours are kid-friendly, though the latter may appeal more to older children. **SeaWorld** tours are offered on a first-come, first-serve basis, so reserve a place at the Guided Tour Information desk when you enter the park. They cost $7 for adults and $6 for 3- to 9-year-olds, plus park admission. Call ☎ **800-406-2244** for more information. In June, July, and August, *Camp SeaWorld* offers 200 classes, including some sleepover programs and family courses. Contact ☎ **407-370-1380** for more details.

At **Walt Disney World,** half-day *Disney Day Camp* excursions are divided into two age groups: 7 to 10 and 11 to 15. These tours offer a good chance for you to take a break while your kids interact with peers in programs that range from exploring special effects at **Disney–MGM Studios** to seeing the wonders of China at **Epcot.** The two daily programs take place 8:00 a.m. to noon and 1:30 to 5:00 p.m. A half-day program costs $69; a whole-day program is $99. A box lunch is available, and park admission isn't required. **WDW** also offers a *Family Magic Tour* that's actually an interactive scavenger hunt. The tour costs $25 for adults and $15 for kids ages 3 to 9. Park admission is required. Call ☎ **407-939-8687** for more details.

Cutting Costs — Savings for Seniors

Although Orlando is a kid- and family-oriented zone, many of its hotels, restaurants, and attractions also roll out the red carpet for older travelers. You can find discounts from several sources, which we list in this section.

Saving money on accommodations

If you're not a member of AARP (American Association of Retired Persons), 601 E. St. NW, Washington, DC 20049 (☎ **800-424-3410** or 202-434-AARP; www.aarp.org), do yourself a favor and join. Doing so enables you to receive discounts on car rentals and hotels.

Mature Outlook, P.O. Box 9390, Des Moines, IA 50322 (☎ **800-336-6330**), is an organization similar to AARP, offering discounts on car rentals and many **Holiday Inn, Howard Johnson,** and **Best Western** hotels. The $19.95 annual membership fee also gets you $200 in Sears coupons and a bimonthly magazine. Membership is open to all Sears customers 18 and over, but the organization's primary focus is on the 50-and-over market.

Money-saving publications

A monthly newsletter on senior citizen travel, the *Mature Traveler* is a valuable resource that you can obtain by subscription ($30 a year). For a free sample, send a postcard with your name and address to GEM Publishing Group, Box 50400, Reno, NV 89513 (E-mail: `maturetrav@aol.com`). GEM also publishes a collection of more than 1,000 senior discounts on airlines, lodging, tours, and attractions around the country. You can call ☎ **800-460-6676** to purchase *The Book of Deals* for $9.95.

Another helpful publication is *101 Tips for the Mature Traveler,* available from Grand Circle Travel, 347 Congress St., Suite 3A, Boston, MA 02210 (☎ **800-221-2610**; `www.gct.com`). Grand Circle Travel is one of hundreds of travel agencies that specialize in senior vacations. SAGA International Holidays, 222 Berkeley St., Boston, MA 02116 (☎ **800-343-0273**), offers inclusive tours and cruises for people 50 and older.

If you're 55 or older, you can receive additional Orlando savings through the Magic Kingdom's Gold Club Card. The card's first perk is its cost: $50 for a two-year membership, which is $15 cheaper than the amount that young whippersnappers pay. The card's dividends include 10 to 30 percent discounts at WDW parks, resorts, and restaurants, as well as savings on travel packages, merchandise, and car rentals. Call ☎ 800-563-4763 for more information on the program.

Additional savings for seniors

If you're a senior, here are some additional ways for you to save money:

- ✔ **Hilton's** Senior Honors Program, available to people 60 and older, provides discounts up to 50 percent off hotel rooms. The annual membership is $50 per person, but because spouses stay for free, only one of you needs to join if you travel together. Call ☎ 800-432-3600 7 a.m. to 7 p.m. CST, Monday through Friday.

- ✔ The **Choice Hotels** group (**Comfort, Clarion, Sleep, Rodeway, Econo Lodge,** and **Friendship**) gives travelers 50 and older 30 percent off regular rates if they reserve in advance (10 percent for walk-ins). The hotels set aside only a few rooms for these Senior Saver Discounts, so book early. Call ☎ 800-424-4777 for **Econo Lodge, Rodeway,** and **Friendship** inns, and ☎ 800-221-2222 for the others.

- ✔ Most U.S. airlines sell senior airfare coupons for travelers 62 and older. Each coupon is good for one flight anywhere in the United States. You can buy a packet of four coupons for $542–$596. Each coupon is valid for one-way travel.

> ✔ Amtrak (☎ **800-872-7245**) offers a 15 percent discount on the lowest available coach fare (with certain travel restrictions) to people 62 and over.

Keep in mind that although some of us may look the part, others don't. If you look younger than your years, consider yourself blessed and always carry some form of photo ID so that you can take advantage of discounts wherever they're offered. Minimum ages for discounts vary from 50 on up, so asking never hurts.

Traveling without Barriers

A disability need not prevent you from savoring the magic of Orlando and **Walt Disney World.** Many of the city's attractions and hotels are designed to accommodate the needs of the disabled, whether it be specially equipped guest rooms or audio aids for the sight impaired. A little advance research and planning, however, is a smart idea.

Finding an accommodating accommodation

Every hotel and motel in Florida is required by law to maintain a special room (or rooms) equipped for wheelchairs, but keep in mind that the law is being phased in over time, so some hotels may not yet have rooms for the disabled. A few places, including **Buena Vista Suites** (☎ **407-239-8588**), **Embassy Suites** (☎ **407-239-1144**), and **Sleep Inn** (☎ **407-396-1600**), boast wheel-in showers. **Walt Disney World's Coronado Springs Resort** (☎ **407-934-7639**), which opened in 1997, maintains 99 rooms that are designed to accommodate guests with disabilities, so make your special needs known when making reservations. For other information about special Disney rooms, call ☎ **407-939-7807.**

Getting around

Public buses in Orlando have hydraulic lifts and restraining belts for wheelchairs, and they serve **Universal Studios Escape, SeaWorld,** shopping areas, and downtown Orlando. When staying on Disney property, you can utilize shuttle buses that accommodate wheelchairs from your hotel.

If you need to rent a wheelchair or an electric scooter for your visit, Walker Medical & Mobility Products will deliver one to your room; it offers a model that accommodates guests weighing up to 375 pounds that fits into Disney's transports and monorails, as well as rental cars. For more information, call ☎ **888-726-6837** or visit Walker's Web site at www.walkermobility.com. You can also rent conventional and electric chairs daily at the theme parks (see Chapters 17–25).

Many of the major car rental companies now offer hand-controlled cars for disabled drivers. Avis can provide such a vehicle at any of its locations in the United States with 48-hour advance notice; Hertz requires advance reservations of between 24 and 72 hours at most of its locations. Likewise, Wheelchair Getaways (☎ 800-536-5518 or 606-873-4973; www.wheelchair-getaways.com) rents specialized vans with wheelchair lifts and other features for the physically challenged.

Amtrak (☎ 800-872-7245) will provide you with redcap service, wheelchair assistance, and special seats if you give them 72 hours notice. Travelers with disabilities are also entitled to a 15 percent discount off the lowest available adult coach fare. Documentation from a doctor or an ID card proving your disability is required, however. Amtrak also provides wheelchair-accessible sleeping accommodations on long-distance trains. Amtrak permits service dogs aboard, and they travel free. For a free booklet called *Amtrak's America,* which includes a chapter detailing services for passengers with disabilities, call ☎ 800-872-7245, or go to www.amtrak.com. TDD/TTY service is also available at 800-523-6590, or write to P.O. Box 7717, Itasca, IL 60143.

Greyhound (☎ 800-752-4841; www.greyhound.com) allows a physically challenged passenger to travel with a companion for a single fare. If you call 48 hours in advance, the bus line also arranges assistance along the route of your trip.

Maneuvering through theme parks

Most theme-park rides and shows, especially the newer ones, are designed to be accessible to a wide variety of guests. Likewise, theme parks often give people in wheelchairs (and their parties) preferential treatment so that they can avoid long lines. If you need crutches or suffer from some other medical problem that may restrict your mobility in any way, you're probably better off renting a wheelchair; the amount of walking you'll need to do in the parks may wear you down in just a few hours.

Each park's brochure tells you what to expect when you arrive. All the parks offer parking that is as close as possible to the entrance for people with disabilities. Tell the parking booth attendant about your special needs, and he or she will direct you to the appropriate spot. You can rent wheelchairs at most major attractions, but you'll probably be most comfortable in your chair from home (and save some money, too).

Keep in mind, however, that wheelchairs wider than 24.5 inches may make navigating through some attractions difficult. And, crowds can make getting around tough for any guest.

The following section gives you information about services for the physically challenged at various parks in Orlando:

Walt Disney World

The Magic Mickster goes to great lengths to assist guests with disabilities. The *Guidebook for Guests with Disabilities* details his many services. Disney no longer mails them prior to visits, but you can pick one up at *Guest Services* near the front entrance to any of the four parks. You can also call ☎ **407-824-4321** for answers to any questions regarding special needs. Some examples of Disney services include the following:

- ✔ Almost all Disney resort hotels have rooms for those with disabilities.

- ✔ You can find braille directories inside the **Magic Kingdom** in front of the *Main Street* train station and in a gazebo in front of the Crystal Palace restaurant. You can also pick up complimentary guided-tour audiocassette tapes and recorders at *Guest Services* to assist visually impaired guests.

- ✔ All parks maintain special parking areas for the physically challenged.

- ✔ You can acquire free personal translator units to amplify the audio at selected attractions at WDW parks. Inquire about these units at the guest services desks inside each park.

- ✔ You can rent wheelchairs at all the parks.

- ✔ You can call ☎ **407-827-5141** to gather more information about Telecommunications Devices for the Deaf (TDDs) at **Walt Disney World.**

Universal Studios Escape

If you're physically challenged, go to *Guest Services,* located just inside the main entrance, to get a *Disabled Guest Guidebook,* a Telecommunications Device for the Deaf (TDD), or other special assistance. You can rent wheelchairs from the concourse area of the parking garage. **Universal** also provides audio descriptions on cassette for visually impaired guests and has sign-language guides and scripts for its shows (advance notice is required; call ☎ **407-363-8000** for details). Call as far in advance as possible and no later than 7 days before arriving for the guides only.

SeaWorld

SeaWorld provides a guide, *The SeaWorld Adventure Park Accessibility Guide,* for guests with disabilities, although most of its attractions are easily accessible to those in wheelchairs. You can pick up the guide at Guest Relations inside the park. **SeaWorld** also provides a braille guide for the visually impaired and a very brief synopsis of its shows for the hearing impaired. For information, call ☎ **407-351-3600.**

Nationwide resources

A World of Options, a 658-page book of resources for physically challenged travelers, covers everything from biking trips to scuba outfitters. The book costs $35 and is available from Mobility International USA, P.O. Box 10767, Eugene, OR 97440 (☎ 541-343-1284, voice and TTY; www.miusa.org). Another place to try is Access-Able Travel Source (www.access-able.com), a comprehensive database of travel agents who specialize in disabled travel, that is also a clearinghouse for information about accessible destinations around the world.

If you require special considerations, you may also want to consider joining a tour that caters specifically to the physically challenged. One of the best operators is Flying Wheels Travel, P.O. Box 382, Owatonna, MN 55060 (☎ 800-535-6790; fax 507-451-1685). It offers various escorted tours and cruises, as well as private tours in minivans with lifts. Likewise, another good company is FEDCAP Rehabilitation Services, 211 W. 14th St., New York, NY 10011. Call ☎ 212-727-4200 or fax 212-727-4373 for information about membership and summer tours.

If you're vision-impaired, contact the American Foundation for the Blind, 11 Penn Plaza, Suite 300, New York, NY 10001. Call ☎ 800-232-5463 for information on traveling with Seeing-Eye dogs.

Advice for Gay and Lesbian Travelers

The popularity of Orlando as a destination for gay and lesbian travelers is apparent in the expansion and development of the Gay Day Celebration at **Disney World** into Gay Weekend. Gay- and lesbian-related events are also held at **Universal, SeaWorld,** and **Church Street Station.** These festivals are held the first weekend in June and draw tens of thousands of gay and lesbian travelers to central Florida. In fact, these events are so popular, you can buy a special package from Universal City Travel, ☎ 800-224-3838, which includes tickets to **Universal Studios, SeaWorld,** and **Church Street Station.** You can also find information about the events at www.gayday.com or www.gaydays.com.

You can get information about events for Gay Weekend as well as events that occur throughout the year from Gay, Lesbian & Bisexual Community Services of Central Florida, 934 N. Mills Ave., Orlando, FL 32803. Call ☎ 407-425-4527 or 407-843-4297, or check out www.glbcc.org on the Web for more information. Welcome packets usually include the latest issue of *Triangle,* a quarterly newsletter (☎ 407-849-0099) dedicated to gay and lesbian issues, and a calendar of events pertaining to Florida's gay and lesbian community. Though not a tourist-specific packet, the welcome packet includes information and ads for the area's clubs. *Watermark* is another gay-friendly publication that you can find in many Central Florida bookstores; it can also be ordered online at Amazon.com.

Likewise, you find useful information from GayOrlando Network (www.gayorlando.com) and The Gay Guide to Florida (http://gayguide.com), both of which contain many nightlife listings.

Both the entertainment industry and theme parks have helped build a strong gay and lesbian community in Orlando. Same-sex dancing is acceptable at most clubs at **WDW's Pleasure Island,** especially the large and very popular *Mannequins Dance Club.* Many of **Universal's CityWalk** establishments are similarly gender blind.

Same-sex dancing isn't expressly forbidden at **Church Street Station,** but it won't be welcomed enthusiastically either. Although we don't know of anyone being asked to leave for dancing, the crowd may not make you feel entirely comfortable.

If you're interested in sampling some of the other local gay and lesbian hot spots, check out the following places:

✔ **The Club at Firestone,** 578 N. Orange Ave. (at Concord Street, in a converted garage that still bears the Firestone sign), ☎ **407-872-0066,** www.clubatfirestone.com. Go-go boys dance on lifts converted into raised platforms and a diverse group boogies on the large concrete floor. The Club at Firestone is a serious dance club, with dark lighting, cavernous rooms, and a high-energy atmosphere, which also sometimes features world-renowned DJs. The upper floors, however, were transformed into a separate, more low-key martini bar — The Glass Chamber. Completely enclosed in glass, you can look at the dance floor below while sipping your drink shaken, not stirred. The cover charge varies from $6 to $10. Limited lot parking is available for $3 to $5.

✔ **Parliament House,** 410 N. Orange Blossom Trail (just west of downtown), ☎ **407-425-7571,** www.ParliamentHouse.com. Attached to a hotel of the same name, this is one of Orlando's wilder, and most popular, gay spots. Not a fancy place, the Parliament House shows the wear and tear of years of hard partying. At the Parliament House, you can drink, dance, and watch the infamous "Miss P" hold bawdy court in the packed drag shows (there's a weekly amateur night on Tuesdays). The dance floor is relatively large, but it gets small quickly as the crowd swells. Parliament House also has a small piano lounge, but the show is a big draw and seats go fast. Cover is $7 Friday and Saturday; $3 on Sunday. Drag shows are Friday, 10:00 p.m. and midnight; Saturday, 9:30 p.m., 11:00 p.m., and 12:30 a.m.; and Sunday 9:00 p.m. and 11:00 p.m.

✔ **Sadie's Tavern,** 415 S. Orlando Ave., Winter Park, ☎ **407-628-4562.** This intimate lesbian bar draws a laid-back crowd, and weekend entertainment usually consists of a local artist playing an acoustic guitar. Cover charge varies, but entry is free most nights and parking is free.

✔ **Southern Nights,** 375 S. Bumby Avenue (between Anderson Street and Colonial Drive), ☎ **407-898-0424.** Southern Nights has theme nights that pack in women on Saturdays and men on Sundays. Friday nights feature three female-impersonator shows. This club doesn't have a cover.

Part II
Ironing Out the Details

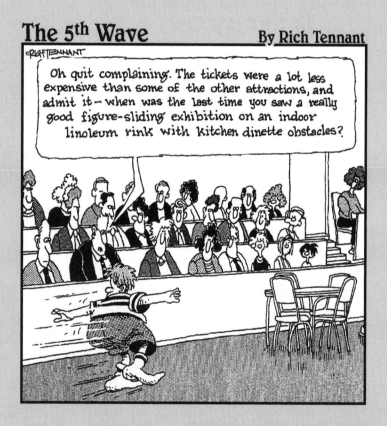

The 5th Wave   By Rich Tennant

©RICH TENNANT

Oh quit complaining. The tickets were a lot less expensive than some of the other attractions, and admit it – when was the last time you saw a really good figure-sliding exhibition on an indoor linoleum rink with kitchen dinette obstacles?

In this part . . .

*O*kay, it's nitty-gritty time. In this section, we chat a little about travel agents, package tours, and how you can get the best airfare. We also help you search for a place to rest your bones: We explore central Florida's neighborhoods, zero in on a room that's right for you, book it, and send you packing.

Chapter 5

Planes, Trains, and Automobiles: Getting to Orlando

. . . .

In This Chapter

▶ Using a travel agent — or not

▶ Checking out package tours: the pros, the cons, and where to get them

▶ Getting the best airfares

▶ Arriving in Orlando on land

. . . .

*G*etting to your destination *isn't* always half the fun of your trip, but your journey doesn't have to be an expensive hassle, and it doesn't require a master's degree in planning either. In this chapter, we eliminate the travel double-talk, chop the useless options, and make sure that you have a fun and easy time planning your getaway.

Acquiring Travel Agent Services

The first task you need to complete after you decide where you want to go on vacation is deciding whether you want to book your vacation yourself or use a hired gun. Many Internet-savvy travelers choose to research and book airfares and hotel accommodations online, but if you prefer discussing your options with an expert, working with a travel agent is your best bet.

Finding a good travel agent is hard to do, but they prove invaluable once you find the right one. The best way to find a travel agent is word of mouth. Ask a friend who travels frequently if he or she has a favorite.

All travel agents can find you bargain rental-car rates, accommodations, or airfares. Good travel agents stop you from choosing the wrong deal, even if it is cheap. The best travel agents can help you with all aspects of your vacation: arranging decent rental rates, budgeting your times, booking better hotels with comparable prices, finding cheap flights that don't require five layovers, and recommending restaurants.

Travel agents work on commission, which is good news and bad news. The good news: You don't have to pay the commission — the airlines, resorts, and tour operators take care of payment. The bad news: Unscrupulous agents will try to persuade you to book vacations that earn them the most commission while at the same time taking the least amount of their time. Unfortunately, the fact that travel agents are paid commission leads to ugly news, too.

The ugly news: Over the past few years, many airlines and some resorts have started eliminating or limiting travel-agent commissions. Therefore, don't bother to book these services unless you specifically request them. In fact, some travel analysts predict that if more players in the travel industry follow suit, agents may start charging customers for their services. When and if that day arrives — and even now — consider using reservation agents associated with airline frequent-flier clubs. However, make sure that you receive a good deal. To do so, call the airlines two or three times (most have toll-free numbers), get a 24-hour confirmation number for any rate that differs from previous quotes, go with the best rate, and cancel the others.

If you want to grade a travel agent, do a little homework. Flip through our sections on accommodations in this book (see Chapter 8) and choose a few that appeal to you. If you have access to the Internet, check prices on the Web (see " Getting the Best Deals on Airfare — Plane and Simple," later in this chapter). You can then take your notes and ask a travel agent to make the arrangements for you. Because they have access to resources better than the most complete travel Web site, travel agents should be able to offer you a price that's better than one you can get yourself. Likewise, travel agents can issue your tickets or vouchers on the spot, and if they can't get your No. 1 hotel, they can recommend an alternative.

Travel agents do receive a commission when it comes to Disney vacations, and they're usually a better source of information than Disney receptionists, who will answer your questions but won't volunteer any money-saving tips. Shop around among the airlines, too (see the appendix in the back of this book for the toll-free numbers and URLs of the major airlines). Delta is Disney's official airline and a big player in its packages.

After you've digested the information on package tours in the next segment, you can ask your travel agent to book the same package (at no added cost to you), plus add-ons such as airport transfers and side trips. Doing so makes life much easier — and cheaper — for you.

Discovering the Ins and Outs of All-in-One Packages

Package tours give you the opportunity to buy airfare, accommodations, and add-ons (if you choose) at the same time. We discuss the ins and outs of package deals in the following sections.

Why buy a package tour?

For popular destinations such as **Walt Disney World,** packages can help save you money — especially packages that roll your hotel, airfare, and round-trip airport transportation into one mix.

Packages can save you money because they're sold in bulk to tour operators, who resell them to the public. The idea behind package tours resembles shopping at one of those membership discount clubs, except the tour operator is the person who buys 1,000 options (hotel rooms, airline tickets, and so on) in bulk and resells them 10 at a time for a cost that undercuts what you'd normally pay.

Package tours vary as much as salad dressing flavors. Some packages offer flights on scheduled airlines, whereas others book charters. Some offer lower prices rather than a better class of hotel. Likewise, with some packages, you can choose between independent and escorted vacations, or add an escorted side trip to your itinerary. However, with some packages, your choice of accommodations and travel days may be limited.

If you choose to buy a package, think strongly about purchasing travel insurance, especially if the tour operator asks you to pay up front. But don't buy insurance from the tour operator! If they don't fulfill their obligation to provide you with the vacation you've paid for, you have no reason to think they'll fulfill their insurance obligations either. Obtain travel insurance through an independent agency. See Chapter 9 for more information on buying travel insurance.

Where can I find travel packages?

If you've decided that you want to give package tours a try, your next course of action is to find the travel package that fits your travel needs. To find travel packages, check the ads in the back of national magazines such as *Travel & Leisure* and *Condé Nast Traveler,* or those magazines that include travel arm sections, such as *Elegant Bride.* You can also check the travel section of your Sunday newspaper, but your best bets are the choices we outline in this section.

The Orlando market is ultracompetitive, so don't overlook a package because it has features you won't use. You may find you can fly from New York to Orlando and pick up your rental car, while discarding the four hotel nights (to stay with relatives or friends), yet still pay less than if you booked your airfare and rental car separately.

Theme park offerings

Disney offers a dizzying array of packages that include airfare, accommodations on or off Disney property, theme-park passes, a rental car, meals, a Disney cruise, and/or a stay at Disney's beach resorts at Vero Beach or Hilton Head. You can call ☎ **800-828-0228** or 407-828-8101 to find out more information about Disney packages (see Chapter 7). **Disney** offers season packages, as well as specially themed vacations, such as golf, honeymoons, spa makeovers, and so on.

Here are some of the positive aspects of booking a Disney package tour:

✓ Using **Disney** as your source for an all-Disney vacation is hard to beat, especially if you receive other discounts, such as those associated with the Magic Kingdom Gold Club Card (see Chapter 7) or if you're a Disney shareholder. However, if you want to see more of Orlando than **Walt Disney World** (and most people do), you should compare the offerings of a Disney agent with a regular travel agent. A motivated travel agent can put together a package of Disney and non-Disney accommodations and attractions for less than the amount that **Disney** charges. Of course, given Mickey's knack for emptying wallets, finding something cheaper is a no-brainer.

✓ Nobody knows the Diz better than its staffers.

✓ You can wrap all sorts of adventures (including cruises and far-away options such as **Disneyland,** Disney Vero, and more) into your package.

✓ Disney reps can offer accommodations in all price ranges ($74 and up).

However, be aware of the following drawbacks to Disney package deals:

✓ Resort guests receive the same perks, whether you buy your Disney package from **Disney** or someone else.

✓ You have to prod Disney reservation agents for details. If you don't ask about them to begin with, the agents usually overlook volunteering suggestions, such as the possibility that you can save money if you start your Disney vacation a day earlier or later.

✓ Some WDW package perks aren't worth a nickel. For example, if they say that you get your picture taken with Mickey as part of the deal, expect that you can find a better deal elsewhere and pay for your own photo.

For detailed information on Disney packages, write to **Walt Disney World,** Box 10000, Lake Buena Vista, FL 32830-1000, call ☎ **800-828-0228** or 407-828-8101, or go online to http://disney.go.com/DisneyWorld/intro.html to order a *Walt Disney World Vacations* brochure or a video. You'll find a dizzying menu of options from which to choose.

Although not on the same scale as Disney, Universal Studios' packages have improved greatly with the addition of the **Islands of Adventure** park (see Chapter 24), the **CityWalk** food-and-club district (Chapters 14 and 29), and the **Portofino Bay Hotel** (Chapter 8). Your package choices include resort stays, VIP access to the parks, and discounts to other non-Disney attractions. **Universal** also offers packages with Carnival Cruise Line out of Port Canaveral, and some include travel and transportation. Contact **Universal Studio Vacations** at ☎ **888-322-5537** or 407-224-7000, or surf online to www.usevacations.com.

SeaWorld also offers three-night packages that include rooms at a handful of Orlando hotels, car rental, tickets to **SeaWorld** (Chapter 25), and in some cases, other parks. You can get information at ☎ **800-423-8368**, or online at www.seaworld.com.

Airline packages

You can also tap airlines as a good resource for packages, as well as a reason to shop outside WDW parks. Many airlines package their flights with lodging and other accommodations. And, when you pick an airline, you can choose one that offers frequent service to your hometown and allows you to accumulate frequent-flyer miles.

Delta Dream Vacations, the big fish in the pond and the official Disney airline, offers selections that can include round-trip airfare, lodging (including tax and baggage tips), a rental car with unlimited mileage or round-trip transfers from the airport, admission to some or all Disney parks for the length of your visit, accommodations, and so on.

Prices for Delta Dream Vacations usually vary depending on the package, property, departure city, and season. Call ☎ **800-872-7786,** or visit online at deltavacations.com/disney.html.

Continental Airlines Vacations offers several packages that include airfare, car rental, and hotel stays at numerous central Florida hotels and WDW resorts. You can apply the airline's frequent-flyer program to some packages, and you can make reservations with or without air service. Call ☎ **800-525-0280** for general information, or check out www.coolvacations.com online.

For other airline-package possibilities, see the phone numbers and Web sites for the various airlines listed in Appendix B in the back of this book.

Other places to find packages

Beside airline and theme park package offerings, you can also find vacation packages elsewhere. One option is American Express, the official credit card of **Walt Disney World. American Express Vacations** (☎ **800-941-2639**; http://travel.americanexpress.com/travel/personal) allows card holders to book reservations at WDW resorts while throwing in a variety of perks, including discounts on merchandise, dinner shows, and certain Disney tours.

Other package specialists include:

- ✔ **SunStyle** (☎ **888-786-7895**; www.sunstyle.com) is a wholesale operator that offers a variety of packages targeting **Disney, Universal Studios Escape, SeaWorld,** and hotels located near those parks. You can buy tickets and book airfare and car rentals through this agency.

- ✔ **Touraine Travel** (☎ **800-967-5583**; www.tourainetravel.com) offers a wide variety of tour packages to **Disney** and Disney properties, **Universal Studios Escape, SeaWorld,** and the **Disney Cruise Line.**

✔ If you're a linkster, you have several packagers from which to choose. **Golf Getaways** (☎ 800-423-3657; www.golfgetaways.com), **Golf Travel Online** (☎ 888-486-4653; www.gto.com), **Golfpac Vacations** (☎ 800-327-0878; www.golfpacinc.com), and **Golf.Com** (www.golf.com) offer a slate of play-and-stay packages — from the most basic to the extraordinarily comprehensive.

Getting the Best Deals on Airfare — Plane and Simple

Buying airfare is a lesson in capitalism. Rarely do you pay the same fare for your ticket as the person sitting next to you on the plane. Airline ticket prices are based on the market — that means you — which translates into a roll of the dice, unless you know how to shop.

Business travelers and others who require flexibility usually pay the full fare price. However, if you can book your flight well in advance, don't mind staying over a Saturday night, or are willing to travel on a Tuesday, Wednesday, or Thursday, you will usually pay a fraction of the full fare price. Likewise, if you can take advantage of the discounts that flying with only a few days' notice offers, you can enjoy the benefits of cheaper airfare. On most flights, even the shortest hops, full-price fare is close to $1,000 or more, but an advance-purchase ticket, sometimes purchased as few as 7 or 14 days before the trip, can cut your ticket cost to $200 to $300. Obviously, planning ahead pays.

Periodically, airlines lower prices on their most popular routes. Although these sale-price fares have date-of-travel restrictions and advance-purchase requirements, you can't beat buying a ticket for (usually) no more than $400 for a cross-country flight. To take advantage of these airline sales, watch for ads in your local newspaper and on TV and call the airlines or check out their Web sites (see Appendix B for Web addresses and phone numbers). Keep in mind, however, that airline sales often take place during low-travel volume seasons. In fact, finding an airline sale around the holidays or around the peak summer vacation months of July and August is rare. On the other hand, November, December, and January (excluding holidays) often bring discounted and promotional fares, with savings of 50 percent or more.

Here are some tips for discovering the best values on airfare to Orlando:

✔ Ask the airlines for their lowest fares and inquire about discounts for booking in advance or at the last minute. Decide when you want to go before you call, because many of the best deals are non-refundable. Also, call more than once. Yes, being on hold that long is frustrating, but you'll probably get different rates each time, and one may be a bonanza.

- ✔ The more flexible you are about your travel dates and length of stay, the more money you're likely to save. Flying at off times (at night, for instance) saves you money.

- ✔ Visit a large travel agency to find out about all your available options. Sometimes a good agent knows about fares you won't find on your own. Internet providers offer travel sections that can provide pricing comparisons.

- ✔ Several so-called no-frills airlines — low fares but no meals or other amenities — fly to Florida. The biggest is Southwest Airlines (☎ 800-435-9792; www.iflyswa.com), which has flights from many U.S. cities to Orlando.

- ✔ Consider joining a travel club, such as **Moment's Notice** (☎ 718-234-6295) or **Sears Discount Travel Club** (☎ 800-433-9383 for information or 800-255-1487 to join), that supplies unsold tickets to their members at discounted prices. (You pay an annual fee to receive the club's hot line number.) Of course, your choices are limited to what's available, so you have to be flexible. Keep in mind, however, that you may not have to join these clubs to get such deals, because some airlines now unload unsold seats directly through their Web sites.

Cutting ticket costs by utilizing consolidators

Consolidators, also known as bucket shops, can be a good place to find low fares. *Consolidators* buy seats in bulk and sell them to the public at prices below the airlines' discounted rates. Their small, boxed ads usually run in the Sunday travel sections of major newspapers, at the bottom of the page. Before you pay, however, ask for a confirmation number from the consolidator, and then call the airline to confirm your seat. Be prepared to book your ticket with a different consolidator — there are many to choose from — if the airline can't confirm your reservation.

Also, be aware that bucket-shop tickets are usually non-refundable or rigged with stiff cancellation penalties, often as high as 50 to 75 percent of the ticket price. Among consolidators, **Council Travel** (☎ 800-226-8624; www.counciltravel.com) and **STA Travel** (☎ 800-781-4040; www.statravel.com) cater especially to young travelers, but people of all ages can take advantage of their bargain-basement prices. **Travel Bargains** (☎ 800-247-3273; www.1800airfare.com), formerly owned by TWA, offers deep discounts on many other airlines with a four-day advance purchase. Other reliable consolidators include **1-800-FLY-CHEAP** (☎ 800-359-2432; www.1800flycheap.com); **TFI Tours International** (☎ 800-745-8000 or 212-736-1140), which serves as a clearinghouse for unused seats; or rebators, such as **Travel Avenue** (☎ 800-333-3335 or 312-876-1116) and the **Smart Traveler** (☎ 800-448-3338 or 305-448-3338), which rebate part of their commission to you.

Arriving in Orlando

If you're flying to Orlando, the best place to land is Orlando International Airport, ☎ **407-825-2001** (unless a rental car and 90 minutes of interstate driving from Tampa is in your game plan). The Orlando airport offers direct or nonstop service from 70 U.S. and 25 international cities. Forty scheduled airlines and as many charters feed 28 million people into its gates annually.

Orlando International Airport connects to highways, Interstate 4, and toll roads that get you (whether you're driving or being driven) into the heat of battle within 30 or 40 minutes.

Finding great deals online

On the Internet, you can find great deals not only on airfare, but also on hotels and car rentals. Among the leading travel sites are: **Arthur Frommer's Budget Travel Online** (www.frommers.com); **Lowestfare** (www.lowestfare.com); **Microsoft Expedia** (www.expedia.com); **Priceline** (www.priceline.com); **Travelocity** (www.travelocity.com); **The Trip** (www.thetrip.com); and **Smarter Living** (www.smarterliving.com).

Each Web site has its own little quirks, but all provide variations of the same service. Simply enter the dates that you want to fly and the cities that you want to visit, and the computer searches for the lowest fares. Several other features are standard at these sites as well, including the ability to check flights at different times or dates in hopes of finding a cheaper fare; e-mail alerts when fares drop on a route that you've specified; and a database of last-minute deals that advertises super-cheap vacation packages or airfares for those who can get away at a moment's notice.

Using Other Methods to Arrive in Orlando

Can't stand to fly? Can't afford the extra expense? You're not alone. Each year, many people drive a car or hop a train to get to Orlando. In this section, we explore the details of taking to the open road or riding the rails.

Driving a car to Orlando

Driving to Orlando is a less expensive, and potentially more scenic option, unless the distance is so great that making the road trip eats up too much of your vacation.

The comfort zone

Flying is fun for some folks, but if you're like us, you consider flying a necessary evil for getting to the real party. Some airlines have been adding an inch or so of legroom, but tourist class remains cramped, the cabin temperature is often too hot or too cold, and the air is dry enough to suck the spit out of a Saint Bernard. However, here are a few things you can do — some while you book your flight — to make your trip more tolerable.

- **Bulkhead seats** (the front row of each cabin compartment) have a little more legroom than normal plane seats. However, bulkhead seats also have some drawbacks. For example, bulkhead seats don't provide you with a place to put your carry-on luggage, except in the overhead bin, because there's not a seat in front of you. Likewise, you may find that this isn't the best place to see an in-flight movie.

- **Emergency-exit row seats** also offer extra room. Airlines usually assign these seats at the airport on a first-come, first-serve basis, so ask when you check in whether you can sit in one of these rows. Remember though, that in the unlikely event of an emergency, you're expected to open the emergency-exit door and help direct traffic. This, of course, doesn't count in-air emergencies. You'll be jeered or even wrestled to the ground by fellow passengers if you try to open the emergency door in mid-flight.

- **Wear comfortable clothes.** Be sure to dress in layers, because "climate controlled" aircraft cabins vary greatly in temperature and comfort levels. You won't regret taking a sweater or jacket that you can put on or take off as your onboard temperature dictates.

- **Bring some toiletries aboard on long flights.** Cabins are notoriously dry places. If you don't want to land in Orlando with the complexion of King Tut, take a travel-size bottle of moisturizer or lotion to refresh your face and hands at the end of your flight. If you're taking an overnight flight (the red-eye), don't forget to pack a toothbrush to combat your breath upon arrival.

  Although some toiletries are helpful on airplane trips, some are dangerous. *Never* bring an unsealed container of nail polish remover into an airline cabin, because the cabin pressure causes the remover to evaporate and damage your luggage; the resulting smell won't help you gain any friends on your flight either. Likewise, if you wear contact lenses, wear your glasses for the flight, or at least bring some eye drops. Your don't want to spend your hard-earned cash to have your "soft" lenses surgically removed at an Orlando hospital.

- **Jet lag** usually isn't a problem for flights within the United States, but some people coming from the West Coast are affected by the three-hour time change. The best way to combat this time warp is to acclimate yourself to local time as quickly as possible. Stay up as long as you can the first day, and then try to wake up at a normal time the second day. Likewise, drink plenty of water during your first few days in town, as well as on the plane, to avoid dehydration.

- **If you're flying with kids,** don't forget chewing gum for ear-pressure problems (adults with sinus problems should chew as well), some toys to keep your angels entertained, extra bottles or pacifiers, and diapers. Even if your kids aren't coming with you, keep in mind that many people on Orlando flights *are* bringing their little darlings. Inbound, kids are often swinging from overhead compartments, excited about their journey to see Mickey Mouse. Outbound, they can fill all the luggage racks with souvenirs and stuffed toys before you can stow your briefcase.

Here's how far several cities are from Orlando: Atlanta, 436 miles; Boston, 1,312 miles; Chicago, 1,120 miles; Cleveland, 1,009 miles; Dallas, 1,170 miles; Detroit, 1,114 miles; New York, 1,088 miles; and Toronto, 1,282 miles.

Need directions? No problem.

- From Atlanta, take I-75 South to the Florida Turnpike to I-4 West.

- From Boston and New York, take I-95 South to I-4 West.

- From Chicago, take I-65 South to Nashville and then I-24 South to I-75 South to the Florida Turnpike to I-4 West.

- From Cleveland, take I-77 South to Columbia, South Carolina, and then I-26 East to I-95 South to I-4 West.

- From Dallas, take I-20 East to I-49 South, to I-10 East, to I-75 South, to the Florida Turnpike, to I-4 West.

- From Detroit, take I-75 South to the Florida Turnpike to I-4 West.

- From Toronto, take Canadian Route 401 South to Queen Elizabeth Way South to I-90 (New York State Thruway) East to I-87 (New York State Thruway) South to I-95 over the George Washington Bridge, and continue south on I-95 to I-4 West.

AAA (☎ 800-222-4357) and some other automobile clubs offer free maps and optimum driving directions to their members.

Arriving by train

Amtrak trains (☎ 800-872-7245) pull into two central stations: 1400 Sligh Blvd., between Columbia and Miller streets in downtown Orlando (about 23 miles from **Walt Disney World**), and 111 Dakin Ave., at Thurman Street in Kissimmee (about 15 miles from **Walt Disney World**). Amtrak's Auto Train allows you to bring along your car to Florida without having to drive it all the way. The service begins in Lorton, Virginia — about a four-hour drive from New York, two hours from Philadelphia — and ends at Sanford, Florida, about 23 miles northeast of Orlando. The Auto Train departs Lorton and Sanford daily at 4:30 p.m., arriving at the other end of the line the next morning at 9:00 a.m. Rates for hauling your car range from $142 to $330; passenger rates are $93 to $182.

As with airline fares, you can sometimes receive discounts if you book train rides far in advance. However, you may find some restrictions on travel dates for discounted train fares, mostly around the very busy holiday periods. Amtrak offers money-saving packages, including accommodations (some at WDW resorts), car rentals, tours, and so on. For package information, call ☎ 800-321-8684.

Central Florida

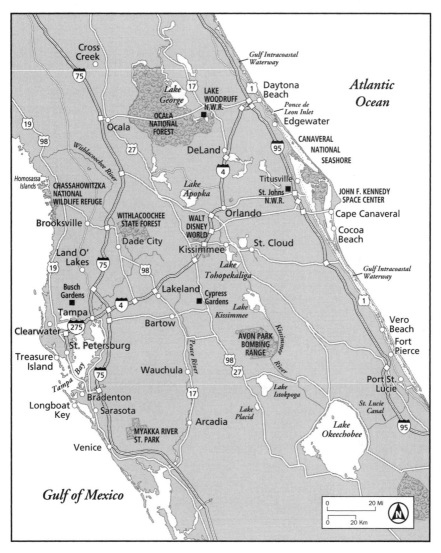

Chapter 6

Finding the Hotel That's Right for You

● ●

In This Chapter

▶ Finding a hotel room that meets your needs

▶ Choosing the neighborhood in which you want to stay

▶ Selecting a hotel that falls in your price range

● ●

*W*here you plant yourself during your vacation helps determine many things about your trip, including your itineraries, how much money you spend, and whether you need to rent a car.

However, you can take one thing to the bank: Unlike the seedier or less competitive areas of Florida, almost every hotel in Orlando has been built or renovated in the past 20 years, so you can expect reasonably modern trimmings. (Hotel appliances won't shock you, and you don't need rabbit ears to see what's on the tube.) Most places in Orlando also try to make kids feel as if they're Mickey's personal guests. Therefore, the factors that decide where you rest your head for the night boil down to location and price. Although you'll pay more for the best locations, you may find these hotels worth the convenience. The closer your hotel is to the things you want to do and see, the less time you waste getting to your destination.

In this chapter — and in Chapters 7 and 8 — we help you separate the tacky from the tasteful Orlando accommodations, so sharpen your pencil and read on.

Deciding Where to Stay

Deciding where to stay in Orlando isn't easy, because rooms come in many different flavors: hotels, motels, bed and breakfasts, and so on. Orlando's more than 100,000 rooms make choosing a room seem a bit overwhelming. The following section gives you a profile of the lodging players.

Evaluating chain hotels versus independent hotels

Galactic chains such as **Holiday Inn, Sheraton, Marriott, Hyatt,** and others are a bit like fast food joints — what you get at one is a lot like what you get at another (the exception being upscale models at the higher end of the **Marriott** and **Hyatt** chains). Throughout the Orlando area, you find a lot of these chain-type hotels, which are favorites of business and convention travelers. (See the appendix at the back of this guide for a list of the major hotel chains' toll-free numbers.)

Independent motels and inns often target select varieties of travelers, such as those traveling with kids, travelers on a budget, visitors looking for hipper surroundings, or older couples who visit friends annually.

Comparing hotels versus motels

Both hotels and motels offer service and amenities. Hotels tend to include more amenities, offer higher-priced rooms, and, in a few cases, feel snobbier than motels, though that attitude can be a fatal flaw in the competitive Orlando market, where you'll likely see more Goofy hats than Gucci. Motels often have a chain or mom-and-pop façade, come in one- or two-story models, include free parking, and some emit a friendly atmosphere that's likely to remind you of home. Those on the lower end of the price scale don't offer many doodads other than soap, towels, and — if you're lucky — coffeemakers, but their rates don't require that you take out a second mortgage, either. And, many motels are quite comfortable if you're not spending a lot of time in the room.

Finding the Perfect Location

Disney maintains the corner on the Orlando hotel market, boasting a 92 percent occupancy rate (compared to 80 percent elsewhere in town) in its 17 Disney-owned-and-operated resorts (with more to come over the next few years) and the 10 official hotels that are located on WDW property. Most folks choose to stay at **Disney**, especially if they're toting children to the parks.

The other four popular areas for guests are Lake Buena Vista, International Drive, and to a lesser degree, Kissimmee, and downtown Orlando. (See Chapter 10 for specifics about downtown neighborhoods.)

Choosing where to stay in Disney World

Where you stay in the Land of the Mouse will depend on which parks you want to visit and what your budget allows. This section includes some options that should help you whittle down your choices.

Most of Disney's pricier accommodations — the **Grand Floridian Resort & Spa, Polynesian Resort, Contemporary Resort,** and **Wilderness Lodge** — are situated on the doorstep of the **Magic Kingdom.** The first three offer the advantage of being on Disney's monorail system, so you can literally lodge a subway stop away from the parks.

Many of the more moderately priced resorts are near **Disney West Side, Pleasure Island, Downtown Disney Marketplace,** and **Typhoon Lagoon.** These resorts include **Dixie Landings, Port Orleans,** and **Old Key West.** The official Disney hotels, including the **Wyndham Palace Resort & Spa, Doubletree Guest Suites,** and **Courtyard by Marriott,** are also in the same area, but they're more expensive.

Disney's Boardwalk, Caribbean Beach Resort, and **Yacht and Beach Club Resort** are closest to **Epcot** and **Disney–MGM Studios,** as are the **Walt Disney World Swan and Dolphin.** (In this group of hotels, the **Caribbean** is in the mid-price range, while the others are more expensive.)

The relatively low-priced **All-Star** (with rooms from $74) and **Coronado Springs** resorts are near **Animal Kingdom** and **Blizzard Beach.** However, they're also a considerable hike from everything else at **Walt Disney World.**

The perks of staying with Mickey

The Disney resorts are a wonderland of creativity, from larger-than-life cowboy boots decorating stairwells and scrubs shaped like dancing hippos to buildings topped with giant birds and fish. Staying on Disney property has benefits and drawbacks.

The benefits of lodging in Mickey's backyard include

- ✔ Unlimited free transportation via the Disney Transportation System's buses, monorails, ferries, and water taxis to and from the four theme parks, resorts, and smaller attractions.

- ✔ Surprise Mornings, where selected parks open early for resort guests on rotating days.

- ✔ Free parking inside theme park lots (other visitors pay $6 a day).

- ✔ Reduced-price children's menus in most restaurants.

- ✔ A guest-services desk where you can buy tickets to all WDW theme parks and attractions to avoid standing in the park lines.

- ✔ As far as proximity is concerned, you can't get much closer to ground zero.

Drawbacks of staying with the Mouse include

- ✔ The Walt Disney World Transportation System can be slow.
- ✔ Resort rates are about 30 percent higher than the prices at comparable hotels and motels located farther away from the parks.
- ✔ You may wind up a prisoner of Disney's other stiff pricing schemes for restaurants, trinkets, and so on.
- ✔ If you don't spend a little time away from the Wizard of Diz, you'll miss the "real" Florida.
- ✔ Mickey, Mickey, MICKEY . . . *ack*! Living in the Disney Dimension can get old after a few days.

Deciding where to stay in Lake Buena Vista

The Lake Buena Vista area borders **Walt Disney World** from the northeast to the southeast along Florida 535. Hotel Plaza Boulevard in Lake Buena Vista is home to many of the 10 official Disney hotels — those that are on Disney property but not owned by Mickey. These hotels are all situated near **Downtown Disney Marketplace, Disney West Side, Pleasure Island,** and **Typhoon Lagoon.** They include **Courtyard by Marriott, Wyndham Place Resort & Spa, Doubletree Guest Suites,** and the **Grosvenor Resort.** Each of these hotels includes free shuttle service to WDW theme parks. Hotels in the official Disney category have larger rooms, more amenities, and fall in the moderate to expensive range, but rates at these hotels range from $99 to $304.

Lake Buena Vista also includes major chains like **Hyatt, Best Western,** and **Comfort Inns.** The **Hyatt Regency Grand Cypress Resort** and **Grand Cypress Villas** are outstanding resorts, with large rooms, patios or balconies, and a ton of amenities, including golf courses, five-star restaurants, and an equestrian center, but they're also on the high end of the price chain. The **Holiday Inn Sunspree,** which caters to families — they even have Kidsuites — is closer to the middle of the price pack (see the index, later in this chapter, for more specific pricing information).

The perks to staying in the Lake Buena Vista area include

- ✔ This area is close to **WDW** but not quite as expensive.
- ✔ There are a number of non-Disney restaurants that offer savings but still feature bargain kids' meals.
- ✔ If you choose an official property, you receive free transportation to **Disney.**

Drawbacks include

> ✔ If you don't choose an official property, you have to rent a car or pay a fee to be shuttled to the parks.
>
> ✔ Though a little cheaper than **Disney,** the hotels and motels in Lake Buena Vista are still high.

Determining where to stay in the International Drive area

The hotels and resorts on International Drive (I-Drive) are seven to ten miles north of the Walt Disney World parks (via I-4) and one to three miles from **Universal Studios Escape** and **SeaWorld.** The northern end of I-Drive is congested and hard to navigate during high seasons and is also covered wall to wall in T-shirt and jeans shops, burger barns, and second- or third-tier attractions. On the other hand, the southern end of I-Drive is more relaxed and less cramped. I-Drive hotels range from low to moderate (**Country Hearth Inn,** $89 to $139) to the luxuriously appointed, home away from home **Peabody Hotel** (a mere pittance at $330 to $1,350). This area includes plenty of restaurants (see Chapter 14), shopping (Chapter 27), and entertainment options (Chapters 29 through 31).

Advantages to lodging on International Drive include

> ✔ You can consider I-Drive a vacation destination unto itself.
>
> ✔ The area offers something for everyone's price range.
>
> ✔ You can stay on International Drive without renting a car if your hotel offers shuttles to the parks that interest you.

Drawbacks include

> ✔ The area is very congested, and big events at the convention center cause congestion, making it even harder to see the sites.
>
> ✔ The northern end tends to be glitzy and chintzy.
>
> ✔ The area is close to **Universal** and **SeaWorld,** but if you're mainly interested in **Disney,** you're seven to ten miles from the heat of the action.
>
> ✔ If you decide not to rent a car and your hotel's shuttle service isn't free, prepare to pay up to get to the parks.
>
> ✔ Crooks love working this area.

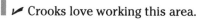

Figuring out where to stay in the Kissimmee-St. Cloud Area

Kissimmee is east of **Walt Disney World.** The town straddles U.S. 192/Irlo Bronson Memorial Highway and is very family and budget friendly. It has a branch of just about every chain restaurant and fast-food outlet known to civilization. If you're traveling with kids and looking for something special, we suggest **Holiday Inn Hotel & Suites Main Gate East,** which offers specially designed Kidsuites — a space for your little ones that's within your room. Other lodging in Kissimmee includes several **Best Westerns, Comfort Inns,** and **Days Inns.** Rates for these chains run from $50 to $130.

Good reasons to stay in the Kissimmee area include

- ✔ Kissimmee is close to **Disney,** and many of its motels will shuttle you there for a fee.

- ✔ Portions of it have a small-town feel.

- ✔ You can eat and sleep in Kissimmee without blowing your entire bankroll.

Drawbacks include

- ✔ Small-town in the case of Kissimmee sometimes means cow town.

- ✔ Many of the storefronts and some of the motels are a little on the tacky side.

- ✔ Many motels are no-frills.

Finding places to stay downtown in O-town

The star of downtown Orlando is **Church Street Station,** an entertainment, dining, and shopping area that has spawned other restaurants, shops, and clubs. The quaint **Antique Row** is nearby. Hotels in this area are, on average, moderately priced, catering mostly to business travelers. (See the following index for additional pricing information on Orlando's best hotels grouped according to location.)

The upside to staying downtown includes:

- ✔ Unlike some downtowns, Orlando offers loads of entertainment, and it's close to non-glitter attractions, such as museums and sports venues.

- ✔ Shopping in Orlando is far less touristy than in the theme parks.

- ✔ Orlando has a broad selection of cuisine from which to choose.

Drawbacks include

- ✔ Limited hotel choices.
- ✔ You're far from **Universal** and **SeaWorld,** even farther from **Disney,** and the traffic is usually wicked on the way to the parks.
- ✔ A rental car is probably a necessity.

Choosing a Hotel That's Right on the Money

Every hotel, motel, and bed and breakfast listing in the following sections (as well as in Chapter 8) have a $ symbol to help you find your price window. The $ symbols are based on *rack rates* (non-discounted rates), and they usually reflect the average of a hotel's high-low rates. Unfortunately, room prices are subject to change without notice (and they often do), so the rates that we quote in this book may change by the time you call the hotel for reservations. Don't be surprised if the rate the hotel offers is lower than the rack rates listed in this book. Likewise, don't be too alarmed if the price has crept up a little.

Here's your scorecard:

$ ($50–$100): Accommodations at this level generally include basic trimmings and limited space. They also tend to lean toward the no-frills side. Those at the higher end may offer amenities such as hair dryers, coffeemakers, cable TV, a midsize pool, a kids' play area, and continental breakfast. If they're multistory, they also usually have an elevator.

$$ ($100–$200): Lodgings in this price range probably will offer you a choice of king-size or double beds, a full range of amenities (coffeemakers, hair dryer, two TVs in the two-room models, multiline phones and possibly a modem line, VCRs, free daily newspaper), designer shampoos, and room service. Rooms are slightly larger, and a Jacuzzi and fitness center may accompany the pool. The continental breakfast probably includes fresh fruit, granola, and muffins rather than day-old doughnuts and little boxes of cereal. The hotel may also have a palatable on-site restaurant.

$$$ ($200–$250): Hotels at this level add a guest-services desk for attraction tickets and restaurant reservations. Likewise, they usually include a large, resort-style pool with multiple Jacuzzi tubs (some of the higher-end rooms have their own), a fitness center, and occasionally a small spa. Rooms have multiple phones, beds, and TVs, as well as minibars, a bath, *and* separate shower.

$$$$ ($250 and Up): Nothing in this price range is outside the realm of possibility, including a Body by Jake gym (the **Walt Disney World Dolphin,** see Chapter 8, has one). In addition to the nicer amenities in the previous categories, many of these hotels offer concierge levels, extra large rooms, 24-hour room service, gorgeous pool bars, and live entertainment in their lounges. Some also include full-service spas, gourmet restaurants, and tight security.

The following section presents a listing of hotel recommendations by neighborhood and price. Use the map following Table 6-1 to get a more specific fix on where each hotel is located in relation to what you want to see and do while you're in Orlando.

Hotel index by location

Downtown Orlando

Four Points Hotel Downtown Orlando ($$)
Radisson Plaza Hotel Orlando ($$)

International Drive Area

Country Hearth Inn ($$)
Hampton Inn at Universal Studios ($$)
Peabody Hotel ($$$$)
Portofino Bay Resort ($$$$)
Radisson Twin Towers ($$)
Renaissance Orlando Hotel ($$–$$$$)
Summerfield Suites ($$$)

Lake Buena Vista (including Official Disney Hotels)

Best Western Lake Buena Vista Hotel ($$)
Blue Tree Resort ($$–$$$)
Courtyard by Marriott ($$)
Doubletree Guest Suites Resort ($$–$$$$)
Grosvenor Resort ($$)
Hilton at Walt Disney World Village ($$$)
Holiday Inn Sunspree Resort Lake Buena Vista ($–$$)
Homewood Suites Maingate ($$)
Hotel Royal Plaza ($$)
Hyatt Regency Grand Cypress Resort ($$$$)
Perrihouse Bed & Breakfast ($$)
Villas of Grand Cypress ($$$$)
Wyndham Palace Resort & Spa ($$$–$$$$)

U.S. 192/Kissimmee

Best Western Kissimmee ($)
Celebration Hotel ($$–$$$)
Holiday Inn Hotel & Suites Main Gate East ($–$$$)
Holiday Inn Nikki Bird Resort ($–$$)
The Unicorn Inn ($)

Walt Disney World

Disney's All-Star Movie Resort ($)
Disney's All-Star Music Resort ($)
Disney's All-Star Sports Resort ($)
Disney's Beach Club Resort ($$$$)
Disney's BoardWalk ($$$$)
Disney's Caribbean Beach Resort ($$)
Disney's Contemporary Resort ($$$)
Disney's Coronado Springs Resort ($$)
Disney's Dixie Landings Resort ($$)
Disney's Fort Wilderness Resort and Campground ($–$$$)
Disney's Grand Floridian Resort & Spa ($$$$)
Disney's Old Key West Resort ($$$$)
Disney's Polynesian Resort ($$$$)
Disney's Port Orleans Resort ($$)
Disney's Wilderness Lodge ($$–$$$)
Disney's Yacht Club Resort ($$$$)
Hilton at Walt Disney World Village ($$–$$$$)
Walt Disney World Dolphin ($$$$)
Walt Disney World Swan ($$$$)

For a complete description of these hotels, see Chapter 8.

Walt Disney World & Lake Buena Vista Hotels

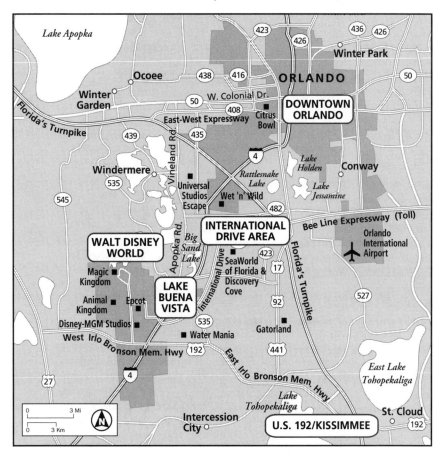

If cost matters most, refer to the following section for a listing of Orlando hotels by price.

Hotel index by price

$$$$ ($250 and up)

Disney's Beach Club Resort
  (Walt Disney World)
Disney's BoardWalk
  (Walt Disney World)
Disney's Contemporary Resort
  (Walt Disney World)
Disney's Grand Floridian Resort & Spa
  (Walt Disney World)
Disney's Old Key West Resort
  (Walt Disney World)

Disney's Polynesian Resort
  (Walt Disney World)
Disney's Wilderness Lodge
  (Walt Disney World)
Disney's Yacht Club Resort
  (Walt Disney World)
Hyatt Regency Grand Cypress Resort
  (Lake Buena Vista)
Peabody Hotel
  (International Drive area)

Portofino Bay Resort
(International Drive area/
Universal Studios)
Villas of Grand Cypress
(Lake Buena Vista)
Walt Disney World Dolphin
(Walt Disney World)
Walt Disney World Swan
(Walt Disney World)

$$$ ($200 to $250)

Celebration Hotel
(U.S. 192/Kissimmee)
Hilton at Walt Disney World Village
(Lake Buena Vista/
Official WDW Hotel)
Summerfield Suites
(International Drive area)
Wyndham Palace Resort & Spa
(Walt Disney World)

$$ ($100 to $200)

Best Western Lake Buena Vista Hotel
(Lake Buena Vista/
Official WDW Hotel)
Blue Tree Resort
(Lake Buena Vista)
Country Hearth Inn
(International Drive area)
Courtyard by Marriott
(Lake Buena Vista)
Disney's Caribbean Beach Resort
(Walt Disney World)
Disney's Coronado Springs Resort (Walt
Disney World)
Disney's Dixie Landings Resort
(Walt Disney World)
Disney's Fort Wilderness
Resort & Campground
(Walt Disney World)
Disney's Port Orleans Resort
(Walt Disney World)
Doubletree Guest Suites Resort
(Lake Buena Vista/
Official Disney Hotel)

Four Points Hotel Downtown Orlando
Sheraton (Downtown)
Grosvenor Resort
(Lake Buena Vista/
Official Disney Hotel)
Holiday Inn Hotel and Suites
Main Gate East
(Kissimmee)
Holiday Inn Nikki Bird Resort
(Kissimmee)
Holiday Inn Sunspree Resort
(Lake Buena Vista)
Homewood Suites Maingate
(Lake Buena Vista)
Hotel Royal Plaza
(Lake Buena Vista/
Official Disney Hotel)

$$ ($100 to $200)

The Perrihouse
(Lake Buena Vista)
Radisson Plaza Hotel Orlando
(Downtown)
Radisson Twin Towers
(International Drive area)
Renaissance Hotel Orlando
(International Drive area)

$ ($50 to $100)

Best Western Kissimmee
(U.S.192/Kissimeee)
Disney's All–Star Movie Resort
(Walt Disney World)
Disney's All–Star Music Resort
(Walt Disney World)
Disney's All–Star Sports Resort
(Walt Disney World)
Hampton Inn at Universal Studios
(International Drive area)
The Unicorn Inn
(Kissimmee)

Chapter 7

Booking the Best Hotel Room Your Money Can Buy

In This Chapter

▶ Getting a good deal on your hotel room

▶ Shopping for a hotel on the Internet

▶ Arriving in town without a reservation

Some folks call a hotel, ask for a rate, and pay it — no questions asked. These are also the same people who go to a car lot and pay sticker price. You, however, won't do the same as these people because we're going to show you how to find the best hotel rates.

The Truth about Rack Rates (and Why You Don't Have to Pay Them)

Rack rates are the standard rates that hotels charge for their rooms. If you call a hotel for a rate or walk into a hotel to get a room for the night, you pay the room's rack rate. Hotels also post their rack rates on the backs of room doors (unless the spring breakers took it home as a souvenir).

You don't have to pay rack rates. In fact, hardly anyone does. Perhaps the best way to avoid paying the rack rate is surprisingly simple: Ask for a cheaper or discounted rate. The hotel's answer may pleasantly surprise you.

Room rates usually depend on many factors, not the least of which is how you make your reservation. For example, a travel agent may be able to secure a better price with certain hotels than you can, because hotels sometimes give agents special discounts as a reward for bringing in a lot of return business.

Seasons also affect room rates, especially as occupancy rates rise and fall. If a hotel is nearly full, it's less likely to offer you a discount. Likewise, if it's nearly empty, the hotel may negotiate a room rate with you. Some resorts offer mid-week specials, and downtown hotels often offer cheaper weekend rates.

Orlando, for the most part, doesn't have a normal winter-summer pattern of high- and low-travel seasons. Blame two things for that: Disney's year-round tourist appeal, and a convention schedule that never takes a breather. These factors especially impact moderately priced accommodations outside **Walt Disney World** (see Chapter 2, "Deciding When to Go," for more on this). Many non-Disney hotels and motels, however, tend to offer lower rates from early January through March, from just past Labor Day to just before Thanksgiving, and the first two weeks of December.

Room prices can change without notice, so the rates that we quote in this book may differ from the actual rate you receive when you make your reservation.

Throughout this book, we provide $ symbols for an at-a-glance price comparison of the various hotels (see the Introduction for an explanation of the $ rates). However, finding a place to hang your sneakers for $50 is hard. The average rate for hotels in Orlando runs about $90 to $95 per night for a double. The Walt Disney World average is about $20 to $25 higher ($110 to $115).

Getting the Best Room at the Best Rate

Finding the best hotel rate requires a bit of detective work. For example, reserving a room through the hotel's 800-number, rather than calling the hotel directly, may result in a lower rate. However, the central reservations number may not know about discounts at specific locations. Case in point: Some franchises may offer a special group rate for a wedding or family reunion, but they may neglect to tell the central booking line. Your best bet is to call the local number *and* the 800-number to see which one gives you a better deal.

If you're a student, senior, military or government employee, or a member of AAA or AARP, ask about discounts. Also, if you own Disney stock, call Shareholder Relations ☎ 818-553-7200 to see if you're eligible for a price break or other perks. The Orlando/Orange County Convention and Visitors Bureau's free Magicard, ☎ 800-551-0181, is good for a family of six and up to $500 in discounts on accommodations, car rentals, attractions, and restaurants.

As a rule, Disney resorts, villas, and official hotels don't offer regular discounts other than for seasonal variations. One of the best ways to catch a break from Mickey is through a package (see Chapter 5, "The Ins & Outs of Package Tours"). **Disney** offers numerous vacation plans that can include meals, tickets, recreation, airfare, rentals, dinner shows, and other features. Call the **Walt Disney World Travel**

Company (☎ **800-828-0228** or 407-828-8101) to book single rooms or resort packages. You can also write to **Central Reservations Operations,** P.O. Box 10000, Lake Buena Vista, FL 32830-1000, or call ☎ **407-934-7639.** This service offers general information about **WDW,** including packages, vacation brochures, and videos.

The Magic Kingdom Gold Club Card can be a good investment if you're planning multiple visits or staying at least a week. Check out Chapter 3 for more details on the card.

When booking your room, don't forget to allow for the area's combined sales and bed taxes. In Orange County (Orlando, Winter Park, and Maitland), the tax equals 11 percent. In Osceola County (Kissimmee/ St. Cloud), the taxes add 12 percent to your bill.

Once you've made your reservation, asking one or two more pointed questions can go a long way toward making sure you have the best room in the house. For example, always ask for a corner room. They're usually larger, quieter, closer to the elevator, include more windows and light than standard rooms, and don't always cost any more. Likewise, ask if the hotel is renovating; if so, request a room away from the renovation work. You can also ask about the location of the restaurants, bars, and discos in the hotel — these may be a source of irritating noise. If you aren't happy with your room when you arrive, talk to the front desk. If they have another room, they should be happy to accommodate you, within reason, of course.

Surfing the Web for Hotel Deals

The Internet offers numerous sites from which you can retrieve information on hotels or resorts in Orlando. The biggest advantage that you get from using the Internet is that you can see the hotel or resort before you book your trip. Plus, you can book online and save yourself the aggravation of listening to a slew of annoying automated voice systems.

The Disney site, `http://disney.go.com/disneyworld/index2.html`, allows you to click on a link, "See the World," to find the resorts, which are divided into five categories: Value, Moderate, Deluxe, Select, Luxury.

Each individual resort link leads you to more information that includes rooms, rates, restaurants, recreation, and so on. Use the "book your trip" link to make reservations online.

At the Universal Studios Escape site, `www.uescape.com`, you can find information on the new **Portofino Bay Hotel,** including room rates, packages, amenities, and a room locator. You can also preview other planned Universal resorts, including the **Hard Rock Hotel** and the **Royal Pacific Hotel.**

Although **SeaWorld** doesn't have its own resort, at `www.seaworld.com`, you can find offers for three-night money-saving packages that include rooms at a handful of Orlando hotels, car rental, and tickets.

The Orlando Convention and Visitors Bureau, in conjunction with the *Orlando Sentinel* newspaper, has a site (www.go2orlando.com) that offers a substantial number of discounts. On the main page, click "Where to Stay" to find hotels, family-friendly motels, and resorts. The link leads you to a form where you fill in your desired type of room (from budget to luxury), the area in Orlando where you want to stay, and other options that you want at your hotel. It then provides a list of accommodations that fit your needs. You can also click picture links to see specific hotels and resorts.

Here are a few other sites where you may find discounts:

- **Orlando.com** (www.orlando.com/vacation) provides links for reservations, accommodations, and special deals. Use the "accommodations" link to find a list of hotels and resorts from budget places to deluxe vacation rentals and villas.

- **Florida Travel Online** (www.orlandotravel.com) is a wholesaler for hotel rooms, suites, and homes. Click the "places to stay" link to find a large database of hotels, which lists prices and other information on approximately 30 hotels and resorts. Clicking the individual hotel links gives you detailed information on each property.

- **Hotel-Lodging Net** (www.orlando.hotel-lodging.net/), lists a number of Orlando resorts, including the **WDW Swan** and **Dolphin,** the **Sheraton World Resort,** and other expensive hotels. The hotel listing is easy to use and provides links that allow you to check rates, get information, and view maps. Click the "hotel info" buttons to see pictures of the hotel and rooms, as well as a detailed listing of amenities at the resorts.

- **hoteldiscount!com** (www.180096hotel.com) lists bargain room rates at hotels in more than 50 U.S. and international cities, including Orlando. The cool thing is that hoteldiscount!com pre-books blocks of rooms in advance, so sometimes it offers rooms — at discount rates — at hotels that are "sold out." This site is notable for delivering deep discounts in cities where hotel rooms are expensive. The toll-free number is printed all over this site (☎ 800-96-HOTEL); call it if you want more options than are listed online.

- **TravelWeb** (www.travelweb.com) lists more than 26,000 hotels in 170 countries, focusing on chains such as Hyatt and Hilton, and you can book almost 90 percent of these online. TravelWeb's Click-It Weekends, updated each Monday, offers weekend deals at many leading hotel chains.

Arriving without a Reservation

Our first bit of advice: Don't come to Orlando without a reservation. If you do, you're more likely to end up feeling like Grumpy than Happy. This is especially true if it's high-travel season, when rooms are both pricey and scarce. If you do, however, decide to head for Orlando on a spur-of-the-moment inspiration, here are a few tips that will save you from having to camp out in your car.

The Orlando Information Center is related to the Orlando/Orange County Convention and Visitors Bureau. These folks find last-minute rooms for nonplanners. Room rates, depending on the seasons, can be a bargain. However, you can only get a room for the night you visit the center, and you have to come in person to find out what, if anything, is available. The Information Center is located in Orlando at 8723 International Drive, a mile west of Sand Lake Road. (☎ **407-363-5872** for information only.)

Other reservation services include the **Central Reservation Service** (☎ **407-740-6442**); **Orlando Magic Vacations** (☎ **407-390-7330**); **Orlando.com** (☎ **407-999-9800**); and **Vacation Works** (☎ **407-396-1883**).

Web wanderers can also find last-minute rooms at **Hotel Con-N-ions** (www.hotelxonxions.com). **Accommodation Search Engine** (www.ASE.net), offers discounts of up to 30 percent off room rates. Fill out a form that records your choices in several categories — rates, types of hotels, facilities, recreation amenities, and so on. After the form is filled out, click the search button on the page, and you receive a list of hotels or resorts that fits your selections.

Chapter 8

Orlando's Best Hotels

● ●

In This Chapter

▶ Taking a look at Orlando's best hotels

▶ Exploring some additional lodging choices

● ●

*W*e've scouted hundreds of places to stay in Orlando and whittled them down to the best — a few dozen that we mention in this chapter — so you don't have to waste your time wading through reviews of places that aren't worth looking at. You may think we're martyrs to the hotel cause, but that's what we get paid for; and thankfully, martyrdom no longer requires getting our heads chopped off or being burned at the stake.

Choosing a Hotel That's within Your Budget

When we mention hotel prices in this book, we refer to the hotels' rack rates, which you should easily be able to beat if you shop for discounts (see Chapter 7 on getting the best hotel room rates for your money). And, to make it easy for you to recognize pricey versus moderately priced hotels, each of the following entries includes one or more $ symbols. The cheapest hotels we list have one $ symbol, and the most expensive have $$$$ symbols. But remember, use our $ symbols only as a general guideline for hotel comparisons. If you visit Orlando in the off-season, buy a package, or find a discount deal, you can stay at $$$$ hotels for $$ rates. Likewise, you can also find $$$$ rooms or suites in $ and $$ hotels.

All the rates in this chapter are per night double, but many accommodations, including all Disney resorts, allow kids to stay free with their parents or grandparents (as long as the number of guests doesn't exceed the maximum occupancy of the room). However, always ask about kid rates when booking your room, just to be safe.

In general, expect higher hotel prices on the more upscale digs as well as those in or near the attractions. Also, although this is a kid-friendly town, we've added a Kid Friendly icon for the hotels, motels, and resorts that roll out the red carpet for their younger guests.

Keep in mind, you are going to Florida, so every hotel that we list has air-conditioning and at least one pool. They also have television (most have cable, and some offer in-room movies for a fee) and telephones. Likewise, many have hair dryers, coffeemakers, and in-room safes.

If you're considering booking a room at a Disney resort, be sure to ask when calling **Central Reservations** (☎ 407-934-7639) or the **WDW Travel Company** (☎ 800-828-0228) about any discounts available to members of AAA or other auto clubs, AARP, frequent-flyer programs, or other groups. Also, ask about special days (yes, they have a day for almost everyone, including Florida residents, emergency personnel, fire, police, and others — so ask). And, ask about meal plans — they can save you money — or packages that include a room, tickets, and airfare.

The Many, Many Hotels of Orlando

Best Western Kissimmee

$ U.S. 192/Kissimmee

This budget inn is close to all the Disney attractions. The rooms are blatantly basic — small, with cramped bathrooms — but the price is hard to ignore. There are two pools, and breakfast and dinner buffets are served in a family-style restaurant where kids under 10 eat free with a paying adult. Transportation to the Disney parks is available for a fee.

2261 E. Irlo Bronson Memorial Hwy. (U.S. 192, located 15 minutes from Orlando, near the Florida Turnpike). ☎ *888-511-7081 or 407-846-2221. Fax: 407-846-1095.* http://orlando.hotelguide.net/data/h101504.htm. *282 units. Parking: Free. Rack rates: $50–$60. Check for AAA and package rates. AE, DISC, MC, V.*

Best Western Lake Buena Vista Hotel

$$ Lake Buena Vista/Official WDW Hotel

This 18-story high-rise is a great place to view the Disney fireworks without braving the crowds in the parks. The lakefront hotel is located on prime property along Hotel Plaza Boulevard and is within walking distance of **Downtown Disney Marketplace.** The rooms are large, and some come with balconies and views of the lake. Amenities include Nintendo, coffeemakers, free local calls, an on-site restaurant, several pools, a playground, baby-sitting service, and free shuttles to Disney parks.

2000 Hotel Plaza Blvd. (between Buena Vista Dr. and Apopka–Vineland Rd./Fla. 535, across from the Doubletree Hotel). ☎ *800-348-3765 or 407-828-2424. Fax: 407-828-8933.* www.orlandolodging.com. *325 units. Parking: Free. Rack rates: $109–$199. Ask about AAA discounts and packages. AE, CB, DC, DISC, JCB, MC.*

Blue Tree Resort

$$-$$$ Lake Buena Vista

This sprawling 16-acre complex is mostly made up of time-share units that their owners rent. Accommodations include one- and two-bedroom units as well as standard hotel-type rooms; all come with free local telephone privileges, so you get a bit more bang for your buck here. The one- and two-bedroom units include pull-out sleeper sofas and range from 786- to 987-square feet — perfect for families. Amenities include four pools, recreational and exercise facilities, as well as free transportation to attractions and shopping. Larger units come with full kitchens, and the lower floors have patios.

*12007 Cypress Run Rd. (located off Fla. 535 on Palm Pkwy., about ½ mile from the entrance to **Downtown Disney Marketplace**).* ☎ *800-688-8733 or 407-238-6014. Fax: 407-239-2649.* www.bluetreeresort.com. *390 units. Parking: Free. Rack rates: $119–$250. Discounts including AAA are available. AE, DISC, MC, V.*

Celebration Hotel

$$-$$$ U.S. 192/Kissimmee

Located in the Disney-run town of Celebration, this hotel has a three-story, wood-frame design straight out of 1920s Florida. All rooms have TVs with Nintendo, speaker phones with voice mail and data ports, high-speed Internet access, ceiling fans, safes, hair dryers, and makeup mirrors. Suites and studios have refrigerators and wet bars. Other amenities include a pool, Jacuzzi, and fitness center. Breakfast is available in the Plantation Room (not included with the room rate). The Celebration shops, 18-hole golf course, and several restaurants are within walking distance.

700 Bloom St. (Take I-4 to exit 25A/U.S. 192, go east to second light, then right on Celebration Ave.). ☎ *888-499-3800 or 407-566-6000. Fax: 407-566-1844.* www.celebrationhotel.com. *115 units. Parking: Free. Rack rates: $165–$255 ($205–$470 for studios and suites). AE, DC, DISC, MC, V.*

Country Hearth Inn

$$ International Drive

This spot is a bargain by I-Drive standards. Some rooms have a patio or balcony, sofa beds, and refrigerators. They're also outfitted with hair dryers, in-room safes, and coffeemakers. The inn has shopping and restaurants within walking distance, and it's a short drive to **Universal, SeaWorld,** and **Wet 'N' Wild. Disney** is 15 to 20 minutes south. A continenal breakfast is included in the rates. Mears Transportation offers shuttle service to the various parks for $5–$15.

9861 International Dr. (located on the south end of I-Drive, between Sand Lake Road and the Beeline Expressway, across the street from the Orange County Convention Center). ☎ *800-447-1890 or 407-352-0008. Fax: 407-352-5449.* www.vacationspot-orlando.com/orlando_hotel_info/country_ hearth_info.html. *150 units. Parking: Free. Rack rates: $89–$139. AE, CB, DISC, DC, MC, V.*

Courtyard by Marriott

$$ Lake Buena Vista

The Courtyard is a moderately priced hotel located close to **Downtown Disney Marketplace**'s shops and restaurants. The Marriott chain has broken the mold with the Courtyard, which attracts more families than business travelers. Rooms are standard size (not microscopic, but you won't forget you're in a hotel), and most come with balconies. There's a small reception area located in a 14-story atrium, a full-service restaurant, a cocktail lounge, and a deli that specializes in pizza. Ask about the route schedule for the free transportation to WDW parks at the guest-services desk.

1805 Hotel Plaza Blvd. (between Lake Buena Vista Dr. and Apopka–Vineland Rd./ Fla. 535, close to the Hilton Royal Plaza Hotel). ☎ *800-223-9930 or 407-828-8888. Fax: 407-827-4623.* http://courtyard.com/MCOLB/. *323 units. Parking: Free. Rack rates: $99–$169. Discounts for AAA members, check for package rates. AE, CB, DC, DISC, JCB, MC, V.*

Disney All-Star Movie Resort

$ Walt Disney World

Kids aren't the only ones amazed by the, uh, aesthetics of this resort. When did you last see architecture as inspiring as Goliath-size Dalmatians leaping from balconies? If you're not saying "Oh, brother!" by now, you may enjoy the larger-than-life versions of a host of other characters that decorate the buildings here, and the low (by Mickey standards) rates will thrill some parents. *The All-Star resorts that follow this listing are pretty much the same* — expect small rooms and postage-stamp bathrooms. But you're still "on property," and you're enjoying the lowest prices your Mouse bucks can buy. This All-Star hotel has a food court that serves pizza, pasta, sandwiches, and family-dinner platters. There's a full-size pool with a *Fantasia* theme. Babysitting and activities for children are also available.

1991 W. Buena Vista Dr. (Disney All Star Resorts are located close to Animal Kingdom, Blizzard Beach, *and* Winter Summerland*).* ☎ *407-934-7639 or 407-939-7000. Fax: 407-939-7111.* http://asp.disney.go.com/disneyworld/ db/seetheworld/resorts/facilities/index.asp?id=813. *1,900 units. Parking: Free. Rack rates: $74–$104. AE, MC, V.*

U.S. 192/ Kissimmee Hotels

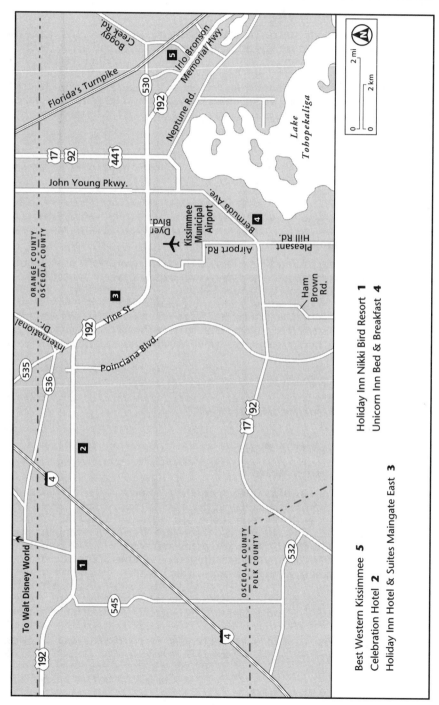

Best Western Kissimmee **5**
Celebration Hotel **2**
Holiday Inn Hotel & Suites Maingate East **3**

Holiday Inn Nikki Bird Resort **1**
Unicorn Inn Bed & Breakfast **4**

Disney's All-Star Music Resort

$ Walt Disney World

If you insist on staying on Disney property and are on a tight budget (or don't care about those few hours of in-room time), beating the All-Star's rates is hard. But you'd better be a fan of family togetherness, because the tiny rooms here mean you'll be up close and personal. The rooms start at 260 square feet or about what you get on a cruise ship if you choose a low-price cabin. (If you've never been on a cruise ship, go to the smallest bedroom in your house and imagine living inside it for seven days.)

1801 W. Buena Vista Dr. (at World Dr. and Osceola Pkwy.). ☎ *407-934-7639 or 407-939-6000. Fax: 407-939-7222.* http://asp.disney.go.com/disneyworld/db/seetheworld/resorts/facilities/index.asp?id=813. *1,920 units. Parking: Free. Rack rates: $74–$104. AE, MC, V.*

Disney's All-Star Sports Resort

$ Walt Disney World

Adjacent to the All-Star Music Resort, this 82-acre property draws sports fans looking for a vacation and visual overload. Rooms are housed in buildings decorated in football (huge helmets protect stairwells from rain), baseball, basketball, tennis, and surfing motifs. They come with double beds, sports action paintings, and in-room safes. Amenities include a brightly decorated food court, room service (pizza only), babysitting, a guest-services desk, two pools, a video arcade, and a playground.

1701 W. Buena Vista Dr. (at World Dr. and Osceola Pkwy.). ☎ *407-934-7639 or 407-939-5000. Fax: 407-939-7333.* http://asp.disney.go.com/disneyworld/db/seetheworld/resorts/facilities/index.asp?id=813. *1,920 units. Parking: Free. Rack rates: $74–$104. AE, MC, V.*

Disney's Beach Club Resort

$$$$ Walt Disney World

The Beach Club is within walking distance of **Epcot,** a plus for those who want to spend more than a day at the *World Showcase* and *Future World.* It has a quintessential Victorian Cape Cod theme and a posh atmosphere. Kids and adults love the resort's three-acre, free-form swimming pool, Stormalong Bay. Guest rooms are roomy and come with one king-size or two queen beds. All units come with double vanities, a tub/shower combination, ceiling fans, and balconies. This is a nice upscale resort destination, even more so if you want to stay only a short distance from the Disney parks. For eats, the Cape May Café is a nice calling card; it offers character breakfasts and authentic New England clambake buffet dinners.

1800 Epcot Resorts Blvd. (The Beach Club is off Buena Vista Dr., west on Epcot Resorts Blvd.). ☎ *407-934-7639 or 407-934-8000. Fax: 407-934-3850.* http://asp.disney.go.com/disneyworld/db/seetheworld/resorts/facilities/resorts.asp?id=280. *597 units. Parking: Free self and valet. Rack rates: $269–$545. AE, MC, V.*

Disney's BoardWalk Inn

$$$$ Walt Disney World

More than any other Disney property, the BoardWalk appeals to couples and singles looking for a sliver of yesterday. Night owls appreciate the entertainment options, couples like the romantic atmosphere, and large families may find this a cost-effective place to stay. The 1920s-era "seaside" resort overlooks a village green and lake. The bed-and-breakfast-style accommodations are larger than those in the moderate Disney resorts, with rich cherry-wood furnishings, two queen beds, a child-size daybed, a midsize bathroom, balconies, and ceiling fans. The Innkeepers Club provides concierge service, and amenities include babysitting, several pools, a free daily newspaper, and recreational facilities, such as tennis, fishing, boating, bike rental, and even a moonlight cruise. The villas here sleep up to 12, and some have kitchens, washer-dryers, and whirlpool baths. The atmosphere is homey, but the creature comforts are first class.

The property connects to a quarter-mile boardwalk that offers shops, restaurants, and street performers, which means there's plenty to do after the sun goes down. There are also a number of dining options (see Chapter 14 for a listing) here, as well as a number of clubs and nightspots (see Chapter 28 for the lowdown on Orlando's nightlife). Note that rooms overlooking the Boardwalk have the best views, but tend to be noisy thanks to the action below.

2101 N. Epcot Resorts Blvd. (north of Buena Vista Dr., on Epcot Resorts Blvd.). ☎ *407-934-7639 or 407-939-5100. Fax: 407-934-5150.* http://asp.disney.go.com/disneyworld/db/seetheworld/resorts/facilities/resorts.asp?id=281. *378 units, 532 villas. Parking: Free self and valet. Rack rates: $269–$730. AE, MC, V.*

Disney's Caribbean Beach Resort

$$ Walt Disney World

This moderately priced hotel's amenities aren't as extensive as those at some of **Disney**'s higher-end properties (or those in the same class outside the **World**), however, the Caribbean Beach offers a good value for families. Units are grouped into five distinct villages, some with water views. The 340-square-foot rooms are brightly colored and feature two double beds, ample-sized bathrooms, and double vanities. Parents with little ones will enjoy the swimming pool, which resembles a Spanish-style Caribbean fort, and Parrot Cay Island, with its short nature trail, an aviary of tropical birds, and picnic area. For dining, there's one full-service restaurant, the Captain's Tavern, and a food court.

900 Cayman Way. (off Buena Vista Dr. toward Epcot on Sea Breeze Dr. and Cayman Way). ☎ *407-934-7639 or 407-934-3400. Fax: 407-934-3288.* http://asp.disney.go.com/disneyworld/db/seetheworld/resorts/facilities/resorts.asp?id=276. *2,112 units. Parking: Free. Rack rates: $124–$189. AE, MC, V.*

Disney's Contemporary Resort

$$$-$$$$ **Walt Disney World**

If location is a priority, the Contemporary is one of your better bets in the **World** because the monorail literally runs right through the hotel, allowing you a fast track to **Epcot** or the **Magic Kingdom.** The 15-story A-frame resort on the Disney-created Seven Seas Lagoon was the first Disney resort built in Florida. The neutrally decorated rooms are among **WDW's** biggest, a plus for families, and most come with two queen-size beds, a daybed, and great views of the lake and **Magic Kingdom.** The pool area is virtually a mini water park. There are three restaurants, including one that offers character meals (see Chapters 14 and 15), a health club, and a marina.

4600 N. World Dr. (the Contemporary is located at the far northern end of Mickeyville, close to the Magic Kingdom *off World Dr.).* ☎ *407-934-7639 or 407-824-1000. Fax: 407-824-3535.* http://asp.disney.go.com/disneyworld/ db/seetheworld/resorts/facilities/resorts.asp?id=83. *1,121 units. Parking: Free self and valet. Rack rates: $219–$325. AE, MC, V.*

Disney's Coronado Springs Resort

$$ **Walt Disney World**

This moderate Disney resort has an American Southwest theme, and a slightly more upscale feel than the other moderately priced resorts thanks to the 95,000-square-foot convention center on premises. Rooms are housed in four- and five-story hacienda-style buildings with terra-cotta tile roofs and palm-shaded courtyards. Some overlook the 15-acre Golden Lake and the better your view, the higher the price. Rooms feature two double beds, (the décor differs in each section, but the layout is the same), with in-room coffeemakers, hair dryers, and modem ports. There are 99 rooms specially designed to accommodate travelers with disabilities, and nearly three-fourths of the rooms are nonsmoking. If you like to swim, you'll delight in the Mayan temple-inspired main pool. Dining options include the Pepper Market food court and the Maya Grill restaurant.

1000 Buena Vista Dr. (Disney's Blizzard Beach *off Buena Vista Dr.).* ☎ *407-934-7639 or 407-934-6632. Fax: 407-939-1001.* http://asp.disney.go.com/disneyworld/ db/seetheworld/resorts/facilities/resorts.asp?id=277. *1,967 units. Parking: Free. Rack rates: $124–$189. AE, MC, V.*

Disney's Dixie Landings Resort

$$ **Walt Disney World**

If you're traveling with children, this is a great place to stay. Low rates, extensive child-oriented facilities, and a food court make the Dixie Landings very popular with families. The rooms are midsize and the bathrooms rather small. About half of all rooms also have trundle beds that can sleep one child (although these rooms cost $15 extra per night).

This resort shares the banks of the mighty Sassagoula River with the Port Orleans Resort. There's a recreation area called Ol' Man Island, which has an immense swimming pool with waterfalls cascading from a broken bridge. Kids love the waterslide, wading pool, and playground. Adults enjoy the whirlpool and a fishin' hole where they can rent poles and get bait to try to catch a fish (real, though Disney stocked). There's Cajun cuisine available at Boatwright's Dining Hall, as well as a food court and a lounge. Boats travel, free of charge, from here to **Pleasure Island, Port Orleans,** and the **Disney Village Marketplace.**

1251 Dixie Dr. (Dixie Landing is located at the north end of Bonnet Creek Pkwy.). ☎ *407-934-7639 or 407-934-6000. Fax: 407-934-7777.* http://asp.disney. go.com/disneyworld/db/seetheworld/resorts/facilities/resorts. asp?id=278. *2,048 units. Parking: Free. Rack rates: $124–$189 for up to four. AE, MC, V.*

Disney's Fort Wilderness Resort and Campground

$-$$$ Walt Disney World

This woodsy, 780-acre resort delights campers, but it's quite a hike from most of the Disney parks, except the **Magic Kingdom.** Even so, there's more than enough to keep you busy at the resort. Guests enjoy extensive recreational facilities, ranging from a riding stable to a nightly campfire program hosted by Chip 'n' Dale. Secluded campsites offer 110/220-volt outlets, barbecue grills, picnic tables, and children's play areas. There are wilderness cabins and rustic one-bedroom cabins that can sleep up to six people, with living rooms, fully equipped eat-in kitchens, picnic tables, and barbecue grills.

Trails End has buffet meals and the cozy Crockett's Tavern features Texas-style grub. During summer, guests enjoy a dazzling electrical water pageant, seen from the beach at 9:45 p.m. If that's not enough, the rambunctious *Hoop-Dee-Doo Musical Revue* takes place in Pioneer Hall every night of the week.

3520 N. Fort Wilderness Trail (located off Vista Blvd., off Fort Wilderness Trail). ☎ *407-934-7639 or 407-824-2900. Fax: 407-824-3508.* http://asp.disney.go. com/disneyworld/db/seetheworld/resorts/facilities/resorts. asp?id=290. *784 campsites, 408 wilderness cabins. Parking: Free. Campsites: $36–$74; Cabins: $214–$289. AE, MC, V.*

Disney's Grand Floridian Resort & Spa

$$$$ Walt Disney World

You won't find a more luxurious address — in a Victorian sense anyway — than this 40-acre *Great Gatsby*-era resort on the shores of the Seven Seas Lagoon. It's a great choice for couples seeking a bit of romance, especially honeymooners who aren't on a tight budget. The Grand Floridian is **Walt Disney World's** upper-crust flagship, and it's as pricey as it is plush. You'll be charmed from the moment you set foot inside. The opulent, five-story domed lobby hosts afternoon teas accompanied by piano music. In the evenings, an orchestra plays big-band tunes. The large guest rooms are richly furnished with chintz and mahogany, and include either sunny private balconies or verandas overlooking formal gardens.

The Grand Floridian has a first-rate health club and spa, a marvelous swimming pool, and offers numerous recreational activities. When your stomach rumbles, you have several restaurants to choose from, including **Disney**'s finest eating establishment, Victoria and Albert's (see Chapter 14). The hotel is on the Disney monorail system, so you're only a few stops away from both **Magic Kingdom** and **Epcot.**

4401 Floridian Way (located in the far northwest corner of the WDW property, on Floridian Way just north of the Polynesian Resort). ☎ *407-934-7639 or 407-824-3000. Fax: 407-824-3186.* http://asp.disney.go.com/disneyworld/db/ seetheworld/resorts/facilities/resorts.asp?id=282. *933 units. Parking: Free self and valet. Rack rates: $304–$480. AE, MC, V.*

Disney's Old Key West Resort

$$$$ Walt Disney World

If you can swallow the price, the reward is some peace and quiet away from the Disney insanity. This is a timeshare property that mirrors turn-of-the-century Key West. Units are rented to tourists when their owners are not using them, and they're a good choice for large families or long stays. Accommodations are villas or homes away from home, with one to three bedrooms, living rooms, full kitchens, and furnished patios with views of the water or the Buena Vista Golf Course. Enjoy the sandy playground, swimming pools, tennis courts, video arcade, and health club. Olivia's Café overlooks a canal and serves breakfast, lunch, and dinner. Good Food to Go and The Gurgling Suitcase offer light snacks. Free Disney movies play nightly in the recreation center.

1510 N. Cove Rd. (off Bonnet Creek Pkwy. on Community Dr.). ☎ *407-934-7700 or 407-827-7700. Fax: 407-827-7710.* http://asp.disney.go.com/ disneyworld/db/seetheworld/resorts/facilities/resorts.asp? id=288. *709 units. Parking: Free. Rack rates: $234–$600 and up. AE, MC, V.*

Disney's Polynesian Resort

$$$$ Walt Disney World

The Polynesian was built when **Disney** first opened its doors, and it's still a great place to stay. It offers the convenience of monorail access to the parks, combined with the privacy of spread-out accommodations that seem far more off the beaten path than they really are. The resort does a great job of re-creating the lushness of Hawaii — the lobby is a virtual rain forest of tropical plants. The rooms are reasonably large, and most have balconies or patios, and canopied beds with bamboo and rattan furnishings. The Neverland Club is a cool baby-sitting service, with an adult-supervised activity program, that offers kids a great place to play while their parents have a night out on the town (open from 4 p.m. to midnight). The resort offers particularly good dining options (see Chapters 14 and 15), including several character meals and dinner shows. There are also numerous recreational activities from which to choose, such as fishing and boat rentals.

1600 Seven Seas Dr. (off Floridian Way across from Shades of Green and Magnolia Palm Dr.). ☎ *407-934-7639 or 407-824-2000. Fax: 407-824-3174.* http://asp.disney.go.com/disneyworld/db/seetheworld/resorts/ facilities/resorts.asp?id=283. *853 units. Parking: Free self and valet. Rack rates: $279–$550 and up. AE, MC, V.*

Disney's Port Orleans Resort

$$ Walt Disney World

This resort, resembling turn-of-the-twentieth-century New Orleans (okay, a cleaned-up version), is a good bet for families and shares a site on the banks of the Sassagoula with Dixie Landings (described earlier in this chapter). And, as is the case with the resorts at this level, it's pretty much a clone of the others. The midsize rooms have small bathrooms and two double beds, cherry-wood furnishings, and wrought-iron balconies. Kids love the larger-than-Olympic-size Doubloon Lagoon swimming pool and its serpent-shaped waterslide. Gardeners will appreciate the land-scaping, which features stately oaks, formal boxwood hedges, azaleas, and jasmine. The Bonfamille's Café (Creole cuisine) serves breakfast and dinner. Scat Cat's Club, a cocktail lounge off the lobby, airs *Monday Night Football* and features family-oriented live entertainment. A food court and pool bar round out the facilities.

2201 Orleans Dr. (off Bonnet Creek Pkwy., next to the Dixie Landings Resort). ☎ *407-934-7639 or 407-934-5000. Fax: 407-934-5353.* http://asp.disney.go. com/disneyworld/db/seetheworld/resorts/facilities/resorts. asp?id=279. *1,008 units. Parking: Free. Rack rates: $124–$189 for up to four. AE, MC, V.*

Disney's Wilderness Lodge

$$$-$$$$ Walt Disney World

Here's an option for those who like the great outdoors but would rather stay indoors than in a tent. The Wilderness Lodge reminds most folks of a rustic national park lodge, in part because it's patterned after the one at Yosemite. Its main drawback: It's difficult and time-consuming to get to other areas via the WDW Transportation System.

A lakefront sand beach and an immense serpentine swimming pool, seemingly excavated out of the rocks, make up for the rooms' modest size; rooms feature two queen-size beds and a mission-style décor. Some have bunk beds and patios or balconies overlooking the lake, woods, or a meadow. Continuing the Yellowstone theme, geysers shoot water into the sky every hour on the hour — just like Old Faithful. There are sev-eral dining options (see Chapter 14) and a plethora of recreational activ-ities. The Cubs Den, a Western-themed entertainment club for children ages 4–12, will keep your kids occupied if you want to sneak out for an evening. It includes a kid buffet, movies, live animal shows, and video games. It's open 5:00 p.m. to midnight and costs $8 per child.

901 West Timberline Dr. (on Seven Seas Dr., south of the Contemporary Resort on the southwest shore of Bay Lake east of the Magic Kingdom). ☎ **407-934-7639** *or 407-824-3200. Fax: 407-824-3232.* http://asp.disney.go.com/ disneyworld/db/seetheworld/resorts/facilities/resorts.asp? id=284. *728 units. Parking: Free self and valet. Rack rates: $185–$600 and up. AE, MC, V.*

Disney's Yacht Club Resort

$$$$ Walt Disney World

If you hanker for a lot of entertainment and sports options, this is the place for you. The resort resembles a turn-of-the-twentieth-century New England yacht club, and is located off a 25-acre lake it shares with the Beach Club (also listed in this chapter). The rooms are relatively large, with sleeping space for up to five adults. They are decorated in nautical themes, with hardwood and brass furnishings, and outfitted with patios or balconies. There's a full range of recreational activities, a marina, an eye-popping swimming pool, and a health club. There are two restaurants to choose from — The Yachtsman Steakhouse (see Chapter 14) and The Yacht Club Galley — as well as several lounges.

1700 Epcot Resorts Blvd. (off Buena Vista Dr.). ☎ **407-934-7639** *or 407-934-7000. Fax: 407-924-3450.* http://asp.disney.go.com/disneyworld/db/ seetheworld/resorts/facilities/resorts.asp?id=285. *642 units. Parking: Free self and valet. Rack rates: $269–$455 and up. AE, MC, V.*

Doubletree Guest Suites

$$-$$$$ Lake Buena Vista/WDW Official Hotel

This seven-story, all-suite hotel is a good choice for large families. Young patrons get their own check-in desk, where they receive a chocolate-chip cookie. There's also a children's theater, game room, and video arcade. The one-bedroom suites can sleep up to six adults and are delightfully decorated. You'll also find a TV in the bathroom, a wet bar, refrigerator, microwave oven, and full living rooms and dining areas. You also have access to several recreational facilities, including two pools, a whirlpool, fitness room, and tennis courts.

The festive Streamers restaurant serves buffet and à la carte breakfasts and dinners featuring American fare with southwestern specialties. The location is excellent — within walking distance of **Downtown Disney** — and there is free transportation to all the parks.

2305 Hotel Plaza Blvd. (just west of Apopka–Vineland Rd./Fla. 535; turn into the entrance to Downtown Disney Marketplace*).* ☎ **800-222-8733** *or 407-934-1000. Fax: 407-934-1011.* www.doubletreeguestsuites.com. *229 units. Parking: Free self and valet. Rack rates: $169–$399. AE, CB, DC, DISC, JCB, MC, V.*

International Drive Area Hotels

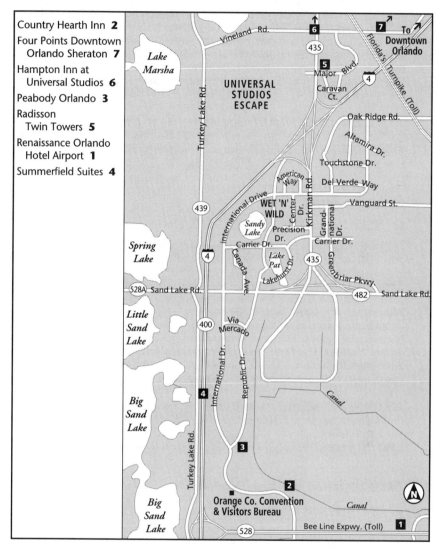

Country Hearth Inn **2**

Four Points Downtown Orlando Sheraton **7**

Hampton Inn at Universal Studios **6**

Peabody Orlando **3**

Radisson Twin Towers **5**

Renaissance Orlando Hotel Airport **1**

Summerfield Suites **4**

Four Points Hotel Downtown Orlando Sheraton

$$ Downtown Orlando

Recently purchased by the Sheraton chain, this hotel has a number of rooms with great views of Lake Eola. The location isn't bad either — it's only 15 minutes from Orlando International Airport and about 25 minutes from Disney attractions (when the traffic gods are smiling). The elegant Mediterranean décor of the public rooms is painted in soft coral, salmon, and green. The guest rooms have rich wood fixtures and soft colors; 20 of them are one-bedroom suites. There's also an executive level, complete with concierge lounge service. The first floor has a ballroom, for the typical wedding reception and conventioneering activities. You can dine in The Parkside Restaurant and Lounge, which serves American cuisine.

151 E. Washington St. (from I-4 take the Anderson St. exit; the hotel is located off Rosalind directly across from the entrance to Lake Eola Park). ☎ *800-321-2323 or 407-841-3220. Fax: 407-849-1839.* www.sheraton4pts.com. *264 units. Parking: Free self and valet. Rack rates: $99–$109. AE, MC, V.*

Grosvenor Resort

$$ Lake Buena Vista/Official WDW Hotel

For traditional styling, plenty of stay-at-home entertainment, and a moderate price tag for a central location, head for the Grosvenor. This moderately priced resort has a 19-story epicenter that features inviting rooms decorated in shades of mauve and green. There are also five-story wings with tower and garden rooms that are larger and provide better views. Rooms are equipped with coffeemakers, safes, minibars, and VCRs. The Grosvenor also has some funky entertainment: Baskervilles Restaurant houses a Sherlock Holmes museum and hosts a Saturday-night mystery dinner theater; the hotel also offers Disney character breakfasts. Other amenities include a 24-hour food court, a pool bar, and a lounge where sporting events are aired on a large-screen TV.

1850 Hotel Plaza Blvd. (Turn west off Fla. 535 onto Hotel Plaza Blvd.; it's close to Downtown Disney Marketplace). ☎ *800-624-4109 or 407-828-4444. Fax: 407-828-8192.* www.grosvenorresort.com. *626 units. Parking: Free self and valet. Rack rates: $145–$175. AE, CB, DC, DISC, JCB, MC, V.*

Hampton Inn at Universal Studios

$ International Drive

It ain't fancy but it's close (three blocks) to **Universal Studios Escape,** a mile from the heat of International Drive's tourist traps, and four miles from **SeaWorld.** Although it doesn't offer shuttles to Disney parks, you can arrange them for a fee (Mears Transportation is one of the more recognized carriers). Nevertheless, depending on your travel plans, you may find renting a car cheaper. The rooms are smallish and each has a coffeemaker; microwaves and refrigerators are available in some units.

There's a game room, pool, and rates include a complimentary breakfast buffet. For dinner, there are a number of restaurants nearby, including those at **Universal's CityWalk.**

5621 Windhover Dr. (Take I-4 to Exit 30B. Go through two traffic lights; turn right at Shoney's Restaurant. The hotel is a five-story white building). ☎ 800-231-8395 or 407-351-6716. Fax: 407-363-1711. www.go2orlando.com/sponsor/hamptoninn. *120 units. Parking: Free. Rack rates: $69–$99. Ask about special discounts. AE, DISC, DC, MC, V.*

Hilton at Walt Disney World Village

$$-$$$ **Lake Buena Vista/Official WDW Hotel**

The Hilton has a number of amenities that appeal to business and family travelers alike, including telephones with voice mail and modem jacks, coffeemakers, dining choices ranging from simple to splurge, two swimming pools, a kiddie pool, a health club with sauna, tennis courts, and rental boats. It's a short walk to **Downtown Disney Marketplace** and **Disney West Side.** Hilton also offers "Disney Surprise Mornings," which allow guests early entrance into a Walt Disney World park on a rotating basis. There's also free shuttle service to the parks.

1751 Hotel Plaza Blvd. (just east of Buena Vista Dr.). ☎ 800-445-8667 or 407-827-4000. Fax: 407-827-3890. www.hilton.com/. *814 units. Parking: Free self and valet. Rack rates: $150–$320. Ask about packages and weekend rates. AE, CB, DC, DISC, MC, V.*

Holiday Inn Hotel and Suites Main Gate East

$-$$$ **U.S. 192/ Kissimmee**

This is a child- and pet-friendly place that's only three miles from the WDW parks. There's a nice mix of mouse and merriment as well as no-nonsense hospitality. All the rooms are child-safe and come with microwaves, refrigerators, and VCRs; some suites have whirlpool tubs. The specially designed KidSuites offer a playhouse that sleeps up to three children. Shuttles to **WDW** are free, and transportation to other parks is available. The Vineyard Café, a full-service restaurant, offers breakfast and dinner. The Gingerbread House is a just-for-kids landing pad located within the Vineyard Café. Kids under 12 eat free.

5678 Irlo Bronson Memorial Hwy. (Located on U.S. 192, near I-4 on Seralago Blvd.). ☎ 800-366-5437 or 407-396-4488. Fax: 407-396-1296. www.familyfunhotel.com. *Parking: Free. Rack rates: $89–$225. Inquire about off-season rates. AE, CB, DC, DISC, MC, V.*

Holiday Inn Nikki Bird Resort

$-$$ U.S. 192/Kissimmee

Here's another great family base and the closest Holiday Inn to the main gate of **Walt Disney World.** The resident mascot, Nikki, wanders the resort, where kids 12 and under eat free in Angel's Diner as long as they're accompanied by paying adults. Nightly entertainment includes songs, puppet shows, magic shows, and games. It has 75 KidSuites, gift shops, and an outdoor pool. Rooms have a refrigerator, microwave, and safe. Free transportation is provided to WDW parks.

7300 Irlo Bronson Memorial Hwy. (located on U.S. 192 just west of I-4). ☎ *800- 206-2747 or 407-396-7300. Fax: 407-396-7555.* www.americanhotelnetwork. com/florida/orlando/hinbks.html. *530 units. Parking: Free. Rack rates: $89–$139. Discounts for AAA, AARP, and corporate. AE, DISC, DC, MC, V.*

Holiday Inn Sunspree Resort Lake Buena Vista

$-$$ Lake Buena Vista

Also located close to the Disney parks, this Holiday Inn offers the chain's "no surprises" dependability while catering to children in a big way. They check in at their own pint-size desk and receive a free fun bag with assorted goodies and a personal welcome from the hotel's animated raccoon mascots, Max and Maxine. There are 231 KidSuites, which offer children a themed area, with bunk beds, CD players, and Super Nintendo, inside their parents' room. The inn also runs Camp Holiday, an activity center that offers magic shows, clowns, sing-alongs, and arts and crafts for ages 2 to 12 (there's a small daily fee). Parents can arrange for a nightly tuck-in by Max.

13351 Lake Buena Vista (located off Fla. 535 near the Crossroads Shopping Center). ☎ *800-366-6299 or 407-239-4500. Fax: 407-239-7713.* www.kidsuites.com. *507 units. Parking: Free. Rack rates: $69–$159 for up to six people. AE, DISC, JCB, MC, V.*

Homewood Suites Maingate

$$ Lake Buena Vista

These moderately priced family suites are two miles from **Disney** and loaded with such amenities as kitchenettes, refrigerators, icemakers, dishwashers, coffeemakers with coffee, microwaves (they even give you a bag of popcorn), stoves, and utensils. The one-bedroom suites come with a king-size bed or two doubles, and the living area has a sleeper sofa. The hotel has a pool, kiddie pool, gym, a picnic area with gas barbecue grills, and a sandpit for your kids to dig in. A free continental breakfast is served daily. HomewoodSuites will provide free transportation to **Walt Disney World** if scheduled in advance. Pets are welcome.

8200 Palm Pkwy. (located off So. Apopka-Vineland Road/Fla. 535 near Lake Buena Vista). ☎ *800-225-5466 or 407-465-8200. Fax: 407-465-0200.* www.homewood-suites.com/. *Parking: Free. Rack rates: $119–$149 for one-bedroom suites that sleep up to four adults. AE, CB, DC, DISC, MC, V.*

Hotel Royal Plaza

$$ Lake Buena Vista/Official WDW Hotel

Another of the Disney "official hotels" within walking distance of **Downtown Disney Marketplace,** the Royal Plaza has rooms decorated in soft resort hues and bleached oak furnishings that come with VCRs, safes, minibars, coffeemakers, and hair dryers. Pool-view rooms have patios or balconies. Executive rooms on the concierge level have Jacuzzis, full living rooms, and a patio or balcony.

A number of restaurants and bars will satisfy any hunger pangs you may have, and a pool bar is set up during the busy, warm-weather season. The Hotel Royal Plaza also has free shuttle service to Disney parks, room service, a guest-services desk (the desk sells tickets and arranges transport to all nearby attractions), baby-sitting service, a large L-shaped swimming pool, whirlpool, four tennis courts, sauna, and a video game arcade.

1905 Hotel Plaza Blvd. (between Buena Vista Dr. and Apopka-Vineland Rd./Fla. 535). ☎ *800-248-7890 or 407-828-2828. Fax: 407-827-6338.* www.orlandotravel.com/hotels/royal.htm. *394 units. Parking: Free self and valet $7. Rack rates: $139–$209. AE, CB, DC, DISC, JCB, MC, V.*

Hyatt Regency Grand Cypress Resort

$$$$ Lake Buena Vista

A resort destination in and of itself, this is a great place to get away from the Disney/Orlando crowd frenzy, which is only a mile away. The large rooms sport a Southern theme and are decorated with wicker furniture. Sports enthusiasts will delight in the top-notch Grand Cypress Equestrian Center, an award-winning golf course, and numerous other recreational facilities. Adults and kids particularly enjoy the half-acre pool, spanned by a rope bridge, which flows through rock grottoes, with 12 waterfalls and 2 steep waterslides.

When hunger pangs strike, the casual-though-elegant Hemingways serves seafood. At the adjoining Villas of Grand Cypress, the five-star Black Swan Restaurant (see Chapter 14) is an excellent choice.

One Grand Cypress Blvd. (off Fla. 535 past the Disney entrance or Hotel Plaza Blvd., to second light). ☎ *800-233-1234 or 407-239-1234. Fax: 407-239-3800.* www.grandcypress.com. *750 units. Parking: Free self and valet. Rack rates: $315–$435. AE, CB, DC, DISC, JCB, MC, V.*

Peabody Hotel

$$$$ International Drive

Welcome to the home of the famous — drum roll, maestro, *s'il vous plait* — Marching Mallards. Their home is in the thick of all the action I-Drive has to offer, including attractions, restaurants, and shopping. The real-live ducks march into their luxury pool each morning — no kidding! — through the lobby, accompanied by — what else? — John Philip Sousa's marching music. You don't have to be a guest to enjoy the rousing fun, so if you're in the neighborhood, drop in for the show.

The Peabody Hotel is located across from the Convention Center, which makes this hotel especially popular with business travelers. Guest rooms, even the standard ones, are lavishly furnished and decorated in neutral tones of beige, brown, and rust. The suites are fabulous and five times larger than the oversize standard rooms. The concierge-level Peabody Club occupies the top three floors. The hotel's ambiance, which extends to its top-rated restaurants (see Chapter 14), isn't duplicated anywhere in Orlando. Combos play jazz and blues in the atrium Lobby Bar nightly. The lobby hosts afternoon English teas on weekdays, sporting events are aired in the cozy Mallards Lounge, and alfresco jazz concerts take place on the fourth-floor recreation level in the spring and fall. Seniors thinking about staying here should take advantage of the hotel's over-50 price perks.

9801 International Dr. (between the Bee Line Expressway and Sand Lake Rd., across the street from the Orange County Convention Center). ☎ **800-732-3639** *or 407-352-4000. Fax: 407-351-0073.* www.peabody-orlando.com. *891 units. Parking: Free self and valet. Rack rates: $330–$1,000 and up. Ask about packages, holiday/summer discounts, and senior rates for those over 50. AE, CB, DC, DISC, JCB, MC, V.*

Perrihouse

$$ Lake Buena Vista

This quaint eight-bedroom, gray brick house nestled among six acres of flowers and trees is a perfect crash pad for those who want a little peace and quiet after a day in the theme parks. There's an on-site bird sanctuary, which draws good reviews from nature lovers. Each room (all are non-smoking) has either a king-size four-poster bed, or a canopied queen. All rooms have minibars, voice mail, and private bathrooms; cribs are available on request. An expanded continental breakfast is served each morning, and there is a self-service kitchen area available for guest use.

10417 Centurion Ct. (take exit 27 off I-4 to Fla. 535 West, go to the third light, at Texaco station, and turn left; go another three miles to Centurion Ct.). ☎ **407-876-4830.** *Fax: 407-876-0241.* www.perrihouse.com. *Eight units. Parking: Free. Rack rates: $99–$149. Inquire about packages and discounts. AE, DISC, MC, V.*

Portofino Bay Resort

$$$$ International Drive

This lovely resort opened in September 1999. If you're planning on spending the bulk of your time at **Universal** and have deep pockets, this is a good choice. The resort offers eight restaurants/lounges, a spa and fitness center, and a playground. The hotel is designed to look like the Mediterranean seaside village of Portofino, Italy, and has some exquisite touches, such as the Murano crystal chandeliers in the lobby and a brick piazza. You can get to the Universal theme parks via boat along the canals.

The accommodations are top-notch: four-poster beds with cloud-soft pillows, bathrooms outfitted with marble tubs, and tiled foyers. Rooms are state-of-art "smart rooms" that provide security, adjust room temperature, and report malfunctions as they occur. Family suites have kid-theme rooms, and butlers are available in 26 of the villas. Villa guests also get complimentary cocktails and hors d'oeuvres nightly in the Villa Club Lounge. The Portofino Bay's facilities range from bocci ball courts to two swimming pools, including one inside a "fort" with a waterslide.

5601 Universal Blvd. (Located off I-4, take Apopka-Vineland Rd. west to Universal Studios Escape, where the resort is located). ☎ *888-322-5541 or 407-503-1000. Fax: 407-224-7118.* www.uescape.com/resorts/. *750 rooms. Parking: $10 per day. Rack rates: $235–$770 and up. AE, CB, D, DC, MC, V.*

Radisson Plaza Hotel Orlando

$$ Downtown Orlando

This centrally located downtown Radisson is very popular with the business set, but offers a good deal for the leisure traveler as well. The newly redecorated rooms feature two-line telephones and modem ports. 'Lando Sam's Restaurant and Lounge is a good place to refuel and relax. The hotel has two tennis courts, a pool with Jacuzzi and tanning decks, and a fully equipped weight room. It's about 25 minutes from **Disney World;** 10–15 from **Universal** and **SeaWorld.**

60 South Ivanhoe Blvd. (downtown near College Park area north of Colonial Dr.). ☎ *800-333-3333 or 407-425-4455. Fax: 407-843-0262.* http://www.radissonorlando.com. *367 units. Parking: Free. Rack rates: $164. Ask about special packages. AE, CB, DC, DISC, MC, V.*

Radisson Twin Towers

$$ International Drive

This is a great place to stay if you'll be spending all or most of your time at **Universal, SeaWorld,** and the other I-Drive attractions (see Chapters 23 through 26). The large rooms feature two queen beds or one king, hair dryers, ironing boards, voice mail, and spacious bathrooms. There are numerous dining options, including the Citrus Shoppe Deli (open 24 hours), and several bars. Other trimmings include a whirlpool spa, a heated Junior Olympic pool, a children's pool and play area, an exercise facility, a hair salon, and shops. Transportation is provided to **Universal, SeaWorld,** and **Wet 'N' Wild.**

5780 Major Blvd. (directly across the street from Universal Studios Escape on Vineland Rd.). ☎ ***800-327-2110** or 407- 351-1000. Fax: 407-206-1759.* http://www. wwb.com/brochure/bh130268.html. *760 rooms. Parking: Free. Rack rates: $109–$169. AE, CB, DC, DISC, MC, V.*

Renaissance Orlando Hotel

$$-$$$ International Drive

Large rooms, good service, and luxurious surroundings are this hotel's calling cards. Its most valuable feature, however, is a location that's perfect if you're going to **Universal, SeaWorld** (it's right across the street), and to a lesser degree, the second-tier I-Drive attractions. The rooms and marble baths are huge. Each room comes equipped with voicemail, a minibar, and an ironing board; hair dryers and refrigerators are available upon request. There's a health club, swimming pool, and small playground. Baby-sitting and day-care service are available. The hotel has five restaurants and three lounges. It provides transportation to the Disney parks for $8 per person, round-trip.

6677 Sea Harbour Dr. (From I-4 follow signs to SeaWorld; the hotel is across from the attraction). ☎ ***407-351-5555**. Fax: 407-351-9991.* http://www. renaissancehotels.com/. *780 units. Parking: Free. Rack rates: $169–$280. AE, DISC, DC, MC, V.*

Summerfield Suites

$$$ International Drive

These two-bedroom suites can sleep up to eight people (if you're really into togetherness). Balconies overlook a courtyard filled with rustling palms. Sun-seekers will feel immediately at home in a suite that's more than just a bedroom. Take time away from the theme parks to luxuriate in grounds possessing the ambiance of a fine resort. Units have homey features such as an iron and ironing board, full kitchen, TV in the living room and bedrooms, and multiple telephones. A daily continental breakfast is free; you can purchase extra courses. The hotel has a pool, kiddie pool, fitness center, and video arcade. A shuttle to **WDW** costs $7 per person.

8480 International Dr. (between the Bee Line Expwy. and Sand Lake Rd.). ☎ ***800-830-4964** or 407-352-2400. Fax: 407-238-0778.* http://www. summerfieldsuites.com/. *Parking: Free. Rack rates: $209–$319. AE, CB, DC, DISC, MC, V.*

Villas of Grand Cypress

$$$$ Lake Buena Vista

Meet the sister site to the Hyatt Regency Grand Cypress (listed earlier in this chapter). The villas, a short drive from the larger hotel, offer privacy not found in most resorts, great views of the golf courses and canals, and resident ducks that wander onto your patio when they hear the door open (so be prepared with crackers or bread crusts). You can play 45 holes of golf on Jack Nicklaus-designed courses or take lessons at the golf academy. The horse crowd loves the top-of-the-line equestrian center; riding lessons and packages are available. The Mediterranean-style villas, which range from junior suites to four-bedroom affairs, have patios or balconies and Roman tubs. The larger villas have full kitchens. Dining is available in the elegant Black Swan Restaurant (see Chapter 14), which has a view of the ninth green. There is free shuttle service to the Hyatt Grand Cypress and all the resort's recreational facilities, and there's free transportation to the **WDW Parks** and **Universal Studios.**

One North Jacaranda (off Fla. 535, past the Disney entrance on Hotel Plaza Blvd., about a mile on the right). ☎ *800-835-7377 or 407-239-4700. Fax: 407-239-7219.* http://www.grandcypress.com/villas/home-villas.htm. *146 units. Parking: Free. Rack rates: $250–$1,740. Ask about golf, equestrian, family, and getaway packages. AE, CB, D, DC, MC, V.*

Walt Disney World Dolphin

$$$$ Walt Disney World

What a wonderful place for folks a) not on a budget, b) wanting to be close to **Epcot** and **Disney–MGM Studios,** and c) desperate to stay in a place that answers the question: What kind of buildings would Dali have created if he were an architect?

It's hard not to notice the massive, 56-foot twin dolphins on the roof of this resort, which some people feel is unfortunate. Once inside the lobby, you'll encounter prints from the likes of Picasso and Matisse. The rooms are fairly large, with two queen-size beds and first-class amenities; some of the units come with balconies. The grounds are lavishly landscaped, and amenities include 24-hour room service, a health club, lighted tennis courts, a three-mile jogging trail, a children's activity program, and many restaurants. It shares its facilities with the **Walt Disney World Swan** (see listing later in this chapter). Nightlife options include the Copa Banana, where a DJ spins tunes for dancing and karaoke. You can walk to **Epcot** from here, and Disney's **Fantasia Gardens** (see Chapter 21) is just across the street.

1500 Epcot Resorts Blvd. (off Buena Vista Dr., next to Walt Disney World Swan). ☎ *800-227-1500 or 407-934-4000. Fax: 407-934-4884.* www.swandolphin.com. *1,509 units. Parking: Free self and valet. Rack rates: $295–$465 and up. Inquire about packages. AE, CB, DC, DISC, JCB, MC, V.*

Walt Disney World Swan

$$$$ Walt Disney World

Located on the same property as the **Dolphin,** the **World Swan** offers another chance to stay on Magic Mickey's property without being bombarded by rodent decor. This 12-story, Westin-owned hotel is topped with dual 45-foot swan statues and seashell fountains. The **Swan** and **Dolphin** hotels are connected by a canopied walkway. The rooms here are luxurious and decorated in cheerful pastels. They're similar to the **Dolphin's,** but the **Swan's** rooms are a bit smaller. The hotel has a number of excellent restaurants, and guests are encouraged to dine both here and at the **Dolphin.** Nightlife options include Kimono's, which serves a wide selection of sushi and hosts karaoke after 8:30 p.m.

1200 Epcot Resorts Blvd. (off Buena Vista Dr., next door to the Walt Disney World Dolphin). ☎ *800-248-7926, 800-228-3000, or 407-934-3000. Fax: 407-934-4499.* www.swandolphin.com. *758 units. Parking: Free self and valet. Rack rates: $295–$465 and up. Inquire about packages. AE, CB, DC, DISC, JCB, MC, V.*

The Unicorn Inn

$ Kissimmee

Here's an English experience in the midst of this still-rural, cowpoke town. Opened as a bed and breakfast in 1995, the Unicorn is located in a blue-shingled house built in 1901. Each room is uniquely decorated to offer basic accommodations that are clean and cozy. Each room comes with a five-course gourmet breakfast. Guests also have use of the inn's kitchen. Several of the rooms can be doubled up to create a suite large enough for a four-member family. The inn has won several awards for historic preservation.

8 South Orlando Ave. (From Disney go east on U.S. 192, right on Bermuda Ave., left on Emmett St. past the courthouse, right on South Orlando Ave.). ☎ *800-865-7212 or 407-846-1200. Fax: 407-846-1773.* www.bbhost.com:8008/unicorninn/. *Parking: Free. Rack rates: $75–$85. Ask about AARP and AAA discounts and other packages. MC, V.*

Wyndham Palace Resort & Spa

$$$-$$$$ Lake Buena Vista/Official WDW Hotel

The hotel's spacious accommodations — most with lake-view balconies or patios — are within walking distance of **Downtown Disney Marketplace.** It's an ideal spot for honeymooners or those looking for a romantic weekend getaway. The appealing rooms are equipped with bedroom and bathroom phones, safes, and ceiling fans. There also are one- and two-bedroom suites that have living and dining rooms, 65 eco-friendly rooms (rooms that have special air-conditioner filters, filtered water, and are odor free), and 20 special-needs rooms (rooms with roll-in showers, higher sinks, lower light fixtures, and larger doorways).

There are several restaurants to choose from, including Arthur's 27 (see Chapter 14), which offers haute cuisine and panoramic park views. Other venues include pool and snack bars, a pastry shop, and the Laughing Kookaburra Good Time Bar. Amenities include two pools, a child-care program, an arcade, and a fully equipped spa.

1900 Buena Vista Dr. (off Fla. 535, turn in the entrance to Downtown Disney Marketplace; the hotel is on Hotel Plaza Blvd.). ☎ *800-327-2990 or 407-827-2727. Fax: 407-827-6034.* www.bvp-resort.com. *1,014 units. Parking: Free self and valet. Rack rates: $209–$500 and up. AE, CB, DC, DISC, MC, V.*

No Room at the Inn?

Okay, so you may hate organization. You're not going to plan this trip in any way, shape, or fashion. There are rooms available, and you're going to find them, regardless of our warnings to plan ahead.

You probably can find a place to stay, but you'll almost certainly not get the pick of the litter or the price you have in mind.

If you insist on arriving without a reservation and don't want to wear out a set of knuckles on motel doors, the official **Orlando Visitors Center** (☎ **407-363-5872**, but only call for information; you must show up to get a room) at 8723 International Dr., Suite 101, may be able to help you. The Center is open 8 a.m. to 8 p.m. daily, except Christmas. The Center can usually point you to available rooms, sometimes at a discount, but these rates are usually only good for the night you arrive.

Arguably, your best bet for finding a room is to aim for a chain. Here's a list of a few standards, most along the budget corridors of Kissimmee/U.S. 192 and International Drive:

- ✔ **Best Western Maingate,** 8600 W. Irlo Bronson Memorial Hwy., Kissimmee (☎ **407-396-0100**)

- ✔ **Comfort Suites Maingate Hotel,** 7888 W. Irlo Bronson Memorial Hwy., Kissimmee (☎ **407-390-9888**)

- ✔ **Days Inn East of the Magic Kingdom,** 5840 W. Irlo Bronson Memorial Hwy., Kissimmee (☎ **407-396-8669**)

- ✔ **Days Inn West-Maingate,** 7980 W. Irlo Bronson Memorial Hwy., Kissimmee (☎ **407-396-1000**)

- ✔ **Holiday Inn Kissimmee,** 2009 W. U.S. Hwy. 192, Kissimmee (☎ **407-846-2713**)

- ✔ **Holiday Inn Main Gate East,** 5678 Irlo Bronson Memorial Hwy., Kissimmee (☎ **800-366-5437** or 407-396-4488)

- ✔ **Howard Johnson Enchanted Land,** 4985 W. Irlo Bronson Memorial Hwy., Kissimmee (☎ **407-396-4343**)

- ✓ **Howard Johnson,** 4643 W. Irlo Bronson Memorial Hwy., Kissimmee (☎ **407-396-1340**)

- ✓ **Motel 6 Orlando West Kissimmee,** 7455 W. Irlo Bronson Memorial Hwy., Kissimmee (☎ **407-396-6422**)

- ✓ **Motel 6 Orlando,** 5731 W. Irlo Bronson Memorial Hwy., Kissimmee (☎ **407-396-6333**)

- ✓ **Quality Inn on Lake Cecile,** 4944 W. Irlo Bronson Memorial Hwy., Kissimmee (☎ **407-396-4455**)

- ✓ **Quality Suites Maingate East,** 5876 W. Irlo Bronson Memorial Hwy., Kissimmee (☎ **407-870-7374**)

- ✓ **Ramada Plaza Hotel Gateway,** 7470 W. Hwy. 192, Kissimmee (☎ **407-396-4400**)

- ✓ **Days Inn Convention Center SeaWorld,** 9990 International Dr., Orlando (☎ **407-352-8700**)

- ✓ **Days Inn/East of Universal Studios,** 5827 Caravan Ct., Orlando (☎ **407-351-3800**)

- ✓ **Days Inn International,** 7200 International Drive, Orlando (☎ **407-351-1200**)

- ✓ **Holiday Inn Express International Drive,** 6323 International Dr., Orlando (☎ **407-351-4430**)

- ✓ **Holiday Inn International Drive Resort,** 6515 International Dr., Orlando (☎ **407-351-3500**)

- ✓ **Travel Lodge International Drive,** 5859 American Way, Orlando (☎ **407-345-8880**)

Chapter 9

Checking Off Your List: Last-Minute Details and Other Things to Keep in Mind

● ●

In This Chapter

▶ Buying travel and medical insurance

▶ Dealing with illness away from home

▶ Renting a car (or why you shouldn't)

▶ Making reservations and getting tickets in advance

▶ Packing tips

● ●

*Y*ou're almost ready to leave for Orlando. All you need to do is take care of a few last-minute details, plan an itinerary, put the dog in the kennel, stuff your bags with everything that's clean, water the geraniums, pay the mortgage, and finish 50 other eleventh-hour musts.

The information in this chapter will save you from wasting precious vacation hours while you wait in line, call around town, and buy the dental floss you forgot to pack. We also help you make decisions on whether to rent a car and give you advice on what to do if you get sick.

For more information about money issues, discounts, and budget matters, check out Chapter 3. Now, put your seat and tray-table in an upright position.

Buying Travel Insurance: Good Idea or Bad?

There are three primary kinds of travel insurance: trip cancellation, lost luggage, and medical. Trip cancellation insurance is a good idea for some, but lost luggage and additional medical insurance don't make sense for most travelers. Be sure to explore your options and consider the following advice before you leave home:

✔ **Trip cancellation insurance.** Cancellation insurance is a good idea if you've paid a large portion of your vacation expenses up front. If you've bought a package trip, cancellation insurance comes in handy if a member of your party becomes ill or if you experience a death in the family and aren't able to go on vacation.

✔ **Lost luggage insurance.** Your homeowner's insurance should cover stolen luggage if your policy encompasses off-premises theft, so check your existing policies before you buy any additional coverage. Airlines are responsible for $2,500 on domestic flights, but that may not be enough to cover your sharkskin suit. Our best advice: Wear it on the plane, and if you're carrying anything else of substantial value, stow it in your carry-on bag.

✔ **Medical insurance.** Your existing health insurance should cover you if you get sick while on vacation. (However, if you belong to an HMO, check to see whether you're fully covered when away from home).

Some credit cards (American Express and certain gold and platinum Visa and MasterCards, for example) offer automatic flight insurance against death or dismemberment in case of an airplane crash. If you still think you need more insurance, make sure that you don't pay for more insurance than you need. For example, if you need only trip cancellation insurance, don't purchase coverage for lost or stolen property. Trip cancellation insurance costs approximately 6 to 8 percent of your vacation's total value. Here's a list of some of the reputable issuers of travel insurance:

- **Access America**, 6600 W. Broad St., Richmond, VA 23230 (☎ **800-284-8300;** Fax: 800-346-9265; www.accessamerica.com)

- **Travelex Insurance Services,** 11717 Burt St., Suite 202, Omaha, NE 68154 (☎ **800-228-9792;** www.travelex-insurance.com)

- **Travel Guard International,** 1145 Clark St., Stevens Point, WI 54481 (☎ **800-826-1300;** www.travel-guard.com)

- **Travel Insured International, Inc.,** P.O. Box 280568, 52-S Oakland Ave., East Hartford, CT 06128-0568 (☎ **800-243-3174;** www.travelinsured.com)

Combating Illness Away from Home

Finding a doctor you trust when you're out of town is hard. And getting a prescription refilled is no piece of cake, either. So, here are some travel tips to help you avoid a medical dilemma while you're on vacation:

✔ If you have health insurance, carry your identification card in your wallet. Likewise, if you don't think your existing policy is sufficient, purchase medical insurance for more comprehensive coverage.

✔ Bring all your medications with you as well as a prescription for more if you think you'll run out.

✔ Bring an extra pair of contact lenses or glasses in case you lose them.

✔ Don't forget to bring over-the-counter medicines for common travelers' ailments like diarrhea or stomach acid.

✔ If you suffer from a chronic illness, talk to your doctor before taking your trip. For conditions such as epilepsy, diabetes, or a heart condition, wear a *Medic Alert* identification tag to immediately alert any doctor about your condition and give him or her access to your medical records through Medic Alert's 24-hour hotline. Participation in the Medic Alert program costs $35, with a $15 renewal fee. Contact the Medic Alert Foundation, 2323 Colorado Ave., Turlock, CA 95382 (☎ **800-432-5378**; www.medicalert.org).

If your ailment isn't a life-threatening emergency, use a walk-in clinic. You may not get immediate attention, but you'll probably pay around $60 rather than the $300 minimum for just signing in at an emergency-room counter. *Centra-Care,* operated by a locally run Florida hospital, is a reputable medical facility with 13 locations throughout the Orlando area. For information and the nearest location, call ☎ **407-660-8118.**

Be wary of other doc-in-a-box facilities. There have been problems with disreputable companies in the last few years operating in tourist areas. You can get a reputable referral from *Ask-A-Nurse.* Ask-A-Nurse asks whether you have insurance, but that's for information purposes only, so they can track who uses their system. Ask-A-Nurse is a free service open to everyone. In Kissimmee call ☎ **407-870-1700**; in Orlando call ☎ **407-897-1700.**

You can fill your prescriptions at pharmacies such as Eckerd or Walgreen's. Likewise, many discount stores, such as Kmart or Target, also have pharmacies, some with 24-hour service. You can find stores such as these in the White or Yellow Pages of the phone book.

To find a dentist, call *Dental Referral Service* (☎ **800-917-6453**). They can tell you the nearest dentist who meets your needs. Phones are manned daily from 5:30 a.m. to 6:00 p.m.

Weighing Your Rental-Car Options

First off, you have to decide whether you'll need a car for your Orlando vacation (see Chapter 11 for more information about renting a car in Orlando). If you're going to spend most of your time at a resort, especially **Walt Disney World,** you may not need a car. **Disney** has its own transportation system; its buses and monorails are free, but you'll be a prisoner of **WDW's** often slow and indirect schedule.

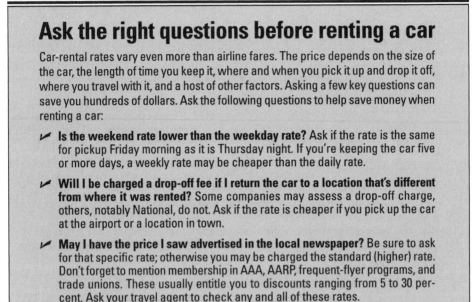

Ask the right questions before renting a car

Car-rental rates vary even more than airline fares. The price depends on the size of the car, the length of time you keep it, where and when you pick it up and drop it off, where you travel with it, and a host of other factors. Asking a few key questions can save you hundreds of dollars. Ask the following questions to help save money when renting a car:

✔ **Is the weekend rate lower than the weekday rate?** Ask if the rate is the same for pickup Friday morning as it is Thursday night. If you're keeping the car five or more days, a weekly rate may be cheaper than the daily rate.

✔ **Will I be charged a drop-off fee if I return the car to a location that's different from where it was rented?** Some companies may assess a drop-off charge, others, notably National, do not. Ask if the rate is cheaper if you pick up the car at the airport or a location in town.

✔ **May I have the price I saw advertised in the local newspaper?** Be sure to ask for that specific rate; otherwise you may be charged the standard (higher) rate. Don't forget to mention membership in AAA, AARP, frequent-flyer programs, and trade unions. These usually entitle you to discounts ranging from 5 to 30 percent. Ask your travel agent to check any and all of these rates.

If you plan to visit **Universal Studios, SeaWorld,** and other attractions or areas of central Florida, you'll need to either rent a car or choose an alternate form of transportation such as one of a number of free hotel shuttles. Other city shuttles charge a fee (the average is $7–$10 per person). Mears Transportation, QuickTransportation, and local taxis are other options (see Chapter 11 for more information on transportation options in Orlando). Getting several people to the parks on a daily basis can be expensive if you choose these routes, but you'll save on car-rental rates, gas, and the $6-per-day parking fee at the major attractions if you take advantage of Orlando's transit system. You also need to decide if the added convenience and mobility of a rental car is worth the added expense. Keep in mind that most car rentals are worth at least 500 miles on your frequent-flier account!

Adding up the cost of renting a car

On top of the standard rental prices, other optional charges apply to most car rentals. The *Collision Damage Waiver (CDW),* which requires you to pay for damage to the car in a collision, is charged on rentals in most states, but is covered by many credit card companies. Check with your credit card company before you go so that you can avoid paying this hefty fee (as much as $15 a day).

Car-rental companies also offer additional liability insurance (if you harm others in an accident), personal accident insurance (if you harm yourself or your passengers), and personal effects insurance (if your luggage is stolen from your car). If you have insurance on your car at home, you're probably covered for most of these unlikelihoods. If your own insurance doesn't cover you for rentals, or if you don't have auto insurance, consider buying additional coverage (car-rental companies are liable for certain base amounts, depending on the state). But, weigh the likelihood of getting into an accident or losing your luggage against the cost of extra coverage (as much as $20 a day combined), which can significantly add to the price of your rental.

Some companies also offer refueling packages, in which you pay for an entire tank of gas up front. The price is usually fairly competitive with local gas prices, but you don't get credit for any gas remaining in the tank. If you reject this option, you pay only for the gas you use, but you have to return the vehicle with a full tank or face charges of $3 to $4 a gallon for any shortfall. If a stop at a gas station on the way to the airport will make you miss your plane, by all means take advantage of the fuel purchase option. Otherwise, skip it.

Booking a rental car on the Internet

As with other aspects of planning your trip, using the Internet can make comparison shopping and reserving a car rental much easier. All the major booking sites — **Travelocity** (www.travelocity.com), **Expedia** (www.expedia.com), **Yahoo! Travel** (www.travel.yahoo.com), and **Cheap Tickets** (www.cheaptickets.com), for example — offer search engines that can dig up discounted car-rental rates. Enter the size of the car you want, the pickup and return dates, and the city where you want to rent, and the server returns a price. You can then make your reservation through these sites.

If you want information about specific rental-car companies serving Orlando, see the Appendix in the back of this book.

Beating the Crowd: Making Reservations and Getting Tickets in Advance

Because time is at a premium in Orlando, and you'll be spending enough of it on attraction lines, the last thing you want to do is wile away precious hours waiting for a restaurant table or a theater ticket. Although, in most cases, an advance reservation is not the mandatory item it is in other cities, having one in hand will certainly make your day run more smoothly.

Reserving a table

Compared to New York and San Francisco, where tables at the best restaurants are snapped up weeks in advance, securing reservations in Orlando is easy. In most instances, you can wait until you get to Florida to make dining reservations. Eateries on the "exceptions" list include Emeril's in **CityWalk** and Victoria & Albert's at **Walt Disney World** (see Chapter 14 for more information about Orlando's fantastic dining scene), where reservations need to be made at least a month in advance. Your hotel's concierge or front desk can help with reservations.

Most Walt Disney World restaurants use a system called Priority Seating. With Priority Seating, you make a reservation that ensures you'll get the next available table after your arrival at the restaurant. Priority Seating reservations differ from a traditional reservation, where an empty table is held for you, but it's far better than just showing up and waiting your turn. For more details on this reservation system, see Chapter 13. You can arrange for Priority Seating for restaurants, including character meals and dinner shows, up to 60 days in advance by calling ☎ **407-939-3463.** You can also make arrangements near the entrances to the theme parks (see Chapters 17 through 20 for detailed park information) or at Disney resorts.

Reserving a ticket and getting event information

Ticketmaster is the key reservations player for most major events in Orlando, including concerts, shows, and pro sports events. If you know of an event that's happening while you're in town, check first with your hometown Ticketmaster outlets to see whether they sell tickets for the event. (If you live as close as Miami or Atlanta, they probably do.) Otherwise, call the Ticketmaster outlet in Orlando at ☎ **407-839-3900,** or go to its Web site at www.ticketmaster.com. Ticketmaster is open from 9 a.m. to 9 p.m. Monday to Friday and 9 a.m. to 7 p.m. Saturday and Sunday.

Dozens of rock, rap, jazz, pop, country, blues, and folk stars are in town during any given week in Orlando. After you're in town, you can find schedules in the *Orlando Sentinel's* **Calendar** section, published every Friday. The newspaper also includes information about local attractions, hotels, restaurants, cultural events, and so on. To get information before you arrive, you can find the newspaper online at www.orlandosentinel.com.

You can also get additional event information from the **Orlando/ Orange County Convention & Visitors Bureau** (☎ **800-643-9492** or 407-363-5871; www.go2orlando.com).

See Chapters 28 through 29 for information about making advance reservations for some of Orlando's best after-dark fun.

Reserving a green

Disney has 99 holes of golf (five regulation, par-72 courses and a nine-hole, par-36 walking course) that are open to the public as well as resort guests. For tee times and information, call ☎ **407-824-2270** up to seven days in advance. (Disney resort guests can reserve up to 30 days in advance.) Golf packages are available, and reservations can be made in advance by calling ☎ **407-934-7639**. Get online details at http://disney.go.com/DisneyWorld/intro.html. (See Chapter 21 for more information.)

You can get information on and make reservations at other non-Disney courses through **Golfpac, ☎ 800-327-0878** or 407-260-2288; www.golfpacinc.com. Or contact **Tee Times USA, ☎ 800-374-8633**; www.teetimesusa.com.

Gearing Up: Practical Packing Advice

To start packing for your trip, take everything you think you'll need and lay it out on the bed. Now get rid of half of it. It's not that the airlines won't let you take it all — they will, with some limits — but why do you want to get a hernia from lugging half your house around with you? And remember, suitcase straps are particularly painful to sunburned shoulders. Use the tips in this section to avoid renting a truck to move your luggage around Orlando.

Florida is a laid-back place. Therefore, you can leave your formal wear — even your tie — at home unless you're planning a special night out. Instead, bring casual clothes, including some comfortable walking shoes (a must) and airy shirts, blouses, shorts, skirts, or pants. If you're coming during the Sunshine State's microscopic winter (that's mainly January and February), you may need to layer your clothing. In fact, bringing a light jacket or sweater and a thin rain poncho anyway is smart. And don't forget all the necessary toiletries, medications (pack these in your carry-on bag so that you have them if the airline loses your luggage), and a camera.

Some airlines allow two pieces of carry-on luggage per person, both of which must fit in the overhead compartment or the seat in front of you, but others restrict passengers to one. (Ask when making your reservation.) Use carry-ons for valuables, medications, and vital documents first. You can then add a book, breakable items you don't want to put in your suitcase, and a snack if you have room. Also, carry the sweater or light jacket with you — cabins can feel like the Arctic one minute and a sauna the next.

Learn the limits on your carry-on luggage

Because lost-luggage rates have reached an all-time high, consumers bring their possessions on board to try to divert disaster. But planes are more crowded than ever, and overhead compartment space is at a premium. Some domestic airlines have started cracking down, limiting you to a single carry-on for crowded flights and imposing size restrictions to the bags that you bring on board. The dimensions vary, but the strictest airlines say carry-ons must measure no more than 22 x 14 x 9 inches, including wheels and handles, and weigh no more than 40 pounds.

Many airports are already furnished with x-ray machines that literally block any carry-on bigger than the posted size restriction. These measures may sound drastic, but keep in mind that many of these regulations are enforced only at the discretion of the gate attendants. If you plan to bring more than one bag aboard a crowded flight, make sure that your medications, documents, and valuables are consolidated in one bag in case you're forced to check the second bag.

Here are some other essential packing tips:

- You can leave the snowshoes, ski masks, and thermal underwear at home; some winter mornings in central Florida do get brisk. The weather usually follows a three-day cycle: wet, windy, and cold; colder and sometimes frosty; bright and beginning to warm. Therefore, *layered clothing* (a sweater, light jacket, and a sweatshirt) is a good idea.

- The most common sign welcoming diners to Florida's restaurants states "Shirt and Shoes Required." It summarizes the Floridian way of life: casual, but not gross. Please, no short-shorts, tank tops, outer-underwear, or see-throughs in the dining room. (You may not care, but the rest of us are trying to eat.) Beyond those, you won't encounter many rules for attire. Classier joints may insist on a coat, fewer yet a tie, but sport coats or — heaven forbid! — suits are pretty much a waste of time and luggage space. Slacks and a nice shirt or blouse are sufficient for almost everywhere, and nice shorts show up everywhere, even at night. Most hosts know that you've spent the day trapped in the theme parks, and they're happy you saved some money for them.

- Sun cover-ups are essential. You can get a blistering burn on the coolest and cloudiest of days in Florida. Bring a hat (preferably one with a brim) and sunglasses, too. Don't forget to bring sunscreen with a 25-rating or higher that's preferably waterproof so that you don't lose its benefits by sweat or the water in pool. Kids especially need protection from the sun.

✔ Don't forget an umbrella or poncho, regardless of the season. Florida is as wet as it is warm, and the umbrella and poncho prices in theme parks can cause a panic attack.

✔ Bring at least two pairs of shoes and plenty of socks so that you can start each day with fresh, dry footwear. Your standby pair of shoes is invaluable after a visit to one of the many theme parks that have water rides. Likewise, waiting in line on hot days is tougher on the tootsies than keeping ice cream from melting on the equator. Many theme-park veterans carry extra shoes and socks with them, changing footwear midway through their day.

✔ If you're visiting Florida from early spring to late fall, bring a lot of lightweight shirts (T-shirts work very well) and shorts to stay cool during the days. And for the sake of your fellow patrons, don't forget an extra swipe of deodorant.

Part III
Settling into Orlando

The 5th Wave   By Rich Tennant

"The hotel said they were giving us the `Indiana Jones' suite."

In this part . . .

Orlando isn't New York or London, but it can seem overwhelming at first. Getting around the tourist areas and downtown Orlando can be quite intimidating. Don't worry, though — it's not as complicated as it looks. In this chapter, we walk you through the city's neighborhoods, tell you where to catch local transportation, and erase any confusion you may have.

Chapter 10

Orienting Yourself in Orlando

In This Chapter

▶ Landing at the airport

▶ Exploring Orlando's neighborhoods

▶ Getting information when you arrive

*A*ll roads in Orlando lead to **Disney** — well, not quite, but you'd be hard-pressed to get lost on an Orlando street without coming across a sign directing you to **WDW**. This, however, does not mean that navigating the city won't drive you to distraction. We'll start off by getting you from the airport to the parks and then clue you in about Orlando's major neighborhoods.

Arriving on the Orlando Scene

While other travelers who didn't read this book are lost in the black hole known as Orlando International Airport (☎ **407-825-2001**), you'll whiz on to baggage claim and your chariot of choice. Our best words of advice: Heads up! You're going to need to pay attention to get out of the airport in a timely fashion.

If you can run a direct route, just follow the signs to baggage claim. (You land at Level 3, so you need to take a shuttle to the main terminal, and then go to Level 2 for your bags. You can catch hotel shuttles or taxis at Level 2; rental-car desks are at Level 1.) *Note*: If you're arriving from a foreign country, you have to go through Immigration before baggage claim and then through Customs after picking up your luggage.

If you need cash, ATMs are located in the arrival and departure terminals near the three pods of gates (1–29, 30–59, and 60–99). There are also ATMs located where the shuttles deposit you in the main terminal. If you need to convert your pounds, francs, and so on to U.S. dollars, you can find currency exchanges (open 9:30 a.m. to 9:00 p.m.) opposite the ATMs at gate pods 1–29 and 60–99 in the air terminal. In the main terminal, they're located where shuttles arrive from gates 1–29.

All major car-rental companies are located at the airport (on Level 1) or nearby. (See the Appendix in the back of this book for the toll-free numbers of the major rental companies.) You can find other vehicle rental company services online at http://fcn.state.fl.us/goaa.

Finding Your Way to Your Hotel

The airport is a 25-minute hop, skip, and long jump from **Disney World,** and 20 minutes from downtown. **Mears Transportation Group** (☎ 407-423-5566) is the major shuttle player. It runs vans between the airport (you board outside baggage claim) and all Disney resorts and official hotels, as well as most other area properties, every 15 to 25 minutes. Round-trip to downtown Orlando or International Drive is $21 for adults ($14 for kids 4 to 11); it's $25 for adults ($17 for kids) to **Walt Disney World/Lake Buena Vista** or Kissimmee/U.S. 192.

Taxis are another option if your party has enough people. The standard rates for **Ace Metro,** ☎ **407-855-0564,** and **Yellow Cab,** ☎ **407-699-9999,** are $2.50 for the first mile and $1.50 a mile thereafter. The one-way charge from the airport to **Disney** for up to five people in a cab or seven in a van is about $42. A trip to International Drive is $26; to downtown, it's $17. Vans and taxis load on Level 2 of the airport.

QuickTransportation/Orlando, ☎ **888-784-2522** or 407-354-2456 (www.quicktransportation.com), offers shuttle service that is a bit more personal. Employees greet you at the airport's baggage claim department (with a sign bearing your name). They're 10 to 15 percent more expensive than Mears, but they're coming for you, not a full load of tourists, and they're going only to your resort. This is a good option for a group of four or more.

Some hotels offer free shuttle service to and from the airport, so make sure to ask when booking your room.

If you're driving a rented car from the airport, take the north exit out of the airport to 528 West (a toll road also known as the Bee Line Expressway). Follow the signs to I-4, then go west to Exit 26 (marked Epcot/Disney Village) and follow the signs toward the Disney attractions. Your ride takes about 20 minutes if traffic isn't too heavy. The WDW exits are clearly marked.

Exploring Orlando by Neighborhood

Orlando's major artery is Interstate 4. Locals call it I-4 or that #@$*%^#!! road, because it's often congested, especially during the weekday rush hour (7 to 9 a.m. and 4 to 6 p.m.). I-4 runs diagonally across the state from Tampa to Daytona Beach. Likewise, exits from I-4 lead to all WDW properties, **Universal, SeaWorld,** International Drive, U.S. 192, Kissimmee, Lake Buena Vista, **Church Street Station,** downtown Orlando, and Winter Park. Most of the exits are well marked, but construction is common, and exit numbers often change. Keep this in mind when you're traveling along I-4, so that you don't end up in the Bahamas.

Orlando Neighborhoods

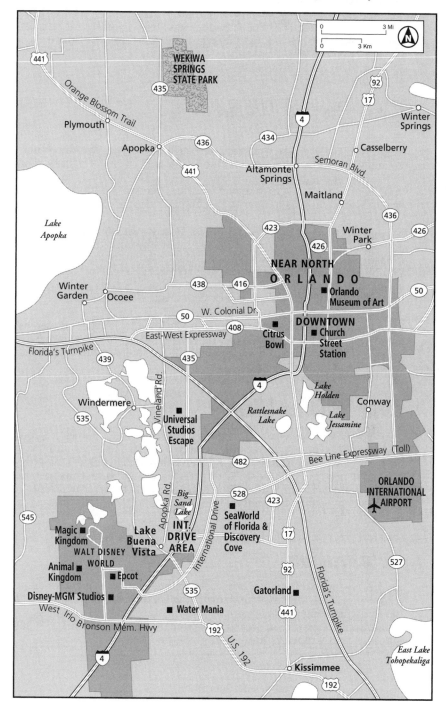

441

WEKIWA
SPRINGS
STATE PARK

435

92

17

Orange Blossom Trail

4

Winter
Springs

Plymouth

Apopka

436

434

Casselberry

441

Altamonte
Springs

Semoran Blvd.

Maitland

436

Lake
Apopka

423

426

Winter
Park

426

NEAR NORTH

ORLANDO

438

416

Orlando
Museum of Art

50

Winter
Garden

Ocoee

50

W. Colonial Dr.

DOWNTOWN

Florida's Turnpike

East-West Expressway

408

Citrus
Bowl

Church
Street
Station

439

435

4

Lake
Holden

Conway

Vineland Rd.

Windermere

535

Universal
Studios
Escape

Rattlesnake
Lake

Lake
Jessamine

Bee Line Expressway (Toll)

482

ORLANDO
INTERNATIONAL
AIRPORT

545

Apopka Rd.

Big
Sand
Lake

528

423

International Drive

INT.
DRIVE
AREA

SeaWorld
of Florida &
Discovery
Cove

17

Magic
Kingdom

Lake
Buena
Vista

WALT DISNEY

WORLD

Animal
Kingdom

Epcot

92

Florida's Turnpike

527

Disney-MGM Studios

535

Gatorland

West Irlo Bronson Mem. Hwy

Water Mania

441

192

U.S. 192

East Lake
Tohopekaliga

4

Kissimmee

192

0   3 Mi

0   3 Km

The Florida Turnpike crosses I-4 and links with I-75 to the north. U.S. 192, a major east-west artery, reaches from Kissimmee to U.S. 27, crossing I-4 near the WDW entrance road. Farther north, the Bee Line Expressway toll road (or Fla. 528) goes east from I-4 past Orlando International Airport to Cape Canaveral and the **Kennedy Space Center.** The East-West Expressway (also known as Florida 408) is another toll road that bypasses the tourist meccas.

Walt Disney World

The empire, its big and little parks, resorts, restaurants, shops, and assorted trimmings are scattered across 30,500 acres. The thing that you may find most surprising is that **WDW** isn't even in Orlando. It's southwest of the city, off I-4 on West U.S. 192. Stay in this area, and you'll learn that convenience has its price. Accommodations here run as much as double as in nearby Kissimmee.

A major section of **Walt Disney World, Downtown Disney** is the general name that **Disney** gives to its two nighttime entertainment areas, **Pleasure Island** and **Disney West Side,** plus its shopping complex, **Downtown Disney Marketplace.** The area is filled with restaurants, shops, and dance clubs of all types and prices. It's actually in Lake Buena Vista, although it's a part of **Walt Disney World.**

Even if you're not staying or driving in Mickeyville, it's a good idea to get a Walt Disney World Transportation Guide Map to see where everything is. They are free and are available at the main or guest-services desk at most Orlando hotels.

Lake Buena Vista

Lake Buena Vista is **Disney**'s next-door neighborhood. It's where you'll find "official" (though not Disney-owned or located) hotels, and it's close to **Downtown Disney** and **Pleasure Island.** This charming area has manicured lawns, tree-lined thoroughfares, and free transportation throughout the realm, though it may take a while to get from Point A to Point B because of a combination of slow shuttle service and heavy traffic.

Celebration

Imagine living in a Disney world. Celebration is an attempt to re-create a squeaky-clean, Mickey magic town. It will eventually have thousands of residents living in Disney homes, which start at about $200,000. Celebration's downtown area is, however, designed for tourists. It has some first-rate, if pricey shops and restaurants.

Kissimmee

Kissimmee has a tacky side: It's loaded with T-shirt shops and every burger barn known to Western civilization. But Kissimmee is just a short drive (roughly 10-15 miles) from the Wizard of Disney and, with plenty of modest motels, it's a good choice for those on a budget. The town centers on U.S. 192/Irlo Bronson Memorial Highway.

International Drive (Highway 536)

Can you say tourist mecca? Known as I-Drive, this area extends seven to ten miles north of the Disney kingdom between Highway 535 and the Florida Turnpike. From bungee jumping and ice-skating to dozens of themed restaurants, this stretch of road is *the* tourist strip in central Florida. I-Drive also offers numerous hotels and shopping areas. It's home to the Orange County Convention Center and offers easy access to **SeaWorld** and **Universal Studios.** I-Drive is already packed, but developers manage to shoehorn more in, year after year.

Downtown Orlando

Right off I-4 East, Downtown Orlando's headliner is the **Church Street Station** entertainment and shopping complex. There are loads of clubs, shops, and restaurants in the heart of the city. Dozens of antiques shops line Antique Row on Orange Avenue near Lake Ivanhoe. Many vacationers take advantage of Lymmo, a free shuttle-bus system that carts you around the downtown area.

Winter Park

Just north of downtown Orlando, Winter Park offers Park Avenue, a collection of upscale shops and restaurants along a cobblestone street. Winter Park has little, if any kid-appeal, and it's too far north to use as a home base if you plan on spending much time at the Disney parks.

Information Please

After you've landed, one of the best places for up-to-date information is the concierge or the front desk at your hotel (and they're even better if you're staying on a Disney property).

If you're in the International Drive area, stop at the official Orlando Visitors Center, ☎ **407-363-5872** for information, 8723 International Drive (four blocks south of Sand Lake Road).

Friday's **"Calendar"** section in the *Orlando Sentinel* also includes a lot of tourist-friendly information on dining and entertainment.

At the Orlando International Airport, arriving passengers can find information at The Magic of Disney and Disney's Flight of Fantastic, two shops located in the A and B terminals, respectively. They sell Disney multiday park tickets, make dinner show and hotel reservations, and provide brochures. Facilities are open daily from 6 a.m. to 9 p.m.

The airport's Universal Studios Store, which is open daily from 6:30 a.m. to 10:00 p.m., provides similar services, as do the SeaWorld stores in the A and B terminals, which are open daily from 6:30 a.m. to 10:00 p.m.

Chapter 11

Getting Around Orlando

• •

In This Chapter

▶ Exploring Orlando's transportation options

▶ Driving in Orlando

▶ Strolling around the city

• •

*O*rlando feeds on adventurers just like you. Tens of millions of travelers arrive every year, and Orlando's tourism czars (prompted by Disney's dollars) want to make getting from Point A to Point B as easy as possible. The faster you can get around town, the more time you can spend in the parks and attractions (and the more money you spend).

However, unless you volunteer for incarceration in Mickeyville, you may have to deal with slowdowns such as rush hour, which runs from 7 to 9 a.m. and 4 to 6 p.m. weekdays, so allow a cushion in your travel plans. During the week, tourist traffic heightens commuter traffic. Most of the parks don't open until 9 a.m. (except **WDW's Animal Kingdom,** see Chapter 20), so you won't miss much if you arrive a little late. Traffic is just as bad on weekends because more vacationers are on the roads as well as nearly as many commuters, because the parks are open daily.

Relying on Orlando's Transportation Network

Your major decision regarding Orlando transportation will be whether to use **Walt Disney World's** transportation network (which is truly useful only to those staying at a **WDW** resort), to rent a car, or to stick to public transportation. What system will work best for you depends on what you want to see, where you are staying, and how much time you want to spend getting around the city.

Traveling with Disney's transportation system

If you plan to stay at a Disney resort or an official hotel (see Chapter 8 for more information on Disney hotels) and will spend the majority of your time visiting Disney parks, you probably can skip a rental car — at least for most of your stay. A free transportation network runs through **Disney World.** Buses, ferries, water taxis, and monorails operate from two hours prior to the parks' opening until two hours after closing. Likewise, Disney offers service to **Downtown Disney, Typhoon Lagoon, River Country, Blizzard Beach, Pleasure Island, Fort Wilderness,** and other Disney resorts. Disney properties also offer transportation to other area attractions, but you'll have to pay extra.

The advantages of utilizing Disney's transportation system include:

- ✔ It's free.
- ✔ You save on car rental and gas charges.
- ✔ You don't have to pay $6 a day to park in the theme park lots.
- ✔ If your party wants to split up, you can board a transport to different areas.

Disadvantages include:

- ✔ You're at the mercy of Disney's schedule.
- ✔ Sometimes you have to take a ferry to catch a bus to get on the monorail to reach your hotel. The system makes a complete circuit, but not necessarily the most direct path for you. It can take an hour or more to get somewhere that's right across the lagoon from you. If you have a little time to spare before making reservations, get a free Walt Disney World Transportation Guide Map (☎ **407-824-4321**). It shows you where various resorts are in relation to the attractions that you want to visit.
- ✔ You have to endure multiple stops, particularly on buses, and at peak periods, crowds may force you to wait for the next bus.

If you plan to travel on the Disney transportation network, verify with the driver or someone at your hotel's information desk that you're taking the most direct route. Keep asking questions along the way. Unlike missing a highway exit, missing a stop on the bus route means you'll have to take another ride on the Mickey-go-round.

Getting around by bus

Lynx (☎ **407-841-8240,** www.golynx.com) bus stops are marked with a paw print. The buses serve **Disney, Universal,** and **International Drive** ($1 for adults, 25 cents for kids and seniors; $10 for an unlimited weekly pass), but their routes are not very visitor-oriented.

Touring by trolley

The I-Ride Trolley on International Drive (☎ 407-354-5656, `www.iridetrolley.com`) runs every 15 minutes, 7 a.m. to midnight (75 cents for adults, 25 cents for seniors, kids under 12 ride free). Due to I-Drive's heavy traffic, this is the best way to get around if you're staying in this area or at least spending the day. It cuts down on the hurry-up-and-wait frustration of bumper-to-bumper traffic.

Using a taxi

Yellow Cab (☎ 407-699-9999) and Ace Metro (☎ 407-855-0564) are among the taxicab companies serving the Orlando area. But for day-to-day travel to and from the attractions, cabs are expensive unless your group has five or more people. Rates cost $2.50 for the first mile, $1.50 per mile thereafter.

Traveling by shuttle

Mears Transportation Group (☎ 407-423-5566) operates shuttle buses to all major attractions, including **Cypress Gardens, Kennedy Space Center, Universal Studios, SeaWorld, Busch Gardens** (yes, in Tampa), and **Church Street Station,** among others. Rates vary by destination.

Maneuvering through town on a motorcycle

If you have a motorcycle license, you can rent bikes at American V Twin (☎ 888-268-8946) or 407-903-0058, `www.amvtwin.com` and Cruise America (☎ 407-931-1409). Their inventory is in short supply, so call ahead. You must be at least 21 years old, have a valid motorcycle license, and have a major credit card. Rentals range from $800 to $1,200 per week and include helmets, locks, and a brief orientation.

Plan months in advance if you're visiting during Bike Week — late February and early March — or Biketober Fest in mid-October. (Both events are in Daytona Beach, but many bikers stay in Orlando.)

Touring Orlando by Car: Expanding Your Sightseeing Horizons

If you're on an extended stay — more than a week — you'll probably want to rent a car for at least a day or two to venture beyond the tourist areas. (Yes, there *is* life beyond the theme parks.) See the Appendix at the back of this book for toll-free numbers of various car rental agencies.

Here are a few additional tips for driving in Orlando.

- ✔ Remember to allow for rush hour traffic between 7 to 9 a.m. and 4 to 6 p.m. on weekdays.

- ✔ I-4 may look like it runs north and south, but Orlando's sign painters say otherwise. To them, you drive west toward Disney and east toward downtown Orlando.

- ✔ In Florida, you can make a right turn on red after coming to a full stop and making sure the coast is clear (unless signs say otherwise). Consider yourself warned: If you're sitting at a red light with your blinker on and not turning right, you'll probably hear horns blaring. Chances are, the drivers are saluting you, too — make sure your path is clear, then *move it.*

- ✔ Posted speed limits are enforced pretty vigorously. Fines for speeding begin at more than $150. Pay particular attention to road construction zones, where speed limits are reduced and signs warn about speeding fines being doubled — they're not kidding.

- ✔ Name Game: International Drive is called I-Drive. Irlo Bronson Memorial Highway is U.S. 192 or just 192. Florida Route 528 is the Bee Line Expressway. State Road 50 is more commonly called Colonial Drive.

- ✔ You must have a Florida handicap permit to park in handicap parking places. Handicap permits from other states are honored, but a disabled license plate alone won't do.

- ✔ Along a 12-mile stretch of U.S. 192 in Kissimmee, 25-foot-high markers start at **Walt Disney World** and extend nearly all the way to **Splendid China** (see Chapter 26), brightly marking the many points of interest. The westernmost marker is Marker 4; the remaining pairs are numbered in sequence and in pairs, one on each side of the highway. If you phone for directions to a restaurant, hotel, or attraction, you'll likely be told the destination's location in relation to these markers. (It's "just past Marker" so and so.)

- ✔ Buckle Up: Florida law demands that you wear a seat belt.

- ✔ In an emergency, you can reach the Florida Highway Patrol on a cell phone by dialing ☎ *FHP.

Watch Your Step: Strolling the Streets of Orlando

 We don't recommend traveling on foot anywhere in Orlando, but occasionally you have to walk across a parking lot or street. *Be very careful.* This city isn't conducive to strolling. Within the safe confines of the theme parks, you have no problems hoofing around (in fact, you're on your feet quite a bit), but walking anywhere outside of the theme parks is a thrills-and-chills experience that most people want to avoid. Orlando is among the most dangerous cities in the country for pedestrians, according to a Washington, D.C.-based research group. Wide roads that are designed to move traffic quickly and a shortage of sidewalks, streetlights, and crosswalks are to blame.

Chapter 12

Monetary Matters

· ·

· ·

*T*ake a moment to ponder the meaning of the most important word in Orlando's economic vocabulary.

Tourism (tooo' riz-um): n. 1. travel, particularly the kind that brings two sides together, one giving food, shelter, and entertainment in exchange for payment from the other; 2. a game of chance in which a bunch of business bigwigs attempt to relieve the unsuspecting of their assets; 3. a puzzling phenomenon in which visitors pay to do things that natives leave town to avoid.

With that in mind, read this chapter for advice on accessing and guarding your money to keep the good times rolling in Orlando.

Finding Funds in Orlando

Even the most thrifty of travelers usually find themselves forking out more money than usual during their Orlando visit, and carrying a fully loaded wallet isn't always the most convenient, or the safest, way to go. Cash, credit, or check; Orlando makes it easy for visitors to access and spend their vacation dollars.

Banking on credit

Disney parks, resorts, shops, and restaurants (but not most of its fast-food counters) accept three major credit cards: American Express, MasterCard, and Visa. **Universal Studios Florida, Islands of Adventure, SeaWorld,** and **Discovery Cove** accept American Express, Discover, MasterCard, and Visa.

You can also receive cash advances off your credit card at any bank. Keep in mind that you'll start paying interest the moment you receive the cash and you won't get frequent-flyer miles on an airline credit card.

At most banks, you don't need to go to a teller; you can get a cash advance at the ATM if you know your personal identification number (PIN). If you've forgotten your PIN or didn't even know you had one, call the phone number on the back of your credit card and ask the bank to send it to you. It usually takes five to seven business days, though some banks will give it to you over the phone if you tell them your mother's maiden name and the number of freckles on your right shoulder or pass some other kind of security clearance.

SunTrust Bank, at 1675 Buena Vista Drive, across from **Downtown Disney Marketplace,** will give you a cash advance on your MasterCard or Visa. It will also cash traveler's checks or personal checks of $25 or less (if drawn on a U.S. bank and if you have a driver's license and major credit card). The bank also exchanges non-U.S. currency. The bank is open 9 a.m. to 4 p.m. weekdays, and until 6 p.m. Thursdays (☎ **407-828-6106**).

Dealing with Disney dineros

If you stay at certain resorts, **Walt Disney World** offers you a debit card that you can use in park shops and restaurants. This is sometimes referred to as a Disney credit card, but it isn't a credit card in the true sense of the word. Items are actually charged to your hotel room, and you have to settle up before checking out, which means you'll have to wait in yet another line.

Although we don't recommend doing so, you can buy Disney Dollars (currency with cute little pictures of Mickey, Goofy, or Minnie on it) at the Guest-Services desk in each of the parks. The bills come in $1, $5, and $10 denominations, and they're good at shops, restaurants, and resorts throughout **Walt Disney World** and in Disney stores elsewhere on the planet. This currency provides no real benefit other than its negligible souvenir value. If you want to trade Disney Dollars for real currency upon leaving **WDW**, you end up facing — you guessed it! — another line.

Locating ATMs

Central Florida is literally peppered with 24-hour automatic teller machines linked to a national network that most likely includes your bank at home. Cirrus (☎ **800-424-7787**) and Plus (☎ **800-843-7587**) are two of the most popular networks. (The back of your ATM card should list its affiliation.) The 800-numbers provide ATM locations where you can withdraw money while on vacation. There's frequently an extra charge for using non-bank ATMs. In Florida, the average is $2.60 if the ATM isn't affiliated with your bank.

In Central Florida, ATMs are about as common as corner phone booths used to be. You can find them on *Main Street* and in *Tomorrowland* in the **Magic Kingdom,** in the *Disney Crossroads Shopping Center,* and at the **WDW All-Star Sports Resort, Disney–MGM Studios, Epcot, Animal Kingdom,** and **Pleasure Island.** They're also located near Guest

Services at **SeaWorld, Universal Studios Florida,** and **Islands of Adventure** (and also at *The Lost Continent* near the bridge to *Jurassic Park.* You also can find them at most of the area's Circle K and 7-Eleven convenience stores and in most major malls. (See Chapter 27 for a few exact ATM locations.)

Maps that the theme parks give you also show you where to find an ATM. Some practically beckon ATM locations in neon. After all, the object is to get you to spend, Spend, SPEND!

If you need to make an eye-to-eye transaction, most local banks are open 9 a.m. to at least 3 or 4 p.m. Monday through Friday and many drive-ins are open 9 a.m. to noon on Saturdays.

Stop, Thief! Reporting Stolen Property

Orlando's wholesome, friendly image persuades many travelers to drop their guard, often with disastrous results. If you're a tourist, you're easy pickings for thieves, and tourist-related crimes are one of Orlando's biggest problems, much as they are in destinations like New York, Las Vegas, and London. Take the same precautions in Orlando that you would take at home, including using ATMs only in well-lighted areas, shielding your access numbers from prying eyes, and never putting anything in the trash that has your account number or other personal information on it.

Almost every credit-card company has a toll-free emergency number that you can call if your wallet or purse is stolen. The credit-card company may be able to wire you a cash advance off your credit card immediately, and in many places, get you an emergency credit card in a day or two.

The issuing bank's 800-number is usually on the back of the credit card. Make note of this number before you leave on your trip and stash it somewhere other than your wallet. If you forget to write down the number, you can call ☎ **800-555-1212** — that's 800 directory assistance — to get the number. And because thieves may not swipe this guidebook — though it's worth its weight in gold — **Citicorp Visa's** U.S. emergency number is ☎ **800-336-8472. American Express** cardholders and traveler's check users need to call ☎ **800-221-7282** for all money emergencies. **MasterCard** holders must call ☎ **800-307-7309.**

If you opt to carry traveler's checks, make sure that you keep a record of their serial numbers in a safe location so that you can handle an emergency.

Odds are that if your wallet is gone, you've seen the last of it, and the police aren't likely to recover it for you. However, after you realize that it's gone and you cancel your credit cards, you should still call the police. You may need their report number for credit card or insurance purposes later.

For more monetary information, see Chapter 3.

Part IV
Dining in Orlando

The 5th Wave   By Rich Tennant

YOUR CHILDS FANTASY RESTAURANT

I'LL START WITH THE BOLOGNA AND COCOA PUFFS, FRUIT ROLL UPS AND A BOWL OF FRENCH JELLY SOUP. FOR AN ENTREE I'LL HAVE SPAGHETTIOS WITH PEANUT BUTTER AND A SIDE OF CHOCOLATE HOT DOGS.

VERY GOOD SIR.

In this part . . .

Few cities offer as many dining options as O-Town. This city's menu features innovative chefs, clever themes, and snappy service. And, because central Florida attracts visitors from every corner of the planet, you're assured of finding literally any kind of cuisine that tickles your taste buds.

In this part, we explore the vast array of dining options Orlando offers, including the kids' favorite, character dining.

Chapter 13

The Scoop on the Orlando Dining Scene

In This Chapter

▶ Making reservations, dressing to dine, and paying the check

▶ Choosing a restaurant by price, location, and cuisine

*T*oday there are almost 4,000 restaurants to choose from in Orlando, with new eateries opening all the time. In this chapter, we provide general pointers about dining in the land of Diz, the dress code, and making reservations. We also give you lists of Orlando's best restaurants by price, location, and cuisine. In Chapter 14, we detail Orlando's A-List eateries, and in Chapter 15, we discuss the quintessential Orlando food experience — character dining.

Making Reservations

Reserving a table is a bright idea for some of Orlando's finest restaurants (see Chapter 14 for a list of the best places to eat), but in most cases, you don't need to make reservations before you leave home or right after you land. There are, of course, some notable exceptions to this rule.

At Disney properties, *Priority Seating* is the buzz word. This practice is the Magic Mickster's way of saying that you get the next available table after you arrive. (Be warned, however. You'll probably have to wait after you get to the restaurant.) We recommended that you *always* call ahead and make a Priority Seating reservation. If you try walking in off the street to find a table, chances are slim that you will succeed before your stomach starts growling at you. Call ☎ **407-939-3463** to stake a claim to a Disney table.

You can also make priority-seating reservations after you're inside the Disney parks. We suggest you do this immediately upon your arrival. At **Epcot,** visit the WorldKey Information Satellite on the main concourse at *World Showcase.* You can also talk to the Guest Relations desk at **Epcot.** In the **Magic Kingdom,** make reservations in person at the individual restaurants — the same holds true for **Disney–MGM Studios,** located on Hollywood Boulevard. At **Animal Kingdom,** visit Guest Relations to make reservations.

Dressing to Dine

You must wear clothes to dine, except, perhaps, at Orlando's one or two nudist resorts. You can, however, leave the penguin suits and long gowns at home. Florida is casual; it doesn't have the same dress codes as Monaco, on the *Queen Elizabeth II,* or at the New York Philharmonic. In most cases, people don't get gussied up to go to dinner in Florida unless they're celebrating a special event or dining at a high-end restaurant that requires formal or semiformal attire. For example, if you eat at Disney's Victoria & Albert's, you need a coat and tie or dressy dress — gender doesn't matter. Likewise, Dux at the Peabody Hotel on I-Drive is another restaurant that requires a little more than casual wear. (See Chapter 14 for details.)

Trimming the Fat from Your Dining Budget

Make sure that you pick up the free magazines and ad books that you see everywhere in Orlando hotels, tourist information centers, most convenience stores, newspaper racks, and so on. These publications include coupons good for a second meal free, discount prices, or a free dessert with a meal. Also, watch for ads from restaurants that offer kids-eat-free specials.

If you enjoy a cocktail before or after dinner, you've probably been to those places that charge almost as much for a drink as liquor stores charge for a bottle. If you want to save a few clams, bring or buy your own stash and have your drink in your hotel room or by the pool instead of paying restaurant prices.

That said, don't ignore places with happy-hour specials, including two-for-one drinks — some at bargain rates. You can find listings in free, handout newspapers in hotel lobbies and other places throughout Orlando.

Cutting food costs inside WDW

Eating at Disney can set you back more than a few bucks. For example, a 16-ounce bottle of cola is $2 and a small bottle of water is $2.50. To save money, buy a bottle of water from a local grocery, which likely costs less than a $1, and take it with you to the park, refilling it at water fountains. Also, in **Animal Kingdom** you can belly up to the bar at the Rainforest Café, order a pop for $1.99, and get a free glass of water. If you're eating lunch, the average price per person is under $10 if you eat at the buffet-style fast-food areas. The cheapest fast food at the park is a smoked turkey drumstick for $4.50; ice cream bars are $2, and a pineapple float is $2.50.

Many of the resorts at Disney offer a refillable mug, which is good for the duration of your WDW visit. The cost for the glass varies from place to place, ranging from $7.50 to $10. At most resorts, the refills are free, though a few of the others charge 90-cents or $1. Some of Disney's water parks have refillable glasses, but refills are limited to the day that you're in the park. (If you hear that you can use your glass for more than one day in some water parks, don't believe it. It's not true.) For more information, call Disney at ☎ **407-824-4321.**

Tackling Tipping and Taxes in Orlando

Sales tax on restaurant meals and drinks ranges from 6 to 7 percent throughout the Orlando area. (These taxes don't apply to groceries.) In addition, the standard tip in full-service restaurants is 15 percent, and a 12 percent tip is usually warranted at a buffet where a server brings your drinks and cleans the table. If you have a pre-dinner drink, leave a small tip to reward the server. The practice of tipping the head waiter has all but disappeared, but if you want a special table in a crowded restaurant, money can talk.

Make sure that you look over your check because some restaurants have started automatically tacking on a gratuity to your bill, especially for larger groups. Examine your check before coughing up more cash. There's no sense in doubling a tip for routine service.

Deciding Where to Dine according to Your Budget

If you're staying in the parks until closing, you may find it more convenient to eat there, but you'll probably pay an average of 25 percent more than in the outside world. All WDW restaurants accept American Express, MasterCard, and Visa, and all of them have children's menus. Bear in mind that all WDW restaurants are *smoke-free.*

The cost of your meal depends not only on what you order but how many courses you order. The $ dollar symbols used on the following pages are the average price for main courses. Allow for the 6 to 7 percent sales tax as well as any appetizers, drinks, or other extras you desire. One $ means the restaurant is among the least expensive; four $$$$ means "youch!"

Inexpensive kids' menus (usually $5 and under) are common at most of Orlando's moderately priced and family-style restaurants. Many offer distractions such as place mats with mazes or pictures to color.

The following index lists some of Orlando's best restaurants by price.

Index by price

$$$$
Chalet Suzanne (Far South)
Victoria & Albert's (Disney's Grand
 Floridian Resort & Spa)

$$$
Arthur's 27 (Lake Buena Vista)
Black Swan (International Drive Area)
Dux (International Drive Area)
Landry's Seafood House (International
 Drive Area)
La Provence (Downtown)
Manuel's on the 28th (Downtown)
Yachtsman Steakhouse (Disney's Yacht
 Club Resort)

$$–$$$
Bergamo's (International Drive Area)
California Grill (Disney's Contemporary
 Resort)
Cinderella's Royal Table (Magic Kingdom)
Citricos (Disney's Grand Floridian
 Resort & Spa)
Coral Reef (Epcot)
Delfino Riviera (Universal's Portofino
 Bay Resort)
Emeril's (Universal Studios/CityWalk)
Fulton's Crab House (Disney's Pleasure
 Island)
La Provence (Downtown)
La Scala (Near North)

$$–$$$
Les Chefs de France Restaurant (Epcot)
Maison & Jardin (Near North)

Michelangelo (International Drive Area)
Morton's of Chicago (International
 Drive Area)
Park Plaza Gardens (Near North)
Tempura Kiku (Epcot)
Wolfgang Puck Café (Disney's Pleasure
 Island)

$$
Artist Point (Disney's Wilderness
 Lodge)
Bonfamille's Café (Port Orleans)
Capriccio (International Drive Area)
Christini's Ristorante (International
 Drive Area)
Flying Fish Café (Disney's BoardWalk
 Resort)
Hollywood Brown Derby (Disney–MGM
 Studios)
House of Blues (Disney's Pleasure
 Island)
La Scala (Near North)
Le Cellier Steakhouse (Epcot)
Liberty Tree Tavern. (Magic Kingdom)
L'Originale Alfredo di Roma Ristorante
 (Epcot)
Marrakesh (Epcot)
Numero Uno (Downtown)
'Ohana (Disney's Polynesian Resort)
Pastamore Ristorante (Universal
 Studios/CityWalk)
Sci-Fi Dine-In Theater Restaurant
 (Disney–MGM Studios)
Spoodles (Disney's BoardWalk Resort)

$–$$

Akershus (Epcot)

B-Line Diner (International Drive Area)

Bahama Breeze (International Drive Area)

Columbia (Lake Buena Vista)

Crystal Palace (Magic Kingdom)

'50s Prime Time Café (Disney–MGM Studios)

Jimmy Buffett's Margaritaville (Universal Studios/CityWalk)

Le Coq Au Vin (South Orlando)

Mama Melrose's Ristorante Italiano (Disney–MGM Studios)

Ming Court (International Drive Area)

Nine Dragons (Epcot)

Pacino's Italian Ristorante (South Orlando)

Pebbles (Downtown, Near North, Lake Buena Vista)

Planet Hollywood (Disney's Pleasure Island)

Portobello Yacht Club (Lake Buena Vista)

Race Rock (International Drive Area)

Rainforest Café (Downtown Disney & Animal Kingdom)

Rolando's (Near North)

Rose & Crown Pub & Dining Room (Epcot)

San Angel Inn (Epcot)

Wild Jacks (International Drive Area)

$

Bob Marley — A Tribute to Freedom (Universal Studios/CityWalk)

Boston's Fish House (Near North)

Bubbaloo's Bodacious BBQ (Near North)

Cafe Tu Tu Tango (International Drive Area)

Little Saigon (Downtown)

L'Originale Alfredo di Roma Ristorante (Epcot)

Lotus Blossom Café (Epcot)

Pastamore Ristorante (Universal Studios/CityWalk)

Plaza Restaurant (Magic Kingdom)

Location, Location, Location: Eating in the Orlando Area

Because you may spend a lot of time in the Walt Disney World area, we've given special attention to dining choices there. (Don't worry. We haven't forgotten to toss in a lot of worthwhile restaurants outside of Mickey's realm — including some new kids under the Universal Studios' umbrella and some old standards elsewhere around town.)

All sit-down restaurants in Disney parks require admission, with one exception: the Rainforest Café at Animal Kingdom. Also, alcohol isn't served in the Magic Kingdom; if you need a drink at the end of the day (and if you have kids, you may), you're out of luck if you stay.

The following index presents a listing of restaurants organized by neighborhood.

Index by location

Downtown

La Provence ($$–$$$)

Little Saigon ($)

Manuel's on the 28th ($$$)

Numero Uno ($$)

Pebbles ($–$$)

Far South
Chalet Suzanne ($$$$)

International Drive Area
B-Line Diner ($–$$)
Bahama Breeze ($–$$)
Bergamo's ($$–$$$)
Black Swan ($$$)
Cafe Tu Tu Tango ($)
Capriccio ($$)
Christini's Ristorante ($$)
Dux ($$$)
Landry's Seafood House ($$$)
Michelangelo ($$–$$$)
Ming Court ($–$$)
Morton's of Chicago ($$–$$$)
Race Rock ($–$$)
Wild Jacks ($–$$)

Lake Buena Vista
Arthur's 27 ($$$)
Pebbles ($–$$)
Portobello Yacht Club ($–$$)

Near North
Boston's Fish House ($)
Bubbaloo's Bodacious BBQ ($)
La Scala ($$–$$$)
Maison & Jardin ($$–$$$)
Park Plaza Gardens ($$–$$$)
Pebbles ($–$$)
Rolando's ($–$$)

South Orlando
Le Coq Au Vin ($–$$)
Pacino's Italian Ristorante ($–$$)

Universal Studios/CityWalk
Bob Marley's (A Tribute to Freedom ($)
Delfino Riviera ($$–$$$)
Emeril's ($$–$$$)
Jimmy Buffett's Margaritaville ($–$$)
Pastamore Ristorante ($$)

Walt Disney World
Akershus (Epcot) ($–$$)
Artist Point (Wilderness Lodge) ($$)

Bonfamille's Café (Port Orleans) ($$)
California Grill (Contemporary Resort) ($$–$$$)
Cinderella's Royal Table (Magic Kingdom) ($$–$$$)
Citricos (Grand Floridian Resort & Spa) ($$–$$$)
Columbia (Celebration) ($–$$)
Coral Reef (Epcot) ($$–$$$)
Crystal Palace (Magic Kingdom) ($–$$)
'50s Prime Time Café (Disney–MGM Studios) ($–$$)
Flying Fish Café (BoardWalk Resort) ($$)
Fulton's Crab House (Pleasure Island) ($$–$$$)
Hollywood Brown Derby (Disney–MGM Studios) ($$)
House of Blues (Pleasure Island) ($$)
Les Chefs de France Restaurant (Epcot) ($$–$$$)
Liberty Tree Tavern (Magic Kingdom) ($$)
L'Originale Alfredo di Roma Ristorante (Epcot) ($$)
Lotus Blossom Café (Epcot) ($)
Mama Melrose's Ristorante Italiano (Disney–MGM Studios) ($–$$)
Marrakesh (Epcot) ($$)
Nine Dragons (Epcot) ($–$$)
'Ohana (Polynesian Resort) ($$)
Planet Hollywood (Pleasure Island) ($–$$)
Plaza Restaurant (Magic Kingdom) ($)
Rose & Crown Pub & Dining Room (Epcot) ($–$$)
San Angel Inn (Epcot) ($–$$)
Sci-Fi Dine-In Theater Restaurant (Disney–MGM Studios) ($$)
Spoodles (BoardWalk Resort) ($$)
Tempura Kiku (Epcot) ($$–$$$)
Victoria & Albert's (Grand Floridian Resort & Spa) ($$$$)
Wolfgang Puck Café (Pleasure Island) ($$–$$$)
Yachtsman Steakhouse (Yacht Club Resort) ($$$)

Culinary Delight: Taking a Taste of Orlando

Whether you hunger for fast food or prefer gourmet meals, there will be at least one restaurant in Orlando where you can find the cuisine of your preference.

The following index lists Orlando's restaurants by cuisine.

Index by cuisine

American

Artist Point (Disney's Wilderness Lodge) ($$)
B-Line Diner (International Drive Area) ($–$$)
Bubbaloo's Bodacious BBQ (Near North) ($)
California Grill (Disney's Contemporary Resort) ($$–$$$)
Chalet Suzanne (Far South) ($$$$)
Cinderella's Royal Table (Magic Kingdom) ($$–$$$)
Citricos (Disney's Grand Floridian Resort & Spa) ($$–$$$)
'50s Prime Time Café (Disney–MGM Studios) ($–$$)
Hollywood Brown Derby (Disney–MGM Studios) ($$)
House of Blues (Disney's Pleasure Island) ($$)
Jimmy Buffett's Margaritaville (Universal Studios/CityWalk) ($–$$)
Le Cellier Steakhouse (Epcot) ($$)
Pebbles (Downtown, Near North, Lake Buena Vista) ($–$$)
Planet Hollywood (Disney's Pleasure Island) ($–$$)
Plaza Restaurant (Magic Kingdom) ($)
Race Rock (International Drive Area) ($–$$)
Rainforest Café (Downtown Disney Marketplace & Animal Kingdom) ($–$$)
Sci-Fi Dine-In Theater Restaurant (Disney–MGM Studios) ($$)
Wild Jacks (International Drive Area) ($–$$)
Wolfgang Puck Café (Pleasure Island) ($$–$$$)
Asian
Little Saigon (Vietnamese; Downtown) ($)
Lotus Blossom Café (Chinese; Epcot) ($)

Asian

Ming Court (Chinese; International Drive Area) ($–$$)
Nine Dragons (Chinese; Epcot) ($–$$)
Tempura Kiku (Japanese; Epcot) ($$–$$$)

Continental

Park Plaza Gardens (Near North) ($$–$$$)
Rose & Crown Pub & Dining Room (Epcot) ($–$$)

French

La Provence (Downtown) ($$–$$$)
Les Chefs de France (Epcot) ($$–$$$)
Le Coq Au Vin (South Orlando) ($–$$)
Maison & Jardin (Near North) ($$–$$$)

Haute Cuisine

Arthur's 27 (Lake Buena Vista) ($$$)
Black Swan (Lake Buena Vista) ($$$)
Cafe Tu Tu Tango (Tapas; International Drive Area) ($)
Dux (International Drive Area) ($$$)
Manuel's on the 28th (Downtown) ($$$)

Victoria & Albert's (Grand Floridian Resort & Spa) ($$$$)

Italian

Bergamo's (International Drive Area) ($$–$$$)
Capriccio (International Drive Area) ($$)
Christini's Ristorante (International Drive Area) ($$)
Delfino Riviera (Portofino Bay Hotel) ($$–$$$)
La Scala (Near North) ($$)
L'Originale Alfredo di Roman Ristorante (Epcot) ($$)
Mama Melrose's Ristorante Italiano (Disney–MGM Studios) ($–$$)
Michelangelo (International Drive Area) ($$–$$$)
Pacino's Italian Ristorante (South Orlando) ($–$$)
Pastamore Ristorante (Universal Studios/CityWalk) ($$)
Portobello Yacht Club (Lake Buena Vista) ($–$$)

Other Ethnic

Akershus (Norwegian; Epcot) ($–$$)
Bahama Breeze (Caribbean; International Drive Area) ($–$$)
Bob Marley — A Tribute to Freedom (Caribbean; Universal Studios/CityWalk) ($)
Bonfamille's Café (New Orleans; Port Orleans) ($$)

Columbia (Cuban; Lake Buena Vista) ($–$$)
Emeril's (New Orleans; Universal Studios/CityWalk) ($$–$$$)
Marrakesh (Moroccan; Epcot) ($$)
Numero Uno (Cuban; Downtown) ($$)
'Ohana (Polynesian; Disney Polynesian Resort) ($$)
San Angel Inn (Mexican; Epcot) ($–$$)
Spoodles (Tapas/Mediterranean; Disney Boardwalk Resort) ($$)

Seafood

Boston's Fish House (Near North) ($)
Coral Reef (Epcot) ($$–$$$)
Flying Fish Café (Disney's BoardWalk Resort) ($$)
Fulton's Crab House (Pleasure Island) ($$–$$$)
Landry's Seafood House (International Drive Area) ($$$)

Steaks

Le Cellier Steakhouse (Epcot) ($$)
Morton's of Chicago (International Drive Area) ($$–$$$)
Yachtsman Steakhouse (Disney's Yacht Club Resort) ($$$)

Chapter 14

Orlando's Best Restaurants from A to Z

• •

In This Chapter

▶ Checking out Orlando's restaurants by the ABCs

▶ Reading full reviews of our favorite Orlando restaurants

• •

*B*rowsing the attractions in and around Orlando can leave you as hungry as an alley cat. You can get so hungry walking around the attractions that you find yourself willing to eat food that no sane person would consider, like pickled beets and pork rinds. Relax. You don't have to resort to such desperate measures as pickled cuisine. In this chapter, we give you our picks for what we think are Orlando's best restaurants and review them in alphabetical order.

Our Favorite Restaurants A to Z

'50s Prime Time Café

$$ Disney–MGM Studios (American Cuisine)

Servers deliver family favorites, including Mom's broiled chicken and meatloaf, Grandma's pot roast, and Dad's chili. The food isn't the best, but the place is so much fun, you may love it anyway. While you eat, you'll be zapped back to the days when you had to finish your vegetables if you wanted dessert (Mom — a.k.a. your server — will scold you if you put your elbows on the table or don't clean your plate.) Desserts include banana splits and s'mores. You can watch *I Love Lucy* reruns that play on the flickering TVs as you eat. The adjacent Tune-In Lounge serves inexpensive light fare.

Near the Indiana Jones Stunt Spectacular. ☎ **407-939-3463.** http://asp.disney.go.com/. *Priority Seating recommended. Parking: $6. Main courses: Dinner $12–$20. AE, MC, V. Open: Daily 11 a.m. to park closing.*

Akershus

$-$$ Walt Disney World/Epcot (Norwegian Cuisine)

A large table spills over with the traditional hot *smarvarmt* and cold *koldt-bord* dishes of a Scandinavian smorgasbord: venison in cream sauce, smoked pork with honey mustard sauce, and *gravlax* (for the culturally impaired, this is a cured salmon whose itty-bitty bones have been yanked out with tweezers). The trimmings include red cabbage, boiled potatoes, and frosty Norwegian beer. Sweets and sandwiches are available across the pavilion courtyard at the Kringla Bakery and Café. Crisp linens, glowing woods, and gleaming crystal surround you. Ask about the child-care center where kids can play while you dine.

In Norway Pavilion. ☎ *407-939-3463. Park admission required. Priority Seating recommended. Parking: $6. Lunch buffet: $12 adults, $5.25 kids 3–9. Dinner buffet: $18.50 adults, $8 children ($5 for children's smorgasbord meals). AE, MC, V. Open: Daily noon to 3:30 p.m. and 4:30 p.m. to park closing.*

Arthur's 27

$$$ Lake Buena Vista/Wyndham Palace Resort & Spa (International Cuisine)

Come first for the 27th-floor sunsets and a spectacular view of the Wizard of Disney's fireworks. Romantic and mellow, this place has the feel of a 1930s supper club, minus the billowing clouds of cigarette smoke. You can choose from selections such as pan-seared breast of squab with chestnut risotto or steamed scallops and poached oysters with black capellini pasta. There's also an impressive wine list.

1900 Lake Buena Vista Dr., just north of Hotel Plaza Blvd. ☎ *407-827-2727.* http://orlando.diningguide.net/data/d101542.htm. *Reservations required. Parking: Free self and validated valet. Main courses: $20–$30; fixed-price menu $49–$60. AE, DC, DISC, MC, V. Open: Daily 6:30–10:30 p.m.*

Artist Point

$$ Disney's Wilderness Lodge (American Northwest Cuisine)

The smell of fresh baked bread greets you upon entering, but eat the hazelnut and sunflower specialties sparingly so that you have room for the main meal. The specialty here is Pacific Northwest cuisine, and the food is great. For starters, try the lamb and lentil stew or the marinated crab and shrimp served in a gazpacho-style sauce of tomatoes, bell peppers, cucumbers, and garlic. For dinner, try the marinated shrimp and chicken, which are grilled on a skewer and served with sea grass and oriental dipping sauce. Other choices include game, steaks, salmon, and other marine delicacies that are grilled over an open, hardwood fire. There's a menu for the health-conscious and character breakfasts, as well as an excellent wine list.

*901 W. Timberline Dr. ☎ **407-824-3200**. Reservations suggested. Parking: Free. Main courses: $15–$25. AE, MC, V. Smoke-free. Open: Daily 7:30–11:30 a.m. and 5:00–10:30 p.m.*

B-Line Diner

$-$$ International Drive Area/Peabody Hotel (American Cuisine)

The décor is straight out of the '50s, with cushioned stool seating at a counter and upholstered booths. Gleaming chrome and tile create a vision of yesterday's roadside diners in this informal and inexpensive gathering place that's popular with visiting celebrities. Kids have their own menu to choose from, and grown-ups can dig into chicken potpie, pan-seared pork (with grilled apples, sun-dried cherry stuffing, and brandy honey sauce), or a ham-and-cheese sandwich on a baguette. There are also health foods and vegetarian specials. Order drinks from the full bar.

*9801 International Dr. ☎ **407-345-4460**. Reservations not accepted. Parking: Free self and validated valet. Main courses: Dinner $8.95–$22. AE, CB, DC, DISC, JCB, MC, V. Open: Daily 24 hours (dinner 5–11 p.m.).*

Bahama Breeze

$-$$ International Drive Area (Carribean Cuisine)

You don't have to try hard to feel like you're in the Bahamas in this informal eatery's straw-market setting. From the people who created The Olive Garden and Red Lobster, this prototype serves paella, coconut curry chicken, Key lime pie, and a mean piña colada pudding. Choose from one of the 50 beer brands or dare a Bahamarita or one of the fruity rum drinks.

*8849 International Dr. ☎ **407-248-2499**. Reservations not accepted. Parking: Valet parking and self parking; parking here is brutal and this joint is always busy, so arrive early. Main courses: $7–$15. AE, MC, V. Open: Sun–Thurs 4:00 p.m.–1:00 a.m., Fri–Sat 4:00 p.m.–1:30 a.m.*

Bergamo's

$$-$$$ International Drive Area/Mercado Shopping Village (Northern Italian Cuisine)

Bergamo's is almost always packed, and the singing waiters here are nearly as much fun as the food. For example, you may find Broadway show tunes and opera mixed with roasted veal and steamed mussels, among other treats. Even if you don't eat, this is a good spot to park your keister and enjoy the show over cocktails.

*8445 International Dr. ☎ **407-352-3805**. Reservations suggested. Parking: Free. Main courses: $12–$37. AE, DC, MC, V. Open: Sun–Thurs 5–10 p.m.; Fri–Sat 5–11 p.m.*

Walt Disney World & Lake Buena Vista Restaurants

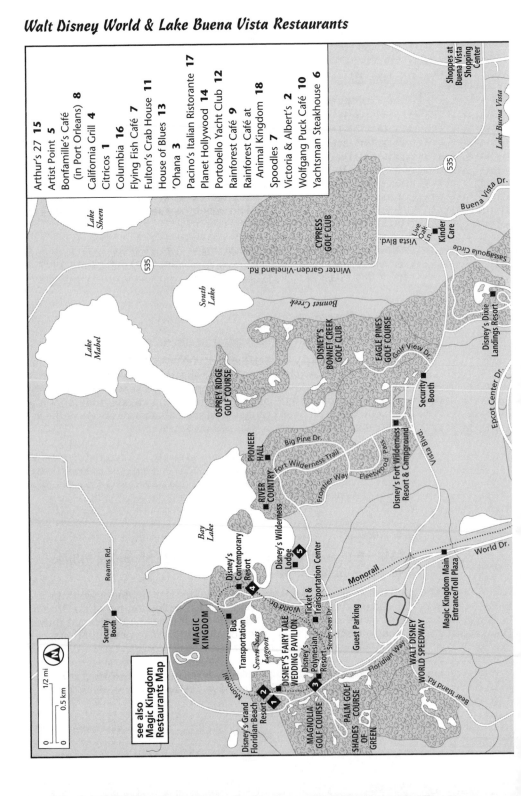

Arthur's 27 **15**
Artist Point **5**
Bonfamille's Café
(in Port Orleans) **8**
California Grill **4**
Citricos **1**
Columbia **16**
Flying Fish Café **7**
Fulton's Crab House **11**
House of Blues **13**
'Ohana **3**
Pacino's Italian Ristorante **17**
Planet Hollywood **14**
Portobello Yacht Club **12**
Rainforest Café **9**
Rainforest Café at
Animal Kingdom **18**
Spoodles **7**
Victoria & Albert's **2**
Wolfgang Puck Café **10**
Yachtsman Steakhouse **6**

see also
Magic Kingdom
Restaurants Map

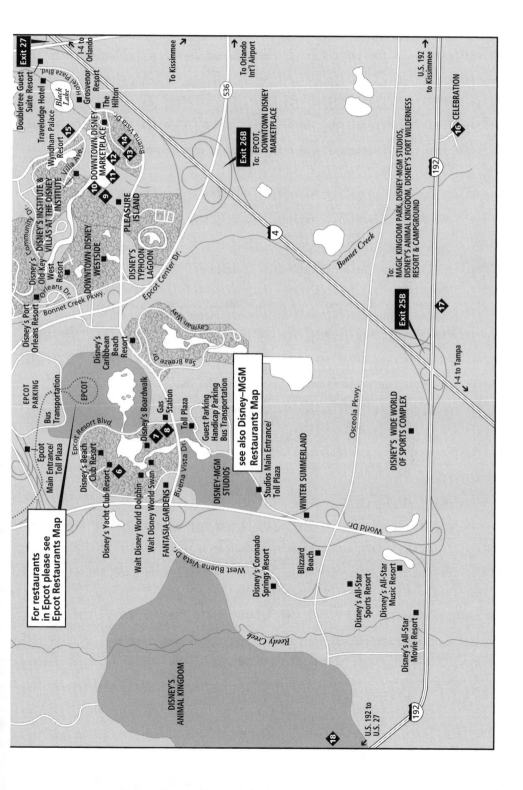

Black Swan

$$$ Lake Buena Vista/Villas of Grand Cypress (Haute Cuisine)

Here's a perfect place for a quiet romantic dinner accompanied by a fine vintage chosen from an extensive wine list. The lodgelike restaurant overlooks the golf course at the Grand Cypress. Try the grilled portobello mushrooms snuggled in a bed of wilted arugula with Asiago cheese, followed by the rack of lamb or Southwestern-style chicken served with black beans, roasted corn relish, and cilantro chili fettuccine. Save room for one of the meal cappers — perhaps an apple tart that's been drenched with caramel sauce and whipped cream or one of the dessert wines or liqueurs.

1 N. Jacaranda (off Fla. 535). ☎ *407-239-1999.* www.grandcypress.com/dining/index.htm. *Reservations recommended. Parking: Free. Main courses: $25–$34. AE, CB, DC, DISC, JCB, MC, V. Open: Daily 6–10 p.m.*

Bob Marley — A Tribute to Freedom

$ Universal Studios/CityWalk (Jamaican)

Bright reds and yellows adorn the walls of this combination club and restaurant that's a replica of the late reggae singer's home in Kingston, Jamaica, complete with tile roof and green window shutters. There's live reggae nightly, but the decibel level doesn't get as high as at Jimmy Buffett's Margaritaville (find info about his restaurant later in this chapter). The small menu has modestly priced light fare including a jerk snapper sandwich served on coca bread with yucca fries; a tomato-based fish chowder; and grouper fingers lightly breaded, fried, and topped with red and green peppers. Of course, most folks don't leave without sipping at least one Red Stripe — Jamaica's national beer.

1000 Universal Studios Plaza. ☎ *407-224-2262.* www.uescape.com/citywalk/. *Reservations not accepted. Parking: $6. Main courses: $6–$9. AE, DISC, MC, V. Open: Daily 5 p.m. to midnight.*

Bonfamille's Café

$$ Disney's Port Orleans Resort (New Orleans Cuisine)

This casual restaurant, faintly reminiscent of New Orleans' French Quarter, is named for a character in Disney's *The Aristocats*. Aesthetics include a courtyard with fountains, exposed-brick walls hung with paintings, big baskets of flowering plants suspended from overhead beams, and Dixieland jazz playing softly in the background. During breakfast it's light and sunny; in the evening, candle lamps provide soft lighting. Louisiana breakfasts range from hot beignets and café au lait to a skillet of crawfish and andouille sausage topped with zesty Creole sauce and melted cheddar. A typical dinner: an appetizer of chicken wings tossed in spicy

Louisiana hot sauce served with celery and blue-cheese dip, followed by grilled Atlantic salmon (served with spicy pecan butter, rice, and sautéed vegetables), and a pudding with strawberry and caramel bourbon sauces for dessert. After dinner, families can head to the hotel's Scat Cats Lounge, where sing-alongs and live music are featured on most nights.

2201 Orleans Dr. (off Bonnet Creek Pkwy.). ☎ *407-939-3463.* http://asp.disney.go.com/. *Priority Seating recommended. Parking: Free. Main courses: Breakfast $5–$7, dinner entrées $6–$22. AE, MC, V. Open: Daily 7:30–11:30 a.m. and 5–10 p.m.*

Boston's Fish House

$ Near North/Winter Park (Seafood)

Fried and broiled seafood dishes play to a packed house because portions here are generous and prices are modest. This is a terrific bargain if you don't need frills. You place your order at a counter and kick back at your table until the meal arrives. If you're a light eater, the hearty seafood chowder can be a meal. There's also a daily catch of salt- or freshwater seafood. Dishes arrive with fixings such as fries, hush puppies, and slaw. This is a good landing zone when you aren't in the mood to return to your room and get gussied up.

6860 Aloma Ave./Fla. 426 (in the Aloma Square Plaza). ☎ *407-678-2107. Reservations not accepted. Parking: Free. Main courses: $7–$12. No credit cards. Open: Fri–Sat 11:00 a.m.–9:30 p.m.; Sun and Tues–Thurs. 11:00 a.m.–8:30 p.m.*

Bubbaloo's Bodacious BBQ

$ Near North (Barbecue)

Smoke billows from the chimney of this real-pit place. The atmosphere is informal, but watch the sauces. Even the mild may be too hot for tender palates; the killer sauce comes with a three-alarm warning — it's meant only for those with asbestos taste buds and a ceramic-lined tummy. The pork platter with fixins is a deal and a half. It comes with beans and slaw. Monday through Friday you'll find daily specials that include chicken, meat loaf, turkey, and open-face roast-beef sandwiches with gravy and vegetables. And, it wouldn't be a barbecue without plenty of brew on hand.

5818 Conroy Rd. (Take I-4 east to Lee Rd., Exit 45, then left.) ☎ *407-295-1212. Reservations not accepted. Parking: Free. Main courses: $5–$8. AE, MC, V. Open: Sun–Thurs 10:00 a.m.–9:30 p.m.; Fri–Sat 10:00 a.m.–10:30 p.m.*

Epcot Restaurants

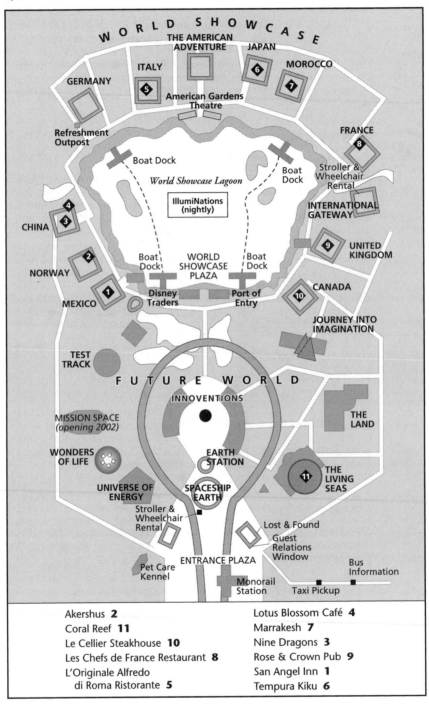

Akershus **2**	Lotus Blossom Café **4**
Coral Reef **11**	Marrakesh **7**
Le Cellier Steakhouse **10**	Nine Dragons **3**
Les Chefs de France Restaurant **8**	Rose & Crown Pub **9**
L'Originale Alfredo di Roma Ristorante **5**	San Angel Inn **1**
	Tempura Kiku **6**

Cafe Tu Tu Tango

$ International Drive Area (Tapas)

Located in the **Doubletree Castle Hotel,** this colorful eatery reminds many of a loft in Barcelona. The all-appetizer menu features treats from Latin America, Asia, the Caribbean, the Middle East, and the United States. This is an ideal spot for sampling different types of cuisine. A tapas (snack) bar, where every order comes in a miniature size, this is a great spot for grazing. Try the Cajun-style egg rolls, tuna sashimi with noodles and spinach in soy vinaigrette, and dozens of other chi-chi appetizers. For dessert, have guava cheesecake with strawberry sauce. *Note:* Ordering several tapas and drinks can turn this into a $$$ restaurant.

8625 International Dr. (just west of the Mercado Shopping Center.) ☎ *407-248-2222. Reservations recommended. Parking: Free. Main courses: Tapas $3.75–$8.55 (even those with small appetites will want two or three). AE, DISC, MC, V. Open: Sun–Thurs 1:30 a.m.–11:00 p.m.; Fri–Sat 11:30 a.m. to midnight.*

California Grill

$$-$$$ Disney's Contemporary Resort (New American Cuisine)

The Grill has the best veggie fare in the World. The constantly changing menu features earth foods blended with pizzas, pastas, and a grand, top-of-the-contemporary panorama of the **Magic Kingdom.** You can sit by the show kitchens and grill (not literally, of course) the chefs, who work magic before your eyes. They serve sushi, sashimi, and unique dishes such as tempura bonsai tuna and salmon roll with spicy organic salad. Legend has it that the art-deco dining room was inspired by Spago of Los Angeles, something that may not mean much to Floridians, but it may impress you if you've visited Spago or at least know it isn't some new health drink. The Grill features a grand wine list (by California standards) and a full bar.

4600 World Dr. ☎ *407-824-1576.* http://asp.disney.go.com/. *Reservations aren't necessary. Parking: Free. Main courses: $13–$30. AE, MC, V. Open: Daily 5:30–10:00 p.m.*

Capriccio

$$ International Drive Area/Peabody Hotel
(Tuscan/Northern Italian Cuisine)

The decor is chic and elegant with a black-and-white tile floor, but the showcase is a kitchen with wood-fired pizza ovens. For starters, try the fried calamari, and then order one of the heavenly pizzas or pastas. The pan-seared tuna with braised fennel and radicchio served with lentil flan is a nice off-speed pitch. When the crusty bread lands on your table, dip it into a puddle of extra-virgin olive oil. For dessert have the *zuppa inglese* (in English: sponge cake layers soaked in rum filled with custard covered with whipped cream and fruit). The wine list is extensive.

9801 International Dr. ☎ *407-352-4000.* www.peabodyorlando.com. *Reservations recommended. Parking: Free self and validated valet. Main courses: $12–$22; Sunday buffet, $29 adults, $13 kids 5–12. AE, CB, DC, DISC, JCB, MC, V. Open: Tues–Sun 6–11 p.m.*

Chalet Suzanne

$$$$ Far South (American Cuisine)

The Chalet, open for 70 years, offers exceptionally good food as well as a quiet, cozy atmosphere, but the prices can induce angina (if not a category-three coronary). It's a hoof from Orlando, about an hour's drive (40 miles), but the eclectic aesthetics and food are worth the time away from Mickey Madness if it fits into your budget. Critics rate the chalet one of Florida's best, as do the real judges — the diners. Sink your fangs into such headliners as grilled lamb chops, lobster thermidor, and shrimp curry. Also, don't miss the world-class soups. The chalet has an A+ wine list.

3800 Chalet Suzanne Lane, Lake Wales. ☎ *800-433-6011* or *863-676-6011.* http://www.chaletsuzanne.com/. *Reservations accepted. Parking: Free. Main courses: Lunch $29–$46, dinner $59–$79. AE, DC, DISC, MC, V. Open: Daily 8–11 a.m.; Tues–Sun 12–5 p.m.; Tues–Thurs and Sun 5:30–8:00 p.m.; Fri–Sat 5:30–9:00 p.m.*

Christini's Ristorante

$$$ International Drive Area (Italian Cuisine)

Numerous awards and trophies, attesting to the high standard of service offered by restaurateur Chris Christini, line this place's walls. If you're one of those who insists on more than atta-boys, count on this restaurant for great service, a gander at show-biz celebrities from down the road at **Disney–MGM** and **Universal,** and a full lounge. For starters, we suggest the special octopus served over polenta. It's hard to decide what to get for the main course, but one of the house specialties is a veal chop, broiled and seasoned with fresh sage, and served with applesauce. Or, if you're in the mood for pasta, try the rigatoni served in a Parmesan fennel cream sauce with shredded sweet Italian sausages.

7600 Dr. Phillips Blvd. ☎ *407-345-8770.* www.christinis.com. *Reservations suggested. Parking: Free. Main courses: $20–$40. AE, CB, DC, MC, V. Open: Daily 6 p.m. to midnight.*

Cinderella's Royal Table

$$-$$$ Magic Kingdom/Main Street (American/English Cuisine)

Cinderella will probably be on hand to greet you before you dine in Gothic splendor under knights' banners hanging from a vaulted ceiling. You can order barbecued tuna, spice-encrusted salmon, chicken, fish, prime rib, or sirloin served with vegetables and soup. For openers, try the elegant breaded Brie with tangy lingonberry. For dessert, get the chocolate mousse. Keep in mind, though, that this is the same inside-the-park fare found in all the other Disney parks. A children's menu offers staples such as macaroni and cheese for less than five bucks.

Inside Cinderella's Castle. ☎ *407-939-3463.* http://asp.disney.go.com/. *Priority Seating recommended. Parking: $6. Main courses: Dinners $17.50–$25.75. AE, MC, V. Open: Daily 11 a.m. to park closing.*

Citricos

$$-$$$ Disney's Grand Floridian Resort & Spa (American Cuisine)

The chef of this bright and airy restaurant makes a statement with citrus- and Mediterranean-infused flavors with a Florida link. Crab and lobster in Parmesan are among the starters. Main courses include red snapper carpaccio with bell pepper-melon salsa or Florida oyster and bay scallop risotto. For dessert, it's hard to resist the citrus soufflé or the chocolate ravioli with licorice ice cream. Citricos has a well-stocked wine cellar that's one of the best inside **WDW**.

4401 Floridian Way. ☎ *407-824-3000.* http://asp.disney.go.com/. *Reservations recommended. Parking: Free. Main courses: $19–$36. AE, MC, V. Open: Daily at 5 p.m.*

Columbia

$-$$ Disney's Celebration (Cuban/Latin American Cuisine)

A large horse stands sentinel inside the dining room of this newest in the chain of Columbia restaurants. The interior is classy and elegant with beige and brown tones, while Spanish pictures adorn the walls. The original Columbia was founded in Tampa in 1905 by the great-grandfather of the present operators (and, frankly, it's by far the best of the mini-chain; but the whole enchilada is still a family affair). You dine on freshly starched linens in a bright room decorated with splashes of old Tampa and Havana: tiles, shiny woodwork, wrought iron, and bent-wood chairs. The 1905 Salad, paella, arroz con pollo, snapper Alicante, Spanish bean soup, and flan (a custard-filled tart) are signatures and offer just cause for celebration. Cigar smokers are welcome.

649 Front St. ☎ *407-566-1505. Reservations recommended. Parking: Free. Main courses: $11–$22. AE, DC, DISC, MC, V. Open: Daily 11:30 a.m.–4:00 p.m. and 4:00–10 :00 p.m.*

Coral Reef

$$-$$$ Epcot/Living Seas Pavilion (Seafood)

Seafood rules at this restaurant that offers fabulous views of the Living Seas aquarium and a dash of classical music to transport diners to a romantic spot under the sea. Start with cream of lobster soup or an under the Seasar salad. Entrées include tuna, sea bass, snapper, and lobster. Meals are unhurried, and most kids don't mind the slow pace because they're captivated by the kaleidoscope of fish, sharks, and rays gliding by the tables.

☎ *407-939-3463.* http://asp.disney.go.com/. *Priority Seating recommended. Parking: $6. Main courses: Lunch $13–$19, dinner $17–$29. AE, MC, V. Open: Daily 11:30 a.m.–3:00 p.m. and 4:30 p.m. to park closing.*

Magic Kingdom Restaurants

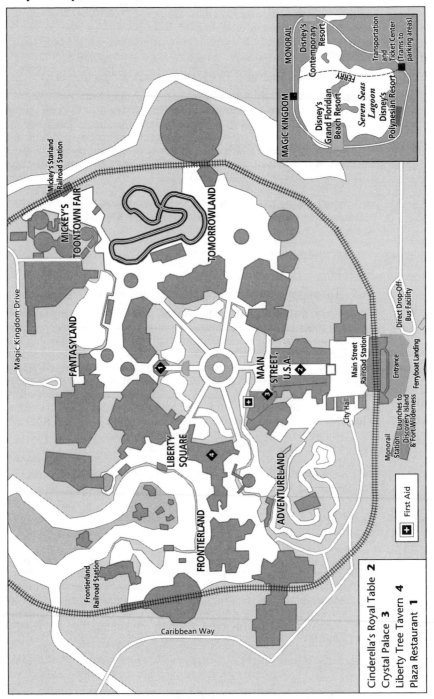

Cinderella's Royal Table **2**
Crystal Palace **3**
Liberty Tree Tavern **4**
Plaza Restaurant **1**

Crystal Palace

$-$$ Main Street/Magic Kingdom (American Cuisine)

This turn-of-the-twentieth-century style restaurant is a kid-magnet that serves a daylong buffet. The changing menu often includes fried chicken, macaroni and cheese, and an assortment of veggies and desserts. The food is filling, though short of overwhelming. The real treats are the characters (see Chapter 15 for more information on Disney character dining) that appear here, but that also means that it's not the place to have a quiet meal.

On Main Street. ☎ *407-939-3463.* http://asp.disney.go.com/. *Priority Seating recommended. Parking: $6. Main courses: Breakfast and lunch $15–$16 adults, $8 kids 3–11; dinner $20 adults, $10 kids. AE, MC, V. Open: Daily 8:00–10:30 a.m., 11:30 a.m.–3:15 p.m., and 4:00 p.m. to park closing.*

Delfino Riviera

$$-$$$ Universal Studios/Portofino Bay Hotel (Mediterranean Cuisine)

Located above a piazza overlooking the other Portofino Bay (not the one in Italy, alas), the atmosphere here is pretty romantic. This is the hotel's signature ristorante, complete with strolling musicians and crooners. The chef's table has six seats, and 20 more can dine on a balcony that offers a view of the commoners sitting below. There's also a terrace for outdoor dining. First-course options include tuna carpaccio with a black pepper and cherry balsamic sauce, champagne-baked oysters, and citrus-cured sturgeon in grapefruit vinaigrette. Try pasta treats such as lobster and champagne risotto and black olive pasta with monkfish and artichoke ragout. For the main course, the chef works magic on sea bass roasted with mushrooms and potatoes in chianti sauce. Venison *osso buco* (veal shanks stewed in white wine) with diced vegetables and polenta (cornmeal mush) is equally good.

1000 Universal Studios Blvd. ☎ *407-503-1415.* www.uescape.com. *Reservations recommended. Parking: $6. Main courses: $20–$32. AE, MC, V. Open: Mon–Sat 6–10 p.m.*

Dux

$$$ International Drive Area/Peabody Hotel (Haute Cuisine)

Think posh with a capital P — that's what comes to mind when you slip inside these walls. The restaurant's name honors a family of live ducks that splashes all day in the marble fountains in the Peabody's grandly formal lobby. This is a favorite of celebrities, who dine here after shooting (movies, not tourists, of course) at **Universal Studios** and **Disney–MGM.** Its eclectic and diverse menu changes with the seasons. Possibilities include dumplings stuffed with mushrooms, scallions, and goat cheese with a garnish of Asiago cheese; lamb chops basted with

Hunan barbecue sauce; grouper grilled in Cajun spices; and a hazelnut meringue napoleon topped with ice cream. Choose a wine from their long, inspired list.

9801 International Dr. ☎ *407-345-4550.* http://www.peabodyorlando.com/. *Reservations recommended. Parking: Free self and validated valet. Main courses: $19–$45. AE, CB, DC, DISC, JCB, MC, V. Open: Daily 6:00–10:30 p.m.*

Emeril's

$$-$$$ Universal Studios/CityWalk (New Orleans Cuisine)

Get a mouthful and eyeful in this ultra-modern showplace, the Florida home of culinary genius Emeril Lagasse, star of *Emeril Live* on cable TV's Food Network. Large abstract paintings cover the walls of a two-story restaurant that looks like an old warehouse. The second floor has a 12,000-bottle wine gallery and a cigar room. If you want a show, we highly recommend trying to get one of the eight counter seats where you can watch the chefs working their Creole magic, but to get one you'll need to make reservations *excruciatingly* early (reserve at least a month in advance).

The lunch menu (it's easier to get a reservation) features many dinner delights, including funky appetizers — Maine lobster cheesecake, to name one — and entrées such as pecan-crusted redfish. Dinnertime best bets include the New Orleans barbecue shrimp for starters, followed by smoked chicken and andouille sausage gumbo. Grilled veal chops, rack of lamb with Creole mustard, and andouille-crusted redfish are other dinner entrées. Something called "A Study of Duck" is, well, quacker overload (with apologies to the residents of Dux, in the previous section). It has seared, sliced duck breast; Hudson Valley foie gras; and a leg of duck confit served with wild mushroom bread pudding. There's also a wood-burning stove for less formal appetites. (Sweet barbecue salmon pizza, anyone?) Jackets are recommended for gents, even though that goes against the grain after a long day in the parks.

1000 Universal Studios Blvd. ☎ *407-224-2424.* www.uescape.com/citywalk/. *Reservations far in advance are a must. Parking: $6. Main courses: $17–$25 lunch, $18–$35 dinner. AE, DISC, MC, V. Open: Daily 11:30 a.m.–2:30 p.m., 5:30–10:00 p.m. (11:00 p.m. Fri–Sat).*

Flying Fish Café

$$ Disney's BoardWalk Resort (Seafood)

Welcome to Coney Island à la Disney. The decorations here are almost as elaborate as the show kitchen, which puts chefs center stage where everyone can see meals being prepared. All seafood — which reigns supreme here (are you surprised?) — is as fresh as it gets in central Florida, so the menu changes frequently. High points include potato-wrapped red snapper and oak-grilled scallops. There are also beef, poultry, and veggie options. For dessert, the Lava Cake has a liquid chocolate center and is a must for chocoholics.

☎ *407-939-3463.* http://asp.disney.go.com/. *Priority Seating recommended. Parking: Free. Main courses: $18–$26. AE, MC, V. Open: Daily 5:30–10:00 p.m.*

Fulton's Crab House

$$-$$$ Downtown Disney/Pleasure Island (Seafood)

Lose yourself in a world of brass, shining mahogany, and river charts while you dine inside a Mississippi Delta-style paddlewheeler. The catch of the day can be presented charcoal-grilled, broiled, fried with a dusting of cornmeal, blackened, or steamed. The cioppino is a feast of lobster, clams, mussels, red potatoes, and corn. Or, have the filet mignon with whipped potatoes. The wine list is comprehensive; there's a full bar. For dessert, don't miss the milk-chocolate crème brûlée.

*Aboard the riverboat at **Pleasure Island** next to the Lego store. ☎ 407-939-3463. www.fultonscrabhouse.com. Reservations not accepted. Parking: Free self; valet parking $5. Main courses: $16–$44. AE, MC, V. Open: Daily 4 p.m. to midnight.*

Hollywood Brown Derby

$$ Disney–MGM Studios (American Cuisine)

It's tough for your eyeballs to dodge the huge derby that marks this restaurant as you square dance into and around **Disney–MGM.** This re-creation of the restaurant where Hollywood's stars gathered in the '30s and '40s is decorated with caricatures of the regulars on its walls. The vittles aren't the best in the solar system, but you may consider grouper served atop a bed of creamy pasta, followed by the famous grapefruit cake with cream-cheese frosting or the white chocolate cheesecake.

Hollywood Blvd. ☎ 407-939-3463. http://asp.disney.go.com/. Priority Seating recommended. Parking: $6. Main courses: $16.50–$23.75; early-bird dinner $15.75. AE, MC, V. Open: Daily 11 a.m. to park closing.

House of Blues

$$ Disney's West Side (Mississippi Delta Cuisine)

Inside this Louisiana clapboard building you find hearty portions of down-home Southern food served in an atmosphere literally shaking with rhythm and blues. Exceedingly crowded on days of big concerts, the music in the nightclub next door is as much a draw as the food. Funky folk art covers the rustic walls from floor to ceiling. The back patio has seating and a nice view of the bay. Food-wise, the spicy jambalaya and gumbo are good bets. The baby back ribs with garlic potatoes and turnip greens are delicious. Sunday's Gospel Brunch ($28 adults, $15 kids 4 to 12, including tax and tip) features foot-stomping music along with omelets, prime rib, jalapeno mashed spuds, cheese grits, and sausage. Brunch is the only time you can make reservations and it sells out fast, *so make them early.*

*Located under the old-fashioned water tower on **Disney's West Side.** ☎ 407-934-2583. http://asp.disney.go.com/. Reservations not accepted (except for Gospel Brunch). Parking: Free. Main courses: $15–$20. AE, DISC, MC, V. Open: Daily 11 a.m.–2 a.m.; club and concert hall, 7 p.m.–2 a.m.*

Disney–MGM Restaurants

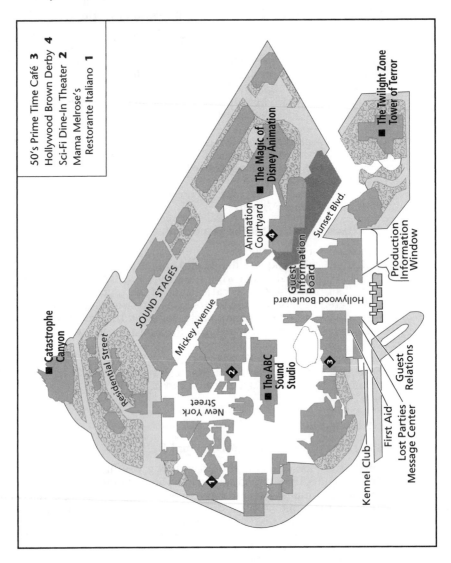

50's Prime Time Café **3**
Hollywood Brown Derby **4**
Sci-Fi Dine-In Theater **2**
Mama Melrose's
Restorante Italiano **1**

The Twilight Zone
Tower of Terror

The Magic of
Disney Animation

Animation
Courtyard

Sunset Blvd.

Guest
Information
Board

Production
Information
Window

Hollywood Boulevard

SOUND STAGES

Mickey Avenue

Catastrophe
Canyon

Residential Street

The ABC
Sound
Studio

New York
Street

Kennel Club

First Aid

Lost Parties
Message Center

Guest
Relations

Jimmy Buffett's Margaritaville

$-$$ Universal Studios/CityWalk (Carribean Cuisine)

After the parrotheads have enough to drink, the noise can make it hard to hear your stable mates, but most folks come to Margaritaville to sing and unwind, not to gab. There are three watering holes: the Landshark Bar, the 12-Volt Bar, and the Volcano Bar, which comes complete with a two-story, margarita-spewing mini mountain.

Despite the renowned cheeseburgers in paradise (yes, they're on the menu at $8), the food has Caribbean leanings. And, although it's not contending for a critic's choice award, it's fairly tasty. Hot numbers include jerk chicken, jambalaya, and a Cuban meat loaf survival sandwich that's a cheeseburger of another kind.

But, watch your tab. At up to $7 a pop for margaritas, the bill can climb to $60 or more for a routine lunch.

1000 Universal Studios Plaza. ☎ *407-224-2155.* www.uescape.com/citywalk/. *Reservations not accepted. Parking: $6. Main courses: $8–$17. AE, DISC, MC, V. Open: Daily 11:30 a.m. to midnight.*

L'Originale Alfredo di Roma Ristorante

$$ Epcot/Italian Pavilion (Italian/Mediterranean Cuisine)

Sample southern Italian cuisine in a seaside Italian palazzo lined with huge murals. Decorated in the warm earth tones characteristic of Florence and Siena, Alfredo's red-brown walls and deeply upholstered armchairs create a friendly atmosphere. The fettucine Alfredo is fittingly executed to perfection. Your best bets include the veal scaloppine with roasted potatoes or a divine linguine pesto and tiramisu for dessert. The early-bird, fixed-price dinner is a bargain. This is the *World Showcase*'s most popular restaurant and it fills up quickly, so Priority Seating is a must.

☎ *407-939-3463.* http://asp.disney.go.com/. *Priority Seating recommended. Parking: $6. Main courses: $9.25–$24.75. A $15.75 fixed-price dinner is served 4:30–6:00 p.m. Open: Daily 11 a.m. until an hour before park closing.*

La Provence

$$-$$$ Downtown Orlando (Classic French Cuisine)

Lace in the windows adds to this restaurant's French motif, but regulars know that the food — not the décor — is the highlight. The Beggar's Pouch appetizer (a buckwheat pancake fashioned into a purse and stuffed with wild mushrooms, shallots, and goat cheese) is a good choice. If you order à la carte, try the authentic foie gras or terrine, then lobster bisque and a fish, game, meat, or vegetarian main dish. The fixed-price options range from the belly-busting *menu gastronomique* to the simpler *menu du marche*. Both offer a parade of courses at reasonably fair prices. Live jazz plays in the library-style lounge.

50 E. Pine St. (one block north of Church St. and just east of Court.) ☎ *407-843-4410. Reservations strongly recommended. Parking: A garage is just east on Pine St., between Magnolia and Rosalind. Main courses: $19–$30. Fixed-price menus $26–$51. Open: Mon–Thurs 5:30–9:30 p.m., Fri–Sat 5:30–10:30 p.m.*

La Scala

$$-$$$ Near North/Altamonte Springs (Northern Italian Cuisine)

An inventive menu beckons diners with offerings such as tender medallions of filet mignon sautéed with roasted garlic, shallots (flavorful onion), and Barolo wine sauce or salmon tossed in a creamy sauce of Chablis, Parmesan, and shallots served over bow-tie pasta. Service can be slow if there's a crowd. And you better be opera-friendly or at least opera-tolerant, because the staff sings while they prepare goodies from the north of Italy. Expect a lot of smiles and a full bar.

205 Loraine Dr. ☎ 407-862-3257. Reservations suggested. Parking: Free. Main courses: $12–$28. AE, DC, MC, V. Open: Mon–Thurs 11:30 a.m.–2:30 p.m. and 5:00–10:30 p.m.; Fri 11:30 a.m.–2:30 p.m. and 5:00–11:00 p.m.; Sat 5:00–10:30 p.m.

Landry's Seafood House

$$$ International Drive Area (Seafood)

The staff here usually rolls out a warm welcome while the kitchen makes seafood specialties with Cajun and Caribbean touches. The catch of the day may be grouper, mahi-mahi, or snapper. Try the seafood-stuffed mushrooms for starters and Key lime pie as a closer.

8800 Vineland Ave. (Fla. 535, east of I-4.) ☎ 407-827-6466. http://www. landrysseafoodhouse.com/. Reservations for parties of eight or more. Parking: Free. Main courses: $12–$16. AE, DC, DISC, MC, V. Open: Mon–Fri 4:00– 11:00 p.m., Sat–Sun 11:30 a.m.–11:00 p.m.

Le Cellier Steakhouse

$$ Epcot/Canadian Pavilion (Canadian Cuisine)

You'll feel welcome in this cozy steak house, which tends to be less crowded — and less manic — than some of **Epcot's** other restaurants. Favorites include a wild mushroom-stuffed fillet or buffalo rib eye served with Parmesan smashed taters. Those preferring marine cuisine may find it hard to resist the maple-glazed Canadian salmon. The à la carte menu offers a number of good selections for families, including burgers for the kids. You can wash down your meal with a Canadian wine, or choose from a selection of Canadian beers. The mouth-watering Butterfinger mousse with raspberry sauce is a dessert favorite.

☎ 407-939-3463. http://asp.disney.go.com/. Priority Seating recommended. Parking: $6. Main courses: $9–$15 lunch; $15–$20 dinner. AE, MC, V. Open: Daily noon to park closing.

Le Coq Au Vin

$$ South Orlando (French Cuisine)

Affordability and good food make this a solid choice for French cuisine if you're on a budget. Owner-chef Louis Perrotte loves country cooking and changes his menu seasonally to include dishes such as a grouper fillet encrusted with toasted pecans bathed in citrus beaurre blanc or a center-cut black-angus steak served with a dollop of peppercorn sauce. You may also run into rack of lamb, braised rabbit, or grilled salmon depending on when you touch down. (If you want to eliminate the mystery, call first.) This restaurant has a bistro atmosphere and regulars who attest to its staying power. Some insist this is Florida's best French restaurant, especially if you're after a bargain. Perrotte serves beer and wine.

4800 So. Orange Ave. ☎ *407-851-6980.* http://www.orlandoweekly.com/dining/results.asp. *Reservations required. Parking: Free. Main courses: $12–$25. AE, DC, MC, V. Open: Mon–Fri 11:30 a.m.–2:00 p.m. and 5:30–10:00 p.m.; Sat 5:30–10:00 p.m.; Sun 5:30–9:00 p.m.*

Les Chefs de France

$$-$$$ Epcot/France Pavilion (French Cuisine)

Three of France's finest chefs supervise the kitchen in this eatery, where the art-nouveau interior is agleam with mirrors and candelabras. Etched-glass and brass dividers create intimate dining areas, and tables are elegantly appointed. Start your gastronomic journey with the seafood cream soup with crab dumplings. Dinner choices include a superb grilled salmon, Mediterranean seafood casserole, braised beef burgundy, and sautéed beef tenderloin with raisins and brandy sauce. Desserts of choice are a sumptuous soufflé Grand-Marnier and crème brûlée (a rich custard covered with a crust of caramelized sugar). There's also a substantial wine list, and you can purchase wines on the list at **Au Palais du Vin,** a wine shop in the France pavilion.

☎ *407-939-3463.* http://asp.disney.go.com/. *Priority Seating suggested. Parking: $6. Main courses: $11–$17 lunch; $20–$30 dinner. AE, MC, V. Open: Daily noon until one hour before the park closes.*

Liberty Tree Tavern

$$ Magic Kingdom/Liberty Square (American Cuisine)

This sit-down restaurant offers the best food in the **Magic Kingdom,** and if you have a large party, it's also more likely than Cinderella's Royal Table to be able to seat you. The Liberty Tree Tavern looks like an eighteenth-century pub, with pegged oak-plank floors, hutches with displays of pewterware, and a vast brick fireplace hung with copper pots. The food is traditional American. Start your meal with a bowl of creamy New England clam chowder or Boston crab cakes. Entrées range from New England pot roast braised in burgundy and served with mashed potatoes and vegetables to a traditional roast turkey dinner with all the trimmings. There are a few heart-healthy options on the menu. There's apple crisp topped with vanilla ice cream for dessert.

☎ *407-939-3463.* http://asp.disney.go.com/. *Priority Seating recommended. Parking: $6. Main courses: $9.75–$14.25 at lunch; fixed price $20 adults, $10 children 3–11 at dinner. Dinners are all-you-can-eat, family-style affairs that include characters (see Chapter 15 about Disney character dining). AE, MC, V. Open: Daily 11:30 a.m.–3:00 p.m. and 4:00 p.m. to park closing.*

Little Saigon

$ Downtown (Vietnamese Cuisine)

Situated in the heart of a tiny Vietnamese neighborhood, this ethnic eatery has been open for more than 12 years and thrives on its regulars. The menu offers everything from appetizers to noodle dishes to stir-fries that mix and match pork, beef, seafood, and vegetables. The combo plates are a good deal. Service and attention depend on the traffic. Order food by number; if you need a description of a dish, you may need to ask for the manager, whose English is better than that of some of the servers. Don't miss the summer rolls with peanut sauce. Beer and wine are available.

1106 E. Colonial Dr. (From I-4, take the Colonial Dr. Exit/Fla. 50 and go east; look for the fish mural between Mills and Thornton.) ☎ *407-423-8539. Reservations required. Parking: Free. Main courses: $4.25–$7. AE, DISC, MC, V. Open: Daily 10 a.m.–9 p.m.*

Lotus Blossom Café

$ Epcot/China Pavilion (Chinese Cuisine)

This open-air cafe's specialty is a combination platter that has stir-fried beef and garden vegetables, an egg roll, and fried rice. That and other options (pork fried rice and stir-fried chicken with vegetables) make it a pleasant and inexpensive self-service outlet. Cooking demonstrations given close-by take place several times a day.

☎ *407-939-3463.* http://asp.disney.go.com/. *Reservations not accepted. Parking: $6. Main courses: Most are $6–$8. AE, MC, V. Open: Daily 11 a.m. to park closing.*

Maison & Jardin

$$-$$$ Near North (Contemporary Continental Cuisine)

Formal and romantic, Maison & Jardin (*House and Garden* just sounds so much prettier in French, doesn't it?) is a time-honored local favorite and a consistent award winner. Alas, this can be a healthy trek, depending on where you're staying (15 minutes from downtown, 30 minutes from Disney). The reward is an atmosphere that's refined for its mature customers (in other words, leave the kids home). Prices are up there on the Richter scale (expect at least $100 for dinner for two, including liquid libations, starters/finishers, tax, and tips), but the vittles are grand and the service matches. The menu has the right blend, including the signature beef Wellington or medallions of elk served with raspberry sauce. The wine list is also pretty impressive.

430 Wymore Rd. (Altamonte Springs/Exit 48 off I-4 to Fla. 436, left at top of ramp, go to second light, left on Wymore Rd. a half-mile on right.) ☎ *407-862-4410.* www.maison-jardin.com. *Reservations recommended. Parking: Free. Main courses: $20–$30. AE, DC, DISC, MC, V. Open: Mon–Sat 6–10 p.m.; Sun brunch 11 a.m.–2 p.m. and dinner 6–9 p.m.*

International Drive Restaurants

B-Line Diner **12**
Bahama Breeze **7**
Bergamo's **4**
Black Swan **13**
Café Tu Tu Tango **5**
Capriccio **11**
Christini's
  Ristorante **3**
Dux **10**
Landry's Seafood
  House **14**
Michelangelo **1**
Ming Court **8**
Morton's of
  Chicago **6**
Race Rock **9**
Wild Jacks **2**

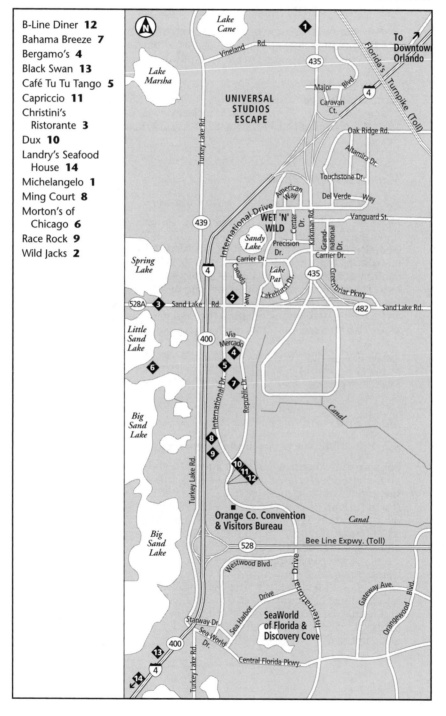

Mama Melrose's Ristorante Italiano

$-$$ Disney–MGM Studios (Italian Cuisine)

The specialty at this cheery Italian trattoria is brick-oven baked pizza, and the menu is fleshed out with assorted pastas, chicken entrées, and seafood dishes. The food isn't very exciting, but it's tasty. Think fast food with flare.

(Close to the Muppet*Vision 3D adventure show). ☎ *407-939-3463.* http://asp. disney.go.com/. *Priority Seating recommended. Parking: $6. Main courses: $8.25–$14.75 lunch, $11.25–$21.50 dinner. AE, MC, V. Open: Daily 11:30 a.m. to park closing.*

Manuel's on the 28th

$$$ Downtown Orlando (Haute Cuisine)

Manuel's is literally the pinnacle of elegance, situated in a posh, panoramic enclave on the 28th floor of the Bank of America building. Come here for a stunning after-dark view of the sparkling, sprawling metropolis that Orlando has become. At most view restaurants, the food can't match the scenery; Manuel's, despite a small kitchen, is an exception. The dozen or more appetizers and entrées hit high notes with duck, lamb, yellowfin tuna, lobster, and filet mignon. Servers will help you pair a great wine with a rack of lamb, the veal chop-and-scampi combination plate, or a steak wreathed in fresh vegetables. Expect a professional staff.

390 N. Orange Ave. (In a bank building.) ☎ *407-246-6580.* http://orlando. citysearch.com/E/V/ORLFL/0001/83/55/. *Reservations required. Parking: Free. Main courses: $24–$32. AE, DC, DISC, MC, V. Open: Tues–Sat 6–10 p.m.*

Marrakesh

$$ Epcot/Morocco Pavilion (Moroccan Cuisine)

For a spot of romance and truly authentic flavor, head for Marrakesh. Of all the Epcot eateries, this venue best typifies the international spirit of the park. Hand-laid mosaics in intricate patterns set the scene for lavish North African dining, complete with belly dancers (Walt may be turning over in his grave). Marrakesh uses a long list of spices including saffron to enhance flavorful specialties. The menu features couscous with chicken, lamb, or a variety of garden vegetables. A favorite appetizer is bastilla, fried pastry that has chicken strips seasoned with almonds, powdered sugar, and cinnamon. The dessert menu includes *bastilla au lait etamandes* with cream and toasted almonds. Try the Moroccan *diffa* (traditional feast) to sample saffron-seasoned harina soup made with lamb and lentils, beef *brewats* in a broth of spices and a cloak of pastry, roast lamb with rice pilaf, chicken with green olives, couscous with vegetables, and mint tea.

☎ **407-939-3463.** http://asp.disney.go.com/. *Priority Seating recommended. Parking: $6. Main courses: $14–$20. A fixed-price menu is served for $17.25 at lunch; $26–$29 at dinner. AE, MC, V. Open: Daily 11:30 a.m.–9:30 p.m.*

Michelangelo

$$-$$$ International Drive Area (Mediterranean Cuisine)

This restaurant has a reputation for being a celebrity hangout; it also has an impeccable atmosphere and an extensive menu. The veal Michelangelo is meltingly tender, and the marinated prime rib is a feast. You can order homemade pastas on the side or as a main dish. The menu has a nice choice of appetizers, soups, entrées, and desserts. There's also a full bar and a decent wine list.

*4898 Kirkman Rd. (In the Kirkman Shoppes, one-quarter mile north of **Universal Studios.**) ☎ **407-297-6666.** Reservations suggested. Parking: Free. Main courses: $14–$29. AE, DC, DISC, MC, V. Open: Daily 6–11 p.m.*

Ming Court

$-$$ International Drive Area (Chinese Cuisine)

Dine in an ethereal setting, graced by lotus ponds filled with glowing goldfish while you're entertained by — get this — zither music. You'll rub elbows with more locals than tourists and find innovative twists on traditional oriental cuisine. The flavors are delicate and probably more balanced than at your neighborhood Chinese place. Try the crisp chicken in tangerine sauce, spicy Szechuan beef or shrimp, or butter-tender filet mignon with crisp-tender vegetables.

*9188 International Dr. (between Sand Lake and Bee Line Expressway). ☎ **407-351-9988.** http://orlando.citysearch.com/E/V/ORLFL/0001/90/72/. Reservations recommended. Parking: Free. Main courses: $8–$17. AE, CB, DC, DISC, MC, V. Open: Daily 11:00 a.m.–2:30 p.m. and 4:30 p.m. to midnight.*

Morton's of Chicago

$$-$$$ International Drive Area (Steakhouse)

Steak-stuffers may be more inclined to go to a Kansas City steak joint, but Morton's is pretty respected locally. Maybe they don't grow the hoofers here, but they know beef, which is served in straightforward meat-and-potatoes style. The cuts are costly, but they're tender and well aged. Side dishes are à la carte, which can add up to an expensive evening if you go overboard. The no-smoking section could be larger — and more smoke-free — but there's a full bar.

*7600 Dr. Phillips Blvd. (In the Marketplace at Dr. Phillips.) ☎ **407-248-3485.** http://orlando.citysearch.com/E/V/ORLFL/0001/89/72/. Reservations recommended. Parking: Free. Main courses: $17–$30. AE, DC, MC, V. Open: Mon–Sat 5:30–11:00 p.m.; Sun 5–10 p.m.*

Downtown Restaurants

Map key:
- Chalet Suzanne **7**
- Lake Wales **7**
- Le Coq Au Vin **6**
- Le Provence **3**
- Little Saigon **2**
- Manuel's on the 28th **1**
- Numero Uno **5**
- Pebbles **4**

Nine Dragons

$-$$ Epcot/China Pavilion (Chinese Cuisine)

This is one of the loveliest of the *World Showcase* restaurants, boasting intricately carved rosewood paneling and an amazing dragon-motif ceiling. Order shredded duck with sweet peppers and Chinese pancakes, spicy Szechuan shrimp, stir-fried chicken with vegetables, or sliced sirloin stir-fried with broccoli and oyster sauce. The menu also has familiar standbys like moo goo gai pan and sweet and sour pork, as well as lobster prepared Cantonese-style, braised and lightly fried duck, honey-roasted spare ribs, and stir-fried grouper and vegetables. The fresh fruit juices are delicious, with or without an alcohol kicker. For dessert, try the sweet red-bean ice cream with fried banana. It's delicious!

☎ *407-939-3463.* http://asp.disney.go.com/. *Priority Seating recommended. Parking: $6. Main courses: $10.50–$23.75. Fixed-price dinner $11.50. AE, MC, V. Open: Daily noon to 9 p.m.*

Numero Uno

$$ Downtown Orlando (Cuban Cuisine)

Some see this family-run Cuban joint as a hole in the wall, but you won't notice the décor after the *paella* hits your table. If that doesn't appeal to you, order *ropa vieja* (literally "old clothes," because the beef is so tender), roast pork, or a remarkable *arroz con pollo* (chicken and rice, usually served with saffron). The trimmings include a lot of Latin favorites like plantains. Dessert is traditional three-milk cake. Beer and wine are the only attitude adjustments.

2499 S. Orange Ave. ☎ *407-841-3840. Reservations recommended. Parking: Tight, but free. Main courses: $8–$19. AE, DC, DISC, MC, V. Open: Mon.–Fri. 11 a.m.– 3 p.m.; Mon.–Sat. 5:30–9:00 p.m.*

'Ohana

$$ Disney's Polynesian Resort (Pacific Rim/Polynesian Cuisine)

Think fun. The whole family will find something to like about 'Ohana 's all-dig-in-pig-out specials. You're welcomed to island hospitality by a server who addresses you as "cousin." That fits, because 'Ohana means *family* in Hawaiian. Located in the Polynesian's main dining room, this nightly luau gives you a chance to see your food being prepared over an 18-foot fire pit. While you wait, someone blows a conch shell and a storyteller arrives on the scene. Then, there are coconut races in the center aisle, you can shake it in hula lessons, and those with birthdays are urged to work out a hula hoop while everyone sings "Happy Birthday" in Hawaiian.

Kids like the hoopla; those seeking intimacy don't.

Soon after you're seated, the feeding frenzy begins in rapid succession (ask your waiter to slow down if the pace is too fast). The vittles include salad, fruit, fresh-baked bread, chicken wrapped in banana leaves, seared salmon, shrimp, grilled sirloin, stir-fried vegetables, banana cream pie, chocolate mousse cake, soft drinks, and coffee. A full bar offers tropical drinks, including nonalcoholic ones for kids, and there's a limited selection of wines.

1600 Seven Seas Dr. ☎ *407/939-3463.* http://asp.disney.go.com/. *Parking: Free. Main courses: Fixed-price family feast, $21 adults, $10 kids 3–11 (see Chapter 15). AE, MC, V. Daily 7:30–11:00 a.m. and 5:00–10:00 p.m.*

Pacino's Italian Ristorante

$-$$ South Orlando/Kissimmee (Italian/Mediterranean Cuisine)

The hand-painted ceiling of this restaurant contains fiber optics to create an aura of dining under the stars, but there's also a patio if you want the real thing. Some servers can be a little aloof, making it really feel like Italy, but the food's price and taste make up for it. House specialties include twin veal chops, ziti with sweet Italian sausage, a challenging 32-ounce porterhouse steak, *fruitti di mare* (a plate literally bursting with clams, calamari, shrimp, and scallops sautéed with white wine and herbs), and Australian lobster tail.

5795 W. Hwy. 192/Irlo Bronson Memorial Pkwy. (2 miles east of I-4). ☎ *407-396-8022.* www.pacinos.com. *Reservations accepted. Parking: Free. Main courses: $10–$27 (most are under $20). AE, MC, V. Open: Daily 4–11 p.m.*

Park Plaza Gardens

$$-$$$ Near North/Winter Park (Continental Cuisine)

The gardenlike atmosphere (look, up in the sky, a glass roof!) is an elegant touch that goes with the cuisine, which is sophisticated and health-conscious. There's also a popular brunch on Sunday, pampering staff, and full bar. Meats range from grilled New York strip steak to Atlantic blue crabs and Maine lobster cakes.

319 Park Ave. South. ☎ *407-645-2475.* www.parkplazagardens.com/home.htm. *Reservations suggested. Parking: Free. Main courses: $18–$30. AE, CB, DC, DISC, MC, V. Open: Mon–Thurs 11 a.m.–2 p.m. and 6–10 p.m.; Fri–Sat 11 a.m.–2 p.m. and 6–11 p.m.; Sun 11 a.m.–9 p.m.*

Pastamore Ristorante

$$ Universal Studios/CityWalk (Italian Cuisine)

Just inside the door you find large display cases full of fresh mozzarella, eggplant, olives, and more that you can order to go or enjoy alfresco on Pastamoré's outdoor patio. This family-style restaurant greets you with statues and Italian artifacts that are scattered about, and the kitchen is open, allowing you a view of the cooks at work. At $15 ($20 if you add shrimp), the antipasto primo is a meal in itself. The mound includes bruschetta, eggplant Caponata, melon con prosciutto, grilled portobello mushrooms, olives, plum tomatoes with fresh mozzarella, a medley of Italian cold cuts, and more. The menu also has traditional features such as veal marsala, chicken parmigiana, shrimp scampi, fettuccine alfredo, lasagna, and pizza. You can also eat on an outdoor patio where pastries, sandwiches, gelato, espresso, and other lighter fare are served 7:30 a.m.–2:00 a.m.

1000 Universal Studios Plaza. ☎ *407-363-8000.* www.uescape.com/citywalk/. *Reservations accepted. Parking: $6. Main courses: $7–$20. AE, DISC, MC, V. Open: Daily 5 p.m. to midnight.*

Pebbles

$-$$ Downtown, Near North/Longwood, Lake Buena Vista (American Cuisine)

This is as close as Orlando gets to a hometown chain. Classy and casual, this downtown spot is like its two sister eateries, offering a menu that ranges from a create-your-own burger (price negotiable) to filet mignon and honey-roasted spare ribs. Owner Manny Garcia offers affordability in the Pebbles line with entrées such as duck, lamb, and pasta dishes, as well as tapas (appetizers), burgers, and soups. The restaurant has a bar, a respectable wine list (order by the glass), a tiki bar and patio outside, and a fun, California atmosphere.

17 W. Church St., ☎ *407-839-0892; 2110 W. Fla. 434,* ☎ *407-774-7111; 12551 Fla. 535,* ☎ *407-827-1111.* http://orlando.citysearch.com/E/V/ORLFL/0001/ 83/86/. *Reservations accepted. Parking: Free. Main courses: $9–$20. AE, CB, DC, DISC, MC, V. Open: Mon–Thurs 11 a.m.–11 p.m.; Fri 11 a.m. to midnight; Sat noon to midnight; Sun noon to 11 p.m.*

Planet Hollywood

$-$$ Disney's Pleasure Island (American Cuisine)

If you go to **Downtown Disney Marketplace,** you can't help but see the giant globe with the lettering screaming *Planet Hollywood* at you. Your kids already know about it — and they're probably clamoring to go, especially if they're teens. This place is part restaurant and part showcase for Hollywood memorabilia. Diners are surrounded by clips from some soon-to-be-released movies and some 300 show-biz artifacts ranging from Peter O'Toole's *Lawrence of Arabia* costume to the front end of the bus from *Speed!* You may expect mediocre food amid the hype, but it's not that bad. You can gnaw on appetizers like hickory-smoked buffalo wings, pot stickers, or nachos, or try out the selection of burgers, sandwiches, pastas, and pizzas. Although the chain has lost its celebrity backers and had financial troubles, this location seems to be alive and well.

1506 E. Buena Vista Dr. ☎ *407-827-7827.* http://orlando.citsearch. com/E/V/ORLFL/0001/92/45/. *Reservations not accepted. Parking: Free. Main courses: $7.50–$19 (most under $13). AE, DC, MC, V. Open: Daily 11 a.m.–2 a.m.*

Plaza Restaurant

$ Magic Kingdom/Main Street (American Cuisine)

Take a breather from the hot sun and teeming crowds in the **Magic Kingdom** and have lunch at this hometown-style restaurant, located appropriately enough at the end of Main Street. The menu offers plain and fancy burgers, hot and cold sandwiches (try the Reuben or the double-decker hot roast beef), salads, and milk shakes in three flavors. Or skip the shakes and leave room for a hot-fudge sundae — the World's best.

☎ *407-939-3463.* http://asp.disney.go.com/. *Priority Seating recommended. Parking: $6. Main courses: $7.75–$10.75. AE, MC, V. Open: Daily 11 a.m. to park closing.*

Near North Restaurants

0 3 Mi	
0 3 Km	

Lake Jessup

Winter Springs 434

4

435

436

434

Apopka

441

❶ ❷

Casselberry

Semoran Blvd.

Altamonte Springs

Maitland

436

❸

423

426

Winter Park

426

❺

❹

426

ORLANDO

❻

50

438 416

50

W. Colonial Dr.

East-West Expressway 408

■ Citrus Bowl

435

Vineland Rd.

Winder-mere

■ Universal Studios Escape

4

Rattlesnake Lake

Lake Holden

Conway

Lake Jessamine

Wet 'n' Wild ■

482

Boston's Fish House **5**
Bubbaloo's Bodacious BBQ **3**
La Scala **1**
Maison & Jardin **2**
Park Plaza Gardens **6**
Rolando's **4**

Portobello Yacht Club

$-$$ Downtown Disney/Pleasure Island (Contemporary Italian Cuisine)

Crispy, thin-crusted pizzas, cooked in wood-burning ovens, are the signature item at this restaurant. The club is a floating trattoria that bills itself as serving nouveau Old World cuisine. That sounds a bit bizarre, but it works thanks to creative chefs and an attentive staff. Try dining on the patio overlooking the water if the weather is good. Inside or out, expect crowds. A full bar, a health-conscious menu, and a lively atmosphere make this a great place for a casual bite.

1650 Buena Vista Dr. ☎ *407-934-8888.* www.portobellorestaurant.com. *Reservations suggested. Parking: Free. Main courses: $10–$17. AE, MC, V. Open: Mon–Sun 11:30 a.m. to midnight.*

Race Rock

$-$$ International Drive Area (American Cuisine)

In case you couldn't guess the theme, it's NASCAR. There are cars and trucks all over the place, and the TV monitors show taped race action. It's *LOUD*. Between the music and racing sounds, it's hard to complete a thought, much less a sentence. But gearheads of all ages love this infield-like pit stop, which features prime rib, big burgers, pizza, egg rolls, soups, salads, and sandwiches. Race Rock's eye candy also includes some drag-sters and hydroplanes. Kids have their own Quarter Midget Menu, complete with games and coloring. Speaking of kids, keeping the sugar away from them here isn't a bad idea; this place lights their little fuses without any ingested assistance.

8986 International Dr., just south of Sand Lake Rd. ☎ **407-248-9876**. http://orlando.citysearch.com/E/V/ORLFL/0001/90/51/. *Reservations only accepted for groups. Parking: Free. Main courses: $7–$8. AE, DC, DISC, MC, V. Open: Daily 11 a.m.–11 p.m. and later if it's crowded.*

Rainforest Café

$-$$ Downtown Disney Marketplace & Animal Kingdom (American Cuisine)

Set amid a jungle with tropical sounds of birds and waterfalls, this is a place to eat that kids love! The food's pretty respectable, but it's really the decor that makes this restaurant. As its name suggests, entering the Rainforest Café is like walking into a jungle — there are lifelike silk plants all over, Animatronic monkeys chattering, and occasional rain and thunder rumblings. The menu offers California-influenced house specialties such as Chicken Monsoon with shrimp and linguine and Rasta Pasta (bow-tie noodles and a variety of vegetables in a creamy garlic-pesto sauce). The barstools resemble zebras, giraffes, and other wild-and-crazy critters.

*1800 E. Buena Vista Dr. (in the **Disney Marketplace**.)* ☎ **407-827-8500**. www.rainforestcafe.com. *Reservations not accepted. Parking: Free. (Also, just outside the entrance to **Animal Kingdom**.* ☎ **407-938-9100**. *Parking: $6.) Main courses: $5.50–$18. AE, DISC, MC, V. Open: Sun–Thurs 10:30 a.m.–11:00 p.m.; Fri–Sat. 10:30 a.m. to midnight.*

Rolando's

$-$$ Near North (Cuban)

The place isn't big on aesthetics — it has plain tables and chairs and a sparse collection of photos of Cuba on the walls — but huge platters of Cuban food make it memorable. Order traditional items such as pork, red snapper, tamale pie, or chicken. Try the hearty rice pudding for dessert. Paella is an option *if* you call an hour in advance and order a minimum of two dinners. The yellow rice is filled with a seafood medley that includes shrimp and lobster, in addition to ham, chicken, and pork.

Standard Cuban sandwiches come with black-bean soup. Entrées are served with freshly baked rolls, salad, rice, and plantains or yucca.

870 E. Semoran/Fla. 436, between Red Bug Rd. and U.S. 17–92. (Take I-4 east to the East-West Expressway, go east, then left on Semoran.) ☎ *407-767-9677.* http://orlando.citysearch.com/E/V/ORLFL/0001/78/34/. *Reservations not accepted. Parking: Free. Main courses: $7.75–$17.50. AE, DISC, MC, V. Open: Tues–Sat 11 a.m.–10 p.m.; Sun 1–8 p.m.*

Rose & Crown Pub & Dining Room

$$ Epcot/United Kingdom Pavilion (British Cuisine)

You can order ale, lagers, and stouts by the pint or (designated-driver alert!) half yard. The Rose & Crown has dark-oak wainscoting, a beamed Tudor ceiling, English folk music, and saucy servers. If you're not too hungry, pick one of the starters — lamb barley soup, fresh mussels, or cheese and fruit. If you're starving, there's London-style fish and chips, Guinness beef with Yorkshire pudding, cottage pie, and walnut chicken with Stilton cream. Other items include vegetable curry, a pork plate, and a beef filled Cornish pastie (meat pie). If you opt for a late dinner, ask for an outdoor table (weather permitting) for a fantastic view of IllumiNations, the fireworks display (see Chapter 18 for more Epcot information). For dessert, try the sherry trifle, a fruit-and-custard cake. Priority seating is recommended for dining, but isn't necessary to stop in at the pub section, a popular drinking spot.

☎ *407-939-3463.* http://asp.disney.go.com/. *Priority Seating recommended for dining room. Parking: $6. Main courses: $10–$14 at lunch; $10–$20 at dinner. Traditional afternoon tea at 3:30 p.m., $10. AE, MC, V. Open: Daily 11 a.m. until one hour before park closes.*

San Angel Inn

$-$$ Epcot/Mexico Pavilion (Mexican Cuisine)

It's always night inside the inn, and you'll eat at one of several romantic candlelit tables located in a hacienda courtyard that is surrounded by dense jungle foliage. The shadow of a crumbling Yucatán pyramid looms in the distance, and you hear the sound of faraway birds while you dine. The ambience of this restaurant, located inside the Mexico Pavilion, is exotic, and the fare is authentic — that's why you won't find nachos or Mexican pizza on the menu. Order an appetizer of *queso fundido* (melted cheese with Mexican pork sausage, served with homemade corn or flour tortillas). Entrées include *mole poblano* (chicken simmered with more than 20 spices and a hint of chocolate) and *filete ranchero* (grilled tenderloin of beef served over corn tortillas with ranchero sauce, pepper strips, Monterey Jack cheese, onions, and refried beans). Combination platters are available at both meals. There's chocolate Kahlúa mousse pie for dessert. Your drinking options include Dos Equis beer and margaritas. A special vegetarian menu is also available.

☎ *407-939-3463.* http://asp.disney.go.com/. *Priority Seating recommended. Parking: $6. Main courses: $9–$17 at lunch; $17–$22 at dinner. AE, MC, V. Open: Daily 11 a.m. to park closing.*

Sci-Fi Dine-in Theater Restaurant

$$ Disney–MGM Studios (American Cuisine)

Horror flicks (which are too hokey to be scary) play on the screen while you dine in a replica of a 1950's Los Angeles drive-in movie emporium, complete with tables ensconced in flashy, chrome-trimmed convertible cars. Gorge yourself on barbecued ribs with vegetables and fries, Cajun-style grilled chicken, free popcorn, and, for dessert, The Cheesecake That Ate New York or 'smores just like you made at camp. You can enjoy a milk shake or order from the full bar. You'll probably give the experience a thumb's up even though the meal isn't five-star (or even four).

Across from Sounds Dangerous Starring Drew Carey. ☎ *407-939-3463.* http://asp.disney.go.com/. *Priority Seating recommended. Parking: $6. Main courses: $8–$15 at lunch, $9.50–$22.75 at dinner. AE, MC, V. Open: Daily 11 a.m. to park closing.*

Spoodles

$$ Disney's BoardWalk Resort (Tapas/Mediterranean Cuisine)

Tapas, pizza, and pasta are the main items on the menu at this Mediterranean-style restaurant. The barbecued Moroccan beef skewers with raisins, toasted almonds, and couscous are drenched in a hot, tangy sauce. The artichoke ravioli with garlic, cherry tomatoes, and arugula is a vegetarian treat. Or try the oven-roasted snapper with artichokes, fennel, and oven-dried tomatoes. Those with heartier appetites should try tapas grande, such as the potato-crusted salmon simmered with wild mushrooms in a veal broth with truffle oil. Disney has gone to great lengths to provide an impressive wine menu. Table-side sangria presentations add something special to the evening. There's a kid's menu featuring a "you make it, we bake it" pizza combination. During the height of the summer tourist season, Spoodles can get crowded, and the wait can be long, even with Priority Seating, so this may not be the best option for famished families coming straight from the parks.

☎ *407-939-3463.* http://asp.disney.go.com/. *Priority Seating recommended. Parking: Free. Main courses: $14–$26. AE, MC. V. Open: Daily 7–11 a.m., noon to 2 p.m., and 5–10 p.m.*

Tempura Kiku

$$-$$$ Epcot/Japan Pavilion (Japanese Cuisine)

The restaurant centers on a teppanyaki steak house where diners sit at grill tables and chefs rapidly dice, slice, stir-fry, and propel cooked food onto your plate with amazing dexterity. Kids especially enjoy watching the chef wield his or her cleaver and utensils. Several parties are seated at the teppanyaki tables, which makes for sociable dining, especially for single travelers looking for conversation. Return guests may remember fixed-price lunches and dinners for two. Those are no longer on the menu, but you still can find treats such as the shrimp appetizer, soybean soup with tofu and mushrooms, grilled fresh vegetables with *udon* noodles, lobster, grilled beef tenderloin, scallops, chicken, steamed rice, chestnut cake, and green tea. Portions are plentiful. Kirin beer, plum wine, and sake are your beverage options, along with specialty drinks, such as *tachibana* (light rum, orange curaçao, and some mandarin orange juice) and nonalcoholic ones for kids. Adjoining the teppanyaki rooms is a U-shaped tempura counter where you can eat shrimp, scallops, chicken, and fresh vegetables that have been lightly battered and deep-fried. Some sushi and sashimi items are served.

☎ *407-939-3463*. http://asp.disney.go.com/. *Priority Seating recommended for teppanyaki; reservations not accepted at tempura counter. Parking: $6. Teppanyaki main courses: $10–$20 at lunch ($5–$6 for kids 3–9), $15–$30 at dinner ($5–$8 for kids). AE, MC, V. Open: Daily 11 a.m. until one hour before park closes.*

Victoria & Albert's

$$$$ Disney's Grand Floridian Resort & Spa (Haute Cuisine)

The setting is Victorian and a nostalgic reminder that dining out was once a treat to be savored in an evening-filling, relaxed, and stylish manner. The chef works wizardry with food from a diverse marketplace. This is the most memorable (and memorably expensive) restaurant in **WDW.** But if money's no object and you're serious about food and romance going hand in hand, head here. The intimate dining room has exquisitely appointed tables. The food is impeccable and presented with a flourish by an attentive and professional staff (each table has a maid named Victoria and a butler named Albert). The fare changes nightly. You may begin with Beluga caviar with toast points or apple-smoked Colorado bison, then have a Dungeness crab cake as a hot appetizer. Antelope consommé may follow, preceding a main course of black bass with toasted couscous or a beef tenderloin with Cipollini onion risotto. Your faithful servers may then bring out English Stilton served with pine-nut bread, port wine, and a pear poached in burgundy, cognac, and cinnamon sugar as a set-up for a dessert of vanilla bean crème brûlée or white chocolate and raspberry Chambord soufflé. (At this point, you explode.) Dinners are usually a two and a half- to three-hour affair, though the later sitting can run longer. If you're inclined to try the chef's table option (you actually dine in the kitchen and watch them prepare your meal), make sure to reserve it weeks, if not months, in advance.

4401 Floridian Way. ☎ *407-939-3463 or 407-824-1089.* http://asp.disney.go.com/. *Reservations required well in advance. Jackets required for men. Not recommended for children. Parking: Free self and validated valet. Main courses: Fixed-price $85 per person, $35 additional for wine pairing; $115 chef's table, $160 with wine. AE, MC, V. Open: Sittings at 5:45 and 9:00 p.m.; chef's table 6:00 p.m. only.*

Wild Jacks

$-$$ International Drive Area (American Cuisine)

You sit family-style at picnic tables with checkered tablecloths while you chow down at this chuckwagon-style eatery. The atmosphere includes mounted buffalo heads, long-dead jack-a-lopes and more dying-calf-in-a-hailstorm, twitch-and-twang country-western music than an average city slicker ought to want to endure in a lifetime. The kitchen is bursting with steaks on an open-pit grill. In addition to the Texas-size hunks of beef served with jalapeño smashed potatoes and corn on the cob, the menu offers a selection of skewered shrimp, tacos, chicken, or pasta, though it's not a good idea to order experimental stuff in a beef house. Wash the meal down with an icy long neck and, for dessert, feast on peach cobbler à la mode. Wild Jacks isn't Orlando's finest steak house, but it's successful enough to have other locations in Altamonte Springs and Kissimmee.

7364 International Dr., between Sand Lake Rd. and Carrier Dr. ☎ *407-352-4407.* http://orlando.citysearch.com/E/V/ORLFL/0001/90/78/. *Reservations not accepted. Parking: Free. Main courses: $9–$20. AE, CB, DC, DISC, JCB, MC, V. Open: Sun–Thurs 4–10 p.m., Fri–Sat 4–11 p.m.*

Wolfgang Puck Café

$$-$$$ Disney's West Side (California Cuisine)

Avant-garde chef Wolfgang Puck brings his West Coast creations to the heart of Florida. You can eat gourmet pizza with a thin, crisp crust and exotic toppings, either on an outdoor patio or inside. You can follow an appetizer of vegetable spring rolls or a sampling from the sushi bar with the fresh-grilled chicken or the Chinois chicken salad. The restaurant is busy and often noisy, so conversation may be difficult. For a lot of folks the food taste doesn't match its eye appeal.

☎ *407-938-9653.* http://asp.disney.go.com/. *Reservations recommended. Parking: Free. Main courses: $9–$29 (many under $20). AE, DC, MC, V. Daily 11 a.m. to midnight.*

Yachtsman Steakhouse

$$$ Disney's Contemporary Resort (Steakhouse)

This restaurant is regarded as one of Orlando's top steak-and-chop houses, a restaurant where diners select their own steaks. It's *the* place to come if you love red meat and are too young or too carefree to worry about arterial blockage. The steaks are aged, the cattle from which they came were grain-fed, and a staff butcher carves the beef. (The porterhouse is tender enough to cut with a fork.) The menu includes grilled lamb chops and Yukon gold angus steak with mashed potatoes and asparagus. (It also has poultry and seafood in case one or more in your party isn't inclined toward red meat.) Desserts include a decadent white chocolate mousse macadamia nut pie. There's a full bar, which offers daily specials. The Steakhouse is prone to crowds, but most folks say that it's worth the wait.

1700 Epcot Resorts Blvd. ☎ *407-939-3463.* http://asp.disney.go.com/. *Reservations suggested. Parking: Free. Main courses: $22–$32. AE, DISC, MC, V. Open: Sun–Sat 6–10 p.m.*

Chapter 15

Disney Character Dining

. . . .

In This Chapter

▶ Budgeting for character dining

▶ Finding the best character meals

. . . .

*T*he eight-and-under crowd usually gets starry-eyed when characters show up to say howdy, sign autographs, pose for photos, and encourage them to eat their okra. Characters turn out at mealtimes at several Disney parks, attractions, and resorts, and these get-togethers are incredibly popular. Translation: One-on-one interaction is somewhat brief.

You may not find a seat if you show up to a character appearance unannounced, so call to make reservations as far in advance as possible.

The Cost of Catching Characters

Prices for Disney character meals are pretty much the same no matter where you dine. Breakfast prices average $14 for adults and $8 to $10 for children 3 to 9. Dinners, which are only available in some places (see the listings later in this chapter), run $19 to $22 for adults and $9 to $13 for children 3 to 9. In general, presentation at all the character meals we list in this chapter rates a B, the food a B–. The character luau at **WDW's Polynesian Resort** (see Chapter 30 for information on this meal and other Disney dinner shows) is a bit better in both categories, so naturally it costs you a few more clams.

To make Priority Seating reservations (these reservations don't lock down a table, but they do give you the next available table after you arrive) for any Disney character meal, call ☎ **407-939-3463**. Character meals accept American Express, MasterCard, and Visa.

You can find all the restaurants mentioned in this chapter on the map "Walt Disney World & Lake Buena Vista Restaurants," located in Chapter 14. You can also find in-depth reviews of their non-character meals and cuisine in that chapter. Additionally, if you're a cyber-sleuth, you can get information at http://disney.go.com/DisneyWorld/intro.html.

The Most Characters Money Can Buy

Although we mention specific characters here, be advised that **WDW** frequently changes its lineups, so don't promise the kids a specific character or you may get burned. Also, keep in mind that you'll have to tack on the price of park admission to all character meals that are held inside the theme parks.

Artist Point

Winnie the Pooh, Tigger, and all their friends from the Hundred Acre Wood host an all-you-can-eat breakfast of scrambled eggs, potatoes, sausage, and bacon. (If you prefer to go with less protein and cholesterol, they also offer a fruit plate in lieu of traditional breakfast fare.) The rustic, lodge-like dining room has a high-beamed ceiling supported by tree-trunk beams and large windows providing scenic lake views.

In Disney's Wilderness Lodge, 901 Timberline Dr. $14.50 adults, $8.75 children 3–9. Open: Daily 7:30–11:30 a.m.

Cape May Café

The Cape May Café is a delightful New England-themed dining room that serves lavish buffet character breakfasts hosted by Admiral Goofy and his crew: Chip 'n' Dale and Pluto (Minnie Mouse occasionally makes an appearance). The buffet is traditional American fare: eggs, pancakes, bacon, and pastries.

In Disney's Beach Club Resort, 1800 Epcot Resorts Blvd. $14.95 adults, $8.50 children 3–9. Open: Daily 7:30–11:00 a.m.

Chef Mickey's

The whimsical Chef Mickey's is the home of buffet breakfasts (eggs, breakfast meats, pancakes, fruit, and so on) where you can meet and be greeted by the Magic Mouse and various pals. Chef Mickey's character buffet dinners come with a salad bar, you-peel-'em-you-eat-'em shrimp, soups, hot entrees, breads, carved meats, vegetables, and an ice cream bar with a great variety of toppings.

In Disney's Contemporary Resort, 4600 North World Dr. Character breakfast $14.95 adults, $7.95 children 3–9; Character dinner $19.95 adults, $8.95 children 3–9. Open: Daily 7:00–11:30 a.m. and 5:00–9:30 p.m.

Cinderella's Royal Table

This Gothic castle — the focal point of the park — is the setting for daily character breakfasts. The menu has standard fare: eggs, bacon, Danish, and fresh breads. Hosts vary, but Cinderella always makes an appearance. This is one of the most popular character meals in the park, so reserve far in advance. This meal is a great way to start your day in the **Magic Kingdom.**

In Cinderella's Castle, The Magic Kingdom. $14.95 adults, $8.95 children 3–9. Open: Daily 8–10 a.m.

Crystal Palace

The real treats here are the characters, Pooh and his pals, who are on location throughout the day. The early menu is typical breakfast fare (omelets, French toast, pancakes, breakfast meats, and — wowser! — breakfast lasagna). Winnie the Pooh holds center stage while the other characters circle the restaurant, providing a lot of love and photo opportunities. At lunch and dinner, standards include fried chicken, macaroni and cheese, and a variety of veggies and desserts. This is one of the worst places to come if you're in dire need of a quiet meal. Pooh and his crew attract jabbering, squealing kids like lovebugs on a wide windshield.

Priority Seating reservations are almost a must here thanks to the crowds.

On Main St., The Magic Kingdom. Breakfast $14.95 adults, $7.95 children 3–9; lunch $14.95 adults, $7.95 children 3–9; dinner $19.95 adults, $12.95 children 3–9. Open: Daily 8:00–10:30 a.m., 11:30 a.m.–3:15 p.m., and 4 p.m. to park closing.

Donald's Prehistoric Breakfast

Here's another all-you-can-shove-in buffet of eggs, bacon, and French toast. Donald Duck, Mickey Mouse, Goofy, and Pluto are on hand to entertain the little ones while they almost eat. *Note:* This is the only place in **Animal Kingdom** that offers a character breakfast.

In Animal Kingdom, Restaurantosaurus, Dinoland U.S.A. Breakfast $13.95 adults, $7.95 children 3–9. Open: Daily 7:40 a.m.–10:30 p.m.

Garden Grill

This revolving restaurant has comfortable, semicircular booths. As you dine, your table travels past desert, prairie, farmland, and rain-forest environments as only Disney imagineers can design them. There's a Momma's-in-the-kitchen theme here: You're given a straw hat as you enter, and the just-folks service staff speaks in country lingo. Hearty family-style meals are hosted by Mickey, Minnie, and Chip 'n' Dale. (Boy, that Mickey sure gets around.) The American breakfast includes scrambled eggs, potatoes with cheese, sausage, ham, biscuits, fresh fruit, and cinnamon rolls. Lunch and dinner offer rotisserie chicken, fish, steak, potatoes, vegetables, salad, and dessert.

In The Land Pavilion, Epcot. Breakfast $14.95 adults, $8.25 children 3–9; lunch $16.95 adults, $9.95 children 3–9; dinner $18.95 adults, $9.95 children 3–9. Open: Daily 8:30 a.m.–8:10 p.m.

Liberty Tree Tavern

This colonial-style, eighteenth-century pub offers character dinners hosted by Mickey, Goofy, Pluto, Chip 'n' Dale, and Tigger (some or all of them). Meals are fixed-price and offer a salad of mixed greens, roast turkey with mashed potatoes, cornbread, and warm apple crisp with vanilla ice cream for dessert.

Food-wise, this is the best character meal in the **World.**

In Liberty Square, The Magic Kingdom. Dinner $19.95 adults, $9.95 children 3–9. Open: Daily 4 p.m. to park closing.

Minnie's Menehune

Traditional breakfast foods (eggs, pancakes, bacon, and more) are prepared on an 18-foot fire pit and served family-style. Minnie, Goofy, and Chip 'n' Dale appear, and there are parades for children to participate in with Polynesian musical instruments.

In Disney's Polynesian Resort, 1600 Seven Seas Dr. $14.95 adults $8.95 children 3–11. Open: Daily 7:30–11:00 a.m. at the Polynesian-themed 'Ohana restaurant. (See Chapters 14 and 30 for more details.)

1900 Park Fare

The exquisitely elegant Grand Floridian resort hosts character meals in the festive exposition-themed 1900 Park Fare. Big Bertha — a 100-year-old French band organ that plays pipes, drums, bells, cymbals, castanets, and the xylophone — provides music. Mary Poppins, Winnie the Pooh, Goofy, Pluto, Chip 'n' Dale, and Minnie appear at the elaborate buffet breakfasts of traditional eggs, French toast, bacon, and pancakes. Beauty and the Beast and friends appear at nightly buffets, which feature prime rib, stuffed pork loin, fresh fish, and more.

In Disney's Grand Floridian Beach Resort, 4401 Floridian Way. Breakfast $15.95 adults, $9.95 children 3–9; dinner $21.95 adults, $12.95 children 3–9. Open: Daily 7:30–11:30 a.m. and 5:30–9:00 p.m.

Part V
Exploring Walt Disney World

"I **know** these are your character's names, but when you're around guests at the theme park, you're neither sleepy, dopey, or grumpy."

In this part . . .

You've made travel plans, picked a hotel, and you know where to eat. At last, you're going to Disney World!

However, the Super Bowl champs and half of their fans, thousands of conventioneers and vacationers, and many locals are going to Disney World, too.

Every year, more than 40 million sweaty bodies invade Disney's four major theme parks, and all of them are hell-bent on riding the same rides and eating in the same restaurants as you are. You'll have a lot more fun if you arrive knowing which parks and attractions suit your tastes as well as knowing which parks you should avoid. In this section, we help you rank the parks' amenities so you can determine where you want to spend the majority of your time.

Chapter 16

Getting an Overview of Walt Disney World

*W*hen the **Magic Kingdom** first opened its gates in 1971, we made the pilgrimage with our one-year-old daughter, Chris, and wandered in slack-jawed awe among the many marvels of Mickeyville.

Today, as our grandsons Jake and Andy enter the mix, we marvel at a different wonder: growth. Walt Disney's legacy has exploded in the last three decades. It has truly become a world, with four theme parks, smaller parks and attractions, nightclubs, hotels, restaurants, shopping districts, and two cruise ships. It's enough to fog your mind, so we're here to put the fun back in your vacation planning.

In this chapter, we introduce you to the parks, tantalize you with ride descriptions, and offer you some suggested itineraries. We also use the JJSays ratings system to give you a pint-sized view of the rides and shows in the parks.

Of course, don't think that ours is the only way to do Disney. We've done it enough times that we know the shortcuts, the duds, and the all-stars. But maybe you can afford a more leisurely pace or prefer a quiet jungle cruise instead of a rock-and-roller coaster. So, make sure that you use this chapter and the rest of Part V to fill in your own dance card.

Welcome to Walt's World

Disney's four main theme parks line the western half of this 30,500-acre world. The **Magic Kingdom** is the original attraction; with 15.2 million visitors a year, it's busier than any other U.S. theme park. **Epcot** is the third busiest theme park welcoming 10.1 million visitors a year, followed by **Disney–MGM Studios** at 8.7 million, and **Animal Kingdom** with 8.6 million visitors a year. Here's a quick look at what you can find in all four Disney parks:

The Lands

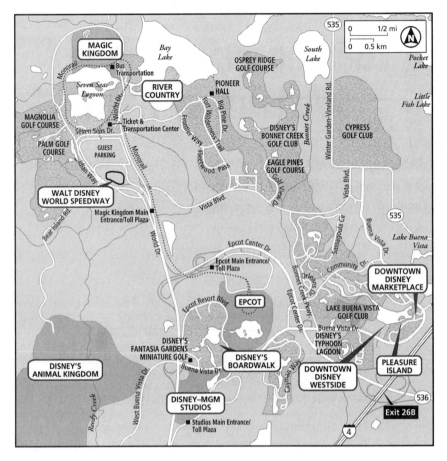

✔ **Magic Kingdom:** Built as Disney's flagship park, the **Magic Kingdom** is divided into seven themed lands. They're laid out like the spokes of a wheel, with the park's icon — Cinderella's Castle — at the hub. Anyone with kids or just young at heart should give the **Magic Kingdom** at least one full day. It offers more for younger children than any other Orlando theme park, but it has broad appeal for first-timers and Disney fans, too. If you fall into these categories, we recommend two days or more, provided you have the time and budget. (See Chapter 17 for more details about the **Magic Kingdom.**)

✔ **Epcot:** Built as an exposition of human achievement and new technology, **Epcot** is symbolized by *Spaceship Earth,* an item usually described as a huge golf ball. *Future World,* the first of Epcot's two sections, has innovative exhibits and rides. The other side of the park, *World Showcase,* has pavilions showcasing the culture of a dozen countries surrounding a lagoon. Allowing two days for the shows, rides, shops, and ethnic restaurants in **Epcot** is a good idea. (See Chapter 18 for more details about **Epcot.**)

This is the least attractive park for young kids, but the best one for adults.

✔ **Disney–MGM Studios:** WDW's third-to-evolve park is reminiscent of the Tinseltown of the '30s and '40s. It blends working studios with shows such as *Indiana Jones Stunt Spectacular* and thrill rides such as the *Twilight Zone Tower of Terror* and *Rock 'n' Roller Coaster.* You can tackle this part of **WDW** in one day. (See Chapter 19 for more details about **Disney–MGM Studios.**)

✔ **Disney's Animal Kingdom:** The newest Disney kid on the block is symbolized by the 14-story *Tree of Life,* which is to this park what *Cinderella's Castle* is to the **Magic Kingdom.** This wildlife exhibit, zoo, and theme park has shows such as *It's Tough to Be A Bug!* and rides such as *Dinosaur.* You won't have trouble touring this park in one day. (See Chapter 20 for more details about **Disney's Animal Kingdom.**)

Have time for more?

In addition to the big four, there are other parks and attractions in the Disney empire, including the following:

✔ **The Walt Disney Wide World of Sports** complex has a 7,500-seat baseball stadium that's the spring training home of the Atlanta Braves. It also has facilities for 30 other sports, including soccer, softball, basketball, and football.

✔ **Walt Disney World Speedway** has a stock car racing track that occasionally showcases races. The Speedway also hosts the *Richard Petty Driving Experience,* where you can ride shotgun or even drive a car at 145 mph. (If you're from Talladega or Darlington, you probably already know how.)

✔ **Three splashy parks** let you float along lazy streams, scream down waterslides, and more. They're especially appealing in summer, when it's 90 degrees and the humidity is 90 percent. The parks are **Blizzard Beach, River Country,** and **Typhoon Lagoon.**

We give you more info about these spots in Chapter 21.

Planet Disney also has several shopping (see Chapter 22) and nightlife (see Chapter 28) venues. For example:

✔ **Disney's BoardWalk** is a good place to stroll the waterfront, dine, dance, or catch a game in the sports bar.

> ✔ **Downtown Disney** comprises **Pleasure Island,** an adult nightclub district; **Downtown Disney Marketplace,** which features dining and shopping; **Disney West Side,** with more shopping, dining, *Cirque du Soleil,* the *House of Blues,* and **DisneyQuest.**

You can get additional information about all WDW properties by calling ☎ **407-824-4321** or visiting its Web site at http://disney.go.com/DisneyWorld/intro.html.

Want to go behind the scenes?

If you'd like to get an insider's look at how the Wizards of Diz make magic, **Behind-The-Scenes Tours** are the way to go. There are so many available options that the Disney folks sometimes have trouble remembering them all.

Here's a sampling. (*Note:* Most tours require park admission.)

> ✔ **Family Magic Tour:** This two-hour scavenger hunt brings you face to face with Disney characters at the **Magic Kingdom** ($25 adults, $15 kids 3 to 9).
>
> ✔ **Camp Disney:** This option (offered as either a half- or full-day excursion) features art, nature, and acting programs for 7- to 15-year-olds ($99 including lunch for two programs, $69 for one).
>
> ✔ **Hidden Treasures of World Showcase:** For $49 to $85 (two to five hours), you can explore the architectural and entertainment offerings at **Epcot.** For the five-hour tour, you won't need to purchase park admission if you depart immediately after your tour finishes; otherwise, you'll also have to pony up the admission fee. This tour is definitely more oriented to adults than to children.
>
> ✔ **Keys to the Kingdom:** Receive a four-hour orientation to the **Magic Kingdom** and a glimpse into the high-tech systems behind Mickey's magic for $45 a person (park admission is not included).
>
> ✔ **Backstage Magic:** At the top of the price chain — $199 per person — *Backstage Magic* is a seven-hour, self- and bus-propelled tour through areas of **Epcot,** the **Magic Kingdom,** and **Disney–MGM Studios** that aren't seen by mainstream guests. If you must know how things work, this tour is for you. You see mechanics repairing and building animatronic beings, and you also venture into **Magic Kingdom** tunnels that aren't only work areas but also paths for the cast to get from one area to another without fighting tourist crowds.

Reservations are recommended, and in many cases essential, for behind-the-scenes tours. You can call ☎ **407-939-8687** to make your reservations.

Finding Your Way to the Fun

If you're driving, Interstate 4's three Disney exits are clearly marked (though the exit numbers periodically change thanks to construction). You can't miss them unless you close your eyes.

Interstate 4 is woefully crowded, especially during rush hour (7–9 a.m. and 4–6 p.m.). In addition to the thousands of people heading for a day at the parks, thousands of locals are heading to work at them. So remember to factor possible delays into your time schedule.

Parking in the theme park lots costs $6 per day and is a snap. Just do what the people in the yellow-striped shirts ask you to do. In the Size XXXL **Magic Kingdom** lot, you'll probably want to ride the tram to the front gate (the trams are a hoot — the seats are made out of petrified plastic so if you lack posterior padding, you'll probably remember the ride for a while). At **Epcot, Disney–MGM,** and **Animal Kingdom,** walking is faster unless you have small children or sore feet.

Don't forget to make a note of your parking area and row. After a day spent standing in line, listening to screaming kids, and being tapped out by cash registers, you'll have a hard time remembering your name, not to mention where you parked.

Traveling the World

If you don't have a car or prefer to skip the drive, many area accommodations offer shuttles that are sometimes free but usually carry a fee.

If you're staying at a WDW resort, you can take the Walt Disney World Transportation System to get to the parks. It's a thorough system that includes buses, monorails, ferries, and water taxis serving the major parks from two hours prior to opening until two hours after closing. The system also serves **Downtown Disney, Typhoon Lagoon, River Country, Blizzard Beach, Pleasure Island, Fort Wilderness,** and other Disney resorts. Disney properties offer transportation to other area attractions as well, but you have to pay for it.

When you call Disney (see Chapter 7 or the individual park descriptions in Chapters 17 through 20), ask them to send you a **Walt Disney World Transportation Guide Map.** This map shows you everything in the kingdom and helps give you an idea of where your hotel is in relation to places that you want to visit. You can also look at the map of WDW's areas in this chapter to help orient yourself.

Preparing for Park Admission Costs

The number of admission options — from one- to multiday tickets — offered at **Walt Disney World** is staggering, and they're all expensive (not college-fund decimating, but close to it). Deciding which option will work best for you depends on the number of days you plan to spend in the parks, what parks and attractions you want to see, and whether you're staying at a WDW resort.

If you choose to buy a single-day admission pass, you're limited to seeing one Disney park; you can't hop to another one in the middle of the day. Disney has instituted a Bounce Back pass option, which enables you to buy a second — and discounted (it's about $5 cheaper) — single-day admission pass at the Guest Relations desk inside the park at the end of your first day. Discounted third- and fourth-day passes are also available under this option; it's a very complicated system, so ask at the Guest Relations desk of the park you're visiting if you're interested. The Bounce Back pass is a pretty good choice if you're staying off property, are only interested in seeing one or two parks, and will spend less than four days at **WDW**. Most people get the best value from four- and five-day passes.

If you're staying at any WDW resort or official hotel (see Chapter 8 for a list of official WDW hotels) you're also eligible for a money-saving *Unlimited Magic Pass,* which is priced according to the length of your stay. The pass also offers special perks, such as early park admission.

If you plan on visiting **Walt Disney World** more than one time during the year, inquire about a money-saving, annual pass ($324 adults, $275 children). For information on a host of WDW passes, see Table 16-1.

WDW considers everyone 10 and older an adult, and the prices that we give you don't include 6 percent sales tax. Also, know that sagging attendance the last few years has prompted **Disney** (as well as **Universal** and **SeaWorld**) to twice bump the single-day admission fee by $2 (it's now $46 for adults, $37 for kids 3 to 9), and there's no guarantee that it won't rise again by the time you arrive. You can get a discount on admission if you have a Magic Kingdom Club Gold Card or are a Disney Shareholder (see Chapter 3 for more information on these discount options).

The average family will spend $100 to $125 per person per day on park admissions, food, and souvenirs alone.

Table 16-1	Walt Disney World Prices	
Admission Option	*Adults*	*Kids (3–9)*
One-day, one-park admission	$46	$37
Four-day Park Hopper Plus Pass (unlimited admission to **Magic Kingdom, Epcot, Animal Kingdom,** and **Disney–MGM**)	$176	$142

Admission Option	Adults	Kids (3–9)
Five-day Park Hopper Plus Pass (unlimited admission as above, plus your choice of two admissions to **Typhoon Lagoon, River Country, Blizzard Beach, Pleasure Island,** or **Disney's Wide World of Sports)**	$236	$192
Six-day Park Hopper Plus Pass (unlimited admission as above, plus your choice of three admissions to **Typhoon Lagoon, River Country, Blizzard Beach, Pleasure Island,** or **Disney's Wide World of Sports)**	$266	$217
Seven-day Park Hopper Plus Pass (unlimited admission as above, plus your choice of four admissions to **Typhoon Lagoon, River Country, Blizzard Beach, Pleasure Island,** or **Disney's Wide World of Sports)**	$296	$242
One-day Pass to **Typhoon Lagoon** or **Blizzard Beach**	$28 adults	$22.50 kids
One-day Pass to **River Country**	$16	$12.50
One-day Pass to **Pleasure Island** Children are not admitted after 7 p.m.	$20, including tax	

Getting the Most Out of Your Trip to the World

The **Magic Kingdom, Epcot,** and **Disney–MGM Studios** usually open at 9 a.m. (sometimes up to 30 minutes earlier) throughout the year. They're open at least until 6 p.m. and often as late as 11 p.m. or midnight during peak periods (holidays and the summer months). **Animal Kingdom** opens at 8 a.m. and closes at 6 p.m. (slightly later during summer). It's a safe bet that the longer a park stays open, the more people will be visiting that day, so planning your schedule before you get to the park is essential. Unfortunately, hours of operation tend to vary, so it's always wise to call ☎ **407-W-DISNEY** ahead of time or to check the official calendar on the Disney Web site at http://asp. disney.go.com/disneyworld/db/seetheworld/hours/index.asp.

Beating the lines

Everyone's looking for a shortcut and no wonder — lines at Disney and the other big parks can be incredibly long and irritating if you come at the wrong time. Twenty minutes is considered cruising when it comes to line time and 45 minutes to one hour is common at the primo rides. In peak periods — summer, holidays, and other times kids are out of school — it can take longer than an hour to reach the front of the line and in three or four minutes, the ride is over.

Here are the best tips we can give you to beat the long lines:

- ✔ Come during off periods.

- ✔ Plan to spend the morning in one section, the afternoon in another. That way you won't waste time and energy running back and forth.

- ✔ Spend *two days* in the park if time and budget allow. Most rides and shows have signs telling you the length of the wait.

- ✔ Ask about or read the health and height restrictions before you get in line in order to avoid wasting time on a ride that isn't for you.

- ✔ Disney parks have tip boards that provide up-to-the-minute information on show times and ride waits. You can find the boards at Main Street, U.S.A. near *Coke Corner* in the **Magic Kingdom,** on Hollywood Boulevard near the entrance to *Sunset Boulevard* in **Disney–MGM Studios,** in the southwest quadrant of *Innoventions Plaza* near **Epcot's** *Future World Fountain,* and in *Safari Village* at **Animal Kingdom.**

Don't want to stand in line as long as other guests, yet not flush enough to hire a stand in? Disney parks have installed a ride-reservation system called FASTPASS. You go to the ride, feed your ticket into a turnstile, and get an assigned time to return. When you go back, you get into a shorter line and climb aboard. This express-lane feature is offered at more than a dozen (and counting) WDW rides. *Note:* This works for only one ride at a time; when you feed a ticket for a reservation, you must go on that ride before you make another FASTPASS reservation.

Utilize E-Ride tickets

The **Magic Kingdom's** *E-Ride Nights* are a bargain for travelers persistent enough to track them down. Only offered in the off season and with little advance notice, E-Ride Tickets cost $10 and give Disney resort guests three hours to ride the nine most popular rides — *Big Thunder Mountain Railroad, Space Mountain,* and *ExtraTERRORestrial Alien Encounter* to name a few — as many times you can. Better still, they only let 5,000 guests into the park during E-Ride Nights. The tickets are sold on a first-come, first-serve basis at the Guest Services desks in the Disney hotels and at the **Magic Kingdom** ticket window (you will be required to show a Disney Resort Guest ID and a valid multiday admission pass). Call ☎ **407-824-4321** for details.

Get a show schedule as soon as you enter the park

Getting a show schedule as soon as you enter the park is essential. Spend a few minutes looking over the schedule as you enter the park, noting where you need to be and when. Many of the attractions in **Walt Disney World** are nonstop, but others occur only at certain times or once a day. You can find maps and schedules at counters on one side or the other of the turnstiles, sometimes at both.

Avoiding the crowds

Crowds are a fact of life at **Walt Disney World,** but that doesn't necessarily mean you'll have to stand in long lines at all the rides and attractions. Forward thinkers can definitely decrease their risk of encountering a major swarm of tourists. Here are some facts to keep in mind as you plan your crowd-avoiding strategy:

✔ Mondays, Thursdays, and Saturdays are the busiest days in **The Magic Kingdom.** Tuesdays, Fridays, and Saturdays are the busy days at **Epcot.** Sundays and Wednesdays are crowded at **Disney–MGM Studios** and **Animal Kingdom.**

✔ Although it's not guaranteed, the parks tend to be less crowded during parts of April to May and October to November. You also have a better chance of avoiding crowds if you have the option to go in the middle of the week. Also, while most people steer clear on rainy days, the parks are less crowded and you won't miss much other than parades (most of the good stuff is indoors).

✔ Guests at Disney hotels get into some of the parks 90 minutes before the swarm during surprise mornings. Ask at your front desk, but these generally occur on each park's busiest days, except **Animal Kingdom,** which doesn't offer this feature.

✔ If you do dine at Disney, make Priority Seating arrangements early in the day to lock in the time you want to eat. (See Chapter 13 for more reservation information.)

✔ Before you leave home, prepare yourself for the long waits in line. Practice standing for an hour at a time, half of it in the sun, shuffling 30 inches every 2½ minutes.

Speaking of lines, while you're standing in them with nothing else to do, look at the faces around you. All of a sudden it doesn't look like magic, does it?

Chapter 17

The Magic Kingdom

● ●

In This Chapter

▶ Locating resources and services in the Magic Kingdom

▶ Checking out the fun: rides, shows, and attractions

▶ Planning for the parades and fireworks

▶ Setting your sites with a suggested itinerary

● ●

*I*f you have young kids or a soft spot for vintage Disney, make your way to this **WDW** signature park first. The **Magic Kingdom** is the most popular of Mickey's enterprises, attracting more than 40,000 people a day! (If you've stood in the beer or bathroom lines at Soldier Field or Yankee Stadium, you have a good idea of what you're in for.)

Proof of the staying power of the **Magic Kingdom** lies in the fact that the park has changed little over the years. Even new attractions, such as *ExtraTERRORestrial Alien Encounter* and *Timekeeper,* fall short of the 3D virtual dynamics you encounter at other theme parks, but the kingdom remains the fairest of them all.

Learning More about the Magic Kingdom

Yes, there are rides, shows, and characters galore, but there are also some practical items you'll need to know about the **Magic Kingdom.**

Arriving early and staying late

Although they say that the **Magic Kingdom** is open every day from 9 a.m. to 7 p.m., there are exceptions. In fact, the gates almost always open earlier than the official opening time. We recommend trying to get to the park early, but not just because of the bonus opening hours. Plotting an early arrival helps counter morning traffic and allows you a more relaxed pace to get from the parking lot to the fun. At the end of the day, closing usually is later than 7 p.m., especially in summer and during holidays. The **Magic Kingdom** may be open as late as midnight for certain special events. Call ☎ **407-W-DISNEY** for more details.

The Magic Kingdom

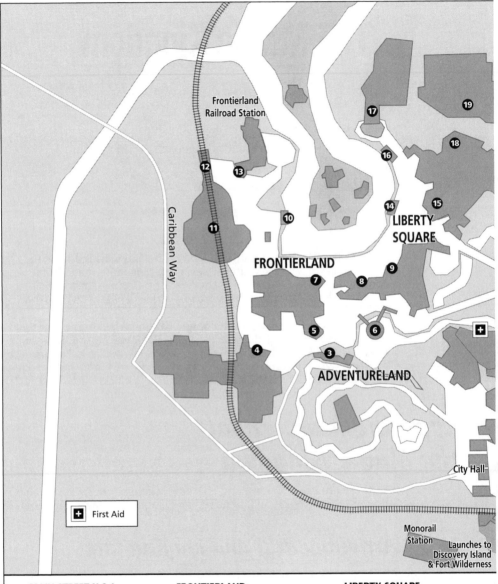

MAIN STREET U.S.A.
Main Street Cinema **2**
Walt Disney World Railroad **1**

ADVENTURELAND
Jungle Cruise **3**
Pirates of the Caribbean **4**
Swiss Family Treehouse **6**
Enchanted Tiki Room **5**

FRONTIERLAND
Big Thunder Mountain Railroad **13**
Country Bear Jamboree **7**
The Diamond Horseshoe
   Saloon Revue **9**
Frontierland Shootin' Arcade **8**
Splash Mountain **11**
Tom Sawyer Island **10**
Walt Disney World Railroad **12**

LIBERTY SQUARE
The Hall of Presidents **15**
The Haunted Mansion **17**
Liberty Belle Riverboat **14**
Mike Fink Keelboats **16**

FANTASYLAND
Castle Forecourt Stage **20**
Cinderella's Castle **21**
Cinderella's Golden Carousel **23**

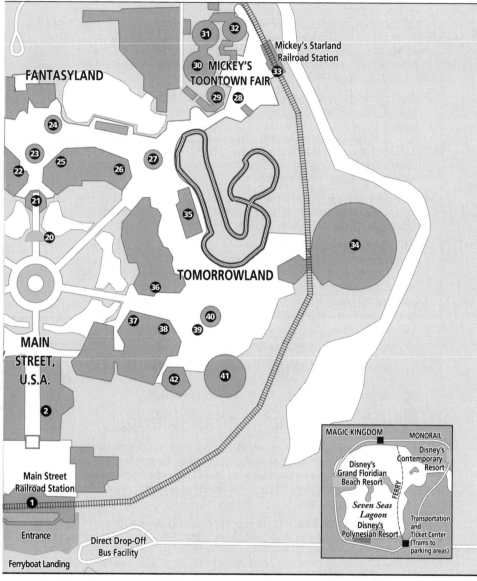

Locating special services and facilities

In case you forgot to bring essential items or need special assistance while at the park, here's a list of services and facilities that you may need:

✔ **ATMs** are located at the main entrance, the SunTrust Bank on Main Street, and in *Tomorrowland.* They honor cards from banks using the Cirrus, Honor, and Plus systems.

✔ You can find **baby-changing facilities,** which include rocking chairs and toddler-size toilets, next to the *Crystal Palace* at the end of *Main Street.* Of course, it's not the most cost-effective place to buy them, but you can purchase disposable diapers, formula, baby food, and pacifiers in the Gerber Baby Center. Changing tables are also located in the center as well as in all women's rest rooms and some of the men's.

✔ **Disposable cameras and film** are available throughout the park. Although once available, you can no longer rent 35mm cameras and camcorders at Disney parks.

✔ You can find **some of your favorite characters** at **Mickey's Toontown Fair.** In *Fantasyland,* look for them in the Fantasyland Character Fest and the Mad Tea Party (on the guide map and schedule that you get when entering the park). Characters also appear in *Frontierland* (the Splash Mountain Courtyard), *Main Street* (Town Square), and *Adventureland.*

✔ **The First Aid Center,** staffed by registered nurses, is located alongside *Crystal Palace* and the Gerber Baby Center.

✔ You can call ☎ **407-824-4321** or visit Disney's Web site, `http://disney.go.com/DisneyWorld/intro.html`, to obtain **additional information about WDW properties.**

✔ You can access **lockers** in an arcade underneath the Main Street Railroad Station. They cost $6, including a $2 refundable deposit.

✔ **Lost Children** are often taken to City Hall or the Baby Care Center, where lost children logbooks are kept. Making kids under 7 wear nametags is a smart idea, because reading name tags is often easier for park staffers than trying to drag a name from a frightened, crying youngin'.

✔ You can send **packages** from any store to Guest Relations in the Plaza area so that you can pick them up at the same place at day's end instead of hauling souvenirs around with you. If you're staying at the Disney resorts, you can have your packages sent straight to your rooms.

✔ **Pets,** except service animals, are prohibited in the parks, but you can board yours for the day or overnight at the Transportation and Ticket Center's kennels.

✔ Make your **Priority Seating** arrangements when you enter the park if you care about having a sit-down meal at a special venue. See Chapter 13 for details.

✔ You can find **a list of special shows** at counters just inside the park entrance, if they're not handed to you as you pass through the park's entrance. Study the *Entertainment Show Schedule,* which lists all the events of the day. You may find special concerts, otherwise unannounced visits from Disney characters, and information about fireworks and parades. Plan these events first, because they're the only ones you won't get a second chance to see.

✔ Rent **strollers** at the Stroller Shop near the entrance for $7 a day, including a $1 deposit.

✔ **Ticket Prices** (at printing time) for a one-day admission are $46 for adults, $37 for kids 3 to 9. See Chapter 16 for more information on park admission prices.

✔ You can rent **wheelchairs** at the gift shop to the left of the ticket booths at the Transportation and Ticket Center, or at the Stroller and Wheelchair Shop inside the main entrance to your right. Cost is $6 plus a $1 deposit; $30 and a $10 deposit for battery-run chairs.

✔ **The prices of consumables** are pretty much standard among Disney parks. The **Magic Kingdom** nails you to the tune of $1.55 for a soda, $2.50 for bottled water, $2.00 for an ice-cream bar, $2.50 for a pineapple float, and $1.15 for a cup of cocoa. Many of these are common prices at **Universal** and **SeaWorld,** as well.

The following section lists all of the fun and exciting attractions housed in the Magic Kingdom by land.

Index of attractions by land

Adventureland

Enchanted Tiki Room
Jungle Cruise
Pirates of the Caribbean
Swiss Family Treehouse

Fantasyland

Cinderella's Castle
Cinderella's Golden Carousel
Dumbo, the Flying Elephant
It's a Small World
Legend of the Lion King
Mad Tea Party
Many Adventures of Winnie the Pooh
Peter Pan's Flight
Snow White's Scary Adventures

Frontierland

Big Thunder Mountain Railroad
Country Bear Jamboree
Diamond Horseshoe Saloon Revue & Medicine Show
Frontierland Shootin' Arcade
Splash Mountain
Tom Sawyer Island

Liberty Square

Boat Rides
Hall of Presidents
Haunted Mansion

Main Street, U.S.A.
Main Street Cinema
Walt Disney World Railroad

Mickey's Toontown Fair
The Barnstormer at Goofy's Wiseacres Farm
Donald's Boat
Mickey's Country House
Minnie's Country House

Tomorrowland
Astro Orbiter
Buzz Lightyear's Space Ranger Spin
ExtraTERRORestrial Alien Encounter
Space Mountain
Timekeeper
Tomorrowland Speedway
Tomorrowland Transit Authority
Walt Disney World Carousel of Progress

Making the Rounds: The Magic Kingdom's Top Attractions

More than three dozen attractions, plus shops and restaurants, are included in this 107-acre package. The following description tour moves counterclockwise from the front gate, going through each of **Magic Kingdom's** seven lands.

Main Street, U.S.A.

Though it's considered one of the kingdom's lands, *Main Street* is more of an entry zone where you can lose yourself in the pleasant nostalgia of yesterday. We recommend passing through it quickly when you arrive. (Get thee to the popular stuff right away before the lines get too long!) You have to make a return voyage on Main Street when you cry "uncle" at the end of the day, so you can browse through the shops at a more leisurely pace before you exit the park. Here are a few highlights of *Main Street, U.S.A.*:

- ✔ **Main Street Cinema:** You don't have to pay admission to watch the theater's cartoons, including vintage films like 1928's *Steamboat Willie*. You will, however, have to stand — there are no seats.

- ✔ **Walt Disney World Railroad:** This steam-powered train makes a free 15-minute loop around the park, with stops in F*rontierland* and at *Mickey's Toontown Fair*. Other transportation along *Main Street* includes horse-drawn trolleys, horseless carriages, jitneys, buses, fire engines, and shoes — yours.

Tomorrowland

In 1994, Disney overhauled *Tomorrowland,* because its vision of the future when the park was designed in the 1960s was starting to look like Yesterville. Originally, Disney imagined a 21st century without computers or answering machines. Thanks to *Star Wars* director George Lucas and others, today's version is more high tech (aliens, robots, and video games, for example), which makes it especially attractive to older kids. Here's a sampling of what you'll find in *Tomorrowland:*

✔ **Astro Orbiter:** Astronaut wannabes, especially those who are 6 years old and under, love whirling high into the galaxy in colorful rockets. Unfortunately, the orbiter has ridiculously long lines, so skip it if you're on a tight timetable.

✔ **Buzz Lightyear's Space Ranger Spin:** On this ride, you go to infinity and beyond in an interactive space adventure in which you help Buzz defend the Earth's supply of batteries from the evil Emperor Zurg. You fly an XP-37 space cruiser armed with twin lasers and a joystick that's capable of spinning the craft. (Space Rangers who get motion sickness should sit this attraction out. There's enough space debris flying around without your help.) While you cruise through space, you collect points by blasting anything that smells remotely like Zurg. Your hits trigger light, sound, and animation effects. Together, you and Buzz trash the Zurgmeister and his evil henchmen, saving the galaxy.

✔ **ExtraTERRORestrial Alien Encounter:** George Lucas helped design this extremely popular ride, which is another white-knuckle treat. After you're locked and loaded, something goes terribly wrong with your teletransporter's aim and it sucks in a disgusting meat-eating creature from part of deep space. The lights alternate on and off, but mainly off, and the alien busts loose. Then, with only a strobe light showing you the way, you're treated to down drafts from its flapping wings, liquid spritzes (mucus if you'd prefer to think that way) on your face, and a little blast of hot breath on the back of your neck near the end.

Uh, no thanks. You guys have fun." No wonder JJ passed. This attraction has a legitimate child warning about it being dark and confining. The recommended age is 10 and older, and although some younger ones may like it, the age limit is a fair recommendation. The confinement part is a hard shoulder plate that lowers over your head to lock you into your tomb, er, seat.

✔ **Space Mountain:** Imagine a roller coaster. Then imagine it in the dark. This ride, *ExtraTERRORestrial Alien Encounter,* and *Big Thunder Mountain Railroad* (we talk about it in the "Frontierland" section, later in this chapter) are the three **Magic Kingdom** attractions that teens and other thrill junkies bolt for first, so get here early or save it for off hours, such as lunch or parade time. It's a classic roller coaster with plenty of plunging and spinning (though it seems faster, it never tops 28 mph). Grab a front seat for the best ride.

Wow, that's double awesome!" It's recommended for those 10 and older, but it's a bit tamer than some of the more modern thrill rides at **Disney–MGM Studios.** However, you must be 44 inches or taller to ride it, and there's a bailout area for those who decide to ditch at the last minute.

✔ **Timekeeper:** IMAX and CircleVision combine with Disney AudioAnimatronics on this 360° movie. *The Timekeeper* is a robotic version of Robin Williams, who has a sidekick named 9-Eyes. Williams' character takes you to the age of dinosaurs, then forward to medieval times, before he inadvertently kidnaps Jules Verne and yanks him on a reluctant trip into outer space.

"That was dumb." It's hard to argue. It *is* boring. You can't even use it as an excuse to rest your feet — you have to stand. Skip it unless you have time to kill.

✔ **Tomorrowland Speedway:** Kids, especially those ages 4 to 9, like slipping into these Indy-car knockoffs; but older children, teens, and adults find the lines and the steering less than stellar — especially those who are used to go-karts or the Malibu Grand Prix. The top speed is 7 mph and there's a thick iron bar separating your tires, so you're pretty much kept on track. You have to be a minimum of 52 inches tall to drive alone.

✔ **Tomorrowland Transit Authority:** This elevated people-mover winds around *Tomorrowland* and into *Space Mountain* on a lazy ride that encourages you to nod off if it's late in the day and you've covered 4 or 5 miles on the old pedometer. There's usually no wait.

✔ **Walt Disney World Carousel of Progress:** A Disney oldie retooled in 1993, this 22-minute show takes up too much time and space for its missing wow power. It uses AudioAnimatronics to trace the technological progress humanity made since the Gas Light era.

Mickey's Toontown Fair

Head off cries of "Where's Mickey?" by taking young kids (2 to 8) to this two-acre site as soon as you arrive. *Toontown* gives kids a chance to meet Disney characters, including Mickey, Minnie, Donald Duck, Goofy, and Pluto. The **Magic Kingdom's** smallest land is set in a whimsical collection of candy-striped tents. *The Barnstormer at Goofy's Wiseacres Farm* is a mini roller coaster designed to look and feel like a crop duster that flies slightly off course and right through the Goofmeister's barn. *Donald's Boat* is an interactive fountain with enough surprises to win squeals of joy (and relief on hot days). *Minnie's Country House* gives kids a chance to play in her kitchen, while *Mickey's Country House* features garden and garage playgrounds, plus a chance to meet the big cheese himself. And *Mickey's Toontown Hall of Fame* offers continuous meetings with Disney favorites.

Fantasyland

The rides and attractions in *Fantasyland* are based on the Disney movies you grew up with way back when, as well as some of the more recent additions to the Disney treasure chest of films. Young kids will want to spend lots of time here, and the attraction lines here ensure that you will. Here's a list of attractions in *Fantasyland:*

✔ **Cinderella's Castle:** This symbol of the **Magic Kingdom** sits at the end of *Main Street* in the center of the park. It's a favorite for family photos, and if you land at the right time, you can meet Cinderella. The interior has a lot of lovely murals and mosaics, but the attraction is visual — there's really nothing to do here but gawk.

✔ **Cinderella's Golden Carousel:** In the late 1960s, Disney imagineers found this old beauty — it was built in 1917 — and brought it to the **Magic Kingdom,** where it was restored in time for the park's opening. It's a delight for kids as well as carousel lovers of all ages. The organ plays — what else? — such Disney classics as "When You Wish Upon a Star" and "Twist and Shout."

✔ **Dumbo, the Flying Elephant:** This attraction doesn't do much for adrenaline-addicted older kids, but it's a favorite for ages 2 through 5. Dumbo's ears keep them airborne for a gentle, circular flight with some little dips. Most kids older than 6 will be humiliated if you even suggest that they ride. If your little ones are dying to ride Dumbo, get here as soon as you enter the park — the wait times for this ride are brutal!

✔ **It's a Small World:** Young kids and most parents love this attraction; teens and other adults find it a real gagger. Nevertheless, pay your dues — every Disney visitor ought to be required to ride it at least once. You glide around the world in small boats, meeting Russian dancers, Chinese acrobats, and French cancan girls — and every one of them sings a tune that eats its way into your brain and refuses to stop playing for months.

✔ **Legend of the Lion King:** Simba and friends star in this jungle stage show. Kids under 4 may get fussy; those over 10 may find it childish. If the wait isn't bad, it's a good place to park yourself for 30 minutes on a hot day. Showtimes are listed outside the theater and on the guide map that's available at the park entrance.

✔ **Mad Tea Party:** You make this tea party wild or mild, depending on how much you choose to spin the steering wheel in the teacup that's your chariot. The ride is based on *Alice in Wonderland* and is suitable for ages 4 and up.

✔ **The Many Adventures of Winnie the Pooh:** Pooh inadvertently created a small storm of protest and plenty of media coverage when the Wizards of Diz picked this ride to replace the popular *Mr. Toad's Wild Ride* last year. *The Many Adventures of Winnie the Pooh* features the cute-and-cuddly little fellow along with Eeyore, Piglet, and Tigger. You board a golden honey pot and ride through a storybook version of the Hundred-Acre Wood, keeping an eye out for heffalumps, woozles, blustery days, and the floody place. This has become a favorite of kids 2 to 8 and their parents.

✔ **Peter Pan's Flight:** Another popular ride among visitors under 8, it begins with a flight over London — adults find the nighttime tableau almost worth the line's long waits — in search of Captain Hook, Tiger Lily, and the Lost Boys. It's one of the old glide rides heralding the technology that was available when the **Magic Kingdom** was born in 1971.

✔ **Snow White's Scary Adventure:** Your journey takes you to the dwarfs' cottage and the wishing well, ending with the prince's kiss to break the evil spell. It's less scary now than it was years ago, when it was really dark, menacing, and surprisingly void of its namesake. She now appears in several friendly scenes, though kids younger than 5 still may get scared.

Liberty Square

Located between *Fantasyland* and *Frontierland,* this re-creation of Revolutionary-era America will infuse you with Colonial spirit shortly after you arrive. Younger guests may not appreciate the historical touches (such as the 13 lanterns symbolizing the original 13 colonies), but they'll delight in seeing a fife-and-drum corps and the opportunity to pose for a picture while locked in the stocks. Here are some other features of *Liberty Square:*

✔ **Boat Rides:** A steam-powered sternwheeler called the *Liberty Belle* and one (sometimes two) Mike Fink keelboats depart *Liberty Square* for scenic cruises along the Rivers of America. The passing landscape sort of looks like the Wild West. Both ply the same route and make a restful interlude for foot-weary park-stompers.

✔ **Hall of Presidents:** American-history buffs age 10 and older most appreciate this show, which can be a real squirmer for young children. The Hall is an inspiring production based on painstaking research. Pay special attention to the roll call of presidents. The animatronic figures are incredibly life-like — they fidget, whisper, and talk to the audience.

✔ **Haunted Mansion:** Although this park favorite has changed little over the years, it continues to offer great special effects and a grand atmosphere. You may chuckle at the corny tombstones lining the entrance, but the ride doesn't get much scarier than spooky music, eerie howling, and things that go bump in the night. (J.J. declined to rate this attraction, but he jumped at the pop-up ghosts.) The ride is best for those 6 and older.

Frontierland

Rustic log cabins, wooden sidewalks, swinging saloon doors, and other Old West trimmings are featured in *Frontierland,* located behind *Adventureland* and adjacent to *Liberty Square.* Attractions in *Frontierland* include the following:

✔ **Big Thunder Mountain Railroad:** The lines don't lie: This rocking railroad is a favorite of the **Magic Kingdom.** The ride is something of a low-grade roller coaster with a lot of corkscrew action. It has enough of a reputation that even first-time visitors make a beeline for it. So, if you can't get to it as soon as the park opens, FASTPASS (see Chapter 16 for more information on beating the long lines) is your best bet. Or, give it a try late in the day (many coaster veterans maintain that the ride is even better after dark) or when a parade pulls most visitors away from the rides.

"Yeeeee-haw!!" Then, "That was awesome!!!" *Thunder Mountain* bounces you around an old mining track, where you barely escape floods, a bridge collapse, rockslides, and other mayhem. (J.J. insists on riding it until everyone in the family turns green or at least begs for a change of scenery.) The ride can be too intense for kids under 6; riders must be at least 40 inches tall.

✔ **Country Bear Jamboree:** The stars of this 15-minute animatronic show are bears that croon country-and-western tunes. The Jamboree is a park standard — a show that's been around since Disney invented dirt. The audience gets caught up in the hand-clapping, knee-slapping, foot-stomping fun as Trixie, decked out in a satiny skirt, laments lost love as she sings "Tears Will Be the Chaser for Your Wine." Teddi Barra descends from the ceiling in a swing to perform "Heart We Did All That We Could," and Big Al moans "Blood in the Saddle."

"Pretty neat." (He was probably just happy to be out of the sun for a while.) He also couldn't resist the Disney vending machines that suckered us out of 50 cents for a flattened penny with a Disney logo. These folks are geniuses at getting everything out of your pockets except the lint. All in all, this attraction works best for the over-age-4 set.

✔ **Diamond Horseshoe Saloon Revue & Medicine Show:** Fancy ladies, honky-tonk pianos, and gamblers entertain you in a seven-times-a-day show that's fun for ages 5 and up. Marshall John Charles sings and banters with the audience, Jingles the Piano Man plays honky-tonk, and there's a magic act — all with lots of humor and audience participation (sit in the balcony if you're not the participating sort). The air-conditioned theater is a great place to dodge the heat, and at lunch, there's a sandwich menu.

✔ **Frontierland Shootin' Arcade:** Combining state-of-the-art electronics with a traditional shooting-gallery format, this arcade presents an array of 97 targets (slow-moving ore cars, buzzards, and gravediggers) in an 1850s boomtown. If you hit a tombstone, it may spin around and mysteriously change its epitaph. To keep things authentic, newfangled electronic firing mechanisms loaded with infrared bullets are concealed in genuine buffalo rifles. When you hit a target, you set off elaborate sound and motion gags. Fifty cents fetches 25 shots.

✔ **Splash Mountain:** If we had to pick one ride as the **Kingdom's** most popular, *Splash Mountain* is it. Although it really doesn't compete with **Sea World's** *Journey to Atlantis* (see Chapter 25) in terms of size and height, *Splash Mountain* is a nifty voyage on a flume that has a substantial vertical drop with a good splash factor (around 200 megatons worth of wet). If you're lucky enough to have some real heavyweights in the front seat, look for a little extra explosion on the 40 mph, five-story downhill.

In summer, this ride can provide sweet relief from the heat and humidity, but in cool weather, parents may want to protect their kids (and themselves) from a chill. *Splash Mountain* is recommended for ages 8 and older. Riders must be at least 44 inches tall.

✔ **Tom Sawyer Island:** You can explore *Injun Joe's Cave* and tackle swinging bridges that threaten to throw you into a gaping chasm. It's a good place for kids to lose a little energy and for moms and dads to relax and maybe indulge in a lunch or a snack at Aunt Polly's, which overlooks the river.

Adventureland

Adventureland is a left-turn off the end of *Main Street.* Kids can engage in swashbuckling behavior while walking through dense tropical foliage (complete with vines), or marauding through bamboo and thatch-roofed huts. Here's a list of some of the attractions at *Adventureland:*

✔ **Enchanted Tiki Room:** Upgraded over the years, the show's newest cast member is Iago of *Lion King* fame. This attraction is set in a large, hexagonal, Polynesian-style dwelling with a thatched roof, bamboo beams, and tapa-bark murals. Other players include 250 tropical birds, chanting totem poles, and singing flowers that whistle, tweet, and warble. The nine-minute show runs continuously throughout the day. Young children are most likely to appreciate this one, but so will nostalgic adults.

✔ **Jungle Cruise:** This ten-minute, narrated voyage on the Congo, Amazon, and Nile offers glimpses of animatronic animals, foliage, a temple-of-doom-type camp, and lots of surprises. The ride passes animatronic pygmies, pythons, elephants, rhinos, gorillas, and hippos that pop threateningly out of the water and blow snot — well, it could've been snot if they weren't robots — on you. This exhibit is nearly 30-years-old, which means it's pretty hokey sometimes.

✔ **Pirates of the Caribbean:** In this oldie-but-goodie, after walking through a long grotto, you board a boat headed into a dark cave. Therein, elaborate scenery and hundreds of animatronic figures re-create a Caribbean town overrun by a boatload of buccaneers. To a background of cheerful yo-ho-ho music, the sound of rushing waterfalls, squawking seagulls, and screams of terror, passengers pass through the line of fire into a raging raid and panorama of almost fierce-looking pirates swigging rum, looting, and plundering.

"I *don't* like that ride." We don't know what scared him when he was 3 or so (it's a pretty slow, calm, and tame attraction), but something did and stuck with him like flies on fried chicken. Therefore, we think kids 5 and under may find a pirate's life a bit too scary. Most kids 6 or older, though, will like it.

✔ **Swiss Family Treehouse:** The story of the shipwrecked Swiss Family Robinson comes alive in this attraction made for swinging, exploring, and crawling fun. It's simple and void of all that high-tech stuff that's popular in today's parks. Be prepared to stand on busy days in a slow-moving line. The attraction is also hard for some physically challenged visitors to navigate. Kids 4 to 12 have a blast.

Parades and fireworks

During fireworks and parades, Disney ropes off designated viewing spots for those with disabilities and their parties. Consult your park map or a park employee at least an hour before the parade or you may have trouble making it through the crowds to get to the designated spots.

Grab a guide map when you arrive in the kingdom. It includes an entertainment schedule that lists all kinds of special goings-on for the day. These include concerts, encounters with characters, holiday events, and other major happenings.

Disney excels at producing fanfare, and the parades and firework displays listed here are among the best of their kind in the world.

✔ **Disney's Magical Moments Parade:** With relatively few floats, all showcasing Disney movies, your interest in this parade depends on how much time you're willing to take away from the attractions. The parade includes lots of dancers and extras, but here's a chance to dodge the mainstream and hit a primo ride while the crowds are thin. If you decide to go, go early — seats on the curb disappear fast. Also, don't forget something soft for your fanny. *Magical Moments* is at 3 p.m. year-round. It runs from *Main Street* to *Liberty Square* and *Frontierland.*

✔ **Fantasy in the Sky Fireworks:** This is an explosive display that's held nightly during the summer and on holidays, as well as selected evenings the rest of the year (consult your schedule). Before the display Tinker Bell flies her magical flight from *Cinderella's Castle.* Suggested viewing areas are *Liberty Square, Frontierland,* and *Mickey's Toontown Fair.* Disney hotels close to the park (**Grand Floridian, Polynesian, Contemporary,** and **Wilderness Lodge**) also offer excellent views.

✔ **Main Street Electrical Parade:** This Disney favorite, which ran for 20 years until 1991, has been brought back with the same floats and costumes that were used for a while at **Disneyland.**

(This parade's WDW predecessor, *SpectroMagic,* was sent to **Disneyland Paris.**) Show times vary with seasons. The 20-minute *Electrical Parade* is held every night during summer and other peak times, Thursday through Saturday in the off season. Twenty-seven batteries fuel its 576,000 lights.

Suggested Itineraries

We provide these itineraries to give you a couple ways of seeing the park. They're designed to be time efficient, but you can add or subtract rides and shows based on your tastes.

Planning a day in the Magic Kingdom with kids

Here's an itinerary for a day in the Magic Kingdom with your young ones.

✔ Consider making a Priority Seating reservation at **Cinderella's Royal Table** (☎ 407-939-3463) if you want to have a sit-down dinner in the park (see Chapter 14 for more details about this restaurant).

✔ If you have very young kids, take the first train out of the Walt Disney World Railroad Station on *Main Street* and get off at **Mickey's Toontown Fair,** where tots can meet Mickey and the gang, ride a mini roller coaster, and visit the Mouse's house.

✔ Go west to **Fantasyland.** Ride *Dumbo, the Flying Elephant; Peter Pan's Flight; It's a Small World; The Many Adventures of Winnie the Pooh;* and *Cinderella's Golden Carousel.* If you're in the mood for a show, see *Legend of the Lion King.*

✔ At lunchtime, you can stop at **Cosmic Ray's Starlight Café** for chicken, a burger, or soup before taking in the stage show.

✔ If you have preteens, skip *Fantasyland* or at least delay it in favor of *Tomorrowland,* where older kids will love thrill rides such as *The ExtraTERRORestrial Alien Encounter, Buzz Lightyear's Space Ranger Spin,* and *Space Mountain.*

✔ If the *Hall of Presidents* and *Haunted Mansion* appeal to you, go to *Liberty Square;* otherwise, head to *Frontierland* for *Splash Mountain* and *Big Thunder Mountain Railroad.*

✔ If time permits, most ages will enjoy a trip to *Adventureland* for *Pirates of the Caribbean, the Jungle Cruise,* and the *Swiss Family Treehouse.*

✔ Watch the *Main Street Electrical Parade* and *Fantasy in the Sky Fireworks* to end your day.

Planning a day in the Magic Kingdom for teenagers and adults

If you no longer belong to the kiddie set, here's a game plan for touring the best the park has to offer you.

- ✔ Consider making a Priority Seating reservation at **Cinderella's Royal Table** (☎ 407-939-3463) if you want a sit-down dinner in the park (see Chapter 14).

- ✔ Beat a path for *Tomorrowland* to ride *Space Mountain, Buzz Lightyear's Space Ranger Spin,* and *The ExtraTERRORestrial Alien Encounter.*

- ✔ Cut through the center of the park to *Frontierland,* where *Splash Mountain, Big Thunder Mountain Railroad,* and *Country Bear Jamboree* are crowd pleasers.

- ✔ The Liberty Tree Tavern is a good lunch stop. Before leaving *Liberty Square,* visit *The Haunted Mansion* and *The Hall of Presidents.*

- ✔ In *Adventureland,* ride the *Jungle Cruise* and *Pirates of the Caribbean,* then watch the show in the *Enchanted Tiki Room.*

- ✔ Bring the day to a rousing conclusion with the *Main Street Electrical Parade* and *Fantasy in the Sky Fireworks.*

Chapter 18

Epcot

· ·

In This Chapter

▶ Highlighting Epcot basics

▶ Experiencing *Future World*

▶ Planning for the *World Showcase*

▶ Examining suggested itineraries

· ·

*G*rab a big pot. Stir in equal measures of theme park and museum, add movies, street performers, and interactive exhibits. What do you have? **Epcot.** Think of **Epcot** as a trip around the world — without the jet lag, though some say it's just as draining if you try to experience it in one day.

Walt Disney wanted this "Experimental Prototype Community Of Tomorrow" to be a high-tech city of 20,000 residents. But, when it was built 15 years after his death, it was more theme park than community and the name was shortened to an acronym, **Epcot,** because, well, it fits on one line in the snazzy brochures that Disney hands out.

If the **Magic Kingdom** is every kid's dream, **Epcot** isn't. **Epcot** is suited for the imaginations and fantasies of older children and adults. It's the least kid-friendly of all the Disney parks. If you have wee ones, we recommend skipping it. If, on the other hand, you have older kids or an inquiring mind yourself, we suggest a two-day visit because it's so big and varied. *World Showcase* lets you experience exotic, far-flung lands without a passport; you can stroll St. Mark's Square in Venice or dine at a sidewalk cafe while munching some of the best pastries this side of Paris. In *Future World,* you can touch, taste, and catch a wave into the third millennium as you find out about cutting-edge technology and the latest thrill rides.

The Essentials: Discovering What You Need to Know about Epcot

Before helping you set off for Epcot's attractions, we should get a few practical matters out of the way.

- **ATM machines** accept cards from banks using Cirrus, Honor, and Plus. You can find them at the front of the park, in *Germany*, and on the bridge between *World Showcase* and *Future World*.

- **The baby-changing area** for Epcot is located in the Baby Care Center near the Odyssey Center in *Future World*. It sells disposable diapers, formula, baby food, and pacifiers. There are changing tables in all women's rest rooms and some men's rooms.

- You can buy **disposable cameras and film** throughout the park. Although once available, you can no longer rent 35mm cameras and camcorders at Disney parks.

- Registered nurses staff the **First Aid Center.** It's located near the Odyssey Center in *Future World*.

- **Epcot's hours** are usually 9 a.m. to 9 p.m., but it's open as late as midnight sometimes.

- You can call ☎ 407-824-4321 or visit Disney's Web site, `http://disney.go.com/DisneyWorld/intro.html`, to obtain **additional information about WDW properties.**

- **Lockers** are located west of *Spaceship Earth,* outside the Entrance Plaza, and in the Bus Information Center by the bus parking lot. The cost is $3 a day, plus a $2 deposit.

- **Lost children** are usually taken to Earth Center or the Baby Care Center. Kids under 7 should wear name tags.

- You can send **packages** from any store in the park to Guest Relations in the Plaza area, allowing you to pick them up all at once at the end of the day. This service is free. Allow three hours for delivery. If you're staying at a Disney resort, you can have your packages sent directly to your rooms.

- You can arrange **pet care** accommodations for $6 a day at kennels just outside the Entrance Plaza at **Epcot.** You must show proof of vaccination.

- You can make **Priority Seating** arrangements (see Chapter 13) at the World Key Terminals just inside the entrance. If you know where you want to eat ahead of time, call ☎ 407-939-3463.

✔ Rent **strollers** from stands east of the Entrance Plaza and at World Showcase's International Gateway. The cost is $7, including a $1 refundable deposit.

✔ **Tickets** to **Epcot** cost $46 for a one-day adult admission, $37 for kids 3 to 9. See Chapter 16 for other options.

✔ Rent **wheelchairs** inside the Entrance Plaza to your left, to the right of ticket booths at the Gift Shop, and at *World Showcase's* International Gateway. They cost $6, including a $1 refundable deposit. Electric chairs cost $30 a day, including a $10 deposit.

✔ The **prices of consumables** are pretty much standard among Disney parks. **Epcot** will nail you to the tune of $1.55 for a soda, $2.50 for bottled water, $2.00 for an ice cream bar, $2.50 for a pineapple float, and $1.15 for a cup of cocoa. Many of these are common prices at **Universal** and **SeaWorld,** as well.

Table 18-1 provides a handy index of **Epcot's** fascinating attractions by park land.

Index of attractions by land

Future World

Innoventions
Journey Into Imagination
The Land
The Living Seas
Spaceship Earth
Test Track
Universe of Energy
Wonders of Life

World Showcase

American Adventure
Canada
China
France
Germany
Italy
Japan
Mexico
Morocco
Norway
United Kingdom

Epcot

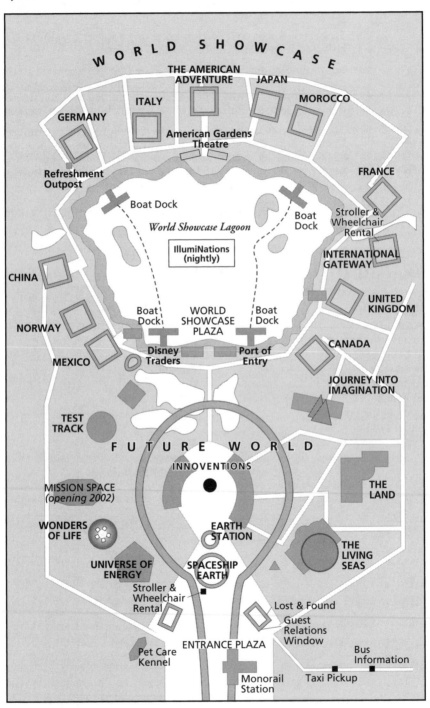

Touring Epcot's Top Attractions

Epcot's 260 acres are vibrantly landscaped, so stop and smell the roses on your way through its two major sections, *Future World* and *World Showcase.*

Epcot is also big enough that walking around it can be exhausting (some people say **Epcot** stands for "Every Person Comes Out Tired"). If you don't spend much time lingering in the *World Showcase,* you can see all of Epcot in one day. A boat launch runs from the edge of *Future World* to *Germany* or *Morocco.* There are also double-decker buses circling the *World Showcase Promenade,* making stops at *Norway, Italy, France,* and *Canada.*

Future World

Most visitors enter **Epcot** through *Future World,* the northern section of the park (although it appears on the bottom of your guide map). *Spaceship Earth,* that thing that looks like a giant, silver golf ball meant for a club the size of Gibraltar, centers *Future World.* Exhibits here focus on discovery, scientific achievements, and technology in areas spanning from energy to undersea exploration.

Innoventions

The crescent-shaped buildings to your right and left, just beyond Spaceship Earth, showcase cutting-edge technology and future products. Robot host Tom Morrow 2.0 welcomes you to nine exhibits, including three-dimensional body images, a huge, high-definition TV screen, and a place where you can create video e-mail to send to your friends. Kids love *Video Games of Tomorrow* — 34 stations sponsored by Sega. There's also an offbeat game show, *The Broadband Connection,* that explains communications in a way a 7-year-old can understand; an area exploring the future of the Internet for kids; and another that gives you a look at cars of tomorrow. It's overwhelmingly commercial, but it's hard to resist the fun.

To the right, the *Discovery Center* includes an area where guests can find out more about **Epcot** attractions, in particular, and **Walt Disney World,** in general. For instance, if after visiting *The Land* you'd like to learn more about hydroponics, they can print out an information sheet for you.

Journey into Imagination

Even the fountains at this attraction are magical — shooting water snakes through the air. There are also a number of high-tech gadgets, but the main attraction is the 3D *Honey I Shrunk the Audience* show, based on the Disney film *Honey I Shrunk the Kids.* Inside, mice terrorize you and, after you're shrunk, a large cat adds to the trauma; then, a giant 5-year-old gives you a good shaking. Vibrating seats and creepy tactile effects enhance the dramatic 3D action. Finally, everyone returns to proper size — everyone, that is, but the family dog, which creates a final surprise.

"I liked that part where the dog sniffed us and acted like he was going to . . ." Well, that's enough from J.J. on that front. We'll save the surprise.

The LandPavilion

If agriculture doesn't interest you, skip *Living with the Land,* a 13-minute boat ride through a simulated rain forest, an African desert, and the American plains. New farming methods and experiments ranging from hydroponics to plants growing in simulated Martian soil are showcased in real gardens. A 45-minute *Behind the Seeds* walking tour is also offered daily, and costs $7 for adults and $4 for kids 3 to 9. Sign up at the Green Thumb Emporium near the entrance to Food Rocks.

Live footage and animation mix in *Circle of Life,* a 15-minute, 70mm motion picture based on *The Lion King.* According to the story line, Timon and Pumbaa are building a monument to the good life called Hakuna Matata Lakeside Village, but their project, as Simba points out, is damaging the savanna for other animals. The environmental message of the film is delivered in an enjoyable manner.

Mock rock performers serenade you with songs about nutrition in *Food Rocks.* Neil Moussaka sings "Don't Take My Squash Away from Me," the Peach Boys harmonize in "Good Nutrition," and Excess, a trio of obnoxious hard rockers, counters by extolling the virtues of junk food.

The Living Seas

The Living Seas pavilion has a 5.7 million-gallon aquarium filled with more than 4,000 sharks, barracudas, rays, dolphins, and other reef fish. You start off with a film demonstrating the formation of the Earth and the seas as a means to support life. You then descend to *Seabase Alpha,* where a short ride offers you stunning views of the pavilion's marine residents. After the ride, you're free to explore an ocean research base of the future. *The Living Seas* also has two manatees living in terribly tight quarters.

Children under 12 soon lose interest at this attraction, unless they're intensely interested in the sea.

Epcot's DiveQuest program allows certified divers to take part in a 3½hour program that includes a 30- to 40-minute scuba dive in the *Living Seas* aquarium for $140. For information, call ☎ **407-937-8687.**

Spaceship Earth

Epcot's icon houses an attraction of the same name. It includes a slow-track journey back to the roots of communications. The 15-minute ride begins with an audio-animatronic Cro-Magnon shaman recounting the story of a hunt while others record it on cave walls. It advances to ancient Egypt, where hieroglyphics adorn temple walls, then to the Phoenician and Greek alphabets, the Gutenberg printing press, the Renaissance, and eventually you're beamed into outer space.

"What's next?" Our sentiments, exactly. This is a real yawner. A lot of folks stop at Spaceship Earth first thing in the morning as they arrive. If you decide you must do it, you can avoid long lines by saving it until later in the day, when, in most cases, you can walk right in.

Test Track

General Motors and Disney sank $60 million into this long-time-coming marvel of GM engineering and Disney imagineering. You can wait in line for more than an hour during peak periods, so consider the FASTPASS option (see Chapter 16 for more information about beating the long lines). During the last 30 minutes of your wait, you snake through displays about corrosion, crash tests, and more. The five-minute ride follows a track that looks like an actual highway. It includes braking tests, a hill climb, and tight S-curves in a six-passenger "convertible." There's also a 12-second burst of speed that gets your heart pumping to the tune of 65 mph.

"That was way fast. Maybe we can do it again, but not this time." In fact, it may be a bit too intense for those under 10.

Universe of Energy

Ellen's Energy Adventure, a 32-minute ride, features comedian Ellen DeGeneres as an energy expert tutored by Bill Nye the Science Guy to be a _Jeopardy!_ contestant. An animated movie depicts the Earth's molten beginnings, its cooling process, and the formation of fossil fuels. You then move back — in solar-powered cars that seat several hundred, no less — 275 million years into an eerie, storm-wracked landscape of the Mesozoic Era, a time of violent geological activity. Giant audio-animatronic dragonflies, pterodactyls, dinosaurs, earthquakes, and streams of molten lava threaten you before entering a steam-filled tunnel deep in the bowels of a volcano. The show ends on an upbeat note — a vision of an energy-abundant future and Ellen as a new _Jeopardy!_ champion.

Wonders of Life

The _Making of Me,_ starring Martin Short, is a captivating 15-minute motion picture combining live action with animation and spectacular in utero photography to create the sweetest introduction imaginable to the facts of life. Short travels back in time to witness his parents as children, their meeting at a college dance, their wedding, and their decision to have a baby. Along with him, we view his development inside his mother's womb and witness his birth.

The presentation may prompt some questions from young children; therefore, we recommend it for ages 10 and up. And, on a different note, the wait to get into the tiny theater may feel like nine months!

Didn't get your fill of being shrunk in _Journey Into Imagination?_ Step into _Body Wars,_ where you're reduced to the size of a cell for a medical rescue mission inside the human immune system. This motion-simulator takes you on a wild ride through gale-force winds in the lungs and pounding heart chambers.

Engineers designed this ride from the last row of the car, so that's the best place to sit to get the most bang for your buck.

(Upon seeing his first white-blood cell) "That's disgusting." Then, near the end of the first half, "Mayday, Mayday." Finally, "That was pretty neat." He was luckier than one of our co-pilots. At the first shake, she giggled. At the first rattle, it became a nervous laugh. At the roll, she started frantically fanning herself. At the exit doors, she looked ready to lose her lunch.

In the funny *Cranium Command,* Buzzy, an audio-animatronic brain-pilot-in-training, is charged with the seemingly impossible task of controlling the brain of a typical 12-year-old boy during traumas that include meeting a girl and a run-in with the school principal. The boy's body parts are played by well-known actors and comedians, including Charles Grodin, Jon Lovitz, and Dana Carvey.

At *Coach's Corner,* you can have your tennis, golf, or baseball swing analyzed by experts, while the *Sensory Funhouse* offers you a chance to test your perceptions. You can also work out on a video-enhanced exercise bike, get a computer-generated evaluation of your health habits, and take a video voyage to investigate the effects of drugs on your heart.

World Showcase

Those who like *World Showcase* (J.J. isn't among them) are mainly adults or older kids with an appreciation of world history and cultural shows. Its 11 miniature nations open at 11 a.m. daily and surround a 40-acre lagoon. All the countries have authentic, indigenous architecture, landscaping, background music, restaurants, and shops. Art exhibits, dance performances, and films are among the area's strongest selling points. All the employees in each pavilion are natives of the country represented.

Most of these nations offer some kind of live entertainment throughout the day. You may see Chinese lion dancers and acrobats, Caledonian bagpipers, Mexican mariachi bands, Moroccan storytellers and belly dancers, Italian living statues and stilt walkers, and colonial fife and drum groups. Check your guide map/show schedule when you enter the park.

You can also find schedules posted near the entrance to each country.

Coming soon

Disney is working with Compaq and NASA on a new out-of-this-world attraction called *Mission: Space.* Located in the Old Horizons center at **Epcot,** its headliner will be a motion simulator like those used by astronauts training for missions. (Think liftoff, g-force, and weightlessness as you visit another planet.) The $150 to $200 million exhibit, not scheduled to open until 2002, will also feature interactive games and programs about space exploration.

The American Adventure

The American Adventure's 29-minute *CliffsNotes* dramatization of U.S. history utilizes a 72-foot rear-projection screen, rousing music, and a large cast of lifelike audio-animatronic figures, including narrators Mark Twain and Ben Franklin. You follow the voyage of the *Mayflower,* watch Jefferson writing the *Declaration of Independence,* and witness Matthew Brady photographing a family that the Civil War is about to divide. You can also witness the stock market crash of 1929, Pearl Harbor, and the *Eagle* heading toward the moon. Teddy Roosevelt discusses the need for national parks; Susan B. Anthony speaks out on women's rights; Frederick Douglass discusses slavery; and Chief Joseph remarks on the situation of Native Americans. The *Voices of Liberty* singers perform folk songs in the Main Hall while you're waiting for the show.

Canada

The pavilion's highlight attraction is *O Canada!* — a dazzling, 18-minute, Circle-Vision 360 film that shows our northern neighbor's scenic wonders, from sophisticated Montréal to the thundering flight of thousands of snow geese departing the St. Lawrence River.

The architecture and landscape in *Canada* include a mansard-roofed replica of Ottawa's nineteenth-century French-style Château Laurier (here called the Hôtel du Canada) and an Indian village complete with a rough-hewn log trading post and 30-foot totem-pole replicas. A steep mountain, cascading waterfall, and forest of evergreens, stately cedars, maples, and birch trees reflect the Canadian wilderness.

China

Epcot's version of this Asian land includes a half-size replica of Beijing's Temple of Heaven, a summer retreat for Chinese emperors. Gardens simulate Suzhou, with miniature waterfalls, fragrant lotus ponds, and bamboo groves.

The highlight is *Wonders of China,* a 20-minute, Circle-Vision 360 film that explores 6,000 years of dynastic and communist rule as well as the breathtaking diversity of China's landscape. The show also includes scenes of the Great Wall, a performance by the Beijing Opera, the Forbidden City, the rice terraces of Hunan Province, the Gobi Desert, and the tropical rain forests of Hainan Island. There's also a gallery of Chinese art, *The House of the Whispering Willows.*

France

This pavilion focuses on France's *belle epoque* (Beautiful Age) period — 1870 to 1910 — when French art, literature, and architecture ruled. You enter the pavilion via a replica of the beautiful cast-iron Pont des Arts footbridge over the Seine, and the grounds include a 1/10-scale model of the Eiffel Tower, which was built from Gustave Eiffel's original blueprints.

The premiere event in the *France* pavilion is *Impressions de France*. Shown in a palatial, sit-down theater à la Fontainebleau, this 18-minute film is a scenic journey through diverse French landscapes projected on a vast, 200° wraparound screen and enhanced by the music of French composers.

Germany

Enclosed by castle walls, *Germany* offers 'wursts, oompah bands, and a rollicking atmosphere. The clock tower is embellished with whimsical glockenspiel figures that herald each hour with quaint melodies. The pavilion's outdoor Biergarten was inspired by medieval Rothenberg and features a year-round Oktoberfest, while sixteenth-century building facades replicate a merchant's hall in the Black Forest and the town hall in Frankfurt's Römerberg Square.

If you're a model-train fanatic or visiting with young kids, don't miss the exquisitely detailed version of a small Bavarian town, complete with working train station, located between *Germany* and *Italy.*

Italy

One of the prettiest *World Showcase* pavilions, *Italy* lures you over an arched stone footbridge to a replica of Venice's intricately ornamented pink-and-white Doge's Palace. Other architectural highlights include the 83-foot bell tower of St. Mark's Square, Venetian bridges, and a central piazza enclosing a version of Bernini's Neptune Fountain. A troupe of street actors often performs a contemporary version of sixteenth-century comedy routines in the piazza.

Japan

The central pagoda is modeled after Nara's Horyuji Temple, built in A.D. 700. The building to its right is a replica of Kyoto's Imperial Palace. If you have some leisure time, enjoy the pebbled footpaths, and other traditional touches. Exhibits ranging from eighteenth-century Bunraki puppets to samurai armor are displayed in the *White Heron Castle,* a replica of the Shirasagi-Jo, a seventeenth-century fortress.

Make sure that you include a performance of traditional Japanese music and dance in your schedule. It's one of the best shows in the *World Showcase.*

Mexico

The music of marimbas and mariachi bands hit you as you approach this festive showcase, fronted by a towering Mayan pyramid modeled on the Aztec temple of Quetzalcoatl (God of Life) and surrounded by dense Yucatán jungle landscaping. Inside the pavilion, you find a museum of pre-Colombian art and artifacts.

El Rio del Tiempo (River of Time) is an eight-minute cruise through Mexico's past and present. Passengers get a close-up look at the Mayan pyramid and the erupting Popocatepetl volcano. Dance performances focusing on the cultures of Mayan, Toltec, Aztec, and colonial Mexico are presented in film segments and by an audio-animatronic cast in vignettes ranging from a Day of the Dead skeleton band to children breaking a piñata.

Morocco

The *Medina* (old city), entered via a replica of an arched gateway, leads to a traditional Moroccan home and the narrow, winding streets of the *souk,* a bustling marketplace where all manners of handcrafted merchandise is on display. The *Medina's* rectangular courtyard centers on a replica of the ornately tiled Najjarine Fountain in Fez, the setting for musical entertainment. There's also a replica of the Koutoubia Minaret, the prayer tower of a twelfth-century mosque in Marrakesh.

The *Royal Gallery of Arts and History* contains an ever-changing exhibit of Moroccan art, and the Center of Tourism has a continuous, three-screen slide show. A guided tour of the pavilion, *Treasures of Morocco,* runs from noon to 7 p.m. daily.

Norway

The *Norway* pavilion's stave church, styled after the thirteenth-century Gol Church of Hallingdal, features changing exhibits. A replica of Oslo's fourteenth-century Akershus Castle, next to a cascading woodland waterfall, is the setting for the pavilion's featured restaurant, Akershus. Other buildings simulate the red-roofed cottages of Bergen and the timber-sided farm buildings of the Nordic woodlands.

Norway includes a two-part attraction. *Maelstrom,* a boat ride in a dragon-headed Viking vessel, travels Norway's fjords and mythical forests to the music of Peer Gynt. Along the way, you see polar bears prowling the shore and are then turned into frogs by trolls that cast a spell on your boat. The watercraft crashes through a narrow gorge and spins into the North Sea, where a storm is in progress (don't worry — this is a relatively calm ride). The storm abates, a princess' kiss turns you into a human again, and you disembark to a tenth-century Viking village to view the 70mm film *Norway.* It's an excellent historical and cultural lesson.

United Kingdom

The *U.K.* pavilion evokes Merry Olde England through its *Britannia Square* — a formal London-style park complete with copper-roofed gazebo bandstand, a stereotypical red phone booth (it really works!), and a statue of the Bard. Four centuries of architecture are represented along quaint cobblestone streets; troubadours and minstrels entertain in front of a traditional British pub where you can grab a pint.

Don't miss the Old Globe Players who present delightfully wacky performances of Shakespeare in the square. The performances include a lot of audience participation and you may be tapped to try your hand at Hamlet — forsooth!

Ending Your Day

Epcot's Millennium Celebration ends December 31, 2000 and with it a special fireworks program, but you won't be disappointed by the usual Epcot end-of-day fanfare.

IllumiNations is a blend of fireworks, lasers, and fountains in a display that's signature Disney. The show is well worth suffering the crowds that flock to the parking lot after the show.

This display is very popular and draws a lot of people, but there are tons of good viewing points around the lagoon. However, it's best to stake your claim to a primo place a half-hour or so before show time, which is listed in your entertainment schedule.

Making the Most of Your Day (s) at Epcot

There's no *one way* to see **Epcot,** and the two itineraries that we offer you in this section are merely options. You can ad lib the following itineraries based on the activities that most appeal to you.

Barnstormer's special: Experiencing Epcot in one day

What an adventurer (or masochist) you are — tackling *Future World* and *World Showcase* in a single bound! Because **Epcot** truly needs two days, you have to move fast and avoid loitering. Here are some tips to help you do so:

- As you enter the park, ask which rides accept FASTPASS (see Chapter 16 for details about bypassing the long lines) and go straight to any that you're dying to ride. If the lines are short, don't bother with FASTPASS.

- Consider making a Priority Seating reservation for lunch and dinner at the World Key terminals in Innoventions East. If you want to arrange seating in advance, call ☎ **407-939-3463.** We suggest the Coral Reef restaurant in *The Living Seas* or the San Angel Inn in the *World Showcase's Mexico* exhibit for lunch; Akershus in *Norway* or the Rose & Crown Pub in the *United Kingdom* for dinner (see Chapter 14 for more options).

- *Future World,* near the front of the park, is the first of **Epcot's** two areas to open in the morning, so start your day there. Skip *Spaceship Earth* at least for now. It's closest to the entrance and that big golf-ball attracts most guests as they enter. Go straight to

Body Wars, which is in the *Wonders of Life* pavilion to the left of *Spaceship Earth,* and *Test Track,* the newest thrill ride, which is just beyond it. Then do a buttonhook west to *Journey Into Imagination* and see *Honey, I Shrunk the Audience.*

✔ Visit the *Living Seas,* where you can watch the huge aquarium forever. But don't. You picked the one-day option and there isn't time.

✔ Head to *World Showcase* next. In our opinion, it's the best part of **Epcot.** *China* has a fabulous 360° movie, *Germany's* Biergarten blares with oompah music, and *Norway* delivers a history lesson and boat ride called *Maelstrom.* Also, take in the show and concerts at the *American Adventure.*

✔ Don't forget *IllumiNations.*

Whew! You made it in record time.

Stop to smell the roses: Exploring Epcot in two days

Ignore the one-day itinerary covered in the previous section, but consider our advice about making Priority Seating reservations and eating at our in-park dining suggestions.

The basic plan of attack for a two-day visit is to hit *Future World* and all of its rides and exhibits on your first day, and then cruise to *World Showcase* the next.

Be sure to ask which rides have FASTPASS (see Chapter 16).

Day one

✔ Skip *Spaceship Earth,* because that's where 75 percent of the park's visitors go first. Head to *Body Wars,* which is in the *Wonders of Life* pavilion to the left of the *Spaceship Earth,* and then visit the *Cranium Command* and *The Making of Me* shows in the same area. *Test Track,* the park's newest thrill ride, is just beyond the pavilion; it'll be crowded, so go get a FASTPASS and come back later. Double back to *Universe of Energy.*

✔ Spend time in *Innoventions,* with its medical, communications, and Internet themes. Enjoy the peaceful tours through the *Living Seas* and *The Land,* then cut to *Journey Into Imagination* for the *Honey, I Shrunk the Audience* ride.

✔ If time permits, try *Spaceship Earth* now that the lines are shorter and return to any rides or shows that you really enjoyed.

Day two

✔ If you arrive when the park opens, go to any *Future World* rides or shows that you missed on your first day or want to repeat. Or, sleep a little later and arrive in time to take up your position at the Port of Entry to the *World Showcase* (it opens at 11 a.m.).

✔ Start in *Canada,* to the far right of the entrance. The movie is uplifting and entertaining. Continue counterclockwise to the *United Kingdom* for street shows, people watching, and a real pub. *France* has a captivating movie and wonderful pastry shop; *Morocco* offers a colorful casbah with merchants, Moorish tile and art, and little passages that put you in Bogartville. (For some, this place is better than the real Casablanca, which is pretty dirty.)

✔ *Japan* has grand architecture but move quickly to *The American Adventure,* a patriotic triumph of audio-animated characters. This is a large theater, so waits are rarely long. Next, head to *Italy* and St. Mark's Square, which comes complete with a 105-foot bell tower.

✔ *Germany* features nonstop Oktoberfest with bands, yodelers, beer, and 'wursts. Don't miss the model railway and the Bavarian-looking shops. Steer yourself to *China,* which offers food, bargain buys, gardens and ponds, and a 360° movie. Continuing counter-clockwise, *Norway* features the *Maelstrom* ride. *Mexico* completes the *World Showcase* circle with a boat-ride into its history.

✔ End your day with the *IllumiNations* fireworks display.

Chapter 19

Disney–MGM Studios

. . . .

In This Chapter

▶ Discovering **Disney–MGM's** extras and essentials

▶ Comparing **MGM** and **Universal Studios**

▶ Reviewing **MGM's** main attractions

▶ Catching shows and parades

▶ Planning a day in the park

. . . .

Disney's ad writers tout **Disney–MGM Studios** as "the Hollywood that never was and always will be." Its movie- and TV-themed shows and props are a large part of the mix, but the park has two bowel-tightening thrill rides, too — the *Twilight Zone Tower of Terror* and *Rock 'n' Roller Coaster*. Its neighborhoods include Hollywood and Sunset boulevards, where art deco movie sets evoke the golden age of Hollywood. New York Street is lined with miniature renditions of the Empire State and Chrysler buildings. It's also an impromptu stage where street actors perform a range of sidewalk slapstick. Likewise, the park is a working studio where shows are in production many days.

Unlike the **Magic Kingdom** and **Epcot,** you can pretty much see **Disney–MGM's** 110 acres of attractions in one day if you arrive early. If you don't get a *Disney–MGM Studios Guidemap* and entertainment schedule as you enter the park, grab one at Guest Services.

Check show times as soon as you arrive and work out an entertainment schedule that appeals to you. Likewise, take a second to plan ahead for mealtime. We describe the park's best restaurants in Chapter 14.

Acquainting Yourself with Disney–MGM Studios

Before we head off for your close-up with the park's rides and attractions, we'll need to dispose of some mundane matters.

> ✔ **ATM machines** accept cards from banks using Cirrus, Honor, and Plus. You can find them on the right side of the park's main entrance.

✔ **The Baby Care Center** in **MGM** is to the left of the main entrance with places for nursing and changing. You can buy disposable diapers, formula, baby food, and pacifiers. Changing tables are also in all women's rest rooms and some men's rooms, and disposable diapers are also available at Guest Services.

✔ You can find **disposable cameras and film** throughout the park. Although once available, you can no longer rent 35mm cameras and camcorders at Disney parks.

✔ **The First Aid Center,** staffed by registered nurses, is in the Entrance Plaza adjoining Guest Services.

✔ **Park Hours** are generally 9 a.m. to at least 7 p.m., with extended hours — sometimes as late as midnight — during holidays and summer.

✔ You can call ☎ 407-824-4321 or visit Disney's Web site, http://disney.go.com/DisneyWorld/intro.html, to obtain **additional information about WDW properties**.

✔ **Lockers** are located near Oscar's Classic Car Souvenirs, to the right of the Entrance Plaza. They cost $6 a day with a $1 refundable deposit.

✔ **Lost children** at **Disney–MGM Studios** are taken to Guest Services. Children under 7 should wear name tags.

✔ The shop clerk can send your **packages** to Guest Services in the Entrance Plaza. Allow three hours for delivery. If you're staying at a Disney resort, you can have your package shipped directly to your room.

✔ Disney offers **pet care** accommodations for $6 a day at kennels just outside the park entrance. Proof of vaccination is required.

✔ **Make Priority Seating arrangements** when you enter the park if you care about having a sit-down meal at a special venue. Or, if you know where you want to chow down in advance, call ☎ 407-939-3463. See Chapter 13 for details on restaurants in the park.

✔ You can rent **strollers** at Oscar's Super Service, inside the main entrance, for $7 including a $1 refundable deposit.

✔ **Admission prices** are $46 for a one-day adult ticket, $37 for children 3 to 9. See Chapter 16 for other options.

✔ **Rent wheelchairs** from the gift shop to the left of the ticket booths at the Transportation and Ticket Center, or at the Stroller and Wheelchair Shop inside the main entrance to your right. Your cost is $6 plus a $1 deposit; $30 and a $10 deposit for battery-run chairs.

✔ **The prices of consumables** are pretty much standard among Disney parks. The **Disney–MGM Studios** will nail you to the tune of $1.55 for a soda, $2.50 for bottled water, $2.00 for an ice cream bar, $2.50 for a pineapple float, and $1.15 for a cup of cocoa. Many of these are common prices at **Universal** and **SeaWorld** as well.

Pitting Disney–MGM Studios Against Universal Studios Florida

If you love movies or the golden age of Hollywood, you'll enjoy wandering the realistic streets, shops, sets, and back lots of **Disney–MGM Studios. Universal Studios Florida** caters more to visitors with little children thanks to *Nickelodeon Studios, Fievel's Playland,* and *Woody Woodpecker's KidZone.* But is this town big enough for two studios? We pity the visitor who has time to visit only one of these stellar parks.

Both parks have good shows and, alas, unavoidably long lines. **Universal** has a slight edge in rides, though *MGM's Rock 'n' Roller Coaster,* is, arguably, the best thrill ride in either park. **Universal** is larger, which means you'll wear out more shoe leather, but it's not as congested. It's also a solid two- or even three-day park, whereas you can finish off **Disney–MGM** in a day, although a second day provides a nice comfort zone.

Our overall evaluation is that **MGM Studios** has some great shows, mainly *Indiana Jones, Star Tours,* the *Muppet 3-D Adventure,* and the backlot tour, but it's a close second to **Universal.**

The following section divides the rides in **Disney–MGM Studios** into two categories. Rides and attractions that are rated G will assuredly entertain the youngest visitors, and in many cases the older ones as well. PG-rated rides are those that are geared to adults (and may bore children) and those that young children are not permitted on.

Index of attractions and rides

G-Rated

Backstage Pass
Bear in the Big Blue House — Live on Stage!
Beauty and the Beast Live on Stage
Disney's Doug Live!
Honey, I Shrunk the Kids Movie Set
Hunchback of Notre Dame: A Musical Adventure
Indiana Jones Epic Stunt Spectacular
Jim Henson's Muppet*Vision 3D
Sounds Dangerous Starring Drew Carey
Voyage of the Little Mermaid

PG-Rated

American Film Institute Showcase
Disney–MGM Studios Backlot Tour
The Great Movie Ride
The Magic of Disney Animation
Rock 'n' Roller Coaster
Star Tours
The Twilight Zone Tower of Terror

Entertaining for the Whole Family: G-Rated Attractions and Rides

Rides and attractions listed in this category are suitable for everyone, but many are especially geared for young kids and may have little appeal to teens or childless adults.

Backstage Pass

A furry flurry of dalmatians and the villainous Cruella De Vil are the stars of Disney's live-action remake of *101 Dalmatians* and this 25-minute walking tour. The stark, eerie movie sets are among the top attractions during the tour, and Wizzer, the most fluid of the canine actors, is featured in a film about the life of a four-pawed star. Taking a cue from **Universal,** where you "Ride the Movies," the special-effects show allows one spectator, usually a tall male, to ride in the movies by re-creating Jeff Daniels' runaway-bike scene. Real dalmatians are also on display.

Bear in the Big Blue House — Live on Stage!

Younger audiences like this 15-minute show, where Bear, Ojo, Tutter, Treelo, Pip, Pop, and Luna perform some of their favorite songs from the whimsical Disney Channel series. The show happens six times a day, and times are in your show schedule.

Beauty and the Beast Live on Stage

A 1,500-seat, covered amphitheater provides the stage for this 25-minute, live Broadway-style production of *Beauty and the Beast* adapted from the movie version. Musical highlights include the rousing "Be Our Guest" opening number and the poignant title song featured in a romantic waltz-scene finale. Sets and costumes are lavish, and the production numbers are spectacular. Arrive early to get a good seat. The park usually hosts six shows a day.

Disney's Doug Live!

Doug, the Nickelodeon star, comes to life on stage, and through his words and actions explains why being 12 is tough. This 30-minute show

Disney–MGM Studios

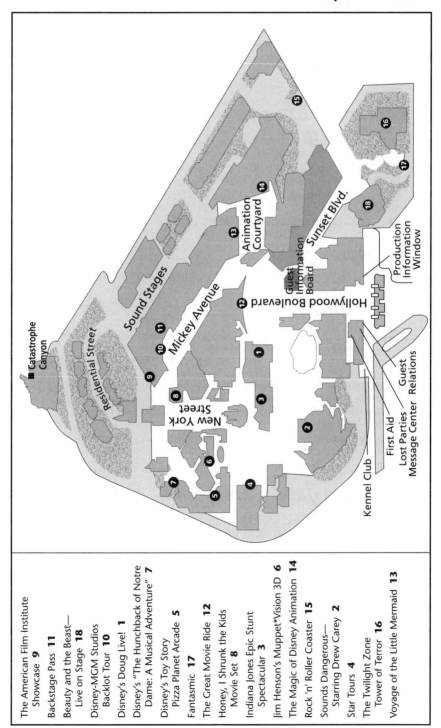

Catastrophe Canyon

Residential Street

Sound Stages

Mickey Avenue

New York Street

Animation Courtyard

Sunset Blvd.

Hollywood Boulevard

Guest Information Board

Production Information Window

Kennel Club

First Aid

Lost Parties Message Center

Guest Relations

combines live performances and animation while Doug and his friends interact. The show is a must-see for Doug show fans, who during audience participation parts answer Doug trivia faster than you can say "The Evil Dr. Rubber Suit." The show requires volunteers: four adults (to play The Beets) and one child (as Quail Man). The music is good and, in summer, the air-conditioning is a blessing. Shows are held six to eight times daily.

Honey, I Shrunk the Kids Movie Set

The *Honey I Shrunk the Kids Movie Set* is an 11,000-square-foot playground where everything is larger than life. A thicket of grass is 30 feet tall, mushroom caps are three stories high, and a friendly ant makes a suitable seat. Play areas include a massive cream cookie, a 52-foot garden hose with leaks, cereal loops 9 feet wide and cushioned for jumping, and a waterfall cascading from a leaf to a dell of fern sprouts (the sprouts form a musical stairway, activated when you step from sprout to sprout). There's also a root maze with a flower-petal slide, a filmstrip slide in a giant film canister, and a huge spider web with 11 levels. This attraction is a great place for your kids ages 2 to 10 to work off their excess energy, while you regain some of your sanity.

Hunchback of Notre Dame: A Musical Adventure

Dozens of singers and dancers tell the story of Quasimodo in a 32-minute live performance geared to all ages. The human cast, aided by puppets, follows the Disney animated score and story line in which Quasimodo ultimately loses more than his beloved Esmerelda. Show up 30 minutes early to ensure a good seat and at least five minutes early to make sure that you get a seat during busy seasons, when the theater fills to capacity.

Indiana Jones Epic Stunt Spectacular

Spectacular is a good word for this 30-minute rock'em sock'em extravaganza guaran-double-teed to keep you entertained and on the edge of your seat. The attraction is held in a big, open-air pavilion and uses lots of adult volunteers. The show begins with Indy rappelling down from the rafters, and the nifty special effects soon have him dodging spikes, falling into a pit of molten something-or-other, surviving two ax-wielding gargoyles, grabbing a priceless amulet, and then outrunning fire, steam, and a large boulder that nearly flattens him — all before the first commercial break. The actors, special effects folks, and director use the breaks to explain what you just saw or are about to see, including stunt secrets. In later scenes, Indy battles the evil Nazis in a Cairo marketplace and at an airport-munitions dump.

"Yeah!" It's definitely an adrenaline booster. Young fans (and most adults) really get into the fun as, true to the film, good triumphs over evil, an airplane propeller chops up a big Nazi, and the ammunition dump does its Fourth of July number. Loud noises, though, may make this show a little too intense for kids under 6.

Jim Henson's Muppet*Vision 3D

Located at *Muppet World Headquarters,* this in-your-face, 25-minute spectacle allows the humor of the late Jim Henson to live on through Miss Piggy, Kermit, and the gang. A delight for all ages, this production is a chuckler that mixes some pretty good 3D effects and sensory gags with puppets and a live-action character or two. In the show, you encounter flying Muppets, cream pies, cannonballs, high winds, fiber-optic fireworks, bubble showers, and even an actual spray of water. Kermit is the host, Miss Piggy sings "Dream a Little Dream of Me," Statler and Waldorf critique the action (which includes numerous mishaps and disasters) from the balcony, and Nicki Napoleon and his Emperor Penguins (a full Muppet orchestra) provide music from the pit. Kids in the first row can interact with the characters.

Sounds Dangerous Starring Drew Carey

Drew Carey provides laughs while dual audio technology provides some incredible hair-raising effects during a 12-minute mixture of movie and live action at ABC Sound Studios. You feel like you're right in the middle of the action of a TV pilot featuring undercover police work and plenty of amusing mishaps. Even when the picture disappears, you follow Detective Charlie Foster's chase via headphones that demonstrate sound effects including a roomful of angry bees, a herd of galloping elephants, and a deafening auto race.

Voyage of the Little Mermaid

Hazy lighting helps paint a picture of an underwater world in a 17-minute show that combines live performances, movie clips, puppetry, and special effects. Sebastian sings "Under the Sea," Ariel performs "Part of Your World," and the evil, tentacled Ursula, 12 feet tall and 10 feet wide, belts out "Poor Unfortunate Soul." The Voyage has some scary scenes, but, just like the movie, the show has a happy ending. You get spritzed with water during the show, making this an especially good experience during hot days.

Exploring PG-Rated Attractions and Rides

Rides and attractions in this category appeal to older children and adults. In some cases, they have age, height, or health restrictions. (*Read:* The shrimp enchiladas you had for lunch may not stay in your stomach.)

American Film Institute Showcase

Waltz through Hollywood history as you gain an appreciation for those behind the movies — editors, cinematographers, producers, and directors whose names blur by in the credits. The walk-through tour also spotlights some of the institute's lifetime achievement winners, including Bette Davis, Jack Nicholson, and Elizabeth Taylor. There are also changing exhibits, such as "Creatures of Distinction," which features puppets and models from movies such as *Star Wars.*

Disney–MGM Studios Backlot Tour

This fun, 35-minute special-effects show starts on foot and finishes in a tram. Two folks out of the audience are outfitted in two-piece rain gear with hoods, then dispatched to a lagoon, where one climbs aboard a tugboat (suitably named Miss Fortune) to endure a rainy, rocky, windy ride, capped by a huge wave that rolls over the pilot house. The footage from that adventure is blended with remote effects on a screen to make it look just like the movies. In real life, the audience member gets a little wet, but rain gear saves him or her from a drenching. The second victim enters a fake submarine where underwater air cannons make you think that depth charges are blowing and machine-gun bullets are riddling across the surface.

After the demonstrations, you board a tram for a ride through Disney's costume department (the world's largest), sets from popular (and not-so-popular) TV shows and movies, and the domain of the special-effects wizards.

Well, his yawns turned to wide eyes and a hearty "WOW!" once we entered *Catastrophe Canyon,* where an "earthquake" causes a tanker truck to explode, rocking the tram. Then a very large, *VERY WET* wave throws 70,000 gallons of water your way.

The Great Movie Ride

A slow journey down **MGM's** memory lane, *The Great Movie Ride* starts in the 1930s and moves forward from there, using incredibly lifelike animatronic versions of Jimmy Cagney, John Wayne, and Clint Eastwood to re-create some of their most memorable roles. Live bandits then show up and blow up the bank. One of the bad guys kidnaps you and your mates, but — revenge is so sweet, isn't it? — he goes the wrong way, into alienville, which has an uncanny resemblance to one of the *Raiders of the Lost Ark* sets. The space thing from *Alien* is waiting in the ceiling, then the right wall, and pretty soon your bank-robbing buddy gets incinerated when he tries to steal the sphinx's jewel. You then jaunt off to Bogie's Casablanca, and Oz, where a remarkable likeness of the witch warns, "I'll get you my pretty, ahahahaha!"

Sorry folks — this time J.J.'s eyes glazed early, and he napped through the ride, but we loved it. Despite the outlaws and alien (which may frighten some youngsters), the 22-minute ride doesn't contain much for kids of any age unless they like old movies.

The Magic of Disney Animation

Disney characters come alive at the stroke of a brush or pencil as you tour glass-walled animation studios and watch artists at work. Walter Cronkite and Robin Williams (guess who plays straight man?) explain what's going on via video monitors. They also star in a very funny eight-minute Peter Pan-themed film about the basics of animation. Animation is painstaking work: To produce an 80-minute film, the animation team must create more than one million drawings of characters and scenery! Original cels (drawings/paintings on celluloid sheets) from famous Disney movies of the past and some of the many Oscars won by Disney artists are also on display here. The 35-minute tour, recommended for ages 8 and up, also includes a grand finale of magical moments from Disney classics such as *Pinocchio, Snow White, Bambi, Beauty and the Beast,* and *The Hunchback of Notre Dame.*

Rock 'n' Roller Coaster

Now it's our turn to say, "WOW!" This inverted roller coaster is one of the best thrill rides that **WDW** has to offer and is certainly not a ride for younger kids or folks with neck or back problems, faint hearts, or a tendency toward motion sickness.

Rock 'n' Roller Coaster is a fast-and-furious, indoor ride that puts you in a 24-passenger stretch limo, outfitted with 120 speakers that blare Aerosmith at 32,000 watts! A flashing light warns you to "prepare to merge as you've never merged before," and faster than you can scream "Stop the music!" (around 2.8 seconds, actually) you shoot from 0 to 60 mph and into the first gut-tightening inversion at 5Gs. The ride's beginning is a real launch (sometimes of lunch) followed by a wild ride through a make-believe California freeway system. One inversion cuts through an "O" in the Hollywood sign, but you won't feel that you're going to be thrown out, because the ride's too fast for that. The ride is so fast, the Disney hype says, that it's similar to sitting atop an F-14 Tomcat. (We've never been in an F-14, so we can't argue.) The ride lasts 3 minutes and 12 seconds, the running time of Aerosmith's hit, "Sweet Emotion." Like *Space Mountain,* all the ride action takes place indoors. Riders must be at least 48 inches tall.

Star Tours

Your journey to a place far, far away begins with a winding walk (a line) through a bunch of *Star Wars* 'droids and a pre-ride warning about high turbulence, sharp drops, and sudden turns. By now, though, you're a seasoned pro of such things and laugh in the face of danger. Once you get through the waiting zone, there's roughly a four-minute final wait at the loading dock while the group in front of you finishes the ride. *Star Tours* is a virtual ride where you go nowhere, but you feel like you do. The ride starts kind of slow, but it finishes fast as you soar through space in a good-guy fighter, with R2-D2 and C3PO helping you make passes through the canals of Lord Vader's mother ship. The special effects include hitting warp speed (you feel like you're going up with a very small G-force) and falling.

JJ SAYS

"I loved that!" It's certainly not as threatening or active as *Rock 'n' Roller Coaster,* but *Star Tours* has a 40-inch height minimum.

The Twilight Zone Tower of Terror

If you like leaving your stomach at several levels, you'll love *The Twilight Zone Tower of Terror.* Its legend says that during a violent storm on Halloween night 1939, lightning struck the Hollywood Tower Hotel, causing an entire wing and an elevator full of people to disappear. And you're about to meet them as you star in a special episode of *The Twilight Zone.* En route to this formerly grand hotel, guests walk past overgrown landscaping and faded signs that once pointed the way to stables and tennis courts; the vines over the entrance trellis are dead, and the hotel is a crumbling ruin. Eerie corridors lead to a dimly lit library, where you can hear a storm raging outside. After various spooky adventures, the ride ends in a dramatic climax: a terrifying, 13-story free fall into *The Twilight Zone!* This thrill ride has a pre-show so authentic that maintenance crews kept fixing leaking pipes designed to drip as part of the ambience. At 199-feet, it's the tallest WDW attraction. You must be 40 inches tall to ride.

Mickey Minutiae

The official scorers at **Disney World** keep track of some pretty odd stuff. Here's a sampling guaranteed to impress the lane lizards at your neighborhood bowling alley when you get back home:

- The four worlds and assorted trimmings of **Walt Disney World** cover 47 square miles, the size of San Francisco or two Manhattan islands. Of **Walt Disney World's** 30,500 acres, only one-quarter is developed; 25 percent of it is a preserve.

- **Disney–MGM Studios'** landmark water tower has its own custom set of mouse ears. They're hat size 342.

- **Disney** sells enough of those signature ear hats annually to cover the head of every human in Pittsburgh and enough T-shirts to put Mickey's mug on the chest of every man, woman, and child in Chicago.

- WDW gift shops sell 500,000 Mickey watches a year.

- Most folks think *Spaceship Earth,* that far-larger-than-life sphere at **Epcot,** looks like a giant golf ball. If **Disney** wanted to match it with a giant golfer, he or she would have to be nearly 2½ miles tall.

- Speaking of *Spaceship Earth,* that huge hunk of aluminum and plastic alloy tips the scales at 16 million pounds, more than the weight of three fully fueled space shuttles.

- **The All-Star Sports Resort** (see Chapter 8 for more details about this hotel) loves big icons. Its symbols include a mammoth tennis ball can that's big enough to hold 9,474,609 real tennis balls and a Coke cup capable of holding 1.9 million gallons of the carbonated beverage.

- WDW guests gobble enough hamburgers and hot dogs to reach from Orlando to Philadelphia if you stretched them end to end. Guests also eat 5 million pounds of french fries and guzzle more than 46 million soft drinks a year.

- An average Disney housekeeper makes 11,680 beds a year.

- One hundred sixty of the Disney characters have costumes to greet park guests, but not all 'toons are created equal. Minnie owns 200 outfits, from evening gowns to cheerleading skirts. Mickey has 175 in his closet. The other characters usually have only one.

- You won't see many bugs on Disney's public properties, because groundskeepers release millions of good bugs to beat up the bad bugs.

- Sunglasses are the hottest commodity at Disney lost and founds. About 100 pairs are turned in daily at the **Magic Kingdom** alone. The oddest recovery was a glass eye. (Yes, it was claimed).

- Disney's parks have six million flowers, trees, and shrubs and three million annuals, which is enough to keep 650 gardeners, pest controllers, and irrigation specialists hopping.

Taking Time Out for Fantastic Parades and Fireworks

In addition to its assortment of rides, **MGM** also offers a daily parade and an exceptional evening display of fireworks.

Fantasmic!

It's hard not to be in awe of the choreography, laser lights, and fireworks that are the core of this 25-minute extravaganza. Shooting comets, great balls of fire, and animated fountains are among the special effects that really charge the audience. The cast includes 50 performers, a giant dragon, a king cobra, and one million gallons of water — most of it orchestrated by a sorcerer mouse that looks very familiar. You'll probably recognize other characters as well as scenes and musical scores from Disney movie classics like *Fantasia, Pinocchio, Snow White and the Seven Dwarfs, The Little Mermaid,* and *The Lion King.* You also see Jafar, Cruella de Vil, and Maleficent in a battle of good versus evil.

 The ample amphitheater holds 9,000 souls. If you want to avoid a real traffic jam after the show, arrive up to 60 minutes early and sit on the right (the theater empties right to left).

Fantasmic! has a lunch/dinner package at no extra charge. Participating restaurants change (at press time they were The Brown Derby and Mama Melrose's Ristorante). If adults in your party order an entrée, you can wiggle into a reserved seating area as much as 10 minutes before show time, but it's not a specific seat, and you can only make arrangements at Guest Services. We think the arrangement lacks merit, unless you're eating at either restaurant anyway and don't want to arrive an hour early for the show.

Mulan . . . The Parade

A short parade celebrating *Mulan*, Disney's 36th full-length animated feature, has replaced the old *Hercules* parade. The parade is based on the story of a young, high-spirited girl who saves her father's life by disguising herself as a man and joining the Chinese army in his place. It's performed afternoons (weather permitting) along Hollywood Boulevard. This parade doesn't touch Magic Kingdom parades in size or scope, so unless you're a big *Mulan* fan, this is a good time to skip over to *Tower of Terror* or *Rock 'n' Roller Coaster,* where the lines are shorter because many guests flock to the parade.

Seeing It All in One Day

Here's a suggested itinerary for helping you make it through
Disney–MGM Studios in one day:

- ✔ Consider making a Priority Seating reservation (at Guest Relations or call ☎ **407-939-3463**) if you want to eat dinner in the park. The Hollywood Brown Derby is a decent sit-down option (see Chapter 14 for a list of Orlando's best restaurants).

- ✔ Head to the *Twilight Zone Tower of Terror.* It's a high-voltage ride that's not for the young or faint of heart. This ride is bad for folks with fears of tight or high places, but it's one of the park favorites. The other is the new *Rock 'n' Roller Coaster,* which blends incredible take-off speed with three inversions.

- ✔ **Disney–MGM Studios** is small, so backtracking isn't a concern. Consider passing up attractions that have long lines, or use FAST-PASS. You may find long lines at *Twilight Zone Tower of Terror, Rock 'n' Roller Coaster*, and *Star Tours.* All are worth your time, as well as the *Indiana Jones Epic Stunt Spectacular.*

- ✔ *Voyage of the Little Mermaid* is a must for the young (in years or yearnings); the same goes for *Jim Henson's Muppet*Vision 3D.*

- ✔ If you're looking for a little lunch action, the '50s Prime Time Café offers a fun show along with staples like meat loaf.

- ✔ Relax at *The Magic of Disney Animation, Doug Live!,* and *Sounds Dangerous Starring Drew Carey;* then go on the ton-of-fun *Backlot Tour.*

- ✔ Check your show schedule for favorites such as *Bear in the Big Blue House, Disney's Hunchback of Notre Dame, Beauty and the Beast,* and, at night, *Fantasmic!*

- ✔ Also check the schedule (weather permitting) for the mid-afternoon *Mulan* parade.

Chapter 20

Animal Kingdom

● ●

In This Chapter

▶ Acquainting yourself with **Animal Kingdom**

▶ Comparing **Animal Kingdom** to **Busch Gardens**

▶ Exploring the attractions in **Animal Kingdom**

▶ Setting an **Animal Kingdom** agenda

● ●

As recently as 1997, what you know as **Animal Kingdom** was a pasture dotted with cow patties and fire-ant mounds. Since then, the patties and mounds have been replaced with a forest, rivers, ravines, savannas, and a ton of nonindigenous animals. If your timing is right, you can see such critters as African lions, giraffes, cheetahs, white rhinos, lowland gorillas, and hippos. You can also bump into a few species that may be new to you, like bongos (the antelopes, not the drums) and naked mole rats (these cuties are pink, nearly hairless, buck-toothed, and they love building subterranean toilets.)

Much of this $800 million park opened in 1998; the final land, Asia, was finished in 1999. Disney CEO Michael Eisner swears it's the next best thing to going to Africa, but don't cancel that safari vacation yet. **Animal Kingdom** is a theme park — even if the exotic wildlife can move out of your view. In this chapter, we give you helpful information about **Animal Kingdom** and its marvels, as well as basic info for visiting the park.

Getting to Know the Kingdom

Before we lead you through the jungle of attractions at **Animal Kingdom,** we thought we'd shell out some nuts-and-bolts information about the park.

> ✔ You can find **ATMs** in **Animal Kingdom** near Garden Gates Gifts to the right of the park entrance. Cards from banks using the Cirrus, Honor, and Plus systems are accepted.
>
> ✔ **The Baby Care Center** is located near *Creature Comforts* in *Safari Village.* As in the other Disney parks, you can also find changing tables in women's rest rooms and some men's. You can also buy disposable diapers at Guest Services.

- **Disposable cameras and film** are available at the Kodak Kiosk in *Africa* and Garden Gate Gifts near the park entrances, as well as in Disney Outfitters in *Safari Village*. You can drop film off for same-day developing at the Kodak Kiosk and Disney Outfitters as well.

- **The First Aid Center,** which is staffed by registered nurses, is located near *Creature Comforts* in *Safari Village*.

- **Business hours** at **Animal Kingdom** are 8 a.m. to 6 p.m., but hours are often extended to 7 a.m. to 7 p.m.

- You can call ☎ **407-824-4321** or visit Disney's Web site, `http://disney.go.com/DisneyWorld/intro.html`, to obtain additional information about WDW properties.

- **Lockers** are located in Garden Gate Gifts to your right as you enter the park. You can also find them to the left, near RainForest Café. Rent lockers for $6 a day.

- **A lost children center** is located near *Creature Comforts* in *Safari Village*. This is also the site of same-day lost and found. Making kids 7 and under wear name tags is a good idea.

- Shop clerks can send your **packages** (there's no charge for this service) to the front of the park at Garden Gate Gifts. Allow three hours for delivery. As in the other Disney parks, if you're staying at a Disney resort, you can have your packages shipped back to your room.

- **Pet care** facilities are located just outside the park entrance. You can board your pet(s) for $6 a day.

- You can make **Priority Seating arrangements** (see Chapter 13 for details on call-ahead dining) at Guest Services just inside the entrance. If you know where you want to eat in advance, call ☎ **407-939-3463**.

- Rent **strollers** at the Garden Gates Gifts shop to the right as you enter the park ($7 with a $1 refundable deposit). There are also satellite locations throughout the park. Ask a Disney employee to steer you in the right direction.

- **Tickets cost** $46 for adults, $37 for children, children under 3 free. See Chapter 16 for other options.

- Rent **wheelchairs** at the Garden Gates Gifts shop that's on your right as you enter the park. Rentals cost $6, including a $1 deposit for a standard wheelchair, and $30 (with a $10 deposit) for electric carts. Ask Disney employees for other locations throughout the park.

- **Consumables** run $1.55 for a soda, $2.50 for bottled water, $2.00 for an ice cream bar, and $1.15 for cocoa.

Understanding the Differences between Animal Kingdom and Busch Gardens

When Disney's fourth theme park opened, it raised two questions: Is it a frontline park worthy of the same sticker shock as Orlando's other major parks, and when does the area have too many?

Sagging attendance at most of the individual parks may answer the latter question. Comparing **Animal Kingdom** to Florida's other big-time critter park, **Busch Gardens** in Tampa, may help answer the first question. Although we take a closer look at **Busch Gardens** in Chapter 26, we also take a few paragraphs in this chapter to compare the **Gardens** to the **Kingdom.**

Animal Kingdom is more a park for animals, a conservation venue as much as an attraction. The short of it is that it's not as easy to see its creatures; they're given a lot more cover than at **Busch Gardens,** so when they want to avoid your probing eyes and the heat, they can. The beautiful foliage used to create that cover also means that **Animal Kingdom** is a lot prettier than its Tampa rival.

The best time to catch the animals out and about at **Animal Kingdom** is in the early morning just after the park opens — usually 7 or 8 a.m. (depending on the season) — or try to see them at closing. Most animals are on the prowl at those times, not at midday (especially during the summer). **Busch's** animals are far easier to see regardless of the time of day.

Animal Kingdom wins the battle of shows with humdingers such as *Tarzan Rocks!* and *Festival of the Lion King.* However, although **Animal Kingdom** has three thrill rides (and we're being kind calling two of them thrilling), **Busch Gardens** pulls ahead with five roller coasters including *Gwazi,* a set of dueling wooden coasters.

Geographically speaking, however, you may not have or want a choice between the two parks. **Animal Kingdom** is located right in the center of the Orlando action. Although we like **Busch Gardens** a tiny bit better, you have to drive or buy other transportation to get to the park, which is about 90 minutes from Orlando, and there isn't as much to see or do in Tampa unless you're into cultural centers, restaurants, and museums. If you're considering a trip to the Tampa Bay area, we recommend buying a copy of *Frommer's Florida* or *Frommer's Portable Tampa & St. Petersburg,* which have a wealth of information about attractions, accommodations, and restaurants on the state's Sun Coast.

Animal Kingdom

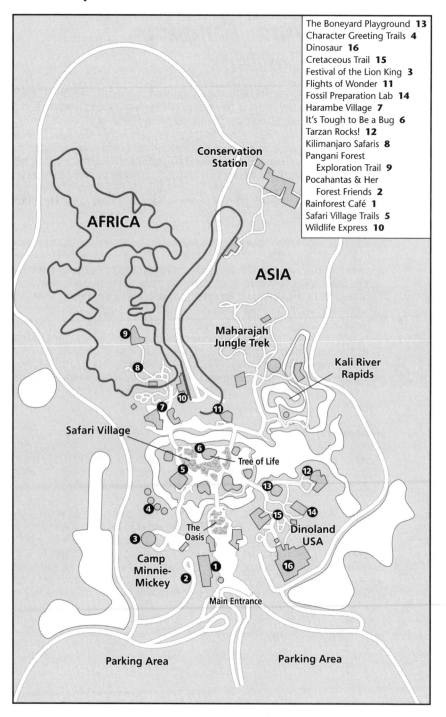

The Boneyard Playground **13**
Character Greeting Trails **4**
Dinosaur **16**
Cretaceous Trail **15**
Festival of the Lion King **3**
Flights of Wonder **11**
Fossil Preparation Lab **14**
Harambe Village **7**
It's Tough to Be a Bug **6**
Tarzan Rocks! **12**
Kilimanjaro Safaris **8**
Pangani Forest
    Exploration Trail **9**
Pocahantas & Her
    Forest Friends **2**
Rainforest Café **1**
Safari Village Trails **5**
Wildlife Express **10**

Conservation
Station

AFRICA

ASIA

Maharajah
Jungle Trek

Kali River
Rapids

Safari Village

Tree of Life

Dinoland
USA

The
Oasis

Camp
Minnie-
Mickey

Main Entrance

Parking Area

Parking Area

Index of attractions by land

The Oasis
Port of Entry and Animal Habitats

Safari Village
It's Tough to Be a Bug!
Safari Trails
Tree of Life

Camp Minnie–Mickey
Character Greeting Pavilions
Festival of the Lion King
Pocahontas and Her Forest Friends

Africa
Conservation Station
Kilimanjaro Safaris
Pangani Falls Exploration Trail

Asia
Flights of Wonder
Kali River Rapids
Maharajah Jungle Trek

Dinoland, U.S.A.
The Boneyard
Cretaceous Trail
Dinosaur
Tarzan Rocks!

Checking Out Animal Kingdom's Top Attractions

The overall conservation theme in this state-of-the-art park is simple but not subtle. Everywhere you turn, you'll find an environmental message, including on the park's signs and in the narratives of the tour guides on rides such as *Kilimanjaro Safaris.* Here, it is the animal's comfort that comes first; they are given plenty of cover, which may make it harder for you to see them. This section provides you with a closer look at the six lands of **Animal Kingdom.**

The Oasis

This is your introduction to **Animal Kingdom,** but a lot of folks, ready to get to the action, launch their way through *The Oasis,* overlooking the fact that this is one of the better places to see animals early in the day. The lush vegetation, streams, grottoes, and waterfalls on either side of the walkway are good places to see wallabies, miniature deer, anteaters, sloths, iguanas, tree kangaroos, otters, and macaws. But a misty fog and the landscaping also give them a lot of room to escape your eyes if they choose.

Safari Village

After you pass through *The Oasis,* you head straight into *Safari Village,* which, like WDW's **Magic Kingdom,** is set up on a hub-and-spoke format with the village as the hub and five lands scattered around **Animal Kingdom.** This is another animal-viewing area (though the thick cover will make it hard to spot any creatures), where you may see wood ducks, flamingos, kangaroos, and small-clawed otters walking around the *Tree of Life,* the Kingdom's 14-story man-made tree (described in detail later in this section).

It's Tough to Be a Bug!

Take the walkway through the *Tree of Life*'s 50-foot base, grab a pair of 3D glasses, and settle into a sometimes creepy-crawly seat. Based on the Disney-Pixar film, *A Bug's Life,* the special effects in this multimedia adventure are pretty impressive. Though it may not be a good choice for kids under 4 (it's dark and loud) or bug haters, this attraction is a fun and sometimes poignant look at life from a smaller perspective. After you put on your bug-eye glasses, all your senses are awakened by the stars, including ants, beetles, spiders, and — oh, no! — a stink bug. Although the video isn't quite on par with *Honey, I Shrunk the Audience* (see Chapter 18 on Epcot attractions), it has some magic moments.

We're sure that J.J. is going to work in pest control when he grows up. He hates bugs. He wanted no part of the show. He fretted a lot while we stood in line. He even threatened to go AWOL, until we explained that our beloved editor would fire us if he didn't bail us out. So he did, reluctantly, and eventually decided it was "well, pretty fun." Same for us. The show includes some spritzes of water, blasts of air, and a foul smell when the stink bug gets its revenge. The seat crawls under your butt when the on-screen insects run amok, causing screams and howls of laughter.

Tree of Life

Like *Cinderella's Castle* at the **Magic Kingdom** (see Chapter 17 for more details) and *Spaceship Earth* in **Epcot** (described in Chapter 18), the 14-story *Tree of Life* is **Animal Kingdom's** icon. The man-made tree and its carved animals are the work of Disney artists, teams of which worked for more than a year on its carved, free-form animal sculptures. It's not as tall or imposing as other icons, but it is impressive. It has 8,000 limbs, 103,000 leaves, and 325 mammals, reptiles, amphibians, bugs, birds, dinosaurs, and Mickeys carved into its trunk, limbs, and roots. The *Tree* seems as if a different animal appears from every angle. One of the creators says he expects it to become one of the most photographed works of art in the world. (He's probably a Disney shareholder.)

Although passing up a detailed survey on your way into the park is hard, we recommended gawking only while standing in line for *It's Tough to Be a Bug!* You have time for a more detailed look — if you so desire — on the way out.

Camp Minnie–Mickey

Youngsters love this place. It's a favorite hangout for several Disney characters from the forest and jungle, including Simba from *Lion King* and Baloo from *The Jungle Book.* Mickey, Minnie, Goofy, Pluto, Donald, Daisy, and a variety of other stars also make appearances from time to time around this woody retreat, which resembles an Adirondack summer camp.

Character greeting pavilions

If you're traveling with children, this is a must do attraction. A variety of Disney characters, from Winnie the Pooh to Timon and Baloo, greet you. Mickey, in recognition of his star status, gets his own pavilion.

Festival of the Lion King

Festival of the Lion King at the Lion King Theater is a rousing 28-minute show that's the best in **Animal Kingdom** and one of the top three in all of **Walt Disney World.** The eight-times-per-day extravaganza celebrates nature's diversity with a talented, colorfully attired cast of singers, dancers, and life-size critters that lead the way to an inspiring sing-along. Based loosely on the animated movie, this stage show combines the pageantry of a parade with a tribal celebration. The action takes place both on stage and around the audience. Even though the pavilion has 1,000 seats, it's best to arrive early.

Pocahontas and Her Forest Friends

The wait to see *Pocahontas and Her Forest Friends* can be nightmarish, and the 15-minute show isn't close to the caliber of *Festival of the Lion King* and *Tarzan Rocks!* In this show, Pocahontas, Grandmother Willow, and some forest creatures hammer home the importance of treating nature with respect. If you must go, go early. The theater has only 350 seats, though they do allow standing-room crowds.

Africa

Enter through the town of Harambe, which means "coming together" in Swahili, which is what happens in this representation of an African coastal village poised on the edge of the twenty-first century. Costumed employees greet you as you enter the buildings. The whitewashed structures, built of coral stone and thatched with reed brought from Africa, surround a central marketplace rich with local wares and colors.

Conservation Station

This area of Africa offers a behind-the-scenes look at how Disney cares for animals inside the park. You walk past a series of nurseries and veterinarian stations. The problem is that these facilities need staff in order to be interesting, and that's not always the case.

Conservation Station includes the Affection Section, where you can cuddle some friendly animals, explore their habitats, and learn how they're cared for and fed.

Time permitting, see *Eco Heroes,* the interactive videos that connect you to endangered animal information and world-famous biologists and conservationists, and *Song of the Rainforest,* which surrounds you with the sounds of the endangered wildlife in a deep jungle. This lecture/audio adventure is kind of interesting, but skip it if there's a long wait.

Kilimanjaro Safaris

This attraction is one of the few rides and the best animal-viewing venue in the kingdom. But remember: The animals are scarce during the middle of the day, especially in the heat of summer.

Also, the time that you spend waiting in line at this attraction can reach 45 minutes or more, so consider using FASTPASS (see Chapter 16), unless you get to it early in the day.

After you reach the end of the line, you board a very large truck (if you're familiar with an Army deuce-and-a-half you get the idea). You're then off on a bouncy ride through what pretends to be an African landscape. (The animals aren't pretending.) Animals in the *Safari* include black rhinos, hippos, antelopes, Nile crocodiles, zebras, wildebeests, and a male lion that, if your timing is right, may offer a half-hearted roar toward some gazelles that are safely out of reach. Predictably, the theme is heavy on the conservation front. There's even a little drama — this is a theme park ride after all — as you and your mates help catch some dastardly poachers.

"I can't wait till we do that again!" But most adults can. This area is called *Harambe,* which means "coming together." And that's just what happens in line and on the *Kilimanjaro Safaris* ride. You have a ton of fun and gain a lot of knowledge, but during the summer months, remember to dress for the Florida heat, especially at midday, even though much of the waiting area is covered and dotted with overhead fans to keep you cool.

Pangani Falls Exploration Trail

You can get a pretty good look at birds and the ever-active mole rats along the trail, but the gorillas are very hard to spot, and small viewing areas in various parts of the other habitats make it hard to see other elusive animals. Lines that grow to three or more people deep also make it hard to see when critters materialize.

Asia

Disney's Imagineers have outdone themselves in creating the mythical kingdom of *Anadapour.* The intricately painted artwork at the front is appealing, and it also helps make the lines seem to move a little faster. Also, watch for (with little prior announcement) the appearance of local youngsters performing Asian dances.

Flights of Wonder

Flights of Wonder is a bird show that mixes live-animal action with a Disney character show including Pumbaa (the warthog) and Timon (a meerkat) of *Lion King* fame. It's a low-key break that has a few laughs, but isn't much by bird-show standards. If you've been to a Florida attraction bird show, you know the plot even if the characters and actors are different. This show isn't very unique. You get close encounters and a journey through what seems like ancient Asia, but the show loses focus fast. The birds, predictably, are trained hams as are the human actors, but at least they're personable.

Kali River Rapids

White-water fanatics will scoff, but for a theme-park raft ride, the *Kali River Rapids* ride is pretty good — slightly better, we think, than *Congo River Rapids* at **Busch Gardens** (see Chapter 28), but not as good as *Popeye & Bluto's Bilge-Rat Barges* in **Islands of Adventure** (see Chapter 24). The *Kali River Rapids* have churning water that mimics real rapids and optical illusions that make you wonder if you're about to go over the falls. The ride begins with a peaceful tour of lush foliage, but soon you're dipping and dripping as your tiny raft tosses and turns. You *will* get wet. The lines are long, but keep your head up and enjoy some of the marvelous art overhead as well as on the beautiful murals. This ride requires a 42-inch height minimum.

Maharajah Jungle Trek

Disney keeps its promise to provide up close views of animals with this exhibit. If you don't show up in the midday heat, you'll see Bengal tigers through the thick glass. Nothing but air divides you from dozens of giant fruit bats hanging in what appears to be a courtyard. Some of the bats have wingspans of six feet. (If you have a phobia, you can bypass this, but the bats are harmless.) Guides are on hand to answer questions, and you also get a brochure that lists the animals you may spot; it's available on your right as you enter the attraction. (An employee will likely ask if you'd like to recycle it as you exit.) You also have chances to see giant Komodo dragons, playful gibbons, and acrobatic siamangs, whose calls have been likened to someone in the throes of pain or passion.

DinoLand U.S.A.

Located to the right of *Safari Village, DinoLand U.S.A.* is Disney's attempt to capitalize on the dinosaur craze inspired by *Jurassic Park* and (ugh) *Barney.* Pass under Olden Gate Bridge, a 40-foot-tall Brachiosaurus reassembled from excavated fossils, to enter. Speaking of fossils, until late summer 1999, *DinoLand* had three paleontologists working on the very real skeleton of *Sue,* a monstrously big

Tyrannosaurus rex unearthed in the Black Hills of South Dakota in 1990. The paleontologists patched and assembled the bones here, mainly because **Disney** helped pay for the project. Alas, *Sue* got a permanent home at the Field Museum in Chicago, but a cast replica of her 67-million-year-old bones is on display.

The Boneyard

Although it's not as inviting at the *Honey, I Shrunk the Kids* play area at **Disney–MGM Studios** (see Chapter 19) or *Woody Woodpecker's KidZone* at **Universal Studios Florida** (see Chapter 23), *The Boneyard* is a great place for parents to catch a second wind. Kids love the play area, and there are plenty of things to wear them down a little. For example, they can slide and climb over a simulated paleontological site, and they can squeeze through the fossils and skeletons of a triceratops and a brontosaurus.

You have to be vigilant about keeping track of your kids. *The Boneyard* is a large area and, although it's monitored by Disney staff at both ends, kids play in a multilevel arena where tube slides can take them from one level to the next in a heartbeat.

Dinosaur

This ride used to be called *Countdown to Extinction,* but it got a new name to go with the Disney motion picture, *Dinosaur.* The ride hurls you through darkness in a CTX Rover time machine, past an array of snarling dinosaurs that are a little hokey. It's far from a smooth ride, and some kids may find the dinosaurs and darkness frightening. However, *Dinosaur* is as close as **Animal Kingdom** comes to a thrill ride — a herky-jerky, twisting-turning, bouncey-jouncey ride in which you and 20 other passengers try to save the last dinosaur worth saving. Evolution, nature's fragility, and potential catastrophe are the punch lines in this lip-biting, armrest-clenching ride against time and some very large lizards (such as a 33-foot carnotaurus, which is named for its favorite food — meat).

"I think I'm gonna puke." That was J.J's comment about halfway through the ride. However, at the end of the ride, J.J. said, "That's the one I like best (in **Animal Kingdom**). Can we do it again?" Riders must be 40 inches — that's 6 inches less than when it was *Countdown to Extinction. Dinosaur* also has a list of warnings aimed at folks with neck and back ailments.

Cretaceous Trail

Wander leisurely back in time as you stroll down a path filled with living plants and animal species that have survived since the dinosaurs. A Chinese crocodile, Florida soft-shelled turtle, and red-legged seriema (a longneck bird) are among the residents on this trail.

Tarzan Rocks!

This 28-minute, five-times-per-day show pulses with music and occasional aerial theatrics. Phil Collins' movie soundtrack supports a cast of 27, including tumblers, dancers, and in-line skating daredevils who

really get the audience into the act. (Go on, try your Tarzan yell —
no one knows you here.) Costumes and music are pretty spectacular,
second in **Animal Kingdom** only to *Festival of the Lion King* in *Camp
Minnie-Mickey.* Our only criticisms: The story line is pretty thin, Tarzan
doesn't appear for 14 minutes, and it's clear by his physique and acting
ability that he's there for eye candy more than anything. The show is
held in the 1,500-seat Theater in the Wild.

Conquering the Kingdom in One Day

The good news is that **Animal Kingdom** is small enough to see in a day,
and here you'll find a plan for viewing the park. It's designed to be time
efficient, but you can add or subtract rides and shows based on your
tastes.

✔ Be here when the gates open, sometimes as early as 7 a.m., but
generally around 8 a.m. (Call Disney information ☎ **407-824-4321**
to check the time.) Arriving early gives you the best chance of
actually seeing animals, because they're most active in the morning air (the next best time to see them is late in the day). If you
want to eat breakfast at the Rainforest Café, make reservations at
☎ **407-939-3463.**

✔ The size of the park (500 acres) means a lot of travel after you
pass through the gates. Don't linger in *The Oasis* area or around
the *Tree of Life;* instead, head directly to the back of the park to be
first in line for the *Kilimanjaro Safaris.* Doing so allows you to see
more animals before it gets hot and the lines become monstrous.
Work your way back through *Africa,* visiting *Pangani Forest
Exploration Trail* and, if you have kids, the train to *Conservation
Station.*

✔ Head to the *Tree of Life* in *Safari Village* next for *It's Tough to Be a
Bug!* (Thrill seekers may prefer to start at *Dinosaur* in *DinoLand
U.S.A.,* a good choice if you get there before the lines or use
FASTPASS.) Younger kids deserve some time at *The Boneyard* in
DinoLand as well as *Camp Minnie–Mickey,* on the other side of the
park. Then see the park's two best shows, *Tarzan Rocks!* and
Festival of the Lion King. If your time allows only one show, *Lion
King* is the best choice.

✔ Restaurantosaurus in *DinoLand* is a fair lunch stop in this area.

✔ Unless you must have a bird-show fix, skip *Flights of Wonder* in Asia,
but don't miss the *Kali River Rapids* and *Maharajah Jungle Trek.* Late
in the day, on your way out, look for smaller animals — iguanas,
anteaters, and sloths to name a few — in the foliage at *The Oasis.*

Chapter 21

Enjoying the Rest of Walt Disney World

● ●

In This Chapter
▶ Invading the **World's** largest video arcade
▶ Experiencing a sports fan's nirvana
▶ Golfing, Disney-style
▶ Splashing into the Disney water parks
▶ Enjoying holiday happenings
▶ Cruising with **Disney**

● ●

*I*n Chapters 17 through 20, you get acquainted with the major parks of **Walt Disney World.** But Walt Disney World also has several small parks and attractions. And while we introduce you to that second tier, we also tell you about a few holiday happenings and the **Disney Cruise Line.**

Playing It Up at DisneyQuest

Meet the world's most interactive video arcade.

From kids just reaching video-game age to teens, reactions to **DisneyQuest** are pretty much the same: "Awesome!" And, although adults enter the five-level arcade thinking they're going to find kids' stuff, many bite the hook as hard as their offspring when they get a gander at the electronic wizardry — everything from old-fashioned pinball with a new-fangled twist to virtual rides.

Here are some of the entrées that you can find at **DisneyQuest:**

▸ *Aladdin's Magic Carpet Ride* puts you astride a motorcycle-like seat while you fly through the 3D Cave of Wonders.

▸ *Hercules in the Underworld* is one of the best interactive games. You and three others assume the roles of Herc, Mel, Pegasus, and Phil, that cute little round guy who seems to be from the same family as Pan. You race through a time-and-space continuum, gathering lightning bolts and dodging obstacles (including Hades) in the underworld. Fail, and you crash and burn — for eternity.

✔ *Invasion: An Extraterrestrial Alien Encounter* has the same kind of theme and intensity as *Hercules in the Underworld.* Your mission is to save colonists from intergalactic bad guys. One player flies the module while others fire an array of weapons. (We're contractually bound to tell you that the Starship Tunstall crashed and burned five times.)

✔ The *Mighty Ducks Pinball Slam* is an interactive, life-size game in which the players ride platforms and use body language to score points.

✔ If you have an inventive mind, stop in *The Create Zone,* where Bill Nye the Science-Turned-Roller-Coaster Guy helps you create the ultimate loop-and-dipster, which you then can ride in a simulator. Bring your own motion-sickness medicine.

✔ If you need some quiet time, sign up at *Animation Academy* for a mini-course in Disney cartooning. There are also snack and food areas. A typical theme-park meal and drink at the food areas runs about $12 per person. There's no specific children's menu, but the servings are plentiful and can easily be enough for two. *Tip*: Crowds are heaviest after dark.

DisneyQuest is located off Buena Vista Dr., adjacent to Pleasure Island and Downtown Disney. ☎ *407-828-4600. Open: Daily 10:30 a.m. to midnight. Admission: $27 adults, $21 kids 3–9 for unlimited play.*

Fielding the Fun at Disney's Wide World of Sports

Disney's Wide World of Sports is a 200-acre, mega-complex that has a 7,500-seat baseball stadium, a separate 4-field complex, 2 Little League fields, 4 softball fields, 6 basketball courts, 12 lighted tennis courts, a track-and-field complex, a golf driving range, and 6 sand volleyball courts.

If you're a true sports fan, write in advance for a package of information about the facilities and a calendar of events. Write to **Disney's Wide World of Sports,** P.O. Box 10,000, Lake Buena Vista, FL 32830-1000 or call ☎ **407-939-1500.**

Here's a sample of options you have at **Disney's Wide World of Sports:**

✔ The *NFL Experience* is open daily from 10 a.m. to 5 p.m. Admission is $9 for adults, $7 for kids ages 3 to 9. Ten drills test running, punting, passing, and receiving skills. You can dodge cardboard defenders and run a pass pattern while a machine shoots you a pass. (A much safer way than risking life and limbs against non-cardboard types.) Depending on your stamina, interest, and the size of the crowds, the experience lasts from 45 minutes to several hours.

✔ The Atlanta Braves started spring training at **Disney's Wide World of Sports** in 1998. There are 18 games during a one-month season that begins in early March. Tickets for the stadium's two areas are $8.50 and $15.50. For information, call ☎ **407-828-3267**; you can get tickets through TicketMaster (☎ **407-839-3900**).

✔ The NFL, NBA, NCAA, PGA, and Harlem Globetrotters also host events, sometimes annually and sometimes more frequently, at the complex.

This sports mecca is located on Victory Way, just north of U.S. 192 (west of I-4). ☎ 407-939-1500. Open: Daily, but hours vary by venue. Admission prices vary by venue.

Gearing Up at the Richard Petty Driving Experience

Test Track is for sissies — this is your chance to race as the pros race, in a 600-horsepower NASCAR Winston-Cup race car. How real is it?

You must sign a two-page waiver with words like DANGEROUS, CALCULATED RISK, and UPDATE YOUR WILL! before getting into a car. At one end of the spectrum, you can ride shotgun for a couple of laps at 145 mph. At the other end, you can spend three hours to two days learning how to drive the car yourself and racing other daredevils in 8 to 30 laps of excitement (for a cool $350 to $1,200). You must be 18 years old to ride in the car.

The Richard Petty Driving Experience is located on World Drive at Vista Blvd. just off U.S. 192, south of the Magic Kingdom. ☎ 800-237-3889. Admission varies by seasons and hours, so call ahead. Admission is $90–$1,200. Only adults are allowed in the race cars.

Preparing for the Masters at Disney Golf

The Magic Mickey offers 99 holes of golf: five regulation par-72 courses and a 9-hole par-36 walking course. All WDW courses are open to the public and offer driving ranges, pro shops, locker rooms, snack bars or restaurants, and PGA-staffed teaching and training programs. For tee times and information, call ☎ **407-824-2270** up to seven days in advance. (Disney resort guests can reserve up to 30 days in advance.) Golf packages are available, and you can call ☎ **407-934-7639** to make reservations in advance.

Other Disney Parks

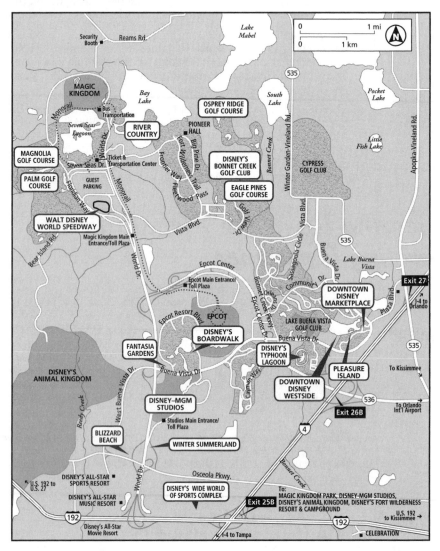

Here's a rundown of some of Disney's best courses. (The following prices, where different, reflect a $5 differential charge for players not staying on Disney property.)

✔ **Palm Course (18 holes).** The Palm is rated one of America's Top 75 Resort Courses and is Disney's toughest to play by the PGA. Set among natural Florida woodlands, the elevated greens, water, and sand traps offer more hazards than Interstate 4. Good luck with the 18th hole, it's rated the fourth toughest hole on the PGA Tour. Greens fees average $120 to $125, with late afternoon twilight rates cut in about half.

✔ **Magnolia Course (18 holes).** This longest course on Disney property is designed in classic PGA style. Wide fairways are deceiving;
you've got to hunker down and whack the ball, but take care:
There are 11 holes with water hazards, and 97 bunkers on the
course. The sixth hole has a special hazard — a sand trap in the
shape of Mickey. Greens fees average around $130 to $135, with
late afternoon twilight rates about half that price.

✔ **Lake Buena Vista Course (18 holes).** This course is a classic country club, with lots of pines spread across a residential area. Well-
bunkered, it's also a challenge that demands accuracy. This course
is one of a few that have hosted a PGA, LPGA, and USGA event.
Greens fees average $120 to $125, with twilight rates half off.

✔ **Eagle Pines Course (18 holes).** Expansive traps and sloping fairways follow the natural lay of the land. Rough pine straw and sand
replace grass rough on this course, along with 16 holes with water
hazards. Greens fees run $140 to $145, with late afternoon rates
about half that price.

✔ **Osprey Ridge Course (18 holes).** This Fazio-designed course
combines rolling fairways cut through forests of scrub oaks, pine,
palmetto, cypress, and bay trees. The Osprey course is ranked as
one of the best public and resort places to play golf in the United
States by *Gold* magazine. Greens fees average $155 to $160.
Twilight rates hit $80 or more.

✔ **Oak Trail Course (9 holes).** If you can't go a day without getting in
a few holes, but don't have time for the 18-hole courses, this is the
place to spank the ball. This 9-hole walking course is designed for
families, or for a quick golf fix. Greens fees are $42.

If this list doesn't give you enough options, or you want to stretch
your legs out of Disney, there are literally 100 other courses within
45 minutes of WDW. You can get additional information and arrange
tee times by contacting *Golfpac* (☎ **800-327-0878** or 407-260-2288;
www.golfpacinc.com), or *Tee Times USA* (☎ **800-374-8633**; www.
teetimesusa.com).

Puttering Around at Disney Miniature Golf

Those too timid to tee off at Disney's majors — or whose big games
aren't yet up to par — can try their putters on the World's miniature
golf courses. There are four whimsically themed courses, and everyone, from novices to master minigolfers, should find at least one to
their liking.

Fantasia Gardens

Fantasia Gardens Miniature Golf, located across the street from the **Swan Hotel** off Epcot Resorts Boulevard, offers two 18-hole miniature courses drawing inspiration from the Walt Disney classic cartoon of the same name. On the *Fantasia Gardens* course, hippos, ostriches, and gators appear, and the Sorcerer's Apprentice presides over the final hole. This is a good course for beginners and kids. Seasoned mini-golfers will probably prefer *Fantasia Fairways,* which is a scaled-down golf course complete with sand traps, water hazards, tricky putting greens, and holes ranging from 40 to 75 feet.

This minicourse is located on Buena Vista Dr., just east of World Drive. ☎ *407-560-8760. Open: Daily 10 a.m.–11 p.m. Admission: $9.25 adults, $7.50 kids 3–9.*

Winter Summerland

Santa Claus and his elves supply the theme at *Winter Summerland,* a miniature golf spread that opened in 1999 with two 18-hole courses. The Winter course takes you from an ice castle to a snowman to the North Pole. The Summer course is pure Florida, from sandcastles to surfboards to a visit with Santa on the Winternet.

Drive East off Buena Vista Dr., just north of Osceola Pkwy. ☎ *407-939-7639. Open: Daily 10 a.m.–11 p.m. Admission: $9.25 adults, $7.50 kids 3–9 per round of miniature golf.*

Making a Splash at Disney's Water Parks

Disney has a trio of magnificent water parks where you can cool off after a day spent trudging through the rest of the **World.**

Here are a few things to keep in mind before you head off for a swim:

- ✔ Go in the afternoons — about 2 p.m., even in summer — if you can stand the heat that long and want to avoid crowds. The early birds are usually gone by then, and lines are short.
- ✔ Go early in the week when most weeklong guests are filling the lines at the major parks.
- ✔ Kids can get lost just as easily at a water park, and the consequences can be worse. All Disney parks have lifeguards, usually wearing bright red suits; but, to be safe, ask how to identify an on-duty lifeguard.
- ✔ If modesty is your policy, women should remember to bring a one-piece bathing suit for the more daring slides. All bathers should

remember the wedgie factor on the more extreme rides, such as Summit Plummet. The wedgie factor is this: You may enter the park wearing baggies and find yourself in a thong.

Blizzard Beach

The newest of Disney's water parks is a 66-acre ski resort in the midst of a tropical lagoon set beneath the 90-foot, uh-oh, *Mount Gushmore.* The base of *Mount Gushmore* has a sand beach with several other attractions, including a wave pool and a smaller, kids' version of the mountain.

Here are brief descriptions of other *Blizzard Beach* attractions:

- ✔ **Cross Country Creek** is a 2,900-foot tube ride around the park.

- ✔ **Runoff Rapids** allows you and your tube to careen down your choice of three twisting-and-turning runs, one of which plunges you into darkness.

- ✔ **Ski-Patrol Training Camp** is designed for preteens. It features a rope swing, an airborne water drop from a t-bar, slides such as the wet and slippery *Mogul Mania,* and a challenging ice-flow walk along slippery floating icebergs.

- ✔ **Slush Gusher** shoots you along a snow-banked gully. It packs a 48-inch minimum height requirement.

- ✔ **Meltaway Bay** is a one-acre, relatively calm wave pool.

- ✔ **Tike's Peak** is a miniversion of *Blizzard Beach* for minivisitors.

- ✔ **Snow Stormers** has three flumes that descend from the top of *Mount Gushmore* along a switchback course through ski-type slalom gates.

- ✔ **Summit Plummet** is wild! Read **every** speed, motion, vertical-dip, wedgie, and hold-onto-your-breastplate warning in this guide. Then test your bravado in a bull ring, a space shuttle, or dozens of other death-defying hobbies as a warm-up. This puppy starts pretty slow, with a lift ride (even in Florida's 100-degree dog days) to the 120-foot summit. Kiss any kids or religious medal you may carry with you because, if you board, you *will be on the world's fastest body slide.* It's a test of your courage and swimsuit that goes virtually straight down and has you moving, *sans* vehicle, at 60 mph by the time you reach the *catch pool* (the stop zone). Even the hardiest of riders may find this slide hard to handle; a veteran thrill-seeker recently described the experience as "15 seconds of paralyzing fear." Minimum height requirement is 48 inches.

- ✔ **Steamboat Springs** is the World's longest white-water raft ride. Your six-passenger raft twists down a 1,200-foot series of rushing waterfalls.

- ✔ **Toboggan Racers** is an eight-lane slide that sends you racing, head first, over exhilarating dips into a "snowy" slope.

All the fun and excitement of Blizzard Beach is located on World Dr., just north of the All-Star Sports and Music resorts. ☎ *407-560-3400. Open: Daily 10 a.m.–5 p.m., extended to 9 a.m.–8 p.m. during peak times such as summer. Admission: $27.95 adults, $22.50 kids 3–9.*

Typhoon Lagoon

Typhoon Lagoon is the ultimate in water theme parks. Its fantasy setting is a palm-fringed tropical island village of ramshackle, tin-roofed structures, strewn with cargo, surfboards, and other marine wreckage left by the great typhoon. A storm-stranded fishing boat (the Miss Tilly) dangles precariously atop the 95-foot *Mount Mayday,* the steep setting for several rides. Every 30 minutes, Tilly's stack blows and shoots a 50-foot geyser of water into the air.

Here are some other sweeteners of the park:

- ✔ **Castaway Creek** is a 2,100-foot lazy river that circles most of the park. Hop onto a raft or an inner tube and meander along through a misty rain forest, then past caves and secluded grottoes. *Water Works,* its theme area, is where jets of water spew from shipwrecked boats and a Rube Goldberg assemblage of broken bamboo pipes and buckets soak you. Tubes are included in the admission.

- ✔ **Ketchakiddie Creek** is a kiddie area designed exclusively for kids under four feet. An innovative water playground, it has bubbling fountains in which kids can frolic, miniwaterslides, a pint-size white-water tubing run, spouting whales and squirting seals, rubbery crocodiles on which to climb, grottoes to explore, and waterfalls under which to loll. This area is also small enough for you to take good home videos or photographs.

- ✔ **Shark Reef** includes a very small snorkeling area with a simulated coral reef that's populated by about 4,000 parrot fish, angelfish, yellowtail damselfish, and other cuties, including small rays. Guests are given free equipment (and instruction) for a 15-minute swim. If you don't want to get in, you can observe the fish via portholes in a walk-through area.

- ✔ **Typhoon Lagoon** is the park's main swimming area. This large and lovely lagoon is the size of two football fields and is surrounded by a white sandy beach. The chlorinated water has a turquoise hue much like the waters of the Caribbean. Large waves hit the shore every 90 seconds. A foghorn sounds to warn you when a wave is coming. Young children can wade in the lagoon's more peaceful tidal pools — *Blustery Bay* and *Whitecap Cove.*

- ✔ **Humunga Kowabunga** consists of three 214-foot *Mount Mayday* slides that propel you down the mountain on a serpentine route through waterfalls and bat caves and past nautical wreckage at 20 mph before depositing you into a bubbling catch pool; each

slide offers slightly different views and thrills. There's also seating
for non-Kowabunga folks whose kids have commissioned them to
"watch me." Women should wear a one-piece on the slides (except
those who don't mind putting on a different sort of show for gawk-
ers). This attraction has a 48-inch height minimum.

✔ **White-Water Rides,** found in *Mount Mayday,* is the setting for three
white-water rafting adventures — *Keelhaul Falls, Mayday Falls,* and
Gangplank Falls — all of which offer steep drops coursing through
caves and passing lush scenery. *Keelhaul Falls* has the most spiraling route, *Mayday Falls* has the steepest drops and fastest water,
and the slightly tamer *Gangplank Falls* uses large tubes so that the
whole family can pile on.

*Typhoon Lagoon is located west of Downtown Disney and south of Lake Buena
Vista Dr., between the Disney Village Marketplace and Disney–MGM Studios.
☎ 407-560-4141. Open: Daily 10 a.m.–5 p.m., extended to 9 a.m.–8 p.m. during peak
periods. Admission: $27.95 adults, $22.50 kids 3–9.*

River Country

One of the many recreational facilities at the Fort Wilderness Resort
campground, this miniwaterpark is themed after Tom Sawyer's swimming hole. *River Country* is usually less crowded than the other Disney
water parks, making it attractive to those who prefer a less hectic place
to swim. Kids can scramble over boulders that double as diving platforms for a 330,000-gallon swimming hole. Two 16-foot slides also provide access to the pool. Here are some other fun features:

✔ Attractions on the adjacent *Bay Lake,* which is equipped with
ropes and ships' booms for climbing, include a pair of flumes —
one 260 feet long, the other 100 feet — that corkscrew through
Whoop-N-Holler Hollow.

✔ *White-Water Rapids* carries inner-tubers along a winding, 230-foot
creek with a series of chutes and pools.

✔ *The Ol' Wading Pool* is a smaller version of the swimming hole
designed for young children.

✔ There are pool and beachside areas for sunning and picnicking,
plus a 350-yard boardwalk trail through a cypress swamp. Beach
towels ($1) and lockers ($5) are available. Light fare is available at
Pop's Place. To get here without a car, take a launch from the dock
near the entrance to the **Magic Kingdom** or a bus from its
Transportation and Ticket Center.

*River Country is located east of Magic Kingdom, on Seven Seas Dr. east of Frontier
Way. ☎ 407-824-4321. Open: Daily 10 a.m.–5 p.m., and sometimes 10 a.m.–7 p.m.
(call the park for details) Admission: $15.95 adults, $12.50 kids 3–9.*

Enjoying the Holiday Season at Disney

Few commercial ventures put folks in the holiday spirit like Disney. Lights, trees, caroling, and special activities begin around Thanksgiving and last until the end of the year.

Three of the best yuletide attractions include the following:

- ✔ **Mickey's Very Merry Christmas Party**, an after-dark ticketed event, takes place on weekends at the **Magic Kingdom** and offers a traditional Christmas parade and a breathtaking fireworks display. The additional charge of $35 per person includes cookies, cocoa, and a souvenir photo. The best part? Shorter lines for the rides.

- ✔ **The Candlelight Procession** at **Epcot** features hundreds of candle-holding carolers, a celebrity narrator telling a Christmas story, a 450-voice choir, and a 50-piece orchestra. Also held on weekends, this is a very moving event. Admission is free with regular park ticket.

- ✔ The **Osborne Family Christmas Lights** came to **Disney–MGM Studios** in 1995 when an Arkansas family ran into trouble with hometown authorities over their multimillion-light display. It seems they'd committed the ultimate Little Rock sin, taking to heart the old hymn that says, "You can't be a beacon if your light don't shine." Their Christmas-light collection of two-million-plus blinkers, twinklers, and strands was so bright that their neighbors complained. There were rumors that air traffic was even disrupted and that the flow of faithful spectators in cars caused mile-long backups. The neighbors, finally seeing the light, went to court. Disney came to the rescue and, in 1995, moved the whole thing to Orlando, adding a million or so bulbs to the display.

Call ☎ 407-824-4321 for information; ☎ 407-934-7639 to inquire about packages. Or, visit the Disney Web site, `http://disney.go.com/DisneyWorld/intro.html`*. Admission: $46 adults, $37 kids 3–9 (park tickets required).*

Sailing the Seas with Disney

It took them a while to catch on, which is unusual for the Disney folks, but they finally discovered another place to expand their empire — the high seas. Despite delays, the **Disney Cruise Line** launched the *Disney Magic* and the *Disney Wonder* in 1998 and 1999, respectively.

The two ships have small differences. The *Magic* is art deco, with a giant Mickey in its three-level lobby and a *Beauty and the Beast* mural in its top restaurant, Lumiere's. The *Wonder* is art nouveau; Ariel commands its lobby, and its featured eatery, Triton's, sports a mural from *The Little Mermaid*.

The restaurants, nightlife, shows, and other onboard activities are very family oriented. One of the ships' unique features is a dine-around option that lets you move among main restaurants (each ship has four) from night to night while keeping the same servers. The *Magic* and *Wonder* stop at Nassau and the WDW-owned Castaway Cay — a 1,000-acre playground for cruise guests.

Subtle differences aside, these two ships are nearly identical twins. Both are 83,000 tons with 12 decks, 875 cabins, and room for up to 2,400 guests. There are adults-only areas but no casinos. Both ships have extensive kid and teen programs — broken into three age groups — that feature state-of-the-art computer equipment. There are also nurseries for 3-month- to 3-year-olds. Activities run from 9 a.m. to 1 a.m.

Three- to eight-year-olds can explore *The Oceaneer's Club*. It's designed to look like Captain Hook's ship, complete with cannons that have sound effects, crow's nests for lookouts, and ceilings painted with Disney-character constellations. There are also costume rooms for dress-up days, story times, and character appearances. When you first sign your kids up, you pick a password that only you know. Your kids also get an identification wristband. When you drop them off, they're logged in, and you're the only one who can pick them up, via password. You're also given a pager that reaches the entire ship, Disney's out island, and parts of Nassau. That way, if the cast needs to reach you, they can just page you with a message.

Disney's *Oceaneer's Lab* is for 9- to 12-year-olds. It's themed with *Toy Story* characters and has a more high-tech atmosphere. There are planned activities and events throughout the day to ensure that your kids enjoy their vacation as much as you do. There are also projects with microscopes, lab experiments, and group explorations throughout the day.

Teen programs are centered on *Common Grounds,* a trendy coffeehouse for their use only. It's not only a hangout, but a place for them to prepare for the comedy hour (the improv pros teach them funny-stuff basics), dances, and play games, including answering enough questions correctly to win the ESPN Sports Challenge.

If you decide to book a Disney cruise, don't be shy. Always ask the magic question: Is that the best rate available? Disney reservationists seldom volunteer anything, but if you ask the right question you usually get the right answer. On an inaugural voyage with journalists, one Disney executive said three-night, cruise-only rates could be as low as $379 if you drive to Port Canaveral, skip the free air, and settle for the lowest-class cabin on board. We're not talking about oar class on a Viking ship. Class on modern cruise ships often is a state of mind.

Fla. 528 at A1A, Cape Canaveral. ☎ **800-939-2784** *or 407-566-3500.* www. disneycruise.com. *Fares: Cruise-only, $559– $2,674 for three nights, $669– $2,864 for four nights; $179– $429 kids 3–17. Seven-day land-sea packages, three or four nights afloat with rest of the week at a Disney resort, $1,049– $4,089 for adults, $399– $699 for kids. Some packages include round-trip airfare and unlimited admission to Disney parks, Pleasure Island, the water parks, and Disney's Wide World of Sports. They also include transportation by bus between Walt Disney World and Port Canaveral. Note: Seven-day voyages to St. Thomas, St. John, St. Marten, and Castaway Cay begin in August 2000. Prices start at $829.*

Chapter 22

Shopping at Walt Disney World

. . . .

In This Chapter

▶ Shopping inside the parks

▶ Cruising the shopping districts

▶ Taking advantage of offbeat shopping options

. . . .

*Y*our kids are begging for 14-carat mouse ears, your mother will have a cow if you don't buy her a pair of Donald Duck slippers, and you've always wanted a Winnie the Pooh cuckoo clock for the den. Then you see the price tags. *Gasp!* How can they get away with that?

You're an emotional and physical captive of a commercial enterprise sprinkled with feel-good pixie dust when you're at **Disney.** We don't know this for sure, but we think Disney's store managers use a simple formula for setting prices: Start with standard retail, then multiply by three.

However, you probably won't escape without a contribution to the stockholders' fund, especially if it's your first trip to **Walt Disney World.** But before you start spending, here are a few things to think about:

✔ If there's a Disney Store near your city, much of what's sold in Disney's parks is available in their stores. Therefore, you don't need to rush into a purchase. (Notable exceptions are goods sold in the *World Showcase* pavilions at **Epcot.**)

✔ At the other end of the spectrum, many WDW shops sell products themed to their area of the park, and it may be hard to find the identical item elsewhere. (But, you get one last chance at the airport. See "Last Chance: Shopping for Disney Doodads at the Airport" at the end of this chapter).

✔ Don't be fooled by someone offering you a "bargain." You usually can't find bargains or discounts in **WDW.** If someone offers you one (especially outside the parks), beware. The bargain or discount may be fake — or worse, a "hot" item.

✔ Theme park shops keep the same hours as the attractions: 9 a.m.–7 p.m. and sometimes later.

✔ Don't forget to allow for 6 percent sales tax on purchases.

Loading Up Your Cart at Walt Disney World

In general, you will find three categories of merchandise in the Disney parks. Souvenirs that scream "Disney!" are the most common. (The number of choices will fog your brain.) Collectibles not related to Disney are another type. You find these in some of the *Main Street* shops in the **Magic Kingdom** as well as around the *World Showcase* in **Epcot.** The last category, merchandise from other countries, is a *World Showcase* specialty.

Don't lug around your loot. Send your purchases from any store to designated areas for pickup as you leave the park to keep your hands free to snap pictures. In the **Magic Kingdom,** you can pick up packages at Guest Relations in the Plaza area. In **Epcot,** you can send your packages to Guest Relations in the Entrance Plaza or the International Gateway for same-day pickup. **Disney–MGM Studios** shop clerks will send your goodies to Guest Relations in front of the park. And, you can pick up your **Animal Kingdom** purchases at Guest Relations in the Entrance Plaza. (Allow at least three hours for delivery.) If you're a Disney resort guest, you can often have your packages delivered to your room for free — ask the shops about this service.

Magic Kingdom

The Emporium on *Main Street's* Town Square has a big selection of *Disneyana* (pricey collectibles, such as Minnie Mouse cookie jars). The *Main Street Athletic Club* offers autographed sports memorabilia and team clothing. You can watch craftspeople create the glass animals and vases sold inside park shops at *Crystal Arts.* The *Main Street Gallery* inside Cinderella's Castle is loaded with family crests, tapestries, suits of armor, and other medieval wares.

Traders of Timbuktu in *Adventureland* carries carved wood and soapstone animals and masks. *Plaza del Sol Caribe,* a Mexican mercado, stocks piñatas, baskets, straw hats, and papier-mâché parrots. *Island Supply,* a Disney version of The Nature Company, offers books, posters, toys, bird feeders, and more. The *House of Treasure* features pirate hats, Captain Hook T-shirts, and ships in bottles.

The *Frontier Trading Post* in *Frontierland* hawks cowboy boots and hats, western shirts, coonskin caps, turquoise jewelry, belts, and toy rifles. Goods in *Prairie Outpost & Supply* include Native American drums, headdresses, and bows and arrows. Visit the *Briar Patch,* under *Splash Mountain,* for Uncle Remus and Winnie the Pooh merchandise.

Liberty Square's *Yankee Trader* is a charming country store that sells Lion King and Pooh cookie jars, Disney cookie cutters, and fancy food items. *Heritage House* offers parchment copies of famous American documents as well as actual historic letters, campaign buttons, Civil War hats, and presidential signatures.

Sir Mickey's in *Fantasyland* is supply central for a variety of Disney-motif trinkets. Wares at *Tinker Bell's Treasures* include Peter Pan merchandise, costumes (Tinker Bell, Snow White, Cinderella, Pocahontas, and others), and collector dolls. *Mickey's Star Traders* is another large Disneyana shop.

Epcot

World Showcase pavilions carry items that represent their pavilion's country.

Heritage Manor Gifts in the *American Showcase,* for instance, sells autographed presidential photographs, needlepoint samplers, afghans and quilts, pottery, candles, Davy Crockett hats, books on American history, historically costumed dolls, classic political campaign buttons, and vintage newspapers with banner headlines such as "Nixon Resigns!" An artisan at the shop makes jewelry out of coins. You can also buy Disney art and character merchandise.

Canada pavilion shops carry sandstone and soapstone carvings, fringed leather vests, duck decoys, moccasins, an array of stuffed animals, Native American dolls and spirit stones, rabbit-skin caps, heavy knitted sweaters, and, of course, maple syrup.

China's Yong Feng Shangdian Shopping Gallery is a bustling marketplace filled with an array of merchandise including silk robes, lacquer and inlaid mother-of-pearl furniture, jade figures, cloisonné vases, tea sets, silk rugs and embroideries, dolls, fans, wind chimes, and Chinese clothing. Artisans demonstrate calligraphy here, too.

Emporia is a covered shopping arcade in *France.* Merchandise includes art, cookbooks, cookware, wines (there's a tasting counter), Madeline and Babar books and dolls, perfumes, and original letters of famous Frenchmen, such as Napoleon.

Germany's shops feature Hummel figurines, crystal, glassware, cookware, cuckoo clocks, cowbells, Alpine hats, German wines (there's a tasting counter) and foods, toys (German Disneyana, teddy bears, dolls, and puppets), and books. An artisan demonstrates molding and painting Hummel figures; another paints detailed scenes on eggs.

Italy's shops have cameo and delicate filigree jewelry, Armani figurines, kitchenware, Italian wines and foods, Murano and other Venetian glass, alabaster figurines, and inlaid wooden music boxes.

The *Mitsukoshi Department Store* (Japan's answer to Macy's) stocks lacquerware, kimonos, kites, fans, dolls in traditional costumes, origami books, samurai swords, Japanese Disneyana, bonsai trees, Japanese foods, Netsuke carvings, pottery, and electronics. Artisans in the courtyard demonstrate the ancient arts of *anesaiku* (shaping brown rice candy into dragons, unicorns, and dolphins), *sumi-e* (calligraphy), and *origami* (paper folding).

Shops in and around the *Plaza de Los Amigos* (a moonlit Mexican *mercado* market with a tiered fountain and street lamps) display an array of leather goods, baskets, sombreros, piñatas, pottery, embroidered dresses and blouses, maracas, jewelry, serapes, paper flowers, colorful papier-mâché birds, and blown-glass objects (an artisan gives glass-blowing demonstrations).

Morocco's streets lead to the *souk*, a bustling marketplace where hand-crafted pottery, brassware, hand-knotted Berber carpets, colorful Rabat carpets, ornate silver and camel-bone boxes, straw baskets, and prayer rugs are sold. You can also catch weaving demonstrations throughout the day.

Norway's shops sell hand-knitted wool hats and sweaters, toys (there's a Lego table where kids can play), wood carvings, Scandinavian foods, pewterware, and jewelry.

High Street and Tudor Lane shops in the *United Kingdom* display a broad sampling of British merchandise, including toy soldiers, Paddington bears, personalized coats of arms, Scottish clothing (cashmere and Shetland sweaters, golf wear, tams, knits, and tartans), fine English china, Waterford crystal, and pub items such as tankards, dartboards, and so on. A tea shop occupies a replica of Anne Hathaway's thatch-roofed sixteenth-century cottage in Stratford-upon-Avon. Other stores represent the Georgian, Victorian, Queen Anne, and Tudor periods.

TIP

Great things to buy at Epcot

Epcot's *World Showcase* shines in the shopping department. While the suggestions here may not necessarily represent bargains — **Disney** never quits trying to lighten your wallet — they are the kind of unique and unusual items you may not find anywhere else.

- ✔ If you're into silver jewelry, don't miss the *Mexico* pavilion. You can find trinkets ranging from simple flowered hair clips to a kidney-shaped, stone-and-silver bracelet.

- ✔ The shops in *Norway* have great sweaters and Scandinavian trolls that are so ugly you're likely to fall in love with them.

- ✔ In *China,* browse through jade teardrop earrings, Disney art, and more. Its merchandise is among the most expensive in **Epcot,** but also among the most fetching.

- ✔ *Italy's* 100 percent silk scarves and ties come in several patterns.

- ✔ Style-conscious teenagers may love a Taquia knit cap, something of a colorful fez-like chapeau, that's available in *Morocco.* You can also find celestial-patterned pottery.

- ✔ Wimbledon shirts, shorts, and skirts are among the hard-to-find items in the *United Kingdom,* which also has an assortment of tea accessories, sweaters, and Beatles memorabilia.

Disney–MGM Studios

The *Animation Gallery* carries collectible cels, books about animation, arts-and-crafts kits for future animators, and collector figurines. *Sid Cahuenga's One-of-a-Kind* sells autographed photos of the stars, original movie posters, and star-touched items, such as a bracelet that belonged to Joan Rivers. Over at *The Darkroom/Cover Story,* you can have your photograph put on the cover of your favorite magazine, anything from *Forbes* to *Psychology Today* to *Golf Digest.* You can also buy costumes. *Celebrity 5 & 10,* modeled after a 1940s Woolworth's, has *Gone With the Wind* memorabilia, MGM Studio T-shirts, movie posters, and Elvis mugs.

Many of the park's major attractions also have merchandise outlets selling *Indiana Jones* adventure clothing, *Little Mermaid* stuffed characters and logo-wear, *Star Wars* souvenirs, and so on.

Few things are free at **WDW.** Their package delivery system, however, is an exception. Send your purchases to Guest Relations in front of the park, where you can collect them at the end of the day. (Allow three hours for delivery.) If you're staying at a Disney resort, you can have your packages delivered to your room.

Animal Kingdom

The *Oasis' Outpost Shop* deals in T-shirts, sweatshirts, hats, and other souvenir items.

Beastly Bazaar in *Safari Village* has a wide selection of items related to the *Tree of Life* and the show, *It's Tough to Be a Bug!. Creature Comforts* sells clothing, stuffed animals, and toys. *Disney Outfitters* carries upscale, animal-theme apparel, jewelry, cameras, and home decorations. *Island Mercantile* offers theme merchandise that represents the park's lands.

Mombasa Marketplace/Ziwani Traders in *Africa* sells *Kilimanjaro Safaris* apparel and gifts as well as realistic animal items and authentic African gifts. *Out of the Wild* features conservation-related clothing, books, stuffed toys and bath-care products.

Chester & Hester's Dinosaur Treasures in *Dinoland U.S.A.* has wild and wacky dinosaur souvenirs, toys, and shirts.

Disney Shopping outside the Theme Parks

Don't think that the enticement to spend money magically disappears when you step outside the theme parks. **Walt Disney World** also encompasses several shopping districts that house a multitude of shops — many of which carry merchandise you can't get anywhere else — that offer you the chance to blow your budget.

Disney West Side

Disney West Side has many specialty stores where you can find unique gifts and souvenirs.

All Star Gear displays a wide array of apparel and accessories, including clothing in which Gretzky, Montana, and Shaq shed plenty of sweat. *Candy Cauldron* looks like a fairy-tale dungeon, but the smells coming out of its show kitchen are anything but punishment. *Guitar Gallery* tempts string-strokers and wannabes with custom guitars and rare collectibles. *Hoypoloi Gallery* is a New Age store offering artsy glass, ceramics, sculptures, and other decorative doodads made from metal, stone, and wood. *Magnetron* is — well, wow! Can there be a market for this many refrigerator magnets? Smoking may be on the way to say-onara-ville, but *Sosa Family Cigars* beckons with sweet smells as well as a tradition reaching back to yesterday's Cuba. Over at *Starabilias,* the main events are jukeboxes, Coke machines, and other lost treasures of the last century. The *Virgin* (as in records) *Megastore* is a movie, music, and multimedia gold mine that also has a café and occasional live (rather than dead) performances.

West Side is on Buena Vista Dr. ☎ 407-828-3800. From I-4, exit on Fla. 536 or Hwy. 535 and follow the signs. It's open 10:30 a.m.-11:00 p.m. Sun.-Thur.; to midnight Fri.-Sat.

Downtown Disney Marketplace

This *Size XXXL* shopping hub on Buena Vista Lagoon is a colorful place to browse, people-watch, have lunch, and maybe buy a trinket.

2R's Reading and Riting delivers shelves of best sellers, bedtime favorites, Disney classics, and so on. *Art of Disney* is a one-of-a-kind gallery that also includes sculpture, crystal, and more. *Discover* sells funky gifts with nature themes. *EUROSPAIN* comes calling with products that crystal and metal artists make before your eyes. *Harrington Bay Clothiers* has traditional men's clothing (but you can probably find Hilfiger, Nautica, and Polo a bit cheaper elsewhere).

The *Lego Imagination Center* is our shopping blue-light special — but not for its bargains. (Remember? There are no bargains in Disneyville.) This is a great place for moms and dads to relax while your young whippersnappers unwind in a free Lego-building area behind the store. *Pooh's Corner* duplicates the merchandise found at the Magic Kingdom ride. Speaking of Disney stuff, *World of Disney* comes with the (don't-hold-it-to-them) promise that if it exists and it's Disney, it's on their shelves.

Downtown Disney Marketplace is on Buena Vista Dr. at Hotel Plaza Blvd. ☎ 407-828-3800. From I-4, exit on Fla. 536 or Hwy. 535 and follow the signs. It's open 9:30 a.m.–11:00 p.m. Sun.–Thurs., and until 11:30 p.m. Fri. and Sat.

Pleasure Island

Most folks see **Pleasure Island** as a party place, but you can shop here, too.

Every nightspot that we tell you about in Chapter 29 also has a theme shop imploring you to buy one last something. Additionally, *Changing Attitudes* next door to Mannequins Dance Palace has some funky clothes for both sexes. *DTV* comes through with fashions for the young and old(er) in any family. *Music Legends* delivers memorabilia, jewelry, hats, and more on a multigeneration sound level, while *Reel Finds* offers collectibles on the video front. *Suspended Animation* is where you can find Disney posters, prints, lithographs, cels, and more.

Pleasure Island is on Buena Vista Dr. ☎ 407-828-3800. From I-4, exit on Fla. 536 or Hwy. 535 and follow the signs. It's open 10:30 a.m.–2:00 a.m. daily.

Sold! Bidding for Bargains at Disney Auctions

From pink Cadillacs to four-foot beer steins, *Walt Disney World's Property Control Department* regularly puts wacky treasures on the auction block . The president of the National Auctioneers Association calls these auctions the best-kept secret at **Disney.** In addition to cast-off goodies from the parks, hotels, and Mickey's other holdings, there are more common items, such as lawn mowers, flatware, and yesterday's props.

Items in Disney auctions fall into two categories: surplus and abused. Surplus means brand-spanking new (Disney bought too much), but how many people need flatware for 400 or a 750-gallon stainless cooking pot? As for the abused element, well, who needs a six-year-old van with enough miles to circle the planet six times? Auctions are held four to six times a year — always on a Thursday, when Disney employees get paid. Some of the more unusual items sold in the past include furniture from Miss Piggy's dressing room, a seven-foot Darth Vader replica, and a motorized surfboard. Call ☎ 407-824-6878 for details.

Disney also houses a store on premises that's normally open only to employees, but it welcomes the public on auction days. Discounts are said to reach 75 percent of park retail prices, but you know how inflated those prices are. However, the sticker price easily beats anything you will find in the theme parks.

Dealing in Collectibles at Disneyana

Anything that's a true collectible or a signature Disney piece doesn't make it to Disney's public auctions (see "Sold! Bidding for Bargains at Disney Auctions," earlier in this chapter). If such items don't wind up in one of the high-end shops within the theme parks, it's stashed away for *Disneyana* — a gathering of collectors and everyday folks who are obsessed with anything of value that bears a Disney character or logo.

Through the years, the Magic Mickey has earned something of a cult-like following, while his souvenirs have gone uptown. Fact is, collectibles are so popular that the annual *Disneyana Convention* is held at **Disney** each September. The convention draws more than 2,000 devotees, including one guy who wears 927 Walt Disney-related tattoos and a woman who has more than 500 Mickey Mouse watches and 10,000 buttons. There's even an auction where yesterday's ho-hum souvenirs sell for small fortunes. If you're a closet worshipper of all things Walt, call ☎ 407-824-4321 for more information on the *Disneyana Convention.*

Last Chance: Shopping for Disney Doodads at the Airport

Argh! You're already at the airport for the trip home and you forgot to buy a stuffed Goofy for Uncle Elmer. Well, you're in luck. **WDW** operates stores at the Orlando International Airport: *Flights Fantastic* (☎ 407-825-6914), and *Magic of Disney* (☎ 407-825-2360), are located in Terminals A and B. These aren't like the Disney Stores in some of your hometowns. They only sell Walt Disney World trinkets — the kind you find in the theme park shops. (Translation: Forget discounts.) They also sell WDW multiday park tickets and can make your dinner show reservations. These stores are open daily from 6 a.m. to 9 p.m.

Part VI

Exploring the Rest of Orlando

The 5th Wave   By Rich Tennant

"SINCE WE LOST THE DOLPHINS, BUSINESS HASN'T BEEN QUITE THE SAME."

In this part . . .

Mickey is still the toughest mouse around, but he doesn't own Orlando anymore. Yes, this is still the town that Disney built. But the fact is, as **SeaWorld** opens its newest theme park, **Discovery Cove,** half of the eight big-league attractions in Orlando don't belong to Disney.

This part of the book explores the rest of Orlando, including the exciting attractions at **Universal Studios Escape,** as well as what you find at **SeaWorld,** the smaller attractions, and some of the best shopping venues outside the parks.

Chapter 23

Universal Studios Florida

* *

In This Chapter

▶ Learning helpful Universal facts

▶ Seeing the best things at **Universal Studios Florida**

▶ Eating and souvenir shopping

▶ Following a suggested one-day itinerary

* *

*1*n Orlando, you soon get the picture, literally and figuratively, about which studio produces what films in the movie business. Both **Universal** and **Disney–MGM Studios** spend a lot of dollars and your time plugging their movies and characters. At **Universal,** that means you can visit *Earthquake, Hercules* (the live-action show, not the animated feature), *Terminator, Back to the Future,* Barney, Yogi Bear, *Jaws, E.T.,* and many more. And remember, **Universal Studios Florida** isn't just a theme park; it's also a working studio where you may get to see a film being made.

Disney–MGM (Chapter 19) and **Universal Studios Florida** are our favorite Orlando theme parks. Even with grown-up, hurl-'em-and-twirl-'em rides such as *Back to the Future, Twister,* and *Earthquake,* **Universal** is a ton of fun for younger visitors, especially since *Woody Woodpecker's KidZone* came along with its pint-size rides, shows, and play areas. And, as an added plus, **Universal** is a working TV and motion-picture studio, so occasionally there's live filming in the park or, more often, at Nickelodeon soundstages. The Nickelodeon soundstages are where cable television's *The Swamp Thing, Clarissa Explains It All*, and the short-lived *SeaQuest DSV* were filmed. And, even if there isn't a film in production when you visit, you can see reel history displayed in the form of actual sets exhibited along Hollywood Boulevard and Rodeo Drive. Hanna-Barbera characters such as Yogi Bear, Scooby Doo, Fred Flintstone, and more are on hand to greet you, as well as a talented troupe of actors portraying Universal stars such as Harpo Marx and the Blues Brothers. Park shows such as *Terminator 2: 3D Battle Across Time* also deliver heart-pumping excitement.

In summer 2000, the big news at **Universal Studios Florida** is the opening of its newest attraction, *Men in Black: Alien Attack,* an interactive, otherworldly show that lets you zap aliens with weapons called alienators.

In this chapter, we give you helpful hints and basic knowledge about visiting **Universal Studios Florida** and experiencing its attractions.

Universal Studios Escape

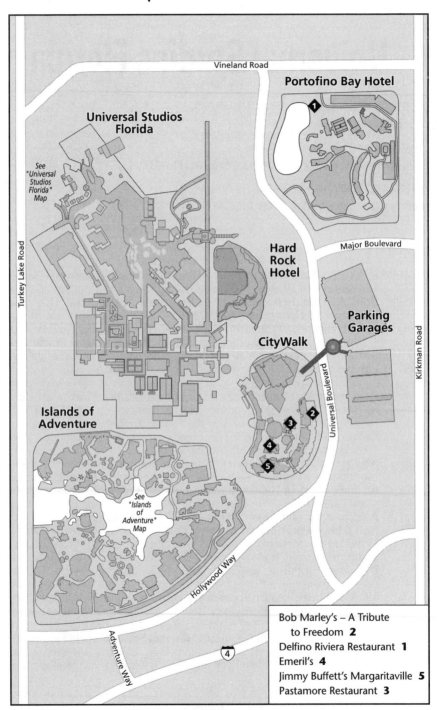

Vineland Road

Portofino Bay Hotel

1

Universal Studios Florida

See "Universal Studios Florida" Map

Turkey Lake Road

Major Boulevard

Hard Rock Hotel

Parking Garages

CityWalk

Kirkman Road

Universal Boulevard

Islands of Adventure

2

3

4

5

See "Islands of Adventure" Map

Hollywood Way

Adventure Way

4

Bob Marley's – A Tribute
   to Freedom **2**
Delfino Riviera Restaurant **1**
Emeril's **4**
Jimmy Buffett's Margaritaville **5**
Pastamore Restaurant **3**

Finding out Important Park Information

In case you forgot to bring essential items or if you need special assistance while at the park, here's a list of services and facilities that may come in handy:

- ✔ **ATMs** accepting cards from banks using the Cirrus, Honor, and Plus systems are on the outside and just inside Universal's entrance.

- ✔ You can find **baby-changing tables** in all men's and women's rest rooms; **nursing facilities** are at Family Services, just inside the main entrance and to the right. (Family Services doesn't sell diapers, so make sure you bring enough of your own.)

- ✔ Disposable **cameras and film** are available at the On Location shop in the Front Lot, just inside the main entrance. One-hour photo developing is available, though we don't recommend paying park prices. You can find many one-hour places around town, including many near tourist-area motels, that are much cheaper.

- ✔ The park provides **car assistance** including battery jumps. If you need assistance with your car, raise the hood and tell any parking attendant your location. Use the call boxes located throughout the parking garage to call for security.

- ✔ **Universal Studios** is located about half a mile north of I-4, Exit 30B, Kirkman Road or Hwy. 435. You may find construction in the area, so keep an eye out for the road signs directing you to **Universal Studios.**

- ✔ **Universal** is trying a new ticket system similar to Disney's FAST-PASS. **Universal Express** offers early admission and faster access to the rides (maximum 15-minute wait) from 7 a.m. to 10 a.m., but it's offered only to folks buying certain multiday passes and only during some seasons. Call ☎ **407-363-8000** for details, or visit www.uescape.com online.

- ✔ You can find **first aid centers** between New York and San Francisco, next to Louie's Italian Restaurant, and just inside the main entrance next to Guest Services.

- ✔ **Park hours** are generally from 9 a.m. to 7 p.m., 365 days a year. Closing hours vary seasonally and depend on special activities within the park. For example, during Halloween Horror Nights, the park closes around 5 p.m., reopens at 7 p.m. (with a new admission fee), and remains open until at least midnight. The best bet is to call before you go so that you're not caught by surprise.

- ✔ **Information** is available at Guest Relations. Call in advance ☎ **407-363-8000,** for information about new travel packages, as well as theme-park information. You can also write to Guest Relations at Universal Studios Florida, 1000 Universal Studios Plaza, Orlando, FL 32819-7601, or visit www.uescape.com online.

✔ Rent **lockers** for $4 a day plus a $2 refundable deposit across from Guest Relations, near the main entrance.

✔ Report **lost children** to Guest Relations near the main entrance or to Security (behind Louie's Italian Restaurant, between *New York* and *San Francisco*). Make children under seven wear name tags in case they forget important information when they're upset.

✔ When **parking** in the multilevel garages, remember the theme and music in your area to help you find your car later. Or, do it the old-fashioned way: Write down your location. Parking costs $6 for cars, $7 for RVs and trailers. Valet parking is available for $12. Universal's garages are connected to its parks and have moving sidewalks, but reaching the gates is still a hoof.

✔ **Pet care** for your small animals is available at the shelter in the parking garages for $5 a day (no reptiles or overnight stays).

✔ You can rent **strollers** in Amity and at Guest Relations, just inside the entrance to the right. The cost is $6 for a single and $12 for a double.

✔ You can choose from several **ticket options.** A one-day ticket costs $46 (plus 6 percent sales tax) for adults, $37 for children 3 to 9. A two-day, two-park unlimited-access escape pass is $79.95 for adults, $64.95 for kids; a three-day, two-park pass is $99.95 for adults, $79.95 for children 3 to 9; and a five-day, three-park pass (including **Wet 'n' Wild**) goes for $119.95 and $95.95. If you're planning to spend more or all of your vacation at **Universal,** or you plan to return within 12 months, a two-park annual pass ($180 adults, $155 children) is the best value. All multiday passes let you move between **Universal Studios Florida** and **Islands of Adventure** during the course of a day.

One other multiday, multipark option is the **FlexTicket.** With the FlexTicket, you pay one price to visit any of the participating parks during a seven- or ten-day period. A seven-day, four-park pass to **Universal Studios Florida, Islands of Adventure, Wet 'n Wild,** and **SeaWorld** is $159.95 for adults and $127.95 for kids 3 to 9. A ten-day, five-park pass, which also includes **Busch Gardens** in Tampa, sells for $196.95 for adults and $157.95 for kids. Call **Universal** at ☎ **407-363-8000** or visit its Web site www.uescape.com to order the FlexTicket and other multiday passes in advance.

✔ **Universal Studios Florida** and **Islands of Adventure** offer five-hour **VIP tours** for $120 per person, including the daily admission charge. These guided tours include line-cutting privileges and pre-ferred seating at several attractions. For more information on the VIP tour, call ☎ **407-224-7750.**

✔ You can rent regular **wheelchairs** for $6 in Amity and at Guest Relations just inside the main gate. Electric wheelchairs are $30, with a $25 deposit.

✔ **Theme-park prices** often reflect the fact that you're a prisoner while inside. Expect to spend $5 for a rain poncho, $7 to $9 for sunscreen, $4.50 for a large beer, and $1.75 for a small bunch of grapes.

Exploring the Top Attractions

Universal matches **Disney** stride for stride, and in some cases is a half step ahead, when it comes to cutting-edge rides. Real, as well as virtual thrills, terrific special effects, mammoth screens, and 3D action are part of its successful mix.

The rides and shows at **Universal** are located in six different zones: *Hollywood, New York, Production Central, San Francisco, Woody Woodpecker's KidZone,* and *World Expo.* You enter the park through the Front Lot. Once you're in line at an attraction, you're entertained by pre-shows that are better than the ones down the road at Disney.

Index of attractions by area

Hollywood
Terminator 2: 3D Battle Across Time

New York
Kongfrontation
Twister . . . Ride It Out

Production Central
The Funtastic World of Hanna-Barbera
Nickelodeon Studios

San Francisco
Beetlejuice's Rock 'n Roll Graveyard Revue
Earthquake — The Big One
JAWS
The Wild, Wild, Wild West Stunt Show

Woody Woodpecker's KidZone
A Day in the Park with Barney
E.T. Adventure
Woody Woodpecker's Nuthouse Coaster

World Expo
Back to the Future the Ride
Men in Black

Hollywood

Hollywood is to the right of the Front Lot, and its main streets include Rodeo Drive, Hollywood Boulevard, and Sunset Boulevard. Here's a list of the best that Hollywood has to offer:

- ✔ **Terminator 2: 3D Battle Across Time.** This attraction is billed as "the quintessential sight and sound experience for the 21st century!" and the park has little need to be modest about its claim. The director who made the movie, Jim Cameron, supervised this $60 million production. After a slow start, it builds to one of the best action shows in Orlando. Live actors and six giant Cyborgs interact with Arnie, who appears on screen (actually there are three huge ones). The crisp 3D effects are among the best in Orlando. (When liquid mercury falls from the screen, cold water really hits your legs.)

  "That's my favorite!" The show could, however, be rated PG for violence and loud noises. Children under six may find the crashing and flying 3D effects too intense.

- ✔ **Gory, Gruesome & Grotesque Horror Make-up Show.** This show is a fantastic Hollywood presentation that gives you a behind-the-scenes look at how monster makeup is done, including the transformation scenes from such movies as *The Fly* and *The Exorcist.*

- ✔ **I Love Lucy, A Tribute.** This show is a remembrance of America's queen of comedy.

New York

New York is near the back of the park and includes rides and shows along 42nd and 57th streets, Park Avenue, and Delancy Street. The premiere attractions in this section are:

- ✔ **Kongfrontation.** King Kong has returned to the Big Apple. As you stand in line in a replica of a grungy, graffiti-scarred New York subway station, CBS newsman Roland Smith reports on Kong's terrifying rampage. Everyone must evacuate to Roosevelt Island, so it's all aboard the tram. Then, well, uh-oh. Cars collide and hydrants explode below, the tram malfunctions, and, of course, you encounter Mr. Banana Breath — all 40 feet and 12,000 pounds of him. He terrifies you and fellow passengers by dangling the tram over the East River. The big ape has 46 movements, including simulated noogies on top of the tram. Long-time New Yorkers will recognize the backdrop — it's Manhattan in 1976, the year Dino DiLaurentis made the second Kong movie, which starred Jessica Lange and Jeff Bridges.

"That ape was pretty stupid." It *was* a tad hokey, but the ride has a 40-inch height minimum and the big gorilla and the dark waiting area may frighten children under six.

✔ **Twister . . . Ride it Out.** The curtain rises in the movie town of Wakita, where Universal engineers have created a five-story funnel cloud by injecting two million cubic feet of air per minute (that's enough to fill four full-size blimps). The sensory elements are pretty incredible. Power lines spark and fall, an oak splits, and the storm rumbles at rock-concert level as cars, trucks, and a cow fly about while the audience watches from just 20 feet away. In the finale, the floor begins to buckle at your feet. Crowds have been known to applaud when it's all over.

"That was pretty scary, but I liked it." This attraction may prove to be a little much for very young children.

Production Central

Production Central is directly behind and to the left of the Front Lot. Its main thoroughfares are Nickelodeon Way and 7th and 8th Avenues. Here are some of the area's highlights:

✔ **The Funtastic World of Hanna-Barbera.** Yogi Bear is the pilot of this motion-simulator/spaceship that travels through the galaxy in an effort to rescue Elroy Jetson from the evil Dick Dastardly. The ride includes lots of rock 'n' roll — dips, dives, and blasts of air when things explode. You hurtle through Bedrock, Scooby's Haunted Castle, and finally Jetsonville before — drat it! — Dick gets foiled again.

"That's awesome!" Although this is supposed to be a kiddie ride, children must be at least 40 inches tall. Prior to the ride, you learn how cartoons are created in a pre-show area. After it's over, you can experiment in an interactive area with animation sound effects — boing! plop! splash! — and color your own cartoons. This is a great place for kids of all ages to take some time and play.

✔ **Nickelodeon Studios Tour.** Tour the soundstages where Nick shows such as *Kenan & Kel* and the *Mystery Files of Shelby Woo* are produced, view concept pilots, visit the kitchen where Gak and green slime are made, play game shows such as *Double Dare 2000*, and try new Sega video games. This 45-minute behind-the-scenes tour is a fun escape from the hustle of the midway, and there's a lot of audience participation. One child volunteer always gets slimed.

"I didn't know slime tasted like applesauce." Fact is, it does. During the tour, guides explain that slime is made from leftover dessert. So if your slimed kid swallows some, green applesauce is probably as bad as the damage gets.

✔ **Other Production Central Shows. Stage 54** is an oft-changing area. If you were here in 1998 you probably saw Hercules & Xena, which then became *The Mummy*. **Alfred Hitchcock's Theater** is a tribute to the master of suspense, in which Tony Perkins narrates a reenactment of the famous shower scene from *Psycho*, and where *The Birds* — as if the movie weren't scary enough — becomes an in-your-face 3D movie. There's also an audience-participation segment in which some volunteers relive frightening scenes. Shows begin at noon.

San Francisco

This L-shaped zone faces the waterfront, and its attractions line The Embarcadero and Amity Avenue.

✔ **Beetlejuice's Rock 'n Roll Graveyard Revue.** Horrible creatures such as Dracula, Wolfman, the Phantom of the Opera, Frankenstein and his bride, and Beetlejuice show up to scare you silly. Their funky rock musical has pyrotechnic special effects and MTV-style choreography. It's loud and lively enough to scare some small children and aggravate many older adults. Young teens seem to like it the most.

✔ **Earthquake — The Big One.** Sparks fly shortly after you board a train. The whopper — 8.3 on the Richter scale! — hits as you pull into the Embarcadero Station, and you're left trapped as vast slabs of concrete collapse around you, a propane truck bursts into flames, a runaway train comes hurtling at you, and the station floods (65,000 gallons of water cascade down the steps). This is *Kongfrontation* (see "New York," earlier in the chapter) minus an ape. Prior to the ride you learn how *Earthquake,* the movie, was made, including a look at a $2.4 million set model. You then shuffle off to a soundstage where seven adult volunteers help re-create the big one.

"I liked that a lot." Children must be at least 40 inches tall. Loud noises, flames, and other special effects may frighten kids younger than six.

✔ **Jaws.** As your boat heads into a seven-acre, five million-gallon lagoon, an ominous dorsal fin appears on the horizon. What follows is a series of attacks from a three-ton, 32-foot-long, mechanical great white shark that tries to sink its urethane teeth into your hide — or at least into your boat's hide. A 30-foot wall of flame caused by burning fuel surrounds the boat, and you'll truly feel the heat in this $45-million attraction. We won't tell you how it ends, but let's just say that in spite of a captain who can't hit the broad side of a dock with his grenade launcher, some restaurant will be serving blackened shark later in the evening. (*Note:* The effects of this ride are more startling after dark.)

Well, it took J.J. a while to spit out his review for this attraction. This ride gave him a stiff neck (from tension) the first time he rode it. He was a little looser the second time around, but he kept hollering: "Gimme the gun! I'll shoot the shark."

✔ **The Wild, Wild, Wild West Stunt Show.** Stunt people demonstrate falls from three-story balconies, gun and whip fights, dynamite explosions, and other Wild West staples. This is a well-performed, lively show that's especially popular with foreign visitors who have celluloid visions of the American West.

Heed the splash zone or you will get very wet.

Woody Woodpecker's KidZone

This section of the park contains rides and attractions sure to please the littlest members of your party. If you're traveling with a number of youngsters, plan on spending a lot of time here. Some of the highlights include:

✔ **A Day in the Park with Barney.** This is Universal's diabolical answer to **Disney**'s *It's a Small World,* one of those attractions that eats the brains and ignites the nerves of anyone but 2- to 6-year-olds and their loving parents. Set in a parklike theater-in-the-round, this 25-minute musical stars the Purple One, Baby Bop, and BJ. It uses song, dance, and interactive play to deliver an environmental message. This show can be the highlight of your youngster's day. The playground next door has chimes to ring, tree houses to explore, and lots of other things to intrigue little visitors.

✔ **E.T. Adventure.** For many families, this ride alone is worth the admission price. On the ride, you soar with E.T., who is on a mission to save his ailing planet, through the forest and into space aboard a star-bound bicycle. You also meet some new characters Steven Spielberg created for the ride, including Botanicus, Tickli Moot Moot, Horn Flowers, and Tympani Tremblies. A cool, wooded forest serves to create one of the most pleasant waits for any ride in central Florida.

✔ **Woody Woodpecker's Nuthouse Coaster.** This is the top attraction in the *KidZone,* an eight-acre concession **Universal Studios** made after being criticized for having too little for young visitors. Sure, it's a kiddie coaster, but the *Nuthouse Coaster* will thrill some moms and dads, too. Although it's only 30 feet at its peak, this ride offers quick, banked turns while you sit in a miniature steam train.

The ride lasts only 50 seconds, and you can wait as long as 30 minutes, but your children probably won't let you skip it.

"... more, More, MORE!" We didn't think J.J. would ever run out of gas. Six trips on this ride and we had to drag him away. Kids have to be 48 inches or above to ride without an adult.

✔ **More to Do in Woody Woodpecker's KidZone. Fievel's Playland** is a wet, western-themed playground with a house to climb and a small water slide. **Curious George Goes to Town** has water- and ball-shooting cannons, plus a huge water tower that empties (after an alarm), drenching anyone who doesn't run for cover. Nearby, **Animal Actors Stage** offers a 20-minute show featuring Babe, Beethoven, Benji, and Lassie.

World Expo

The smallest zone in **Universal Studios Florida** offers a lot of punch in its two rides. World Expo is on Exposition Boulevard, between San Francisco and KidZone. The top attractions here are:

✔ **Back to the Future . . . the Ride.** This ride has more warnings than a centipede has legs. Topping the list: If you have a problem with motion sickness, don't get on. If you don't have a problem with motion sickness, but have a problem with other people getting motion sick on you, you may want to invest $5 in one of those ponchos. (No sense ruining your new Mickey shirt, right?) There also are warnings for would-be riders who are pregnant or become dizzy, as well as those who are claustrophobic or have neck, heart, or back problems. These warnings are all justified.

✔ *Back to the Future* offers you a chance at time travel in a simulator made to look like a DeLorean. Six to eight of you are packed into a car after a video briefing from Christopher Lloyd, also known as Dr. Emmett Brown. Biff the Bully has stolen another DeLorean, and you have to catch him. The fate of the universe is in your hands. The huge screen makes this ride very intense, but if you didn't heed the warnings and begin to feel some of the symptoms, just stick your neck out of your car — literally. You can see the other cars, lending the very true perspective that you're really only in a theater.

✔ "WOW! Can we ride it again?" Maybe later. We forgot our ponchos. By the way, kids must be 40 inches or more to ride.

✔ **Men in Black: Alien Attack.** Board a six-passenger cruiser, and you'll buzz the streets of New York, using laser tag-style guns to splatter 80 kinds of bug-eyed terrorists. This four-minute ride relies on 360-degree spins rather than speed for its thrill factor. At the ride's conclusion, you're swallowed by a giant roach, and you must then blast your way out (getting doused with bug guts — warm water) for your efforts. Will Smith rates you as galaxy defender, atomically average, or bug bait. This ride-through video game is located next to *Back to the Future,* and it has a 42-inch height minimum.

Grabbing a Bite to Eat

There are more than a dozen places to eat at **Universal Studios Florida.** The main food attractions range from lobster to corn dogs. Here are our favorites by category:

- ✔ **Best sit-down meal.** Lombard's Landing, across from *Earthquake,* has a hearty fried clam basket, as well as lobster, steak, pasta, and burgers ($10–$19).

- ✔ **Best counter service.** Universal Studios' Classic Monsters Café is one of the newest eateries in the park and serves salads, pizza, pasta, and rotisserie chicken ($6 to $10). You can find it off 7th Avenue near The Boneyard.

- ✔ **Best place for hungry families.** Similar to a mall food court, the International Food Bazaar offers a variety of ethnic food in one location. With options ranging from stir-fry to fajitas, this is a place where a family can split up and still eat under one roof. There are kid's meals for under $4 at most locations. The food is far from gourmet but a cut above regular fast food ($6 to $11). It's located near the back of *Animal Actor's Studio* near the lagoon and the entrance to *Back to the Future.*

- ✔ **Best Snack.** The Frozen Lemon Slush ($2.35) at Brody's Ice Cream Shop is just the thing to refresh you on a hot summer afternoon. Brody's is located near the *Wild, Wild, Wild West Stunt Show* arena. Carts in Amityville also sell the luscious lemon treat.

See Chapter 15, "The Scoop on Orlando's Dining Scene," for the best places to grab a bite at **Universal's CityWalk.**

Shopping at Universal Studios Florida

If **Disney** can do it, **Universal** can, too. Every major attraction at **Universal** has a theme store attached. Although the prices are relatively high when you consider you're just buying a T-shirt, the Hard Rock Cafe in adjacent **CityWalk** is extremely popular and has a small but diverse selection of Hard Rock everything.

More than 25 other shops in the park sell souvenirs ranging from *I Love Lucy* collectibles to Bates Motel shower curtains. Be warned, however, that, unlike **WDW,** these shops are even more specific to individual attractions — if you see something you like, buy it. You probably won't see it in another store. Here's a sampling of the more unusual gifts available at some of the Universal stores:

Universal Studios Florida

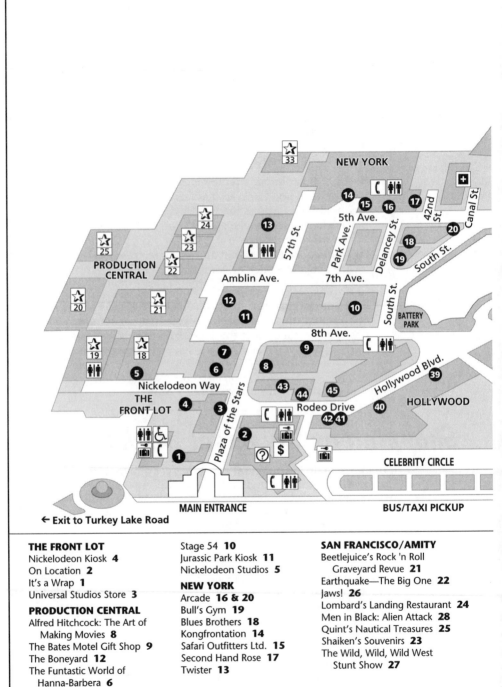

THE FRONT LOT
Nickelodeon Kiosk **4**
On Location **2**
It's a Wrap **1**
Universal Studios Store **3**

PRODUCTION CENTRAL
Alfred Hitchcock: The Art of
Making Movies **8**
The Bates Motel Gift Shop **9**
The Boneyard **12**
The Funtastic World of
Hanna-Barbera **6**
Hanna-Barbera Store **7**

Stage 54 **10**
Jurassic Park Kiosk **11**
Nickelodeon Studios **5**

NEW YORK
Arcade **16 & 20**
Bull's Gym **19**
Blues Brothers **18**
Kongfrontation **14**
Safari Outfitters Ltd. **15**
Second Hand Rose **17**
Twister **13**

SAN FRANCISCO/AMITY
Beetlejuice's Rock 'n Roll
Graveyard Revue **21**
Earthquake—The Big One **22**
Jaws! **26**
Lombard's Landing Restaurant **24**
Men in Black: Alien Attack **28**
Quint's Nautical Treasures **25**
Shaiken's Souvenirs **23**
The Wild, Wild, Wild West
Stunt Show **27**

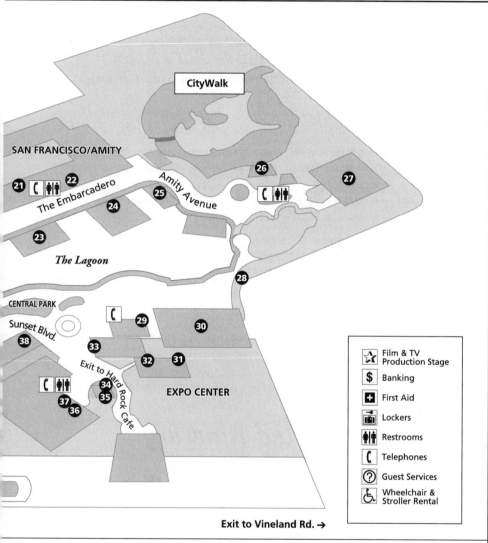

CityWalk

SAN FRANCISCO/AMITY

21 22 The Embarcadero

24

23

The Lagoon

25

Amity Avenue

26

27

28

CENTRAL PARK

Sunset Blvd.

38

29

30

33

32 31

Exit to Hard Rock Cafe

34
35
37
36

EXPO CENTER

Film & TV Production Stage

$ Banking

First Aid

Lockers

Restrooms

Telephones

? Guest Services

Wheelchair & Stroller Rental

Exit to Vineland Rd. →

EXPO CENTER
Animal Actors Stage **33**
Back to the Future Gifts **29**
Back to the Future...The Ride **30**
The Barney Store **32**

WOODY WOODPECKER'S KID ZONE
A Day in the Park with Barney **31**
E.T. Adventure **36**
E.T.'s Toy Closet **37**
Fievel's Playland **34**
Woody Woodpecker's
 Nuthouse Coaster **35**

HOLLYWOOD
AT&T at the Movies **38**
Brown Derby Hat Shop **45**
Cyber Image **40**
The Dark Room **41**
The Gory, Gruesome & Grotesque
 Horror Make-up Show **39**
Lucy, A Tribute **44**
Silver Screen Collectibles **43**
Terminator 2: 3D Battle
 Across Time **42**

✔ **Back to the Future Gifts.** Real fans of the movie series find lots of intriguing stuff here. One of the more interesting is a miniature version of the *Back to the Future* DeLorean.

✔ **The Bates Motel Gift Shop.** When house guests have stayed just a bit too long, you can send a not-so-subtle message by putting out these Bates Motel guest towels.

✔ **E.T.'s Toy Closet.** This is the place for plush, stuffed animals including a replica of the alien namesake.

✔ **Hanna-Barbera Store.** Scooby Doo Slippers and Fred Flintstone T-shirts are great gifts for the young and young at heart.

✔ **Kongfrontation.** A video copy of the original movie that started it all is available, as well as several sizes of cuddly stuffed gorillas.

✔ **Quint's Nautical Treasures.** This is the place to go for a different kind of T-shirt. Tropical colors, with subtle Universal logos, are the hot items here.

✔ **Second Hand Rose.** This is something you will never see at **Disney:** discounted merchandise. Items in this store include last season's hot T-shirts, stuffed animals, and a wide variety of souvenirs at the lowest prices in the park.

✔ **Silver Screen Collectibles.** Fans of *I Love Lucy* will adore the small variety of collectible dolls. There's also a Betty Boop line. For an interesting, practical, and inexpensive little something to take home, check out the Woody Woodpecker back scratcher.

✔ **Universal Studios Store.** This store, near the entrance, sells just about everything when it comes to Universal apparel.

Using Our Suggested Itinerary

Spending one day at **Universal Studios** is sufficient if you arrive early and keep up a steady pace. The following one-day guide will help keep you on track to see the best of **Universal:**

✔ Skip the city sidewalks of the main gate and save *Terminator 2: 3D Battle Across Time* until later. Veer to the left and if the lines are relatively short, see *The Funtastic World of Hanna-Barbera.*

✔ If you're a late arrival, take the 45-minute *Nickelodeon Studios Tour* (4- to 14-year-olds will love it); otherwise, save it for the end of the day.

✔ Continue clockwise around the park, visiting *Twister, Kongfrontation, Jaws,* and *Earthquake.*

✔ Take a break for lunch, watch *The Wild, Wild, Wild West Stunt Show,* and move to *Back to the Future, Men in Black,* and *E.T. Adventure.*

✔ If you haven't already, let your kids burn off some energy in *Woody Woodpecker's KidZone,* go to *Terminator 2,* and, if you didn't catch it earlier, the *Nickelodeon Studios Tour.*

✔ You may have time to revisit another attraction or beat the crowd to the parking lot.

A second day lets you revisit some of your favorite rides and shows or experience the ones you missed. With the pressure to hit all the major rides lessened, you can delay your *Nickelodeon Studios Tour* until day two (the first tour usually isn't until 10:30 a.m.), but in our opinion it's a must-visit if you have kids who watch this network. Visitors sometimes have a chance to participate in the taping of some of Nick's often-sloppy game shows. You can also visit the *Gory, Gruesome & Grotesque Horror Make-up Show* and *Beetlejuice's Rock 'n Roll Graveyard Revue.*

Chapter 24

Islands of Adventure

. . . .

In This Chapter

▶ Knowing the details

▶ Hopping the **Islands**

▶ Finding take-home souvenirs

▶ Traveling around the **Universe** in a day

. . . .

*U*niversal's second park opened in 1999 with a vibrantly colored, cleverly themed collection of fast, fun rides wrapped in a 110-acre package. Roller coasters thunder above its pedestrian walkways, water rides careen through the center of the park, and theme restaurants are camouflaged to match their surroundings, adding to your overall immersion in the various "islands" in this adventure.

From the wobbly angles and day-glo colors of *Seuss Island* to the lush foliage of *Jurassic Park,* **Universal** has also done a good job of differentiating the various sections of the park, making it easier to navigate. (Unlike **Universal Studios Florida,** where it's sometimes hard to tell if you're in *San Francisco* or *New York.*)

This $1 billion park is divided into six areas: the *Port of Entry,* where you'll find a collection of shops and eateries, and the themed sections: *Seuss Landing, Toon Lagoon, Jurassic Park, Marvel Super Hero Island,* and *The Lost Continent.* **Islands of Adventure** has a large menu of thrill rides and coasters, plus a growing stable of play areas for younger guests. The trade-off is that there are few shows and stage productions.

Knowing Essential Park Information

Before you start on your journey through the park's rides and attractions, here are some mundane matters that you may need to know.

> ✔ **AOL Kiosks.** These compact stations allow Islands visitors to send and check e-mail. Look for them near the Confisco Grille in the *Port of Entry,* Mythos Restaurant in *The Lost Continent,* Captain America Diner in *Marvel Super Hero Island,* and in the Discovery Center in *Jurassic Park.* Using the kiosks is free, but there are notes asking you to spend no more than five minutes online. Attendants will shoo you away if you stay too long.

- ✔ **ATMs.** You can find machines accepting cards from banks using the Cirrus, Honor, and Plus systems outside the park's main entrance and in *The Lost Continent* near the bridge leading to *Jurassic Park*.

- ✔ **Baby-changing and nursing facilities.** Baby-swap stations are located at all the major attractions, allowing one parent to wait with their under-age (or under-height) offspring while the other parent rides. Diaper-changing stations are also in all the rest rooms. You can find nursing facilities in the Guest Services building at the *Port of Entry*.

- ✔ **Cameras and film.** Purchase film and disposable cameras at De Foto's Expedition Photography, inside the main entrance to the right.

- ✔ **Car assistance.** If you need assistance with your car, raise the hood and tell any parking attendant your location, or use the call boxes located throughout the garage to call for security. The park provides battery jumps.

- ✔ **Directions to the park.** Universal is about half a mile north of I-4, Exit 30B, Kirkman Road or Hwy. 435. You may find construction in the area, so keep an eye out for the road signs directing you to Universal Studios.

- ✔ **Express Lane. Universal** is trying a new system similar to **Disney**'s FASTPASS. **Universal Express** offers early admission and faster access to the rides (maximum 15-minute wait) from 7 to 10 a.m. However, the service is only offered to folks buying certain multi-day passes and only during some seasons. Call ☎ **407-363-8000** for details; online, go to www.uescape.com.

- ✔ **First aid centers.** You can find first aid centers just inside and to the right of the main entrance as well as in *The Lost Continent*, across from Oasis Coolers.

- ✔ **Hours. Islands of Adventure** is open 365 days a year, generally from 9 a.m. to 7 p.m. Closing hours vary seasonally and depend on special activities within the park.

- ✔ **Information.** Call Guest Relations (☎ **407-363-8000**) before you leave to request information about new travel packages, as well as theme-park information. With the opening of **Islands of Adventure** and the **Portofino Bay Hotel** (see Chapter 8), the availability of good deals should continue, especially for packages that include hotel stays. Ask for details on special offers. You also can write to **Islands of Adventure,** 1000 Universal Studios Plaza, Orlando, FL 32819-7610, or go to www.uescape.com on the Internet.

- ✔ **Lockers.** You can find lockers across from Guest Relations near the main entrance ($4 a day plus a $2 refundable deposit). You'll also find them at some of the more energetic rides (the ones on which you can lose valuables). Lockers located near energetic rides are usually free for an hour and $1 for each additional 30-minute period. If you don't want to stash your life savings in a locker, give your belongings to a nonrider in your party.

✔ **Lost children.** If you lose a child, go to Guest Relations near the main entrance. Make children under seven wear name tags for easy identification in case they're too upset to talk when they're lost.

✔ **Parking.** If you park in the multilevel garages, remember the theme and music in your area to help you find your car later. Or, do it the old-fashioned way and write it down. Parking costs $6 for cars, $7 for RVs and trailers. Valet parking is available for $12. Universal's garages are connected to its parks and have moving sidewalks, but it's still a long walk to the gates.

✔ **Pet care.** You can leave your small animals at the shelter in the parking garages for $5 a day (no overnight stays).

✔ **Strollers.** Look to the left as you enter the park through the turnstiles. Stroller rental costs $6 for a single, $12 for a double.

✔ **Tickets.** You have several available ticket options at **Islands of Adventure.** A one-day ticket costs $46 (plus 6 percent sales tax) for adults, $37 for children ages 3–9. A two-day, two-park (includes **Universal Studios Florida**) unlimited-access Escape pass is $79.95 for adults, $64.95 for kids; a three-day, two-park pass is $99.95 for adults, $79.95 for children 3–9; and a five-day, three-park pass (including **Wet 'n Wild**) goes for $119.95 and $95.95 for kids. If you plan to spend more or all of your vacation at **Universal,** or you plan to return within 12 months, a two-park annual pass ($180 adults, $155 children) is a good value. All multiday passes let you move between **Universal Studios Florida** and **Islands of Adventure** during the course of a day.

One other multiday, multipark option is the FlexTicket. With this option, you pay one price to visit any of the participating parks during a 7- or 10-day period. A seven-day, four-park pass to **Universal Studios Florida, Islands of Adventure, Wet 'n Wild,** and **SeaWorld** is $159.95 for adults and $127.95 for kids 3–9. A 10-day, five-park pass, which also includes **Busch Gardens** in Tampa, sells for $196.95 for adults and $157.95 for kids. Call **Universal** at ☎ **407-363-8000** or visit its Web site, www.uescape.com, to order the FlexTicket and other multiday passes in advance.

✔ **Tours.** Five-hour VIP tours at **Universal Studios Florida** and **Islands of Adventure** cost $120 per person, including the daily admission charge. These guided tours include line-cutting privileges and preferred seating at several attractions. For more information about the VIP tour, call ☎ **407-224-7750.**

✔ **Wheelchairs.** You can rent regular wheelchairs for $6 in the center concourse of the parking garage or to your left as you enter the turnstiles of the main entrance. Electric wheelchairs are $30, with a $25 deposit.

Theme park prices often reflect the fact that you're a prisoner while inside. Expect to spend $5.00 for a poncho, $7.00 to $9.00 for sunscreen, $4.50 for a large beer, and $1.75 for a small bunch of grapes.

Islands of Adventure

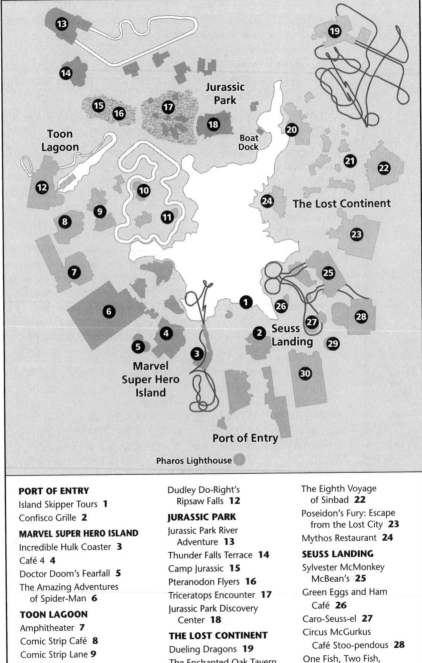

PORT OF ENTRY
Pharos Lighthouse

PORT OF ENTRY
Island Skipper Tours **1**
Confisco Grille **2**

MARVEL SUPER HERO ISLAND
Incredible Hulk Coaster **3**
Café 4 **4**
Doctor Doom's Fearfall **5**
The Amazing Adventures
  of Spider-Man **6**

TOON LAGOON
Amphitheater **7**
Comic Strip Café **8**
Comic Strip Lane **9**
Popeye & Bluto's
  Bilge-Rat Barges **10**
Me Ship, The Olive **11**

Dudley Do-Right's
  Ripsaw Falls **12**

JURASSIC PARK
Jurassic Park River
  Adventure **13**
Thunder Falls Terrace **14**
Camp Jurassic **15**
Pteranodon Flyers **16**
Triceratops Encounter **17**
Jurassic Park Discovery
  Center **18**

THE LOST CONTINENT
Dueling Dragons **19**
The Enchanted Oak Tavern
  (and Alchemy Bar) **20**
Sinbad **21**

The Eighth Voyage
  of Sinbad **22**
Poseidon's Fury: Escape
  from the Lost City **23**
Mythos Restaurant **24**

SEUSS LANDING
Sylvester McMonkey
  McBean's **25**
Green Eggs and Ham
  Café **26**
Caro-Seuss-el **27**
Circus McGurkus
  Café Stoo-pendous **28**
One Fish, Two Fish,
  Red Fish, Blue Fish **29**
The Cat in the Hat **30**

Practical Advice for Island Adventurers

In order to get the most out of your visit to the park, keep the following tips in mind when you're exploring the **Islands of Adventure:**

✔ **Short visitors.** Ten of the 12 major rides at **Islands of Adventure** have height restrictions (from 40 to 54 inches). You can find a baby or child swap at all major attractions, allowing you or your partner to ride while the other watches your tikes, but sitting in a waiting room isn't much fun for the little ones. Take your child's height into consideration before coming to the park or at least some of its islands.

In July 2000, **Universal** added two notable attractions to its lineup to answer criticism that **Islands of Adventure** has too little for young guests. The *Flying Unicorn* is a small roller coaster that travels through a mythical forest and resides next to *Dueling Dragons*. *Storm Force* is a spinning attraction in which guests help Storm harness weather to fight her archenemy, Magneto. Located on *Marvel Super Hero Island, Storm Force*'s special effects include a swirling storm of light and sound.

✔ **Cruising the Islands.** If you hauled your stroller with you on your vacation, bring it with you to the park. It's a very long walk from your car, through the massive parking garage and the nighttime entertainment district **CityWalk,** before you get to the park. Carrying a young child and the accompanying paraphernalia, even with a series of moving sidewalks, can make the long trek seem even longer — especially at the end of the day.

✔ **Read ride restriction warnings.** Make sure that you consider all the ride restrictions. Expectant mothers, guests prone to motion sickness, and those with heart, neck, or back trouble are discouraged from riding several of the biggest attractions. There's still plenty to see and do, but without the roller coasters, the thrill of **Islands of Adventure** is diminished.

✔ **Beat the heat.** Several rides require that you wait outside without any cover to protect you from the sizzling Florida sun. Bring some bottled water with you for the long waits (it costs $2.50 if you buy it in the park) or take a sip or two from the fountains placed in the waiting areas. Also, alcohol is more readily available at this park than at **Disney,** so remember that liquor, roller coasters, and sweltering heat can make for a messy mix.

✔ **Cash in on your AAA card.** You can save 10 percent on your purchases at any gift shop or on a meal in **Islands of Adventure** by showing your AAA (American Automobile Association) card. This discount isn't available at food or merchandise carts. Likewise, tobacco, candy, film, collectibles, and sundry items aren't included in discounts.

Exploring the Top Attractions at Islands of Adventure

Islands of Adventure's six sections, featuring more than 20 rides and attractions, plus numerous restaurants and shops are laid out in a circular pattern around a large lagoon.

Index of attractions by area

Seuss Landing
Caro-Seuss-El
The Cat in the Hat
If I Ran the Zoo
One Fish, Two Fish, Red Fish, Blue Fish

Marvel Super Hero Island
The Amazing Adventures of Spider-Man
Dr. Doom's Fearfall
Incredible Hulk Coaster

Toon Lagoon
Comic Strip Lane
Dudley Do-Right's Ripsaw Falls
Me Ship, The Olive
Popeye & Bluto's Bilge-Rat Barges

Jurassic Park
Camp Jurassic
Discovery Center
Jurassic Park River Adventure
Pteranodon Flyers
Triceratops Encounter

The Lost Continent
Dueling Dragons
The Eighth Voyage of Sinbad
The Mystic Fountain
Poseidon's Fury: Escape
  from the Lost City

Port of Entry

Think of the *Port* as the park's starting line. The entire race is before you, but the creators of **Islands of Adventure** want to juice you slowly. The aesthetics in *Port of Entry* resemble a faraway marketplace that you'd find in *Indiana Jones* — oops, that's *another* movie company. Anyway, this is the garden-variety "now-that-we-have-you-what-can-we-sell-you?" gate area where the park pushes stuff like junk food, souvenirs, and other completely unnecessary things while you're still suffering from ticket shock. From the *Port of Entry,* you can walk to the five other islands dotting the lagoon or, if you want a shortcut, go to *Island Skipper Tours* and catch one of the boats that chug you to the opposite side of the park.

Seuss Landing

The main attractions in **Seuss Landing,** a 10-acre island, are aimed at the younger set, though anyone who loved the good Doctor as a child will enjoy some nostalgic fun on the colorful rides. In addition to those listed here, a new ride will open as this book goes to press and is supposed to give you a bird's-eye view from an aerial train that glides around the island and through a restaurant.

✔ **Caro-Seuss-El.** This not-so-ordinary carousel replaces the traditional wooden horses with seven whimsical Seussian characters (54 total mounts), including Cowfish, the elephant birds from *Horton Hatches an Egg,* and Mulligatawnies. They move up and down as well as in and out. Pull the reins to make their eyes blink or heads bob as you twirl through the riot of color surrounding the ride. The ride also features a rocking-chariot platform and wheelchair-loading system that makes it a fun attraction for guests with disabilities.

✔ **The Cat in the Hat.** All aboard the couch! In this case, the couches are six-passenger futons that steer 1,800 people an hour through 18 show scenes. Any Seuss fan will recognize the giant candy-striped hat looming over the entrance and probably the chaotic journey. Comparable to, but a lot spunkier than, *It's A Small World* at **WDW,** *The Cat in the Hat* has become one of the signature experiences of **Islands of Adventure,** though you may find it tame. Love it or hate it, you have to do it. The couches travel through scenes retelling *The Cat and the Hat* tale of a day gone terribly south. You'll also encounter old favorites like Thing 1 and Thing 2.

"That felt weird. My eyes are still spinning." The ride's highlight is a revolving 24-foot tunnel that alters your perceptions and leaves you feeling woozy. You must be 48 inches or taller to ride alone, and keep in mind that pop-up characters may scare younger children.

✔ **If I Ran the Zoo.** *If I Ran the Zoo* is an interactive playland for kids who enjoy everything from flying water snakes to a chance to tickle the toes of a Seussian animal. The 19 play stations are a nice place to let your kids burn off some excited energy.

✔ **One Fish, Two Fish, Red Fish, Blue Fish.** On this attraction, your controls allow you to move your funky fish up or down 15 feet as you spin around on an arm attached to a hub. Watch out for squirt posts, which spray unsuspecting riders who don't follow the ride's rhyme scheme (and sometimes the ones who do follow it). Riders must be 48 inches or taller to ride without an adult.

Marvel Super Hero Island

If you're a thrill junkie, you'll love the twisting, turning, stomach-churning rides on this island filled with building-tall murals of Marvel Super Heroes. Children can meet some of their favorite heroes in front of *The Amazing Adventures of Spider-Man*. Check your daily guide map, handed out when you enter the park or at guest services, for the times of hero appearances.

- **The Amazing Adventures of Spider-Man.** *The Amazing Adventures of Spider-Man* is a primo ride that combines moving vehicles, filmed 3D action, and special effects themed around the original web master. The script: While you're on a yawn-able tour of the *Daily Bugle* newspaper — *yikes!* — the boys in black hats filch the Statue of Liberty. Your mission is to help Spidey get it back. This ride is similar to *Back to the Future* at **Universal Studios Florida,** but it's not as stationary. For example, cars twist and spin, plunge and soar through this comic book universe. Passengers wearing 3D glasses squeal as real and computer-generated objects alternately fly toward their 12-person cars. There's also a simulated 400-foot drop that feels an awful lot like the real thing.

  Expectant mothers or those with heart, neck, or back problems shouldn't ride the *Amazing Adventures of Spider-Man.*

  "I think I left my stomach back there." J.J. wasn't the only one. Dark scenes and some of the motion effects make this ride unsuitable for very young kids. It also has a 40-inch height minimum.

- **Dr. Doom's Fearfall.** Look! Up in the sky! It's a bird, it's a plane. . . uh, it's you falling 200 feet if you're courageous enough to climb aboard. This towering metal skeleton provides screams that you can hear far into the day and night. The plot line: You're touring a lab when — are you sensing a theme here? — something goes horribly wrong as Doctor Doom tries to cure you of fear. You're fired to the top of the ride, with feet dangling, and dropped in intervals, leaving your stomach at several levels. The fall feels like the *Tower of Terror* at **Disney–MGM Studios,** but with the additional sensation of hanging free.

  If you're an expectant mother or you experience heart, neck, or back problems, you shouldn't ride *Dr. Doom's Fearfall.* Minimum height is 52 inches, and we recommend a minimum age of 10.

- **Incredible Hulk Coaster.** This ride may be for you if you think *Dueling Dragons* (see "The Lost Continent" later in this chapter) is for sissies. *The Incredible Hulk Coaster* is sure to knot your shorts and stomach as it literally rockets from a dark tunnel into the sunlight, while accelerating from 0 to 40 mph in two seconds. Universal's scriptwriters insist that it has the same thrust as an F-16. Although it's only two-thirds the speed of **Disney–MGM's**

Rock 'n' Roller Coaster, this ride is in broad daylight, and you can *see* the asphalt! After you're launched, you spin upside down 128 feet from the ground, feel weightless, and careen through the center of the park over the heads of other visitors. If you're a coaster lover, you'll be pleased to know that this ride, which lasts 2 minutes and 15 seconds, includes seven rollovers and two deep drops. Sunglasses, assorted change, and an occasional set of car keys lie in a mesh net beneath the ride — proof of its motion and the fact that most folks don't heed our locker warning (see "Knowing Essential Park Information," earlier in this chapter). As a nice touch, the 32-passenger metal coaster glows green at night.

Expectant mothers or those with heart, neck, or back problems shouldn't ride.

"No thanks. I'm too young to die." This is another ride that we think is best for riders 10 and older. Children must be at least 54 inches tall to climb aboard.

Toon Lagoon

More than 150 life-size, sculpted cartoon images let you know you've entered **Toon Lagoon,** which is dedicated to your favorites from the Sunday funnies.

✔ **Comic Strip Lane.** Beetle Bailey, Hagar the Horrible, and Dagwood & Blondie are just a few of the 80 characters in this comic-strip neighborhood. This attraction is fun for visuals and passive moments, but it's also one to skip if you're on a tight schedule.

✔ **Dudley Do-Right's Ripsaw Falls.** Although this island is pretty Popeye-happy, the heroic Dudley has a splashy flume ride that drops 75 feet at 50 mph. (Apparently it was a bit too much for some riders who complained. **Universal** temporarily closed it in early 2000 to tame it a bit.) Your mission is to save the fair Nell from Snidely Whiplash. The boats take you around a 400,000-gallon lagoon and plunge you 15 feet below the water's surface, but this is mainly hype — the water is contained on either side of you. *Note:* You *will* get very wet despite the contained water.

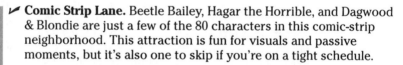

Expectant mothers or people with heart, neck, or back problems shouldn't ride this attraction, and children must be at least 44 inches tall.

✔ **Me Ship, The Olive.** This three-story boat is a family-friendly play-land with dozens of interactive activities from bow to stern. Kids can toot whistles, clang bells, or play the organ. *Sweet Pea's Playpen* is a favorite of younger guests. Kids 6 and up love *Cargo Crane,* where they can drench riders on *Popeye & Bluto's Bilge-Rat Barges* (see "Popeye & Bluto's Bilge-Rat Barges," later in this chapter).

✔ **Popeye & Bluto's Bilge-Rat Barges.** Here's another water special — a churning, turning, twisting, listing raft ride with the same kind of vehicle as *Kali River Rapids* at Disney's **Animal Kingdom** (see Chapter 20), but this one's faster and bouncier. You'll get wet from mechanical devices as well as the water cannons fired by guests at *Me Ship, The Olive* (see "Me Ship, The Olive," earlier in the chapter). The 12-passenger rafts bump and dip their way along a course lined with villains, most notably Bluto, Sea Hag, and a twirling octopus boat wash.

"I think they put ice water in there." He's right, the water is *c-c-cold*, which is a blessing on hot summer days but less so in January, and trust us — you can get completely soaked. Children must be at least 42 inches tall to ride.

Jurassic Park

All the basics from Steven Spielberg's wildly successful films, and some of the high-tech wizardry, are incorporated into this lushly landscaped tropical locale that includes a replica of the visitor's center from the movie. Expect long lines at the *River Adventure* and pleasant surprises at the *Discovery Center,* both described in the following section.

✔ **Camp Jurassic.** This play area, designed along the same lines as *The Boneyard* in Disney's **Animal Kingdom,** has everything from lava pits with dinosaur bones to a rain forest. Watch out for the spitters that lurk in dark caves. The multilevel play area offers plenty of places for kids to crawl, explore, and lose a little steam. Keep a close eye on young children because it's easy to get turned around inside the caverns.

✔ **Discovery Center.** *Discovery Center* is an air-conditioned spot where you can relax while you learn something. The center has life-size dinosaur replicas and some interactive games, including a sequencer that lets you combine your DNA with a dinosaur's, as well as the *Beasaur* exhibit, where you can see and hear as the dinosaurs did. You can also play *You Bet Your Dinosaur* (a game show originally called *You Bet Jurassic*) and scan the walls for fossils. The highlight is watching a tiny velociraptor hatch in the lab. There are a limited number of interactive stations, so keep in mind that this attraction can consume a lot of time on busy days.

✔ **Jurassic Park River Adventure.** The adventure of this attraction begins slowly but soon throws you into a world of stormy skies and five-story dinosaurs, including a T-Rex, the most unrelenting, fearsome bully to walk the planet. This is an improved version of *Kongfrontation* at **Universal Studios Florida** (see Chapter 23) that allows you to literally come face to face with the breathing inhabitants of *Jurassic Park,* including spitters that spit at you. To escape, you take a breathtaking 85-foot plunge in a flume that's steep and quick enough to lift your fanny from the seat. Did we mention that you'll get soaked?

"I don't want to do that again — *ever!*" (At least he was brave enough to ride it through once. At test time, Spielberg made them stop the ride and let him out before the plunge.) Children must be at least 42 inches tall.

✔ **Pteranodon Flyers.** Maybe you remember that childish rhyme: "Birdie, birdie, in the sky; why'd you do that in my eye?" Well, *Pteranodon Flyers* will make you wonder if our cave-dwelling ancestors had to worry about such droppings from things with 12-foot wingspans.

The 10-foot metal frames and simple seats of this high-flying ride look flimsy. The landing is bumpy, and you'll swing side to side throughout. Unlike the traditional gondolas in sky rides, on *Pteranodon Flyers,* your feet hang free from the two-seat, skeletal flyer, and there's little but a restraining belt between you and the ground. Now that we've scared you, this is a kiddie ride — single passengers must be between 36 and 56 inches; adults can climb aboard *only* when accompanying someone that size

This ride launches only two passengers every 30 to 40 seconds so it can consume an hour even in the off-season.

✔ **Triceratops Encounter.** Meet a "living" dinosaur and learn from its trainers about the care and feeding of the 24-foot-long, 10-foot-high Triceratops. The creature's responses to touch include realistic blinks, breathing, flinches, and leg movements. You can touch this heavyweight dino as it turns its head and groans.

The Lost Continent

Although they've mixed their millennia — ancient Greece with medieval forest — **Universal** has done a good job creating a foreboding mood in this section of the park, where the entrance is marked by menacing stone griffins.

✔ **Dueling Dragons.** This is the Islands of Adventure version of a dual-dueling roller coaster. The timer on this puppy is set for only 2½ minutes, but it comes with the usual health warnings and a scream factor of 11 on a 10-point scale. True coaster crazies love this intertwined set of leg-dangling racers that climb to 125 feet, invert five times, and on three occasions, come within 12 inches of each other as the two dragons battle, and you prove your bravery by tagging along. (Ride greeters ought to pass out diapers and a sedative.) The *Fire Dragon* can reach speeds of up to 60 mph, while the *Ice Dragon* makes it to only 55 mph.

For the best ride, try to get one of the two outside seats in each row. Also, pay attention, because the lines for both coasters split near the loading dock so that daredevils can claim the very first car.

You shouldn't ride this ride if you're an expectant mother or if you have heart, neck, or back problems. (Why aren't you surprised?) Children must be at least 54 inches tall.

✔ **The Eighth Voyage of Sinbad.** The mythical sailor Sinbad is the star of a stunt demonstration that takes place in a 1,700-seat theater decorated with blue stalagmites and eerie, gloomy shipwrecks. The show includes six water explosions and 50 pyrotechnic effects including a 10-foot circle of flames. It doesn't, however, come close to the quality of the *Indiana Jones* stunt show at **Disney–MGM Studios.**

✔ **The Mystic Fountain.** This interactive smart fountain delights younger guests. It can see and hear, leading to a lot of kibitzing with those who stand before the stone fountain, suitably named Rocky. If you get close enough, you may even get a surprise shower. It's a real treat for 3- to 8-year-olds.

✔ **Poseidon's Fury: Escape from the Lost City.** Clearly, *Poseidon's Fury* is the park's best show. It exposes you to fire and water in the same manner that *Earthquake* does at **Universal Studios Florida,** but it takes adventure to another level. The Keeper, a ghostly white character, leads you on a journey where you become trapped in a battle between the evil Poseidon, god of the sea, and Zeus, king of the gods. From a small room, you proceed through a 42-foot vortex — where 17,500 gallons of water swirl around you, barrel-style — and into the Temple of Poseidon. In the battle royale, the gods hurl 25-foot fireballs at each other. It's more interesting than frightening but still offers a thrill.

Children must be 48 inches to enter, and some may find the flaming fireballs, explosive sounds, and rushing water a little too intense.

Dining at Islands of Adventure

After all the action and angst of riding rides and visiting attractions, you're probably hungry. There are a number of stands in the park where you can get a quick bite to eat and a handful of full-service restaurants. The park's creators have taken some extra care to tie in restaurant offerings with the theme. For example, the Green Eggs and Ham Café may be one of the few places on earth where you're willing to eat tinted eggs. (They're sold in the form of an egg-and-ham sandwich for $5.95.) Thunder Falls Terrace Restaurant in *Jurassic Park* offers a rib-and-chicken combo as well as other options in the $8 to $12 range.

Here are some of our park favorites:

✔ **Best sit-down restaurant.** At Mythos, selections include jerk grouper, lobster-stuffed potato, pepper-painted salmon with lemon couscous, or pan-fried crab cakes with lobster sauce and basil. This restaurant is best suited for older children and adults. Prices range from $5.50 to $17.50. Open daily 11:30 a.m. to 3:30 p.m.

✔ **Best atmosphere for adults.** The Enchanted Oak Tavern (and Alchemy Bar) has a cavelike interior, which from the outside looks like a mammoth tree, and is brightened by an azure blue skylight with a celestial theme. The tables and chairs are thick planks, and the servers are clad in wench wear. Try the chicken/rib combo with waffle fries for $12.95. You can also choose from 45 brands of beer.

✔ **Best atmosphere for kids.** The fun never stops under the big top at Circus McGurkus Café Stoo-pendous in Seuss Landing, where animated trapeze artists swing from the ceiling. Kids' meals, including a souvenir cup, are $5. The adult menu features fried chicken, lasagna, spaghetti, and pizza. Try the fried chicken platter for $7.50 or the lasagna for $6.79.

✔ **Best vegetarian fare.** Fire-Eater's Grill, located in The Lost Continent, is a fast food stand that offers a tasty veggie falafel for $4.59. You also can get a tossed salad for $2.79.

✔ **Best Diversity.** Comic Strip Café, located in Toon Lagoon, is a four-in-one, counter service-style eatery offering fish and chips, Chinese food, Mexican food, and pizza and pasta ($5.59 to $6.99).

You can also find several restaurants (see Chapter 14) and clubs (see Chapter 28) just a short walk from **Islands of Adventure** at the new entertainment complex, **CityWalk**.

A mealtime adventure

At press time, the Confisco Grille in the *Port of Entry* is the only Universal restaurant where you can join characters for a bite. Yogi, BooBoo, Woody Woodpecker, Rocky and Bullwinkle, Scooby Doo, Fred, Barney, Fievel, and George Jetson are among the characters who may show up. (A rotating collection of characters comes to each lunch, so don't promise the kids a specific character.) The menu is basic — burgers, pork chops, shrimp, and such — but the meals are often less crowded than character meals at **WDW**, so the kids get more one-on-one time with each character. Character lunches at Confisco Grill are held from noon to 2 p.m. daily. You order meals off the menu ($8.95 to $15.95 adults, $3.95 kids 3–11). For more information, call ☎ 407-224-6339. You can make reservations 60 days in advance, and the venue periodically changes, so make sure that you call in advance.

Shopping at Islands of Adventure

The park's 20-something shops have plenty of theme merchandise. You may want to check out *Cats, Hats & Things* and *Dr. Seuss' All The Books You Can Read* for special Seussian material. *Jurassic Outfitters Dinostore* offers an array of stuffed and plastic dinos, plus safari-style clothing. If you're a super hero fan, check out *Marvel Alterniverse.*

You may find theme- or character-specific merchandise in only one store.

Here's a sample of some of the more unusual wares available:

- ✔ **Jurassic Outfitters.** You can find plenty of T-shirts with slogans like "I Survived (the fill-in-the-blank ride)" here.

- ✔ **WossaMotta U.** You can probably bet that no one at the office will have a Rocky or Bullwinkle ceramic mug, available at this store in *Toon Lagoon.*

- ✔ **Spider-Man Shop.** This shop specializes in its namesake's paraphernalia, including red Spidey caps covered with black webs and denim jackets with logos.

- ✔ **Picture This!** Mug for the camera and get Seussian-style, 5 × 7 or 8 × 10 souvenir photos.

- ✔ **Toon Extra.** Where else can you buy a miniature stuffed Mr. Peanut bean bag, an Olive Oyl and Popeye frame, or a stuffed Beetle Bailey?

- ✔ **Treasures of Poseidon.** This shop in *The Lost Continent* carries an array of blue glassware including tumblers, shot glasses, and over-sized mugs, as well as brass sculptures.

Using Our Suggested Itinerary

You can see **Islands of Adventure,** like **Universal Studios Florida,** in one day if you keep up a steady pace. In this section, we provide sample itineraries that can help ensure that you see as much as possible while you're visiting **Islands of Adventure.**

If you have children under 10, try this itinerary to help you keep pace:

- ✔ As soon as you enter the park, go straight to *Seuss Landing,* an island where everything is geared to the young and young at heart. You'll easily spend the morning exploring real-life interpretations of the wacky, colorful world of Dr. Seuss. (The wild colors also make for good photographs.)

   Make sure that you ride *The Cat in the Hat; One Fish, Two Fish, Red Fish, Blue Fish;* and *Caro-Seuss-El.* After all that waiting in line, let the little ones burn off some energy playing in *If I Ran the Zoo.*

- ✔ Grab some lunch at the Green Eggs and Ham Café.

- ✔ Head to *The Lost Continent* and enjoy the shows at *Poseidon's Fury: Escape from the Lost City* and *The Eighth Voyage of Sinbad.*

- ✔ Spend some time at the *Camp Jurassic* play area. If you need a break, explore the *Jurassic Park Discovery Center.*

If your child is older, or you're a childless visitor:

- ✔ Go to *Dueling Dragons* and *Poseidon's Fury* in *The Lost Continent.*

- ✔ Amble over to *Jurassic Park* and visit *the Jurassic Park River Adventure* (the name masks a steep flume ride).

- ✔ Head to *Toon Lagoon* and grab some lunch at the Comic Strip Café before spinning down the river (and getting wet!) in *Popeye & Bluto's Bilge-Rat Barges* and taking the plunge down *Dudley Do-Right's Ripsaw Falls.*

- ✔ End your day at *Marvel Super Hero Island* where you can tackle the *Incredible Hulk Coaster, Dr. Doom's Fearfall,* and *The Amazing Adventures of Spider-Man.*

Chapter 25

SeaWorld and Discovery Cove

● ●

In This Chapter

▶ Understanding the basics

▶ Checking out attractions

▶ Exploring **Discovery Cove**

▶ Deciding where to eat and shop

▶ Using an itinerary

● ●

*F*inishing seventh in a seven-horse race is tough, but **SeaWorld** delivers an off-speed pitch — a more relaxed pace with several animal encounters — to attract 4.7 million visitors a year. This modern marine park focuses more on discovery than on thrill rides, though it offers its share of excitement with *Journey to Atlantis,* a steep flumelike ride, and the new *Kraken,* a floorless roller coaster. **SeaWorld's** more than 200 acres of educational fun offer stars such as Shamu and his family of performing killer whales, polar bears Klondike and Snow, and a supporting cast of seals, sea lions, manatees, penguins, dolphins, and so on. You can also feed the nonperforming critters and feel the crushed-velvet texture of a gentle stingray in various pools throughout the park.

SeaWorld's new park, **Discovery Cove,** opened in summer 2000, and it allows guests to swim with dolphins in an encounter that, at $179 per person, goes off the price chart. But **SeaWorld** is betting a fortune that as many as 1,000 people a day will bite their hook.

Gathering Important Information

Before we start wading through **SeaWorld's** attractions and shows, here's some practical information about the park:

✔ **ATMs.** You can find an ATM machine that accepts cards from banks using the Cirrus, Honor, and Plus systems at the front of the park.

✔ **Baby-changing and nursing stations.** Changing tables are in or near most women's rest rooms and at the men's rest room at the front entrance near Shamu's Emporium. You can buy diapers in machines located near all changing areas and at Shamu's Emporium. Likewise, there's a special area for nursing mothers near the women's rest room at *Friends of the Wild* gift shop, near the center of the park.

✔ **Cameras and film.** You can purchase film and disposable cameras at stores throughout **SeaWorld.**

✔ **Directions.** If you're driving south from Orlando, take exit 28 off I-4 and follow the signs. If you're heading north from Tampa, use exit 27A.

✔ **First Aid Center.** Registered nurses staff centers behind *Stingray Lagoon* and near *Shamu's Happy Harbor.*

✔ **Hours.** The park is open from 9 a.m. to 7 p.m., 365 days a year, and later during summer and holidays, when there are additional shows at night.

✔ **Information.** Write to SeaWorld Guest Services at 7007 SeaWorld Dr., Orlando, FL 32801, call ☎ **800-327-2424** or 407-351-3600, or visit www.seaworld.com to gather park information before you leave. Once inside the park, head for the Information Center, which is on your left as you enter the park.

✔ **Lockers.** You can rent them for $2 a day, next to Shamu's Emporium, just inside the park entrance.

✔ **Lost children.** Lost kids are taken to the Information Center, where a parkwide paging system helps reunite them with their families. Children under 7 should wear name tags.

✔ **Parking.** Parking costs $6 for cars, $7 for RVs and trailers. The parking lots aren't huge, so you can easily walk to the park. Trams also run. Remember to note the location of your car, too. SeaWorld characters such as Wally Walrus mark sections, but it's easy to forget where you parked after you've spent the day barnstorming through attractions.

✔ **Pet care.** Board your pet for the day at the kennel between the parking lot and main gate. The cost is $5 a day (no overnight stays).

✔ **Strollers.** Rent dolphin-shaped strollers at the Information Center near the entrance. They cost $6 for a single, $12 for a double.

✔ **Tickets.** A one-day ticket costs $46 for adults, $37 for kids 3 to 9 (plus 6 percent sales tax). **SeaWorld** sometimes offers specials, such as a second day free.

If you're planning to see a number of non-Disney parks, consider the *FlexTicket*. A seven-day, four-park pass to **Universal Studios Florida, Islands of Adventure, Wet 'n Wild,** and **SeaWorld** is $159.95 for adults and $127.95 for kids 3 to 9. A ten-day, five-park pass, which also includes **Busch Gardens** in Tampa, sells for $196.95 for adults and $157.95 for children. Call ☎ **800-327-2424** or 407-351-3600 for more information.

✔ **Tours.** *SeaWorld's Adventure Express Tour* ($55 adults, $50 children 3 to 9 *plus* park admission) is a 5½ hour guided excursion that includes back-door access to two rides, reserved seating at two animal shows, and a chance to touch or feed penguins, dolphins, stingrays, and sea lions. The tour is the only way to dodge park lines, though these usually aren't as bad as **Disney's** or **Universal's.** You can choose from three one-hour tours — *Polar Expedition Guided Tour, Sharks,* and *To The Rescue* — that are reasonably inexpensive ($7 adults, $6 kids, plus park admission). Additionally, **SeaWorld** offers a 90-minute behind-the-scenes tour of the park's breeding, research, and training facilities and a 45-minute presentation about **SeaWorld's** animal behavior and training techniques. The cost for these tours is also $7 for adults and $6 for children 3 to 9. There are several tours daily, but make reservations when you enter the park. Call ☎ **407-351-3600** for information.

✔ **Wheelchairs.** Regular wheelchairs are available at the Information Center for $6; electric chairs are $30 plus a $25 deposit.

Exploring the Top Attractions

SeaWorld explores the mysteries of the deep in a format that combines wildlife-conservation awareness with laid-back fun. Close encounters with marine life are the major draw here, but you'll also find some excellent shows and thrill rides.

The following section lists an index of **SeaWorld's** attractions.

Index of SeaWorld attractions

Clyde & Seamore Take Pirate Island
Dolphin Interaction Program
Intensity Games Water Ski Show
Journey to Atlantis
Key West at SeaWorld
Key West Dolphin Fest
Kraken

Manatees: The Last Generation?
Penguin Encounter
The Shamu Adventure
Shamu's Happy Harbor
Terrors of the Deep
Trainer for a Day
Wild Arctic

 ## Clyde & Seamore Take Pirate Island

A lovable sea lion-and-otter duet, with a supporting cast of walruses and harbor seals, stars in this fish-breathed comedy that comes with a swashbuckling conservation theme. The show is corny, but don't hold that against the animal actors. Besides, if you're going to spend much time at all at the high-tech rides and shows at the other theme parks, you'll be happy for the break.

Dolphin Interaction Program

If you have a spare $159 (in addition to park admission), you can don a wet suit and wade into waist-deep water to interact with dolphins. This is an extremely popular, two-hour activity each morning, and it has very limited space. If you're interested, call ☎ **407-370-1385** before leaving home. *Note*: You must be at least 10 years old and 52 inches tall to participate.

Intensity Games Water Ski Show

It's hard to top this show, a crowd-pleaser for more than 15 years. The hyper-competition stars some of the most skilled athletes on water. The 20-person team includes world-class skiers, wake-boarders, and stunt men and women from across the United States performing non-stop aquabatics.

Journey to Atlantis

Taking a cue from **Disney's** Imagineers, **SeaWorld** has come up with a flume ride that carries the customary surgeon-general's warning about heart problems, neck or back ailments, pregnancy, seizures, dizziness, and claustrophobia. (Until the seat cushions were padded, there should've been a warning about hemorrhoids, too.) The story line of this attraction involves a battle of good versus evil, but what really matters is the drop — a wild plunge from 60 feet with lugelike curves and a shorter drop thrown in for good measure.

"That scared the heck out of me." The ride carries a 46-inch height minimum, but *Atlantis* isn't as intense as *Splash Mountain* at **Magic Kingdom** (Chapter 17) or *Jurassic Park River Adventure* in **Islands of Adventure** (Chapter 24).

Key West at SeaWorld

It's not quite the way Hemingway saw it, but this five-acre sliver of paved paradise is a tree- and flower-lined Caribbean village that offers island food, street vendors, and entertainers. It has three animal habitats: *Stingray Lagoon,* where you get a hands-on encounter with harmless southern diamond and cownose rays; *Dolphin Cove,* a habitat for bottlenose dolphins set up for visitor interaction; and *Sea Turtle Point,* home to endangered and threatened species. Shortly after this area opened, the dolphins made a game of teasing visitors by swimming just out of arm's reach. But they soon discovered there are advantages to human interaction — namely smelt.

Speaking of smelt, you can get a half dozen of them (to feed the dolphins) for $3 or two trays for $5, and it's real easy to be melted by the dolphins' begging. We've spent half a park admission feeding the dolphins smelt before coming to our senses.

Key West Dolphin Fest

At the partially covered, open-air Whale and Dolphin Stadium, Atlantic bottlenose dolphins perform flips and high jumps, swim at high speeds, twirl, do the back stroke, and give rides to trainers. Some false killer whales, or Pseudocra crassidens, also make an appearance to the accompaniment of calypso music. The tricks are impressive, but if you've seen a traditional tourist-park dolphin show, you already know the plot.

If you go to this show, go before you see Shamu. He puts these little mammals to shame.

Kraken

Launched in summer 2000, this coaster is **SeaWorld's** deepest venture into the worlds of thrill-ride battles. *Kraken* is named for a massive, mythological, underwater beast that Poseidon kept caged. This twenty-first-century version involves floorless and open-sided 32-passenger trains that plant you on a pedestal high above the track. When the monster breaks loose, you climb 151 feet, fall 144 feet, hit speeds of 65 mph, go underground three times (spraying bystanders with water — or worse if you're weak of stomach), and make seven loops over a 4,177-foot course. This ride may be the longest 3 minutes, 39 seconds of your life.

Manatees: The Last Generation?

This exhibit is as close as most people get to the endangered West Indian manatees. Underwater viewing stations, innovative cinema techniques, and interactive displays combine for a tribute to these gentle marine mammals.

Penguin Encounter

The *Penguin Encounter* transports you via a moving sidewalk through Tuxedoville. The stars of the show are on the other side of a Plexiglas shield. You get a glimpse of them as they preen, socialize, and swim at bullet speed in a 22-degree habitat. You can also see puffins and murres in a similar, but separate, area.

The Shamu Adventure

Everyone comes to **SeaWorld** to see the big guy, and he and his friends don't disappoint. This featured event is a well-choreographed show, planned and carried out by very good trainers and very smart Orcas. The whales really dive into their work! The fun builds until the video monitor flashes an urgent "Weather Watch" and one of the trainers utters the warning: "Uh-oh!" Hurricane Shamu is about to make landfall.

At this point, many folks remember the splash-area warnings posted throughout the grandstand. Those who didn't pay attention when they arrived get one last chance to flee. The Orcas then race around the edge of the pool, creating huge waves of icy water that profoundly soak everything in range. Veteran animal handler Jack Hanna also makes an appearance on the huge overhead monitors, compliments of ShamuVision.

"I'm f-f-freezing!" Don't say we didn't warn you about the splash area. Shamu's pool must be 40°F. So, if you want to stay dry, don't sit in the first 14 rows!

Shamu: Close Up! is an adjoining exhibit that lets you get close to killer whales and learn about breeding programs. Don't miss the underwater viewing area. You may get to see a mother with her big baby.

Shamu's Happy Harbor

This three-acre play area has a four-story net tower with a 35-foot crow's-nest lookout, water cannons, remote-controlled vehicles, and a water maze. It's one of the most extensive play areas at any park and a great place for kids to unwind. Bring extra clothes for the tots (or for yourself) because the *Harbor* isn't designed to keep you dry.

Terrors of the Deep

This attraction, formerly called *Shark Encounter,* was improved by the addition of some 220 species. Pools out front have small sharks and rays (feeding isn't allowed). The interior aquariums have big eels, beautiful lionfish, hauntingly still barracudas, and the fat, bug-eyed puffer-fish, which are considered a delicacy in Japan. (They also pack the world's deadliest poison in their liver, kidneys, skin, ovaries, and eyes.)

This tour isn't for the claustrophobic: You walk through a Plexiglas tube beneath hundreds of millions of gallons of water. Also, small children may find the swimming sharks a little too much to handle.

Trainer for a Day

Expect to invest a sizable chunk of your day and budget in this 7½ hour program (7:00 a.m. to 2:30 p.m.). You and one other person work side by side with a trainer, preparing meals and feeding the animals, learning basic training techniques, and sharing lunch. It costs $349 and is limited to two people per day, so make reservations very early. You must be 13 or older, at least 52 inches tall, able to climb, and able to lift and carry 15 pounds of vittles. Call ☎ **407-370-1382** for more information.

Wild Arctic

Wild Arctic combines a high-definition adventure film with flight-simulator technology to evoke breathtaking Arctic panoramas. After a hazardous flight over the frozen north, visitors emerge at a remote research base, home to four polar bears (including star residents and polar twins Klondike and Snow), seals, walruses, and white beluga whales. Kids may find the bumpy ride a little much, but there's a separate line for those who want to skip the thrill-ride section.

More SeaWorld Fun

Other SeaWorld attractions include *Pacific Point Preserve,* a 2½ acre natural setting that duplicates the rocky northern Pacific Coast home of California sea lions and harbor seals (more smelt opportunities here), and *Tropical Rain Forest,* a bamboo and banyan-tree habitat that's home to cockatoos and other birds.

Hawaiian Rhythms is a dance troupe that entertains in an outdoor facility at Hawaiian Village (if you care to join, grass skirts and leis are available). The 5½ acre *Anheuser-Busch Hospitality Center* offers free samples of Anheuser-Busch beers. Next door, stroll through the stables, and you may catch a glimpse of the famous Budweiser Clydesdale horses being groomed.

Checking Out Discovery Cove

SeaWorld's second theme park opened in summer 2000. Its $100-million construction cost is one-tenth the sticker price of **Islands of Adventure,** but **Discovery Cove's** admission price is four times higher. You have two options: $179 per person plus 6 percent sales tax, regardless of age, if you want to swim with the dolphins, or $89 if you can skip that luxury. **Discovery Cove** is an all-inclusive park, which means that you get

✔ Elbow room — there's a limit of 1,000 guests per day.

✔ Ticket prices that include just about everything you'll need, from lunch to your towel and locker to swimming/snorkeling gear and your activities. Activities include

- Swimming near (but on the other side of Plexiglas from) black-tip sharks and barracudas

- Snorkeling around a 1.3-million-gallon tank containing a coral reef with brightly colored tropical fish and another tank with gentle rays

- Touching and feeding 300 exotic birds in the 100-foot-long aviary hidden under a waterfall

- Cooling off under foaming waterfalls

- Soaking up the sun on the beaches
- Enjoying the soothing waters of the park's pools and rivers (freshwater and saltwater)

✔ A 30-minute encounter (guests must be 6 or older, though we recommend at least 8 to avoid scares from things that go bump on and under the water) supervised by a trainer, if you choose the dolphin experience.

✔ Seven days of unlimited admission to **SeaWorld.**

To get to **Discovery Cove,** follow these directions to **SeaWorld:** If you're driving south from Orlando, take exit 28 off I-4 and follow the signs. If you're heading northeast from Tampa, use exit 27A.

For up-to-the-minute information on this new park, call ☎ **877-434-7268** or go to www.discoverycove.com. If you go for this extravagant park, we recommend making a reservation far in advance, just in case many other travelers choose to do the same.

Dining and Shopping at SeaWorld

The *Aloha! Polynesian Luau Dinner and Show,* a full-scale dinner show featuring South Seas food (mahi-mahi, chicken, and pork), song, and fire dancing, takes place nightly at 6:30 p.m. Park admission is required. The cost is $35.95 for adults, $25.95 for children 8 to 12, and $15.95 for children 3 to 7. Reservations are required (☎ **800-327-2424** or 407-363-2559).

There are also several counter-style or sit-down eateries at **SeaWorld.** Most meals cost less than $10 per person. Restaurants include Chicken 'n' Biscuit (fried poultry, salads); Waterfront Sandwich Grill (smoked turkey, burgers); Buccaneer Smokehouse (ribs, brisket); Mama Stella's Italian Kitchen (pasta, pizza, salads); Mango Joe's Café (fajitas, tortillas); The Deli (sandwiches); and Bimini Bay Café (steak, chicken, seafood, salads, sandwiches).

SeaWorld doesn't have nearly as many shops as the other major theme parks, but there are lots of surprisingly cuddly sea creatures. For example, you can buy a stuffed manatee at *Manatee Cove.* The *Friends of the Wild* gift shop near *Penguin Encounter* is also nice, as is the shop attached to *Wild Arctic.* Because of the Anheuser-Busch connection, the gift shop outside the entrance to the park offers a staggering array of Budweiser- and Busch-related items.

Using Our Suggested Itinerary

SeaWorld is a much slower-paced theme park than the other Orlando juggernauts, and there are only two rides where you'll have to fight the kind of crowds found at **Disney** and **Universal:** *Journey to Atlantis* and the new *Kraken.* If you arrive at park opening, we recommend hauling your keister to them straight off (go first to whichever appeals to you most, then suck it up and get in line for the other). Both are to the left of the entrance at the back of the park. If you arrive later or don't want to rush, experience those rides as your tour route allows.

The following itinerary will get you around the park in a convenient and timely fashion:

- ✔ Start with *Pets on Stage* at the SeaWorld Theater (the first show usually is at 10:45 a.m.).

- ✔ Catch the *Shamu Adventure Show* at Shamu Stadium and visit *Wild Arctic.*

- ✔ Watch the *Intensity Games Water Ski Show* at Atlantis Bayside Stadium, and then visit *Clyde & Seamore Take Pirate Island* at the Sea Lion & Otter Stadium, followed by *Cirque de la Mer* at Nautilus Theater.

- ✔ If you've worked up a thirst, visit the *Anheuser-Busch Hospitality Center* and the *Clydesdale Hamlet* next door.

- ✔ After you're refreshed, see *Terrors of the Deep.*

- ✔ Feed the seals and sea lions at *Pacific Point Preserve,* and say hi to the residents at *Penguin Encounter.*

- ✔ Tour *Manatees: The Last Generation?, Key West at SeaWorld,* and *Stingray Lagoon.*

- ✔ Catch the *Key West Dolphin Fest* at Dolphin Stadium to end your day.

Chapter 26

Other Cool Attractions

● ●

In This Chapter

▶ Getting wet outside Walt's World

▶ Trekking through Busch Gardens

▶ Exploring the Final Frontier

● ●

*I*n Chapters 16 through 25, we familiarize you with the major theme-park players in and around Orlando. But, you're probably wondering if there's *anything* that's more relaxed, a little — and we mean little — cheaper, or offers an out-of-this-world experience.

The answer to your question is yes.

In this chapter, we explore an alternative to the Disney water parks, and two attractions that are just 90-minute's drive outside of Orlando: an African safari and theme park, and a magnificent center that recounts the United States' adventures in space.

See Chapter 30 for a list of attractions that are cheaper than the ones we mention in this chapter.

Wipe Out! Orlando's Water Parks

If you want to escape the hullabaloo of **Walt Disney World,** but still want to cool off at a water park, you won't have a problem. **Wet 'n Wild**, the oldest water park in Orlando, is still going strong, and if you combine a visit here with one to **Universal Studios Escape,** you may achieve considerable savings.

Wet 'n Wild is a 25-acre water park where you can jump waves, careen down steep flumes, and run rapids. Among the highlights: *Fuji Flyer,* a six-story, four-passenger toboggan ride through 450 feet of banked curves; *The Surge,* one of the longest, fastest multipassenger tube rides in the Southeast (580 feet of banked curves); *Bomb Bay*, where you enter a bomblike casing 76 feet in the air for a speedy vertical flight straight down; *Black Hole* (step into a spaceship and board a two-person raft for a 30-second, 500-foot, twisting, turning, space-themed reentry through total darkness); *Raging Rapids,* a simulated white-water tubing adventure with a waterfall plunge; and *Lazy River,* a leisurely float trip. The success of this park pushed **Disney** into the water-park game, but **Wet 'n Wild** still has plenty to offer. *Bomb Bay* ranks among one of the best thrill rides in central Florida. Likewise, the park offers flumes, a vast wave pool, a large children's water playground where the rides that we describe previously in this paragraph are re-created in miniature, and a picnic area.

You can buy a multiday **FlexTicket** for entry into **Wet 'n Wild.** A seven-day, four-park pass to **Universal Studios Florida, Islands of Adventure, Wet 'n Wild,** and **SeaWorld** is $159.95 for adults, $127.95 for kids 3 to 9. A ten-day, five-park pass, which also includes **Busch Gardens** in Tampa, is $196.95 for adults and $157.95 for kids.

Wet 'n Wild is located at 6200 International Drive, at Universal Boulevard. (Take I-4 east to Exit 30A and follow the signs.) Call ☎ **800-992-9453** or 407-351-9453 for details, or check out www.wetnwild.com on the Internet. **Wet 'n Wild** is open daily, but hours vary seasonally (be sure to call before you go). Admission is $28.95 for adults, $22.95 for kids 3 to 9, and $14.48 for seniors 55 and older. Tube, towel, and locker rental costs $9 plus a $4 refundable deposit. Parking for cars costs $5 and $6 for RVs.

Fun Outside the City

After a few days in Orlando, it may seem like the city has everything that anyone could want to do. So if an attraction is going to convince you to drive or hitch a ride to something one or two hours away, it probably has to be something special. That's a tall order given all the stuff that's in this World. But we think there are two places worth going out of your way to visit.

Roar! Busch Gardens

This Tampa park grew out of a brewery. In the 1960s, the main (and only) attractions at **Busch Gardens** were a bird show and free beer. (You may be thinking, who could ask for anything more?) Today, however, **Busch Gardens** is one of Florida's top theme parks. Two things set it aside from Disney's **Animal Kingdom:** its coasters and critters.

Busch Gardens has five — count 'em, *FIVE!!* — roller coasters to keep your adrenaline and stomach levels high. The newest is *Gwazi,* a wooden wonder named for a fabled African lion with a tiger's head. This $10-million ride slowly climbs to 90 feet, before turning, twisting, diving, and *va-rrroommming* to speeds of 50 mph — enough to give you air time (also known as weightlessness). Fact is, these twin coasters, the Lion and the Tiger, provide 2 minutes and 20 seconds of thrills and chills, steep-banked curves, and bobsled maneuvers. There are six points on the ride where you're certain you're going to slam the other coaster as you hit 3.5 Gs. (That's science's way of saying that if you weigh 100 pounds, your body will feel like 350.)

The 15-inch seat is smaller than an airline seat, so it's a tight squeeze for thin folks and the next-best-thing to misery for larger models.

Busch's other four roller coasters are made of steel. *Kumba* is a 143-foot-high number that covers 4,000 feet of tract at 60 mph. It jerks you with sudden turns (54-inch height minimum). *Montu* musses your hair at speeds exceeding 60 mph while the G-force keeps you plastered to your seat (54-inch minimum). *The Python* is a tad tamer, running through a double spiraling corkscrew and a 70-foot plunge (48-inch minimum). *The Scorpion* offers a high-speed 60-foot drop and 360-degree loop (42-inch minimum).

Busch's critters have fewer places to hide and, therefore, are easier to see than those at **Animal Kingdom** (Chapter 20). *Edge of Africa* and the *Serengeti Plain* allow views of lions, hippos, crocodiles, hyenas, and other animals that seem to roam free. (The *Serengeti,* by the way, recently got a facelift. It's 29 acres now have hills, 700 trees, 32 kinds of edible grass, and 300 animals that are encouraged to wander closer to the tourist-carrying trains by food, cool shade, and water misters.) *Nairobi's Myombe Reserve* is home to gorillas; this land also has a baby animal nursery, petting zoo, turtle and reptile displays, and an elephant exhibit. *The Congo* features rare white Bengal tigers. For a good view, try the monorail, sky ride, and *Trans-Veldt Railway.*

The park's three water rides are welcome relief from the summer heat. *Tanganyika Tidal Wave* and *Stanley Falls* flume ride are splashy fun. The *Congo River Rapids* ride is very similar to *Kali River Rapids* in **Animal Kingdom.**

In addition to the animals, your kids will love the treehouse, rides (56-inch height maximum), and Dumphrey the Dragon in *Land of the Dragons,* as well as the sandy dig site at *King Tut's Tomb* and the friendly lorikeets of *Lory Landing.*

Buy your tickets in advance at the *Tampa Bay Visitor Information Center,* across Busch Boulevard from the park's entrance, to avoid long lines and save a couple of dollars.

Busch Gardens usually offers a special that lets you buy a second-day ticket for $12 per person.

Did we mention free beer if you're 21 or older? You can sample Anheuser-Busch products at the *Hospitality House.*

Busch Gardens is located at 3000 E. Busch Boulevard. at McKinley Drive/N. 40th Street. From Orlando, take I-4 west to the U.S. 41 exit, go right (north) on Fla. 583. The route to the park is well marked, and it's 90 minutes from Orlando. Park hours are 9:30 a.m.–6:00 p.m. daily; however, the park sometimes opens as early as 9:00 a.m. and closes as late as 8:30 p.m. Admission costs $45.68 for adults, $36.74 kids 3 to 9, including tax. FlexTicket pricing is $196.96 for adults, $157.95 for kids for a ten-day pass that also includes unlimited admission to **Universal Studios Florida, Islands of Adventure, SeaWorld,** and **Wet 'n Wild.** Parking is $6. Call ☎ **800-423-8367** or 813-987-5283 or visit www.buschgardens.com for more information.

Blast off! Kennedy Space Center

Each time a space shuttle blasts into the heavens, someone you know wishes he or she could be an astronaut. Heck — maybe it's you. What a rush, eh? Riding a missile that's slightly more stable than a nuclear warhead, boldly going where no man or woman has gone before. But does your fantasy include these side effects?

- ✔ The liftoff thrust is 7½ million pounds, which is equal to the giddy-up of 20 (that's not a typo) 747 planes. By the time you're in orbit 8 minutes later, you're lickety-splitting at 17,000 mph.

- ✔ Weightlessness makes your lower-body fluids rise like dead fish, bloating your face and causing your sinuses to feel like you've suddenly caught a wicked hangover.

Those are just a couple of the fun facts you may learn on a visit to the **Kennedy Space Center.** Highlights of the center include trips down memory lane and glances into the future of space exploration.

You'll explore the history of manned flights, beginning with the wild ride of Alan Shepard (1961) and Neil Armstrong's 1969 moonwalk. (Lunar Theater's re-creation of Apollo 11 and Firing Room Theater's look at the Apollo 1 fire are gripping.) There are also three 5½-story, 3D Imax theaters that literally shake, rattle, and rock 'n 'roll with special effects. We think the best two movies are *L5,* a fictional look at the first space colony, and *The Dream Is Alive,* a rousing past-and-present focus on the space shuttle program.

The *Kennedy Space Center Visitor Complex* has real NASA rockets and exhibits that look at space exploration into this millennium. There are also hands-on activities aimed at kids, a daily encounter with a real astronaut, several dining venues, and a shop selling a variety of space memorabilia and souvenirs.

Bus tours run continuously. The bus makes stops at the *Vehicle Assembly Building,* where shuttles are prepared for launch; the *LC-39 Observation Gantry,* which has a 360-degree view of shuttle launch pads; and the *Apollo/Saturn V Center,* which includes artifacts, photos, interactive exhibits, and the 363-foot-tall Saturn V rocket.

If you want to go out on the launch pads, take the *Cape Canaveral Then and Now* guided tour. This once daily, two-hour excursion focuses more on the history of the space program and stops at sites where the shuttle buses don't. You explore *Hangar S,* where the Mercury astronauts lived; the launch pads for the Mercury, Gemini, and Apollo missions; the *U.S. Air Force Space and Missile Museum;* and historic *Cape Canaveral Lighthouse.*

On launch day, the **Kennedy Space Center** is closed until after early shuttle launches or, for later ones, it closes six hours before the scheduled liftoff. Launch days aren't good days to tour the facility, which deserves a six- to eight-hour stay. However, launch days are great for seeing history in the present tense. *NASA Parkway*, one of the better launch-viewing areas for spectators, is no longer open to public traffic on launch days. (That's a blessing, because it used to get so crowded there was a two- to four-hour traffic jam.) But for $10, the **Kennedy Space Center** will take you on a two-hour (longer if there's a launch delay) excursion to the Parkway to see the launch and you won't have to fight traffic. If a launch is canceled for any reason, you will receive a pass to return to the center the following day. You must pick up tickets, available five days prior to the launch, on site. For information, call ☎ **321-449-4444.**

Despite 2.8 million visitors a year, the **Kennedy Space Center** feels far less crowded than the Orlando parks or **Busch Gardens.** If you're not driving your own sedan or coming on some other prepaid tour, you can arrange the trip through Mears Transportation (☎ **407-423-5566**).

We recommend this attraction for anyone who's ever dreamed about the final frontier. The **Kennedy Space Center** is also a great day trip for visitors 6 and older. Those ages 3 to 5 will enjoy some play areas but may be bored by the exhibits and even scared by the explosive movies.

To get to the **Kennedy Space Center** from Orlando, take the Beeline Expressway east to Fla. 407, turn left, then right at Fla. 405. Directions to the center are well marked along the roadside. The **Kennedy Space Center** is located at NASA Parkway/Fla. 405, six miles east of Titusville, about one-half mile west of Fla. 3. Hours are 9 a.m. to dusk daily. Admission is free. Bus tours are available for $14 adults, $10 for kids 3 to 11. IMAX movies cost $7.50 for adults, $5.50 for kids. Put the two together (a bus tour and one movie) and pay $19 for an adult admission, $15 for kids. One bus tour and two IMAX movies runs $26 for adults and $20 for kids. The *Then and Now* guided tour (bus and launch pad tours, see below) costs $35 per person. Wheelchairs and strollers are free. Call ☎ **321-452-2121** for general information, ☎ **321-449-4444** for guided bus tours and launch reservations. Visit www.kennedyspacecenter.com online.

Chapter 27

A Shopper's Guide to Orlando

*I*n this chapter, we provide you with a rundown of places outside the Mickey zone where you can blow your cash, assuming that you have the time — and that the theme parks haven't emptied your bank accounts yet. Because **Walt Disney World** is tops in Orlando at separating you from your money, discussing Disney-related shopping requires its own chapter — Chapter 22.

Checking Out the Shopping Scene

Some of you reading this book were no doubt born with a divining rod that guides you to bargains. Orlando is a destination that will test your rod's merit. You can find malls like the ones that you have back home and a few factory outlets. There's also an engaging antique district where it's fun to window-shop. But Orlando, Kissimmee, and much of what lies in between are tourist zones. That's right — they're overrun by T-shirt shacks, jean joints, and souvenir shops promising bargains that don't exist.

The same is true for the theme parks, too. If you line up at the registers at **Disney, Universal,** and the other parks, you pay more than what the merchandise is worth. But, if you must have those mouse ears, we've outlined Disney's shopping options in Chapter 22 and the other major theme parks' merchandise in Chapters 23, 24, and 25.

Orlando Shopping

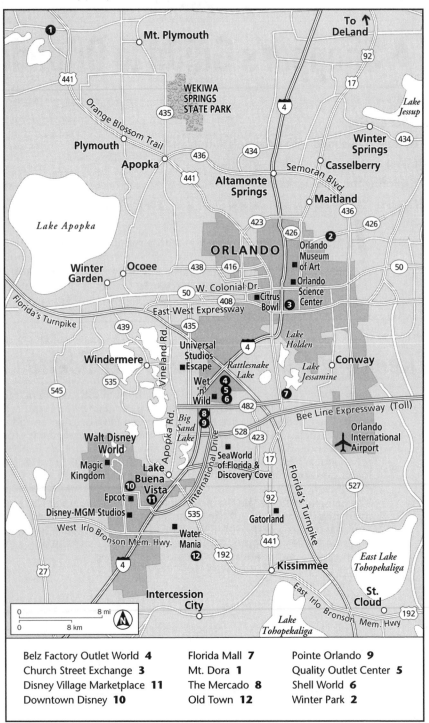

Belz Factory Outlet World **4**	Florida Mall **7**	Pointe Orlando **9**
Church Street Exchange **3**	Mt. Dora **1**	Quality Outlet Center **5**
Disney Village Marketplace **11**	The Mercado **8**	Shell World **6**
Downtown Disney **10**	Old Town **12**	Winter Park **2**

Here are three shopping heads-ups before you get started:

✔ **Sales tax.** In Orange County, which includes the International Drive area and most of the parks, sales tax is 6 percent. Kissimmee and the rest of Osceola County charge 7 percent sales tax.

✔ **Store hours.** Most of the stores that we mention in this chapter are open seven days a week, from 9 or 10 a.m. until 9 p.m. (6 p.m. on Sundays). Small stores, including those in the antique district, usually close around 5 or 6 p.m. and often aren't open on Sunday.

✔ **Money.** Most stores accept major credit cards, traveler's checks, and, of course, cash. However, there may not be an ATM handy, and none of the stores accepts foreign currency or personal checks.

Exploring the Great Shopping Neighborhoods

Orlando doesn't have a central shopping district or districts. Instead, it has tourist areas that are best avoided unless you want cheap goods at high prices, as well as retail neighborhoods where locals shop, such as malls and so on. The following is a list of some of the more frequented shopping zones:

✔ **Celebration.** Think *Pleasantville* with a Mickey touch. This Disney-created town of 20,000 is more of a diversion than a shopper's paradise. The downtown area has a dozen shops, a couple of art galleries, and four restaurants. The shops offer some interesting buys, but the real plus is the atmosphere. From **WDW,** take U.S. 192 east five miles, past Interstate 4. The entrance to Celebration is on the right. Call ☎ **407-566-2200** for more information.

✔ **Kissimmee.** Southeast of the Disney parks, Kissimmee straddles U.S. 192/Irlo Bronson Memorial Highway — a sometimes-tacky strip lined with budget motels, smaller attractions, and every fast-food restaurant known to man. Kissimmee's shopping merit is negligible unless you're looking for a cheap T-shirt or a white elephant gift. (Seashells, anyone?)

✔ **International Drive Area.** This tourist magnet extends seven to ten miles north of the Disney parks between Florida 535 and the Florida Turnpike. The southern end has a little elbow room, but the northern part is a tourist strip crowded with small-time attractions (there's bungee jumping for those who have a death wish), fast fooderies, and souvenir shacks. There are two main shopping draws: *Pointe Orlando* (see listing under "The Malls," later in this chapter) and *The Mercado,* ☎ **407-345-9337,** which has restaurants, music, and shops (Conch Republic, Designer Gear, Classic Characters) in a complex designed like a Mediterranean village.

Locally, International Drive is called *I-Drive*.

✔ **Downtown Orlando.** Orlando's downtown is actually northeast of the parks on I-4. The biggest draws here are the shops in **Church Street Station** and Antique Row (see "Charging it at Church Street" and "Downtown Antiquing" later).

✔ **Winter Park.** Just north of downtown Orlando, Winter Park began as a haven for Yankees traveling away from the cold. Today, Winter Park's centerpiece is Park Avenue, a collection of upscale shops and restaurants along a cobblestone street. Ann Taylor and Banana Republic are among the dozens of specialty shops. Park Avenue also has some art galleries For more information on Winter Park, call ☎ **407-644-8281,** or head over to www. winterpark.org on the Web.

Finding the Big Names in Shopping

Orlando's reputation wasn't built on shopping. In fact, it's not even the number one shopping town in Florida, falling well short of Miami-Fort Lauderdale. But Orlando has attracted some big names, including a very small *Saks* and the promise of a *Bloomingdale's, Macy's,* and maybe a *Harrods.* It also has a growing stable of discount centers.

Factory Outlets

In the last decade, the tourist areas have bloomed with outlets where shoppers can find some name brand bargains — maybe. To borrow advice from a popular rhyme, we suggest: "Things aren't always what they seem; skim milk masquerades as cream."

If you're a smart outlet shopper, you know the suggested retail prices for items before you hit the stores. Therefore, you know what is — and what *isn't* — a bargain. Here's a list of outlet stores and centers in and around Orlando:

✔ **Belz Factory Outlet World.** Belz (☎ **407-354-0126;** www.belz.com), is the granddaddy of all Orlando outlets. Located at 5401 W. Oak Ridge Road (at the north end of International Drive), it has 180 stores in two huge, enclosed malls and four annexes. (The only thing missing is a voting precinct.) The outlet offers 18 shoe stores (including Bass, Bally, and Capezio), 14 housewares stores (such as Corning, Oneida, and Mikasa), and more than 60 clothing shops (London Fog, Jonathan Logan, Guess Jeans, Aileen, Danskin, Jordache, Leslie Fay, Carole Little, Harvé Benard, Calvin Klein, and Anne Klein, for example). You can also buy books, toys, electronics, sporting goods, jewelry, and so on.

Don't kill yourself trying to get to every building. Many of the manufacturers have more than one location here, each with much of the same selection. And unless you're from out of the country, sportswear stores like Nike and Reebok, don't offer much of a deal, especially on shoes.

✔ **Lake Buena Vista Factory Stores.** The three dozen or so outlets here include Casuals (Calvin Klein, Ralph Lauren, and Tommy Hilfiger), Liz Claiborne, GAP, Jantzen, Osh Kosh, and Reebok. Savings are modest. You can find these stores at 15591 S. Apopka-Vineland Road; ☎ 407-238-9301; www.LBVFactoryStores.com.

✔ **Quality Outlet Center.** On the smaller side, Quality Outlet Center has 20 outlets, including Arrow, American Tourister, Corning-Revere, Florsheim shoes, Magnavox, Laura Ashley, Adidas, Great Western Boots, Linens 'n' Things, Mikasa, Royal Doulton, and Villeroy & Boch. Savings here tend to be modest. You'll find the outlet at 5527 International Drive (one block east of Kirkman Road); ☎ 407-423-5885.

✔ **Kissimmee Manufacturer's Outlet Mall.** The 35 stores in this mall include Van Heusen, Bugle Boy, Fieldcrest/Cannon, Bass Apparel, Westport (women's fashions), and Acme Boot. Go to U.S. 192 (a mile east of Fla. 535 in Kissimmee); ☎ 407-396-8900.

✔ **Orlando Premium Outlets.** Opened in July 2000, this 440,000-square-foot center is the newest kid on the block. It's being billed as Orlando's only upscale outlet, with 110 tenants such as Bottega Veneta, Coach, Cole-Haan, Donna Karan, Kenneth Cole, Nike, Polo/Ralph Lauren, Tahari, Theory, Timberland, and Tommy Hilfiger. The center plans twice-a-day shuttles (by reservation) from Disney, International Drive, and U.S. 192. It's located at 8200 Vineland Avenue (just off the southern third of I-Drive), ☎ 407-239-6101; www.PremiumOutlets.com.

The Malls

The Orlando area contains several traditional shopping malls. Like tenants in malls everywhere, these merchants pay a hefty rent, so good buys are elusive. Arguably, a mall's best bargain is people watching, which is free. Here's a list of Orlando's malls:

✔ **Florida Mall.** Fresh off a $70-million expansion, this mall's anchors include Dillard's, Saks, Burdines, JCPenney, Sears, an Adam's Mark Hotel, and more than 200 specialty stores, restaurants, and entertainment venues. You can find the Florida Mall at 8001 S. Orange Blossom Trail (at Sand Lake Road, four miles east of International Drive. Call ☎ 407-851-7234 for details.

✔ **Orlando Fashion Square Mall.** This city-side mall has marblelike walkways, indoor palm trees, and tenants that include Burdines, Gayfers, JCPenney, Sears, 165 specialty shops, and an extensive food court. The mall is five miles from downtown Orlando at 3201 E. Colonial Drive; ☎ **407-896-1131.**

✔ **Altamonte Mall.** Built in the early 1970s, this is the area's second largest mall, behind the newly expanded Florida Mall. Altamonte Mall big-league tenants include Gayfers, Burdines, and JCPenney, as well as 175 specialty shops. You can find it at 451 E. Altamonte Drive (about 15 miles north of downtown Orlando). For information call ☎ **407-830-4400,** or surf over to www.altamontemall.com.

✔ **Pointe Orlando.** Although it's set up like a mall, this complex's two levels of stores, restaurants, and a 21-screen IMAX theater aren't under one roof. Headliners among the 80 shops include Banana Republic, Foot Locker, and a 33,000-square-foot FAO Schwarz, whose exterior is adorned with a 3-story Raggedy Ann. Inside FAO Schwartz, you can find a huge *Star Wars* area, including a seven-foot Darth Vader that retails for a cool $7,000, and a Barbie collection so large it makes some folks crazy — if they don't die of sticker shock first. Pointe Orlando is located at 9101 International Drive; ☎ **407-248-2838.**

Charging It at Church Street

The Exchange Shopping Emporium is part of **Church Street Station.** Built in an ornate Victorian style, with hardwood oak floors and hand-painted tin ceilings, it offers 40 specialty shops and restaurants spread over three floors. Although there are some mall standards such as Victoria's Secret, most offer more unusual wares. *Black Market Minerals,* for example, sells an infinite variety of things made from semiprecious gems and beads. *The Gothic Shop* sells angel figures, gargoyles, and Greek and Roman images made of plaster.

Just across the tracks, *Church Street Market* offers a collection of 30 shops and eateries. *Behr's Chocolates* sells homemade confections; *Hit or Miss* specializes in woman's clothing; and *Brookstone* is an upscale shop offering electronic gadgets that you can try out.

To find the shopping complexes from the attractions, take I-4 east to downtown Orlando. Exit at Anderson Street (Exit 38). Turn left on Boone Avenue, then left on South Street. Turn right on Garland Avenue. Parking is available in a city-owned lot between South Street and Garland Avenue. Note your parking space and pay at the machines located at the end of the lot.

Antiquing Downtown

If you can think of nothing better than a relaxing afternoon of sifting through yesterday's treasures, check out *Antique Row* on Orange Avenue in downtown Orlando.

Flo's Attic (☎ **407-895-1800**) and *Pieces of Eight Emporium* (☎ **407-896-8700**) sell traditional antiques. *Art's Cigars* (☎ **407-895-9772**) is a two-story leather-and-tweed kind of place where you're encouraged to light up and enjoy the view of Lake Ivanhoe. *Wildlife Gallery* (☎ **407-898-4544**) sells pricey, original works of art, including sculpture. And the *Fly Fisherman* (☎ **407-898-1989**) sells — no surprise here — fly-fishing gear. You can sometimes watch people taking lessons in the park across the street.

All the stores we mention in this section are spread over three miles along Orange Avenue. The heaviest concentration is between Princeton Street and New Hampshire Avenue, although a few are scattered between New Hampshire and Virginia avenues. The more upscale shops extend a few blocks beyond Virginia. To get to *Antiques Row* from the theme parks, take I-4 east to Princeton Street (Exit 43). Turn right on Orange Avenue. Parking is limited, so stop wherever you find a space along the street.

As for hours of operation, most of the stores on *Antique Row* are open from about 9 a.m. to 6 p.m., Monday to Saturday. (Storeowners usually run the stores, so hours can vary. A small number are open on Sunday, but it's not worth the trip from the resorts.)

Part VII

Living It Up After the Sun Goes Down: Orlando Nightlife

The 5th Wave   By Rich Tennant

"Actually, they started out as just bickering pianos."

In this part . . .

Orlando's action used to literally rise and set with the sun, but that's hardly the case now. We tip our hats to those of you who still have the pizzazz for a nighttime adventure after a day in the parks. Whether you prefer rocking the night away, dancing until dawn, or dining while you watch knights rescue damsels in distress, you can liven up your evenings in Orlando, and this part of the book shows you how.

Chapter 28

Hitting the Clubs and Bars

• •

In This Chapter

▶ Rocking the night away at **Walt Disney World**

▶ Cruising the clubs at **CityWalk**

▶ Sampling Orlando's Old Guard nightlife

▶ Exploring hot spots inside Orlando's hotels

▶ Finding a few more places to boogie down

• •

Sure, you came for the sunrise-to-sunset rides, shows, and corn dogs. But you're still under

A. 30

B. 40

C. __ (write it in — we won't squeal)

Although Orlando has a reputation as a daylight destination, it's night-side menu continues growing as fun-seekers like you insist on a place to howl at the moon.

Clubs such as *Mannequins* and *House of Blues* at **Pleasure Island** and **West Side** rock well into the wee hours. **Universal Studios** entered the after-dark game in 1999 with its **CityWalk** entertainment district and such nightspots as *the groove* and *CityJazz*. ***Church Street Station's Rosie O'Grady's*** is a long-time after-hours favorite. *The Mercado* on International Drive and a handful of stand-alone clubs also add to the rocking mix.

 Many of the clubs that we list in the following section are open to anyone 18 or older, but remember: The minimum drinking age in Florida is 21, and the clubs will check your ID.

Walt Disney World Nightlife

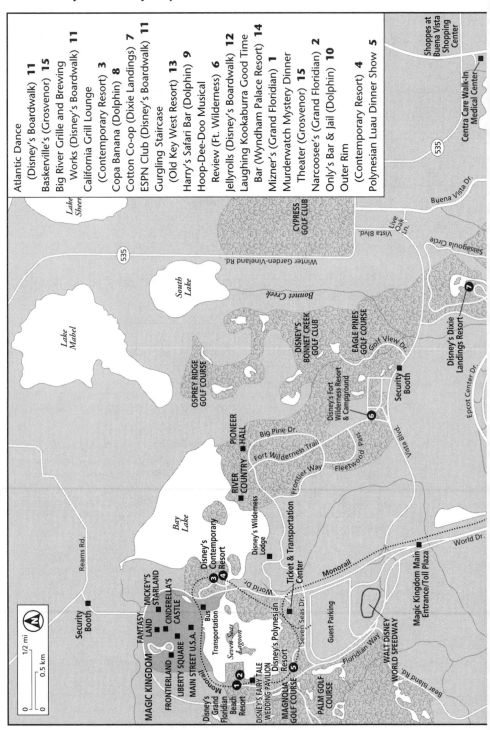

Atlantic Dance
(Disney's Boardwalk) **11**
Baskerville's (Grosvenor) **15**
Big River Grille and Brewing
Works (Disney's Boardwalk) **11**
California Grill Lounge
(Contemporary Resort) **3**
Copa Banana (Dolphin) **8**
Cotton Co-op (Dixie Landings) **7**
ESPN Club (Disney's Boardwalk) **11**
Gurgling Staircase
(Old Key West Resort) **13**
Harry's Safari Bar (Dolphin) **9**
Hoop-Dee-Doo Musical
Review (Ft. Wilderness) **6**
Jellyrolls (Disney's Boardwalk) **12**
Laughing Kookaburra Good Time
Bar (Wyndham Palace Resort) **14**
Mizner's (Grand Floridian) **1**
Murderwatch Mystery Dinner
Theater (Grosvenor) **15**
Narcoosee's (Grand Floridian) **2**
Only's Bar & Jail (Dolphin) **10**
Outer Rim
(Contemporary Resort) **4**
Polynesian Luau Dinner Show **5**

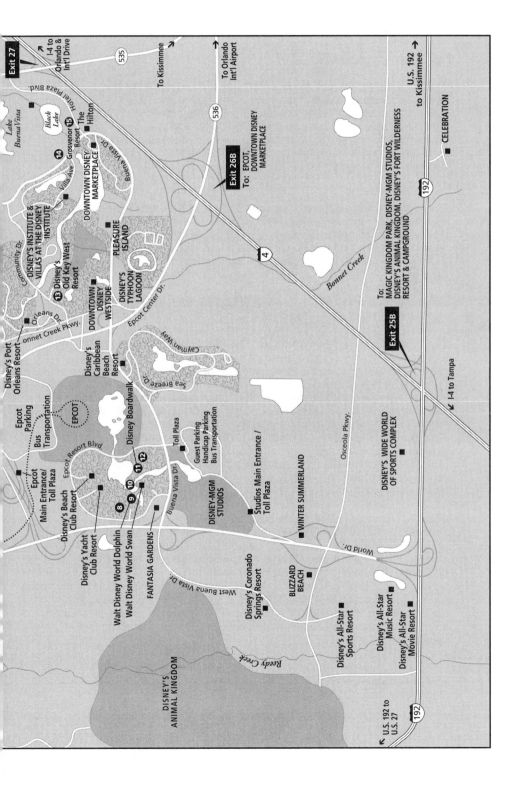

Enjoying the Pleasures of Pleasure Island

This six-acre, sometimes gated, entertainment district is the home of several nightspots. Admission to the island is free from 10 a.m.–7 p.m. Admission is $20, including tax, after 7 p.m., when the clubs open (admission is included if you have an All-In-One-Hopper pass — see Chapter 16 for information on Disney admission passes). Self-parking is free. For information on **Pleasure Island,** call ☎ **407-934-7781,** or check out Disney's Web site at http://disney.go.com/DisneyWorld/intro.html.

Mannequins Dance Palace is the main event on **Pleasure Island,** and it's a high-energy club with a big, rotating dance floor. Being a local favorite makes it hard to get into, so arrive early, especially on weekends. Three levels of bars and mixing space are adorned with elaborately dressed mannequins. The DJ plays contemporary tunes loud enough to wake the dead.

You must be 21 to get into *Mannequins Dance Club,* and the staff is *very* serious about that.

The *Adventurers Club* is a multistory building that, according to WDW legend, was designed to be the library and archaeological trophy room for Pleasure Island founder and explorer, Merriweather Adam Pleasure, who was lost at sea in 1941. The club is decorated with early aviation photos, hunting trophies, and a mounted yakoose — a half yak, half moose that speaks, whether you're drinking or not. Also on hand are Pleasure's zany band of globetrotting friends and servants, played by skilled actors who interact with guests while staying in character. Improvisational comedy and cabaret shows are performed in the Library. You can easily hang out here all night, sipping potent tropical drinks in the library or the bar, where elephant-foot barstools rise and sink mysteriously.

If you're a fan of the BET Cable Network, you'll probably love *BET Soundstage* (☎ **407-934-7666**), which offers traditional R&B and the rhyme of hip-hop. You can dance on an expansive floor or kick back on an outdoor terrace. Cover charge for the *Soundstage* is included in the Pleasure Island pass, except for major concerts.

A very talented troupe — the Who, What and Warehouse Players — are the main event at the *Comedy Warehouse.* The group performs 45-minute improvisational shows based on audience suggestions. They do five shows a night.

Disco and polyester rule at *8Trax,* a 1970s-style club where 50 TV screens air diverse shows and videos over the dance floor. A DJ plays everything from "YMCA" to "The Hustle."

The Wildhorse Saloon attracts country connoisseurs with some of the millennium's best boot-scootin' music. If you don't know how to scoot, the Wildhorse Dancers can show you the moves before you hit the 1,500-square-foot dance floor. The cover charge is included in Pleasure Island admission except on nights of big concerts. Call ☎ **407-934-7781** to find out if anyone is performing while you're in town.

Exploring the West Side

Immediately adjacent to **Pleasure Island, Disney West Side** is a slightly newer district, where you'll find clubs, restaurants, and **DisneyQuest** (see Chapter 21).

Singer Gloria Estefan and her husband, Emilio, created *Bongo's Cuban Café* (☎ **407-828-0999;** www.bongoscubancafe.com), an eatery/nightspot where a Desi Arnaz look-alike may show up to croon a few tunes. The upbeat salsa music makes this place noisy, so flee to the patio or upstairs if you want privacy. All in all, this isn't one of Florida's better Cuban restaurants, so you're better off coming for the atmosphere rather than the food (which will run you about $10–$26). The *Café* is open daily from 11 a.m. to 2 a.m. and doesn't take reservations. You can also find plenty of free self-parking.

Cirque du Soleil isn't your ordinary circus. It doesn't have any lions, tigers, or bears. But you won't feel cheated. This Circus of the Sun is nonstop energy. At times, it seems as if all 64 performers are on stage simultaneously, especially during the frenetic trampoline routine. Trapeze artists, high-wire walkers, an airborne gymnast, a posing strongman, mimes, and two clowns cement a show called *La Nouba* into a five-star performance. But if you're on a tight budget, this is gut-check time: Can you blow one or two day's entertainment budget on 90 minutes of fun? Tickets are $62 for adults and $38 for kids 3 to 9, yet there's rarely an empty seat in the 1,671-seat arena. Show times are at 6 and 9 p.m., Wednesday through Saturday; 3 and 6 p.m. on Sundays. For information, call ☎ **407-939-7600,** or go visit their Web site at www.cirquedusoleil.com.

The walls and rafters in the *House of Blues* literally shake with rhythm and blues. The *House* is decorated with colorful folk art, and the patio has a nice view of the bay. If you like spicy food, the jambalaya and gumbo ($15–$20) are treats. Sunday's Gospel Brunch ($28 for adults and $15 kids 4 to 12) has foot-stomping music served with omelets, prime rib, jalapeno smashed potatoes, cheese grits, and sausage. Brunch is the only time you can make reservations. Call ☎ **407-934-2583** to make your reservations early. The *House of Blues* is open daily 11 a.m. to 2 a.m., and offers free self-parking.

Downtown Disney

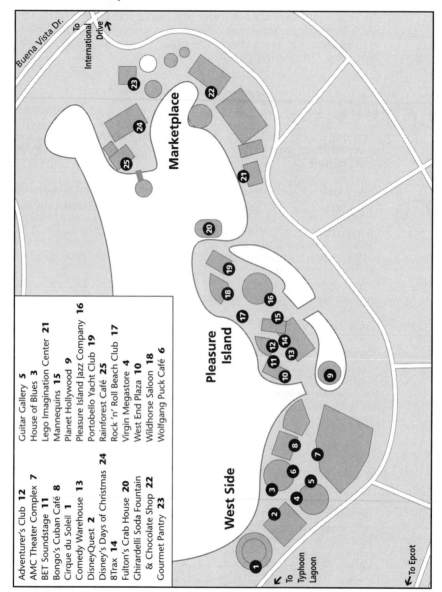

Marketplace

Pleasure Island

West Side

To Buena Vista Dr.

To International Drive

To Typhoon Lagoon

To Epcot

Adventurer's Club **12**
AMC Theater Complex **7**
BET Soundstage **11**
Bongo's Cuban Café **8**
Cirque du Soleil **1**
Comedy Warehouse **13**
DisneyQuest **2**
Disney's Days of Christmas **24**
8Trax **14**
Fulton's Crab House **20**
Ghirardelli Soda Fountain
 & Chocolate Shop **22**
Gourmet Pantry **23**

Guitar Gallery **5**
House of Blues **3**
Lego Imagination Center **21**
Mannequins **15**
Planet Hollywood **9**
Pleasure Island Jazz Company **16**
Portobello Yacht Club **19**
Rainforest Café **25**
Rock 'n' Roll Beach Club **17**
Virgin Megastore **4**
West End Plaza **10**
Wildhorse Saloon **18**
Wolfgang Puck Café **6**

Strolling along Disney's BoardWalk

This is part of the same-named resort (see Chapter 8). The **BoardWalk** is a great place for a quiet stroll or more. Street performers sing, dance, juggle, and make a little magic most evenings. *Atlantic Dance* (☎ **407-539-5100**) offers retro-swing and contemporary Latin music ($3 cover charge). The rustic, saloon-style *Jellyrolls* (☎ **407-939-3463**), offers dueling pianos (no cover). If you need a game fix, *ESPN Sports* (☎ 407-939-3463; www.disneyworld.com) has 71 TV screens, a full-service bar, food, and a small arcade, all without a cover charge.

Dancing the Night away at CityWalk

Universal's answer to **Pleasure Island** is a two-level collection of clubs and restaurants located between its two theme parks. **CityWalk** (☎ 407-363-8000; www.uescape.com/citywalk/), is open 11 a.m. to 2 a.m. daily. There's no admission, but several clubs have cover charges after 5 or 6 p.m., and some aren't open earlier than that. If you're planning to see only a few clubs, it's cheaper to pay individually. Club hoppers are better off buying the *CityWalk Party Pass,* which for $18 including tax, allows entry to all the clubs. Call ☎ 800-711-0080 for information on the pass. Parking costs $6 in the Universal garage.

Bob Marley — A Tribute to Freedom (☎ 407-224-2262) has architecture said to replicate Marley's home in Kingston. Local and national reggae bands perform. Light Jamaican fare is served under umbrellas. Hours are 5 p.m. to 2 a.m. Monday to Friday and 11 a.m. to 2 a.m. Saturday to Sunday. There's a cover of $4.25 after 8 p.m.; cover prices increase for concerts on special nights.

The collection of memorabilia at the *Downbeat Jazz Hall of Fame* ranges from Buddy Rich to Ella Fitzgerald. The adjoining *Thelonious Monk Institute of Jazz* is a performance venue that's also the site of workshops. You can browse through 500 pieces of memorabilia reaching from Dixieland, swing, bebop, and modern jazz. Nationally acclaimed acts perform frequently. On the food side of the equation, look for tapas, sushi, and lamb chops. *The Institute of Jazz* is open 7:30 p.m. to 2:00 a.m.

the groove (☎ 407-363-8000) is **CityWalk's** answer to **Pleasure Island's** *Mannequins,* though it's not as crowded. The sound system is guaranteed to blow your hair back, and the dance floor is in a room gleaming with chrome. Music-wise, *the groove* features hip-hop, jazz fusion, techno, and alternative. A DJ plays tunes on nights when recording artists aren't booked. In addition to the main room, three alcoves have their own unique designs, bars, and specialty drinks to fit the mood. The *blue lounge* is retro icy and cool, the *red lounge* is hot and spicy in a Victorian sense, and the *green lounge* brings back the 70s.You must be at least 21 to enter, and it will cost you a cover charge of $5.25 for the privilege. The club is open from 9 p.m. to 2 a.m.

CityWalk's *Hard Rock Cafe* (☎ 407-351-5483) is the largest in the world, and the adjoining *Hard Rock Live* is the first concert hall bearing the name. There's also a free exhibit area in the cafe, where you can browse through displays of rock memorabilia, including the platform heels, leather jumpsuits, and tongue action of KISS. Cover charge varies by act. They are open daily 11 a.m. to 2 a.m.

Flip-flops plus flowered shirts equals *Jimmy Buffett's Margaritaville* (☎ 407-224-2155). Canned music is piped through the building, with a Jimmy sound-alike strumming on the back porch. Bar-wise, you have three options. *The Volcano* erupts (we're not kidding) margaritas; the *Land Shark* has fins swimming around the ceiling; and the *12 Volt,* is, well, a little electrifying. The menu screams Key West. It includes cheeseburgers in paradise, mahimahi, and key lime pie. See Chapter 14 for more on the vittles. *Margaritaville* is open from 11 a.m. to 2 a.m., and there's a $3.25 cover after 10 p.m.

Guessing the focus of a place that has a one-page food menu and a booklet filled with drinks doesn't take a genius. Just like the French Quarter's version, drinking is the highlight at **CityWalk's** *Pat O'Brien's* (☎ 407-224-2122). You can enjoy dueling pianos and a flame-throwing fountain while you suck down the signature drink — the Hurricane. No one under 21 is permitted after 7 p.m. *Pat O' Brien's* offers a limited menu of sandwiches, snacks, and treats like jambalaya and shrimp Creole. A meal will set you back $6–$10. Hours are 4 p.m. to 2 a.m., and there is a $2 cover charge after 9 p.m.

All Aboard for Church Street Station

The first Orlando nightspot, the success of **Church Street Station** prompted **Disney** and **Universal** to enter the night games. The **Station** is a cobblestoned city block with real turn-of-the-century buildings. This club-and-dining complex offers 20 live shows and street performers, and its interiors have a magnificent collection of woodwork, stained glass, and antiques.

Church Street Station is located at 129 W. Church Street (off I-4, between Garland and Orange avenues in downtown Orlando). Admission is free before 5 p.m.; after 5 p.m., it's $17.95 ($11.95 for kids 4 to 12). Entry to the restaurants, the *Exchange Shopping Emporium,* and the Midway game area is free. Clubs are open 7:15 p.m. to 2:00 a.m., shops 11 a.m. to 11 p.m. Metered parking is $1-an-hour, or you can use valet parking for $7. To find **Church Street Station,** take I-4 east to Exit 38 (Anderson St.), stay in the left lane, and follow the signs.

Dixieland bands, banjo players, and cancan girls keep your blood from coagulating inside *Rosie O'Grady's Good Time Emporium,* an 1890s-style gambling hall and saloon. As for eye candy, the train benches came from an old rail station, the back-bar mirrors from a Glasgow pub, and the bank tellers' cages from a nineteenth-century bank.

If you like folk and bluegrass, try *Apple Annie's Courtyard,* a brick-floor building with arched trusses from an early nineteenth-century New Orleans church; 12-foot, hand-carved filigree mirrors created in Vienna around 1740; and an eighteenth-century French communion rail that serves as the front bar.

Nightlife in Downtown Orlando

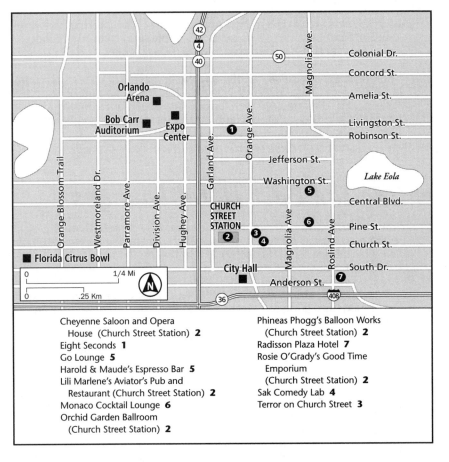

Cheyenne Saloon and Opera
  House (Church Street Station) **2**
Eight Seconds **1**
Go Lounge **5**
Harold & Maude's Espresso Bar **5**
Lili Marlene's Aviator's Pub and
  Restaurant (Church Street Station) **2**
Monaco Cocktail Lounge **6**
Orchid Garden Ballroom
  (Church Street Station) **2**

Phineas Phogg's Balloon Works
  (Church Street Station) **2**
Radisson Plaza Hotel **7**
Rosie O'Grady's Good Time
  Emporium
  (Church Street Station) **2**
Sak Comedy Lab **4**
Terror on Church Street **3**

Phineas Phogg's Balloon Works is a whimsical bar with hot-air balloons over the dance floor and loud, pulsating music surrounding it. No one under 21 is admitted.

A three-level bar with balconies, the *Cheyenne Saloon and Opera House* is crowned with a lofty stained-glass skylight and Western art throughout, including 11 Remington sculptures. The *Cheyenne* has the best show of the bunch, with a tight country band that really knows how to kick up its heels. Thursdays mean $2 beer and $2 barbecue sandwiches from 4:30 p.m. to 7:30 p.m.

Dreams of *The Great Gatsby* permeate the *Orchid Garden Ballroom,* where a Victorian mood is the setting for an oldies dance club. A DJ plays rock 'n' roll classics such as "Great Balls of Fire" and "Let's Go to the Hop," interspersed with live bands.

Do It All at The Mercado

By day, *The Mercado* is a mild shopping arena (8445 International Boulevard, south of Sand Lake Road); by night, it's home to free entertainment in Center Court (at 7:30 p.m.), a special spot to toss back a beer.

The *Cricketers Arms Pub* (☎ **407-354-0686;** www.cricketersarmspub.com.), is a bit quieter. But, *Cricketers* is a good place to sip a pint of Boddingtons, Fullers, ESB, Old Speckled Hen, or one of a dozen other imports while you enjoy some U.K. camaraderie and maybe feast on steak-and-ale pie or a bloody-good plate of fish-and-chips ($6–$12).

Locating the Best Hotel Lounges

Some of Orlando's best nightlife is located in its hotels. Even the locals head to the resort areas for fun after dark. If you're staying at one of the places listed in this section, you can do an evening on the town without ever getting behind the wheel.

In WDW hotels, *Cotton Co-Op* at **Dixie Landings** serves up live music and Cajun food until midnight. In the **Grand Floridian,** *Mizner's* has an orchestra until 1 a.m. and a wood-paneled interior. *Narcoossee's* offers Victorian décor and beer by the yard or half-yard. *Outer Rim* in the **Contemporary Resort** is trendy and close to the monorail. *Kimono's* in the **Swan** becomes a karaoke bar after 8:30 p.m. *Copa Banana* in the **Dolphin** offers a DJ, dancing, and karaoke.

The *Laughing Kookaburra Good Time Bar* in the **Wyndham Palace, Lake Buena Vista** (☎ **407-827-3722**), is open from 7 p.m. to 2 a.m., with live music and a DJ most nights. The piano bar in *Arthur's 27* (☎ **800-327-2990** or 407-827-2727), also in **Wyndham Palace,** has a great view of Disney's fireworks. *Baskerville's* (☎ **407-827-6500**), in the **Grosvenor Resort Hotel, Lake Buena Vista,** features jazz nights Wednesday through Friday, 7 p.m. to 9 p.m., and a solve-it-yourself mystery show on Saturday at 6 p.m. and 9 p.m. (See Chapter 29 for more info about this dinner show.) The *Lobby Bar* (☎ **407-352-4000**), at the **Peabody Orlando,** is a popular gathering spot with piano music.

Exploring Orlando's Other Hot Spots

Orlando offers many other hot spots where you can enjoy the nightlife. Here's our list of favorites:

- **Cairo.** 22 S. Magnolia Avenue (one block off Orange Avenue.) One of the newer arrivals downtown, this popular club has bars on three levels. You can find lots of '70s retro clothes and kids trying to look older than their age. Reggae plays on the rooftop during the weekends. The club also offers ladies' and Latin nights. (☎ **407-422-3595.** Open 8 p.m. to 2 a.m. Friday to Sunday, $5 cover charge. Street parking available.)

Nightlife on International Drive

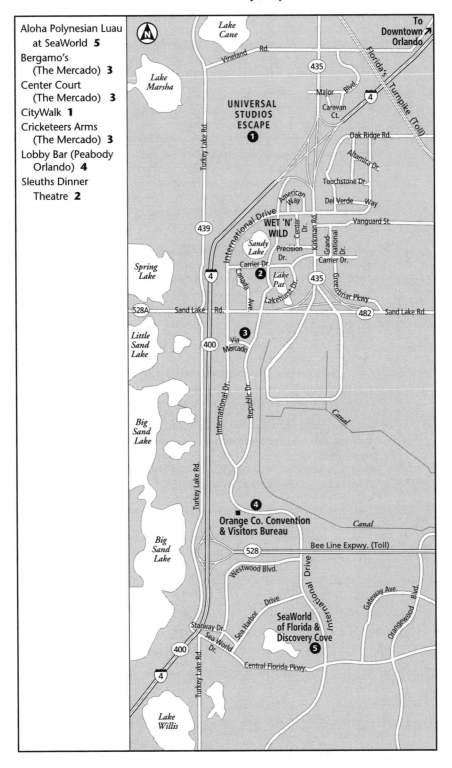

✔ **Club La Vela.** 5100 Adanson Street in Orlando (just north of downtown) is another recent arrival. *Club La Vela* is a 40,000-square-foot venture with a 2,500-seat concert hall. The decibel level, bikini pageants, and ladies' nights make this club more attractive to the spring-break crowd than others. Cover charge is $5 to $10 depending on the night and event. (☎ **407-629-4779;** www/clublavela.com.)

✔ **8 Seconds.** 100 W. Livingston Avenue Orlando. This honky-tonk has a cavernous interior and a huge dance floor where you can get free line-dancing lessons early in the evening. If you go, take the side trip to the parking lot on "Buckin' Bull Nights," when cowboys provide some extra entertainment in the ring. You can also find monster-truck pulls in the back lot. Country stars sometimes perform outside the ring. (Open 7 p.m. Friday to Saturday, $5 cover, 21 and older; $7 under 21. Parking in city lot $3. ☎ **407-839-4800;** www.8-seconds.com.)

✔ **Howl at the Moon Saloon.** 55 W. Church Street. This is a fun bar that's open 6 p.m. to 2 a.m. daily. Your best bet: Go on a full moon — even if you're too shy to cock your head back and howlllll with the best. (☎ **407-841-9118;** www.howlatthemoon.com. $2 to $4 cover, Wedneday to Saturday)

✔ **Kit Kat Club/Globe Lounge/Harold & Maude's.** 25 Wall Street Plaza (off Orange Avenue), Orlando. This three-for-one hotspot includes a hangout for the Generation X crowd (*Kit Kat*); an Irish (and other) coffee and sandwich bar (*Harold & Maude's*); and a small, alternative dance club (*Globe Lounge*). ☎ **407-422-1669.** Only the *Globe Lounge* requires a cover (usually under $5).

✔ **Sapphire Supper Club.** 54 N. Orange Avenue, Orlando. Some major-league acts perform at this downtown venue, including jazz legend and used-to-be-Orlando resident Sam Rivers. This joint is cool and jazzy, offering cigar and martini nights that young professionals and music lovers of every age dig. (☎ **407-246-1419;** www.sapphiresupperclub.com.) **Cover prices vary.**

Chapter 29

Dinner and a Show: The Orlando Theater Scene

● ●

In This Chapter

▶ Finding out the truth about Orlando dinner shows

▶ Seeing the best shows

▶ Getting tickets

● ●

*I*f a day at the theme parks isn't enough to satisfy your appetite for entertainment, Orlando's dinner-theater circuit serves up a diverse menu of amusements that will keep you entertained as you chow down. Solve a "murder," learn to hula, or cheer on a knight at a medieval joust.

Finding Out the Inside Scoop

Disney and Orlando have a reasonably busy dinner-show scene, but their offerings aren't like what you'll find in such high-flying cultural centers as Paris, New York, and London. Shows at **Disney** and in Orlando offer fun, not critically acclaimed drama. Most focus on entertaining the number one VIP: Kids. Therefore, in many instances, theater in Orlando is a little like eating in front of the television set.

Eating adds another element of adventure to theater in Orlando. Dinner-show fare, especially outside **Disney**, is right off the rubber-chicken circuit. Food at dinner-show theaters usually consists of a choice of two or three entrées and school-lunch caliber side dishes. Your choice of food may explain why some theaters serve free wine and beer — to dull your palate — after you're seated, and before dinner is served.

The prices of the shows that we list in this chapter include food and pedestrian drinks, but not tax or tips.

Now Playing

In addition to the dinner shows listed in this section, there will also be another theater soon. Dolly Parton plans to enter the mix in 2001 with a *Dixie Stampede & Dinner Show* similar to the ones she owns in Pigeon Forge, Tennessee; Branson, Missouri; and Myrtle Beach, South Carolina. The opening of the *Dixie Stampede & Dinner Show* means there's going to be 32 horses starring in a show that has plenty of riding, roping, wagon racing, and a North-South rivalry that puts the audience on opposite sides of the Mason-Dixon line. The $20 million attraction will have 1,000 seats and won't serve alcohol.

Arabian Nights

If you're a horse fan, this show is a winner. It stars virtually every breed on the planet, from chiseled Arabians to muscular quarter horses to Royal Lippizaner stallions. Many locals rate this number one among Orlando dinner shows. On most nights the show opens with a ground trainer working one-on-one with a black stallion. The continuous action includes Wild West trick riders, a dual-dressage performance, a cowgirl thrill show, Native American riders, and treats such as horse skiing, soccer, and chariot races. The meal, served during the two-hour show, includes salad, prime rib, vegetables, rolls, dessert, sodas, and wine.

6225 W. Irlo Bronson Memorial Hwy. (U.S. 192, east of I-4 at Exit 25A). ☎ *800-553-6116 or 407-239-9223.* www.arabian-nights.com. *Reservations recommended. Shows held daily, times vary. Admission: $37 adults, $24 kids 3–11. Free parking.*

Hoop-Dee-Doo Musical Revue

This is **Disney's** most popular show, so make your reservations early. Feast on a down-home, all-you-can-eat barbecue (country-fried chicken, smoked ribs, salad, corn on the cob, baked beans, baked bread, strawberry shortcake, and coffee, tea, beer, sangria, or soda). While you stuff yourself silly in Pioneer Hall, performers in 1890s garb lead you in a foot-stomping, hand-clapping, high-energy show that includes a lot of jokes you haven't heard since second grade. *Tip:* Be prepared to join in the fun, or the singers and the rest of the audience will humiliate you. If you catch an early show, go to the *Electrical Water Pageant* at 9:45 p.m., which you can view from the Fort Wilderness Beach.

3520 N. Fort Wilderness Trail (at WDW's Fort Wilderness Resort and Campground). ☎ *407-939-3563.* http://disney.go.com/DisneyWorld/intro.html. *Reservations required. Shows: 5:00, 7:15, and 9:30p.m. Admission: Adults $44, kids 3–11 $22. Free self-parking.*

Medieval Times

This is the Orlando branch of the restaurant that Jim Carrey visited in the movie, *The Cable Guy*. Pig out on barbecued ribs, herb-roasted chicken, soup, appetizers, potatoes, dessert, and a beverage. But because this is the eleventh century, you eat with your fingers from plates while mounted knights run around the arena, jousting to please the fair ladies. Arrive early and take a look at Medieval Village, a re-created Middle Ages settlement.

4510 W. Irlo Bronson Memorial Hwy. (U.S. Hwy. 192, 11 miles east of the main Disney entrance, next to Wal-Mart). ☎ ***800-229-8300*** *or 407-396-1518.* www.medievaltimes.com. *Reservations recommended. Performances nightly, times vary. Admission: $38.95 adults, $23.95 kids 3–12. Free parking.*

MurderWatch Mystery Theatre.

Located in Baskervilles Restaurant, this all-you-can-eat-prime-rib buffet also offers chicken, fish, and a children's buffet while diners try to solve the mystery. The restaurant, by the way, has a nineteenth-century décor and also houses a Sherlock Holmes museum.

In the Grosvenor Resort at 1850 Hotel Plaza Blvd. (Turn west off Fla. 535 onto Hotel Plaza Blvd.; it's close to Downtown Disney Marketplace.) ☎ ***800-624-4109*** *or 407-827-6534,* www.grosvenorresort.com. *Reservations recommended. Admission: $34.95 adults, $10.95 kids 3–11. Shows: Sat., 6 and 9 p.m. Free parking.*

Pirates Dinner Adventure

The special effects at this show include a full-size ship in a 300,000-gallon lagoon, circus-style aerial acts, music, and a little drama. Afterward, you're invited to the Buccaneer Bash dance party. Dinner includes an appetizer buffet with the pre-show, followed by chicken, beef, rice, vegetables, dessert, and coffee.

6400 Carrier Dr. (from Disney, take I-4 to Sand Lake Road, go east to International Drive, then north to Carrier). ☎ ***800-866-2469*** *or 407-248-0590.* www.orlandopirates.com. *Reservations recommended. Admission: $37.95 adults, $22.95 kids 3–11. Free parking. Shows: 6:30 and 10:00 p.m.*

Polynesian Luau Dinner Show

This delightful two-hour dinner show is a big favorite with kids, all of whom are invited on the stage. It features a colorfully costumed cast of hyperactive entertainers from New Zealand, Tahiti, Hawaii, and Samoa performing hula, warrior, ceremonial, love, and fire dances on a flower-filled stage. The show takes place in an open-air theater (dress for night-time weather) with candlelit tables, red-flame lanterns meant to resemble torches, and tapa-bark paintings adorning the walls. Arrive early: There's a pre-show highlighting Polynesian crafts and culture (lei making, hula lessons, and more). The all-you-can-eat meal includes a big platter of fresh island fruits, barbecued chicken, roast pork, corn, vegetables, red and sweet potatoes, pull-apart cinnamon bread, beverages, and a tropical ice-cream sundae.

1600 Seven Seas Dr. (at Disney's Polynesian Resort). ☎ ***407-939-3463.*** http://disney.go.com/DisneyWorld/intro.html. *Reservations required. Shows: 5:15 and 8:00 p.m. Tues. through Sat. Admission: Adults $44, $22 kids 3–11. Free self- and valet parking.*

Getting Tickets

In some cases, you can make a reservation for dinner shows on the same day you want to attend. Sometimes, you can just walk up to the ticket window and buy a ticket (though we don't recommend it). However, in all but spur-of-the-moment cases, we recommend using the numbers in the listings in this chapter to book seats.

When it comes to **Walt Disney World** dinner shows, always make a Priority Seating reservation, ☎ **407-939-3463** (see Chapter 13). Disney's shows fill up fast, sometimes weeks in advance for weekend performances.

Part VIII
The Part of Tens

The 5th Wave   By Rich Tennant

Tell them we work at one of the theme parks, and maybe they won't ask too many questions.

In this part . . .

Ah, tradition. The Part of Tens chapters are to Dummies books what hangovers are to New Year's Day — an integral part of the experience. In this part of the book, we feed you plenty of useful and fun information that we think is especially handy.

In the following chapters, we talk about some budget attractions that can stretch your dollars, tourist traps you should avoid (such as three-day-old seafood), and some fun ways to keep active when you're not at the theme parks.

Chapter 30

Top Ten Cheap Alternatives to the Parks

• •

In This Chapter

▶ Spending some time at a museum

▶ Strolling through a "real" park

▶ Taking a leisurely boat tour

• •

*W*hile everyone else is emptying their wallets in the theme parks around Orlando, in this chapter, we give you suggestions for great places to dodge crowds and save a few bucks.

Central Florida Zoological Park

The 400 critters that live in this 21-acre zoo include wreathed hornbills, kookaburras, bald eagles, mandrills, siamangs, black howler monkeys, Asian elephants, two-toed sloths, clouded leopards, cheetahs, caracals, and American crocodiles. The headliner is a lovable hippopotamus named Geraldine.

The park is located at 3755 N. U.S. 17/92 (in Sanford). Call ☎ **407-323-4450** for more information or visit www.centralfloridazoo.org on the Web. Admission is $7 for adults, $4 for seniors 60 and over, and $3 for kids 3 to 12. (Guests enter for half price every Thursday before 10 a.m., and seniors visit for half price every Tuesday.) The park is open daily 9 a.m. to 5 p.m.

Charles Hosmer Morse Museum of American Art

Although it's not a New York-quality house, Charlie's Place has a big collection of Louis Tiffany glass, created for the 1893 Colombian Expo in Chicago. The collection was expanded in 1999 when it moved to the 800-square-foot Tiffany Chapel in the Charles Hosmer Museum. A huge electrified chandelier and six stained-glass windows from that exposition are on display.

You can find the museum at 445 Park Avenue N., Winter Park. (Take the I-4 Fairbanks Avenue exit east to Park Avenue, go left and through four traffic lights.) Call ☎ **407-645-5311** or 407-645-5324 (a telephone recording) for more details, or check the museum's site on the Web at www.inusa.com/tour/fl/orlando/morse.htm. Admission is $3 for adults, $1 for students, and kids under 12 get in free. The museum is open Tuesday through Saturday 9:30 a.m. to 4:00 p.m. and Sunday 1 to 4 p.m.

Cornell Fine Arts Museum

This showplace has 6,000 works on display, making it one of Florida's most distinguished and comprehensive art collections. The museum also conducts lectures and gallery-talk walks.

The museum is located at the east end of Holt Avenue on the Rollins College campus in Winter Park. (Take I-4 Exit 45/Fairbanks Avenue east to Park, turn right, then left on Holt.) Call ☎ **407-646-2526** or visit www.rollins.edu/cfam for more information. Admission is free, and the museum is open Tuesday through Friday, 10 a.m. to 5 p.m., and Saturday and Sunday from 1 to 5 p.m.

Eatonville and the Zora Neale Hurston National Museum of Fine Arts

America's oldest black municipality is located just north of Orlando. Eatonville is the birthplace of Hurston — a too-little heralded, African-American author. The city hosts an annual festival in January honoring her and her work. A small gallery on the site displays periodically changing exhibits of art and other work, and you can grab a map for a walking tour of the community, established in 1887. *Make sure to call in advance to confirm the museum's business hours.*

The museum is at 227 E. Kennedy Boulevard, Eatonville. (Take I-4 to Exit 46 and make a quick left onto Lee Road, then left on Wymore, and then right on Kennedy. It's one-quarter mile down the road on the left.) Call ☎ **407-647-3307** or visit www.cs.ucf.edu/~zora for more information. The museum accepts donations as admission. The museum is open Monday through Friday 9 a.m. to 4 p.m.

Farmers Market

Farmers Market is a fun Saturday-morning breakfast or lunch excursion. Peddlers sell fruit, vegetables, bagels, cheese, coffee, and more in a friendly back-on-the-block setting.

The market is located at New York Street at New England Avenue, Winter Park. (Take I-4 exit 45/Fairbanks east to New York, then left two blocks to the market.) Call ☎ **407-623-3200** for more information. Admission is free, and the market is open Saturdays from 7 a.m. to noon.

Florida Audubon Center for Birds of Prey

This bird sanctuary — one of the biggest rehabilitation centers in the Southeast — flies under the radar of most tourists, making it a great place to get to know the winged wonders (owls and eagles) that earn their keep by entertaining the few visitors who do visit. The center is closed while a new, state-of-the-art rehab center and permanent residence are being built, but it's scheduled to reopen in fall 2000, so make sure that you call ahead before visiting.

The center is at 1101 Audubon Way, Maitland. (Take I-4 to Lee Road/ Exit 46, turn right, at first light/Wymore Road, go left, then right at the next light/Kennedy Boulevard Continue one-half mile to East Ave., turn left, and go to the stop sign at Audubon Way. Turn left, and the center is on the right.) Call ☎ **407-644-0190** or visit www.adoptabird.org/ for more information. The center accepts donations: $5 adults, $3 children 3 to 12. Visitor hours are Tuesday through Sunday, 10 a.m. to 5 p.m.

Holocaust Memorial Resource and Education Center

Exhibits at this center illustrate pre-war Jewish communities in Europe, Hitler's rise to power, the concentration camps, and the lives of camp survivors. There's also a memorial wall made from stone imported from Jerusalem.

The center is at 851 N. Maitland Avenue, Maitland. (Take I-4 to Exit 47, go east through merge with Maitland Boulevard, right at first light onto Maitland Avenue It's in the Jewish Community Center at Maitland Blvd. and Maitland Avenue) Call ☎ **407-628-0555** or visit www.holocaustedu. org for more information. The center accepts donations as admission Monday through Thursday, 9 a.m. to 4 p.m. and Friday, 9 a.m. to 1 p.m. The center is also occasionally open Sundays. Call ahead to confirm.

Kissimmee Sports Arena & Rodeo

The Kissimmee Sports Arena & Rodeo is a good way to fill a Friday night dance card, and it's only 20 minutes from the major theme parks. Events include saddle bronc and bull riding, calf roping, and barrel racing.

The arena is located at 958 South Hoagland Boulevard, Kissimmee. (Take I-4 Exit 25A/U.S. 192 east to Hoagland, and then go south one mile to the arena.) Call ☎ **407-933-0020** or visit www.ksarodeo.com for more details. Admission is $15 for adults, $7.50 for children 12 and under. The fun begins every Friday at 8 p.m.

Lake Eola Park

This quiet hideaway in downtown Orlando offers the city's skyline as a backdrop. The lake has a cascading fountain that features a 12-minute evening light show. The park has a .9-mile walking and jogging path, a playground, and paddleboats for rent ($7 per half hour). FunnyEola features comedy acts the second Tuesday of each month at 7:30 p.m. There are also a variety of other performances, most of which are free (call ahead for more details). The Shakespeare Festival (April to early May) costs $5 to $30 nightly. Call % 407-893-4600 for more information about the festival.

The park is located at Washington Street and Rosalind Avenue, Orlando. (Take I-4 to Anderson Street, exit right, turn left at the fourth light/ Rosalind. The amphitheater is on the right.) Call ☎ **407-246-2827** for more information about the park. Admission is free, and the park is open daylight hours daily, sometimes later. Call the park before you visit to confirm business hours.

Lakeridge Winery & Vineyards

This working vineyard produces some of Florida's more noteworthy vintages. Tours include a look behind the scenes and a video presentation. Tastings offer a sample of three or more wines.

The winery is located at 19239 U.S. 27, Clermont. (Take U.S. 192 west of the **WDW** parks to U.S. 27, turn right and go 20 miles north.) Call ☎ **352-394-8627** for more information. Admission to the tours and tastings is free, and the winery is open Monday through Saturday, 10 a.m. to 5 p.m. and Sunday, 11 a.m. to 5 p.m.

Winter Park Scenic Boat Tour

This peaceful water voyage has been operating since 1938. The narrated, one-hour cruises showcase the area's beautiful lakes and canals, Rollins College, Kraft Azalea Gardens, and a number of historic mansions.

The boat tour launches from 312 E. Morse Boulevard, Winter Park. Call ☎ **407-644-4056** for additional information about the tour. Admission is $7 for adults and $3 for children under 12. The daily tours run every hour from 10 a.m. to 4 p.m.

Chapter 31

Top Ten Fitness Activities (Other than Walking the Parks)

· ·

In This Chapter

▶ Enjoying water-related activities

▶ Getting land-based exercise

· ·

*W*ant some exercise other than walking the parks? **Walt Disney World** and surrounding areas offer plenty of activities to keep you busy. The majority of these activities are most convenient for guests of Disney resorts and official hotels, but many other large resorts also offer comprehensive facilities (see Chapter 8 for more details). The WDW facilities described in this chapter are open to the public, no matter where you're staying. For further information, call ☎ 407-939-7529.

Bicycling

Bike rentals (single- and multispeed bikes for adults, tandems, and children's bikes) are available from the Bike Barn (☎ 407-824-2742) at **Fort Wilderness Resort and Campground. Fort Wilderness** has extensive and well-kept bike trails. Rates run $5 per hour or $12 per day; rates include tandems. You can also rent bicycles with training wheels and baby seats. Helmets are available at no additional charge.

Boating

Along with a ton of man-made lakes and lagoons, **WDW** owns a navy of pleasure boats. You can rent Water Sprites, canopy boats, and 20-foot pontoon boats ($20 to $30 for 30 minutes) at **Walt Disney World Village Marina.** For information, call ☎ 407-828-2204. **Fort Wilderness'** *Bike Barn* (☎ 407-824-2742) rents canoes and paddleboats ($6 per half hour, $10 per hour). See Chapter 8 for additional boating options.

Fishing

WDW offers a variety of fishing excursions on the various Disney lakes, including Bay Lake and Seven Seas Lagoon. These lakes are stocked, so you may catch something, but if you're a true angler, you probably won't find it much of a challenge. You can call the **Walt Disney World Village Marina** (☎ 407-824-2621, open weekdays from 10 a.m. to 6 p.m. in the winter and fall, 10 a.m. to 7 p.m. in the summer) 2 to 14 days in advance to arrange an excursion. A license isn't required. The fee is $150 for up to five people for two hours, including refreshments, gear, guide, and tax. Bait is extra.

The **Dixie Landings** and **Port Orleans** resorts offer early morning and evening sunset fishing trips for $55 a person. The price includes refreshments, guide, equipment, and artificial bait. Call ☎ **407-939-7529** during weekdays from 9 a.m. to 5 p.m.

Here's a less-expensive alternative: Rent fishing poles at the *Bike Barn* (☎ **407-824-2742**), and try your luck in **Fort Wilderness'** canals. A license isn't necessary.

Golf

Walt Disney World operates five 18-hole, par-72 golf courses and one 9-hole, par-36 walking course (see Chapter 21). All are open to the public and include pro shops, equipment rentals, and instruction. Rates range from $100 to $125 per 18-hole round for resort guests; the fee is $5 more if you're not staying at a WDW property. For tee times and information, call ☎ **407-824-2270** up to seven days in advance (up to 30 days for Disney-resort and official-property guests). Call ☎ **407-934-7639** for information about golf packages.

Elsewhere around town, you can find more than 125 other golf courses, some of them designed by Arnold Palmer, Jack Nicklaus, Tom Fazio, Pete Dye, Robert Trent Jones, and others. *Golf* magazine recognized the 45 holes designed by Nicklaus at the **Villas of Grand Cypress** resort as among the best in the nation. Tee times begin at 8 a.m. daily. Special rates are available for children under 18. For information call ☎ **407-239-1909.** The course is generally restricted to guests or guests of guests (at an average cost of $165), but there's limited play available to those not staying at the resort, and those fees begin at $225.

Also consider contacting **Golfpac,** (☎ **800-327-0878** or 407-260-2288; www.golfpacinc.com), an organization that packages golf vacations with accommodations and other features, and prearranges tee times at more than 40 Orlando-area courses. The further in advance you call (months, if possible), the better your options. **Tee Times USA** (☎ **800-374-8633;** www.teetimesusa.com) is another company that couples course and package information with a reservations service.

Online, you can visit the following URL to find a course that fits your budget: www.virtualvoyages.com/usa/fl/orlando/orl_golf.htm.

Hiking

The nice thing about hiking is that you can do it almost anywhere that has trails or sidewalks. You can use the trails that we list later in this chapter under "Jogging," or visit one of our favorite spots at **Walt Disney World,** the Hotel Plaza Boulevard. This small town avenue is lined with huge shade trees, and its winding sidewalks pass many official Disney hotels. You can find the Hotel Plaza Boulevard northeast of **Downtown Disney Marketplace.**

Horseback Riding

Disney's Fort Wilderness Resort and Campground offers 45-minute guided trail rides six times a day ($23 per person). Kids must be at least 9 years old, and there's a maximum weight limit of 250 pounds for riders. For information and reservations up to 30 days in advance, call ☎ **407-824-2832.**

The **Villas of Grand Cypress** also opens its equestrian center to outsiders. You can go on a 45-minute, walk-trot trail ride at 10 or 11 a.m. and 1 or 2 p.m. for $35. A 30-minute private lesson is $55, and an hour's lesson is $95. Call ☎ **407-239-4700** and ask for the equestrian center.

Jogging

Many Disney resorts offer scenic jogging trails. For instance, the **Yacht** and **Beach Club** resorts share a 2-mile trail; the **Disney Institute** has a 3.4-mile course with 32 exercise stations; the **Caribbean Beach Resort's** 1.4-mile promenade circles a lake; **Dixie Landings** offers a 1.7-mile riverfront trail, and **Fort Wilderness'** tree-shaded 2.3-mile jogging path has exercise stations about every quarter mile. Pick up a jogging trail map at any Disney property's guest-services desk.

Swimming

The local YMCA offers a full fitness center, racquetball courts, and an indoor Olympic-size pool. Admission is $10 for children and adults; $25 for families. For information call ☎ **407-363-1911.** The YMCA is located at 8422 International Drive (Take I-4 to Exit 29, turn right, and then right again on International Drive. Turn right at second light.)

Tennis

Twenty-two lighted tennis courts are scattered throughout the Disney properties. Most are free and available on a first-come, first-serve basis. If you're willing to pay, you can reserve courts up to several months in advance at two Disney resorts: the **Contemporary**

(☎ 407-824-3578) and the **Grand Floridian** (☎ 407-824-2435). Both charge $15 per hour; you can also reserve lesson times with the resident pros. The **Contemporary** offers a large pro shop, a ball machine, rebound walls, and equipment rentals.

Waterskiing

You can call ☎ 407-824-2621 to arrange water-skiing trips (including boats, drivers, equipment, and instruction) at **Walt Disney World.** Make reservations up to 14 days in advance. The cost is $100 per hour for up to five people.

You can also get time behind a boat at **Ski World** near downtown Orlando. Lessons are $35 for 20 minutes. For information, call ☎ 407-894-5012. To get there, take I-4 to downtown, and then take Exit 43, Princeton Street. Turn right at the bottom of the ramp. Turn right at the first light, and **Ski World** is about a mile on your left. The lake is on your right.

Appendix

Quick Concierge

• •

*T*his handy section is where we've condensed the practical and
pertinent information — from airline phone numbers to mailbox
locations — you'll need to make certain you have a successful and
stress-free Orlando vacation. And, for those of you who believe in being
really prepared, we also give you some additional resources to check out.

Orlando A to Z: Facts at Your Fingertips

AAA: American Automobile Association members can contact their
local offices for maps and optimum driving directions or call
☎ 800-222-4357 and asked to be transferred to the office nearest you.
Online, you can find information at www.aaa.com.

American Express: You can call ☎ 800-297-3429 or go to its Web site at
www.americanexpress.com/travel to reach the card company's Travel
Service offices nationally. In Orlando, call ☎ 407-843-0004. American
Express is the official card of **Walt Disney World;** it has windows at each
of the four WDW theme parks (see Chapters 17–20 for locations).

ATMs: Machines honoring Cirrus, Honor, Plus, and other systems
are common in all of Orlando's theme parks (see Chapters 17–20 and
23–25 for locations). They're also at many banks, shopping centers, and
convenience stores (see Chapter 3).

Babysitters: Many family-friendly accommodations have some kind of
sitting services and several have on-premise child-care facilities with
counselor-supervised activity programs. Disney uses **KinderCare** sitters (see Chapter 4). ☎ 407-827-5444.

Camera Repair: Southern Photo (☎ 407-896-0322), in the downtown
area, is one of the best in central Florida. Closer to the parks, try **Photo
Time** (☎ 407-352-1818), on International Drive.

Convention Center: The Orange County Convention Center (9800
International Drive; ☎ 407-345-9800), almost always has something
going on and most events are open to the public. The Disney resorts,
as well as some other hotels, provide rides there for a fee. You can also
use **Mears Transportation** (☎ 407-422-4561). Once there, you can ride

around the neighborhood on the **I-Ride Trolley** (☎ 407-354-5656. www.iridetrolley.com). It runs about every 15 minutes, 7 a.m. to midnight (75 cents for adults, 25 cents for seniors, and kids under 12 are free) on International Drive and is a good way to avoid the heavy traffic facing I-Drive motorists.

Credit Cards: Disney is fickle with credit cards, taking only American Express, MasterCard, and VISA in all of its parks and most of the other venues. The list of cards accepted is larger in other places. (See Chapter 3 for general information.)

Customs: Every visitor 21 years of age or older may bring in to the United States, free of duty, the following: one liter of wine or liquor; 200 cigarettes or 100 cigars (but no cigars from Cuba) or 3 pounds of smoking tobacco, and $100 worth of gifts. These exemptions are offered to travelers who spend at least 72 hours in the United States and who haven't claimed the same exemptions within the preceding 6 months. You can't bring food (particularly cheese, fruit, cooked meats, and canned goods) and plants (vegetables, seeds, tropical plants, and so on) into the country. Foreign tourists may bring in or take out up to $10,000 in U.S. or foreign currency with no formalities; you must declare larger sums to Customs upon leaving.

Doctors: You don't need us to tell you to go to the hospital in an emergency (see "Hospitals," later in this chapter). For lesser problems, local walk-in clinics usually cost five times less than the $300 minimum just for signing in at an emergency-room counter. **Centra-Care,** operated by a local hospital, is a reputable clinic with 13 locations throughout Orlando. For more information including the nearest location, call ☎ 407-660-8118. If you want a direct feed to a doctor, try **Ask-A-Nurse.** They'll ask if you have insurance, but that's for information purposes only — so they can track who uses the system. Ask-A-Nurse is a free service open to everyone. In Kissimmee, call ☎ 407-870-1700; in Orlando call ☎ 407-897-1700.

Emergencies: All of Florida uses ☎ 911 as the emergency number for police, fire departments, ambulances, and other critical needs. There's also a 24-hour, toll-free number for the **Poison Control Center,** ☎ 800-282-3171. Call ☎ 407-238-2000 for in-room, 24-hour medical service at Disney resort properties. For less urgent requests, call ☎ 800-647-9284, a number sponsored by the **Florida Tourism Industry Marketing Corporation,** the state tourism promotion board. With operators speaking more than 100 languages, this service can provide general directions and help with lost travel papers and credit cards, medical emergencies, accidents, money transfers, airline confirmation, and much more.

Hospitals: Sand Lake Hospital, 9400 Turkey Lake Road (☎ 407-351-8550), is about two miles south of Sand Lake Road. From the WDW area, take I-4 east to Exit 29, turn left onto Sand Lake Road, and make a left on Turkey Lake Road. The hospital is two miles on your right. **Celebration Health** (☎ 407-764-4000), located in the Disney-owned town Celebration, is at 400 Celebration Place. From I-4, take Exit 25A. At the first traffic light, turn right onto Celebration Avenue. At the first stop sign, take another right.

Information: To receive local telephone information, call ☎ 411. The other most common sources of information are **Walt Disney World,** Box 10000, Lake Buena Vista, FL 32830-1000 (☎ 407-934-7639, http://disney.go.com/DisneyWorld/intro.html), and the **Orlando/Orange County Convention & Visitors Bureau,** 8723 International Drive, Suite 101, Orlando, FL 32819 (☎ 407-363-5871, www.go2orlando.com).

Internet Access and Cyber Cafes: Have a laptop? To check your e-mail, all you need is a data port, e-mail address, or free-mail account. You have to pay local and long-distance charges (expect up to 95 cents a minute, plus the $7 connection fee). Some places, such as the **Marriott Orlando World Center,** offer a flat 24-hour fee ($10), and some hotels without in-room connections have business centers where you can connect for an hourly fee.

If you already have a primary e-mail account, you can set your browser to forward mail to your free e-mail account while you're away.

In the parks, **Universal's Islands of Adventure** (see Chapter 24) has **AOL kiosks** — compact stations located throughout the park where you check and send e-mail. Look for them in **CityWalk** near the port of entry at the Confisco Grille, the Mythos Restaurant in *The Lost Continent,* Capt. America Diner in *Marvel Super Hero Island,* and in the *Discovery Center* in **Jurassic Park.** They're free but have notes that ask you to spend five minutes or less. For information, call ☎ 407-363-8000.

In Mickeyville, **DisneyQuest** (☎ 407-938-6237) in **West Side** (Chapter 21) offers Internet access in the *Wired Wonderland Café,* where you can send postcards and play games in five-minute blocks (*Note:* You can't check free-mail accounts here). Epcot's *Innoventions* kiosks (Chapter 18) let you send and receive e-mail.

Another way to access e-mail without logging on is using **MyTalk.com,** (www.mytalk.com). MyTalk.com is really a voice mail service that lets you retrieve your e-mail via telephone from anywhere in the United States. You can reply to your messages as well. Local calls are limited to two minutes per call, and long-distance toll charges apply.

Liquor Laws: Orlando's liquor laws are pretty straightforward. You can get into bars at an early age (don't worry if you're coming in diapers), but, in most cases, the Disney and Universal club districts that we list in Chapter 28 require guests to be 18 (or more) to enter after the sun goes down. Florida law also requires revelers to be 21 before they consume alcohol.

Mail: If you want to receive mail on your vacation and you aren't sure of your address, you can have your mail sent to you, in your name, in care of General Delivery at the main post office of the city or region where you expect to stay. **Orlando's main post office** (☎ 800-275-8777) is located at 1040 Post Office Boulevard. **Lake Buena Vista's main post office** (☎ 800-275-8777) is at 12133 S. Apopka-Vineland Road. You must pick up your mail in person and produce proof of identity (driver's license, passport, and so on).

Maps: AAA (see "AAA," earlier in this appendix) and other auto clubs usually provide maps for members. You can also find them in bookstores and libraries in your hometown.

Newspapers/Magazines: Check out the Sunday travel section in your hometown paper (or the one in the biggest city nearby) for bargains, ideas, and tips. After you land in O-Town, you can find a lot of bargains in the *Orlando Sentinel* (online, check out www.orlandosentinel.com) throughout the week. The paper's Friday **"Calendar"** section is a literal gold mine for current information on the area's accommodations, restaurant, nightclub, and attractions front. And don't overlook all of those handout (free) coupon books and throwaway magazines in restaurant and hotel lobbies (as well as at attractions and in free newspaper racks around **WDW** and Orlando). Everyone you run into in Orlando wants to give you a coupon — just make sure there isn't a timeshare attached to it.

Pharmacies: Walgreen's drugstore, 1003 West Vine Street (Hwy. 192), just east of Bermuda Avenue (☎ 407-847-5252), operates a 24-hour pharmacy. There's also an Eckerd drugstore at 7324 International Drive (☎ 407-345-0491) and 1205 West Vine (☎ 407-847-5174) that's open 24 hours a day.

Police: In any emergency, call ☎ 911. If you have a cellular phone and need help, dial ☎ *FHP for the **Florida Highway Patrol.** Otherwise, call the Orlando police **nonemergency line** at ☎ 407-246-2414 or the **Orange County Sheriff's Office** at ☎ 407-649-8400.

Rest rooms: Foreign visitors often complain that public toilets are hard to find, but Orlando isn't any worse than most U.S. cities. True, there aren't any public rest rooms on the streets, but you can usually find one in a bar, restaurant, hotel, museum, department store, convenience store, attraction, fast food barn, or service station — and it'll probably be clean. In particular, Mobil service stations have made a public pledge to provide spic-and-span bathrooms, most decorated with homey touches. Note, however, that restaurants and bars in resorts or heavily visited areas may reserve their rest rooms for the use of their patrons. To qualify as a patron, pay for a cup of coffee or a soft drink, and you'll avoid arguments. Within the theme parks, rest rooms are clearly marked on the park maps. Don't panic if you see that the flushing handle is missing. Many new toilets are installed with lasers that trigger the flush automatically when you leave the stall.

Safety: Don't let the aura of Mickey Mouse allow you to lower your guard. Orlando has a crime rate that's comparable to other major U.S. cities. Stay alert and remain aware of your immediate surroundings. Keeping your valuables in a safe-deposit box (inquire at your hotel's front desk) is a good idea, although nowadays many hotels are equipped with in-room safes. Keep a close eye on your valuables when you're in a public place, such as a restaurant, theater, or even an airport terminal. Renting a locker is always preferable to leaving your valuables in the trunk of your car, even in the theme park lots. Be cautious and avoid carrying large amounts of cash in a backpack or fanny pack, which thieves can easily access while you're standing in line for a ride or show. If you're renting a car, carefully read the safety instructions that the rental company provides. Never stop in a dark area, and remember that children should never ride in the front seat of a car equipped with air bags.

Smoking: If you smoke, you most likely know to expect a diminishing playground. Restaurant space and hotel rooms for smokers are evaporating. The Wizard of Diz not only cut space and stopped selling tobacco years ago, but it has also started establishing precious few "you can smoke here" areas in the outside world. Light 'em while and where you can.

Special Diets: Some local restaurants will arrange for special meals including kosher if you call in advance. **Disney** (☎ 407-939-3463) excels at this.

Taxes: Expect to add 11 or 12 percent to room rates; and 6 to 7 percent on most everything else — except groceries and health supplies or medical services.

Taxis: Yellow Cab (☎ 407-699-9999) and **Ace Metro** (☎ 407-855-0564) are among those cabs serving the area. But for day-to-day travel, cabs are expensive unless your group has five or more people. Rates are $2.50 for the first mile, $1.50 per mile thereafter.

Telephone: Local calls within the 407 area code require **10-digit dialing**, even if you're trying to get the store right across the street. You must dial 407 plus the local number. If you're making a long-distance call, it's just like anywhere else in the United States: dial 1 (or 0 for an operator-assisted call), followed by the area code and seven-digit number.

Time Zone: Orlando is on eastern standard time from late fall until mid-spring, and on eastern daylight time (one hour later) the rest of the year. That means, when both of Mickey's gloved hands are on 12 noon in Orlando, it's 7 a.m. in Honolulu, 8 a.m. in Anchorage, 9 a.m. in Vancouver and Los Angeles, 11 a.m. in Winnipeg and New Orleans, and 6 p.m. in London.

Transit Info: Lynx (☎ 407-841-8240. www.golynx.com) bus stops are marked with a paw print. The buses serve **Disney, Universal,** and **International Drive** ($1 for adults, 25 cents for kids and seniors; $10 for an unlimited weekly pass), but they're not very tourist-oriented.

Weather: Call ☎ 321-255-0212 to get forecasts from the **National Weather Service.** When the phone picks up, punch in 412 from a touch-tone phone, and you'll get the Orlando forecast. Also check with The Weather Channel if you have cable television or go to its Web site, www.weather.com.

Toll-Free Numbers & Web Sites

Airlines

Air Canada
☎ 888-247-2262;
www.aircanada.ca

America West Airlines
☎ 800-235-9292;
www.americawest.com

American Airlines
☎ 800-433-7300;
www.americanair.com

British Airways
☎ 800-247-9297
(☎ 0345-222-111 in
Britain); www.british-airways.com

Canadian Airlines International
☎ 800-426-7000;
www.cdair.ca

Continental Airlines
☎ 800-525-0280;
www.continental.com

Delta Air Lines
☎ 800-221-1212;
www.delta-air.com

Northwest Airlines
☎ 800-225-2525;
www.nwa.com

Southwest Airlines
☎ 800-435-9792;
www.iflyswa.com

Trans World Airlines (TWA)
☎ 800-221-2000;
www2.twa.com

United Airlines
☎ 800-241-6522;
www.ual.com

US Airways
☎ 800-428-4322;
www.usairways.com

Virgin Atlantic Airways
☎ 800-862-8621 in the
Continental United States
(☎ 0293-747-747 in
Britain); www.fly.virgin.com

Car-Van-Truck-Rental agencies

Advantage
☎ 800-777-5500;
www.arac.com

Alamo
☎ 800-327-9633;
www.goalamo.com

Avis
☎ 800-331-1212 in the
Continental United States
(☎ 800-879-3847 in
Canada); www.avis.com

Budget
☎ 800-527-0700;
www.budgetrentacar.com

Dollar
☎ 800-800-4000;
www.dollar.com

Enterprise
☎ 800-325-8007;
www.enterprise.com

Hertz
☎ 800-654-3131;
www.hertz.com

National
☎ 800-227-7368;
www.nationalcar.com

Payless
☎ 800-729-5377;
www.paylesscar.com

Rent-A-Wreck
☎ 800-535-1391;
www.rent-a-wreck.com

Thrifty
☎ 800-367-2277;
www.thrifty.com

Major hotel and motel chains

Best Western International
☎ 800-528-1234;
www.bestwestern.com

Clarion Hotels
☎ 800-252-7466;
www.hotelchoice.com

Comfort Inns
☎ 800-228-5150;
www.hotelchoice.com

Courtyard by Marriott
☎ 800-321-2211;
www.courtyard.com

Days Inn
☎ 800-325-2525;
www.daysinn.com

Doubletree Hotels
☎ 800-222-8733;
www.doubletreehotels.com

Econo Lodges
☎ 800-553-2666;
www.hotelchoice.com/

Fairfield Inn by Marriott
☎ 800-228-2800;
www.fairfieldinn.com

Hampton Inn
☎ 800-426-7866;
www.hampton-inn.com

Hilton Hotels
☎ 800-445-8667;
www.hilton.com

Holiday Inn
☎ 800-465-4329;
www.holiday-inn.com

Howard Johnson
☎ 800-654-2000;
www.hojo.com/hojo.html

Hyatt Hotels & Resorts
☎ 800-228-9000;
www.hyatt.com

ITT Sheraton
☎ 800-325-3535;
www.sheraton.com

Marriott Hotels
☎ 800-228-9290;
www.marriott.com

Quality Inns
☎ 800-228-5151;
www.hotelchoice.com/

Radisson Hotels International
☎ 800-333-3333;
www.radisson.com

Ramada Inns
☎ 800-272-6232;
www.ramada.com

Red Roof Inns
☎ 800-843-7663;
www.redroof.com

Residence Inn by Marriott
☎ 800-331-3131;
www.residenceinn.com

Rodeway Inns
☎ 800-228-2000;
www.hotelchoice.com/

Super 8 Motels
☎ 800-800-8000;
www.super8motels.com

Wyndham Hotels and Resorts
☎ 800-822-4200;
www.wyndham.com

Finding More Information

If you want more detailed information on attractions, accommodations, or just about anything else that's in Orlando, you won't find getting it difficult. In this section, we give you some excellent sources for tourist information, maps, and brochures.

Orlando/Orange County Convention and Visitors Bureau

The convention and visitor's bureau can answer tourist questions and send you maps and brochures, such as the *Official Visitors Guide, African-American Visitors Guide, Area Guide to Restaurants, Official Accommodations Guide,* and *Discover the Unexpected Orlando!* You should receive the packet in about three weeks, and it will include the Magicard, which is good for up to $500 in discounts on accommodations, car rentals, attractions, and more.

8723 International Dr., Suite 101, Orlando, FL 32819. ☎ *407-363-5871 (voice — you can talk to a real person!),* 800-643-9492 *or* 800-551-0181 *(automated).* www.go2orlando.com.

Walt Disney World

This umbrella designation includes the **Magic Kingdom, Epcot, Disney–MGM Studios,** and **Animal Kingdom,** as well as **Disney's** water parks and secondary attractions, resorts, restaurants, the **Disney Cruise Line,** and so on. You can order vacation brochures and information for or about guests with special needs (Chapter 4), sleep-over guests (Chapters 7 and 8), dining with characters in Mickeyville (Chapter 15), the attractions (see Chapters 16 through 20), Disney shopping (Chapters 21 and 22), and **Pleasure Island** (Chapter 28).

Box 10000, Lake Buena Vista, FL 32830-1000. ☎ *407-934-7639.* http://disney.go.com/DisneyWorld/intro.html.

Universal Studios Escape

This pit stop has information on **Universal Studios Florida** (Chapter 23), **Islands of Adventure** (Chapter 24), and **CityWalk,** Universal's new nighttime party-and-eat-hearty place (Chapter 28). **Escape** also offers vacation brochures, including information on restaurants and accommodations.

1000 Universal Studios Plaza, Orlando, FL 32819. ☎ *800-837-2273.* www.uescape.com.

SeaWorld

Ask for vacation brochures with information on **SeaWorld's** (Chapter 25) restaurants, hotel partners, and Shamu's new Kingdom, **Discovery Cove,** where you can swim with dolphins.

7007 SeaWorld Dr., Orlando, FL 32801. ☎ 800-327-2424 *or 407-351-3600.* www.seaworld.com. *For Discovery Cove,* ☎ 877-434-7268. www.discoverycove.com.

Kissimmee – St. Cloud Convention and Visitors Bureau

Call for a package of maps, brochures, coupon books, and a guide to local accommodations and attractions.

1925 E. Irlo Bronson Hwy./U.S. 192, Kissimmee, FL 34744, or P.O. Box 422007, Kissimmee, FL 34742-2007. ☎ 800-327-9159. www.floridakiss.com.

Visit Florida

This is the state's official tourism office. Because it's a statewide endeavor, it's not terribly Orlando specific, but it offers some good information, and you can order a copy of the *Florida Vacation Guide* as well as brochures on golf, fishing, camping, biking, and the Black Heritage Trail.

661 E. Jefferson St., Suite 300, Tallahassee, FL 32301 ☎ 888-735-2872. www.flausa.com.

Frommer's

Get more information about Walt's World and Orlando from these other works by IDG Books: *Frommer's Walt Disney World & Orlando, Frommer's Irreverent Guide to Walt Disney World, Unofficial Guide to Mini Mickey, Unofficial Guide to Walt Disney World, Unofficial Guide to Walt Disney World for Grown-ups, Unofficial Guide to Walt Disney World for Kids, Inside Disney,* and *Beyond Disney.* You can also visit the Frommer's Web site at www.frommers.com.

Orlando Sentinel

The city's daily newspaper publishes *Orlando Sentinel* Online at www.orlandosentinel.com. It offers entertainment information ranging from restaurants and hotels to theme parks and the performing arts.

Outside the United States

You can find Orlando Tourism Offices outside the United States in: London, ☎ 171-486-6464; Mexico ☎ 5-208-1517; Brazil ☎ 31-441-9083; Japan ☎ 3-3501-7245; Germany ☎ 261-973-0673; Belgium ☎ 2-705-7897; and Argentina ☎ 11-4805-5582.

Fare Game: Choosing an Airline

Travel Agency: _____ Phone: _____

Agent's Name: _____ Quoted Fare: _____

Departure Schedule & Flight Information

Airline: _____ Airport: _____

Flight #: _____ Date: _____ Time: _____ a.m./p.m.

Arrives in: _____ Time: _____ a.m./p.m.

Connecting Flight (if any)

Amount of time between flights: _____ hours/mins

Airline: _____ Airport: _____

Flight #: _____ Date: _____ Time: _____ a.m./p.m.

Arrives in: _____ Time: _____ a.m./p.m.

Return Trip Schedule & Flight Information

Airline: _____ Airport: _____

Flight #: _____ Date: _____ Time: _____ a.m./p.m.

Arrives in: _____ Time: _____ a.m./p.m.

Connecting Flight (if any)

Amount of time between flights: _____ hours/mins

Airline: _____ Airport: _____

Flight #: _____ Date: _____ Time: _____ a.m./p.m.

Arrives in: _____ Time: _____ a.m./p.m.

Notes

Making Dollars and Sense of It

Expense	Amount
Airfare	
Car Rental	
Lodging	
Parking	
Breakfast	
Lunch	
Dinner	
Babysitting	
Attractions	
Transportation	
Souvenirs	
Tips	
Grand Total	

Notes

Sweet Dreams: Choosing Your Hotel

Enter the hotels where you'd prefer to stay based on location and price. Then use the worksheet below to plan your itinerary.

Hotel	Location	Price per night

Places to Go, People to See, Things to Do

Enter the attractions you most would like to see. Then use the worksheet below to plan your itinerary.

Attractions	Amount of time you expect to spend there	Best day and time to go

Going "My" Way

Itinerary #1

☐ _____
☐ _____
☐ _____
☐ _____

Itinerary #2

☐ _____
☐ _____
☐ _____
☐ _____

Itinerary #3

☐ _____
☐ _____
☐ _____
☐ _____

Itinerary #4

☐ _____
☐ _____
☐ _____
☐ _____

Itinerary #5

☐ _____
☐ _____
☐ _____
☐ _____

Itinerary #6

- ☐ _____
- ☐ _____
- ☐ _____
- ☐ _____

Itinerary #7

- ☐ _____
- ☐ _____
- ☐ _____
- ☐ _____

Itinerary #8

- ☐ _____
- ☐ _____
- ☐ _____
- ☐ _____

Itinerary #9

- ☐ _____
- ☐ _____
- ☐ _____
- ☐ _____

Itinerary #10

- ☐ _____
- ☐ _____
- ☐ _____
- ☐ _____

Menus & Venues

Enter the restaurants where you'd most like to dine. Then use the worksheet below to plan your itinerary.

Name	Address/Phone	Cuisine/Price

Notes

Index

Accommodations Index

Refer to page 62 for a hotel index by location.

Kid-Friendly Restaurants

IDG BOOKS WORLDWIDE
BOOK REGISTRATION

Register
This Book
and Win!

We want to hear from you!

Visit **http://my2cents.dummies.com** to register this book and tell us how you liked it!

- Get entered in our monthly prize giveaway.

- Give us feedback about this book — tell us what you like best, what you like least, or maybe what you'd like to ask the author and us to change!

- Let us know any other *For Dummies*® topics that interest you.

Your feedback helps us determine what books to publish, tells us what coverage to add as we revise our books, and lets us know whether we're meeting your needs as a *For Dummies* reader. You're our most valuable resource, and what you have to say is important to us!

Not on the Web yet? It's easy to get started with *Dummies 101*®: *The Internet For Windows*® *98* or *The Internet For Dummies*®3 at local retailers everywhere.

Or let us know what you think by sending us a letter at the following address:

For Dummies Book Registration
Dummies Press
10475 Crosspoint Blvd.
Indianapolis, IN 46256

™

BESTSELLING
BOOK SERIES